·HARDY· GERANIUMS

OTHER GARDENING
BOOKS PUBLISHED BY
CROOM HELM

·HARDY· GERANIUMS

PETER·F·YEO

Croom Helm, London and Sydney
Timber Press, Portland, Oregon

© 1985 Peter F. Yeo
Croom Helm Ltd, Provident House, Burrell Row,
Beckenham, Kent BR3 1AT
Croom Helm Australia Pty Ltd, First Floor, 139 King Street,
Sydney, NSW 2001, Australia

British Library Cataloguing in Publication Data

Yeo, Peter F.
  Hardy geraniums.
  1. Geraniums
  I. Title
  635.9'33216   SB413.G35

  ISBN–0–7099–2907–2

First published in the USA in 1985 by
Timber Press
PO Box 1631
Beaverton, OR 97075
ISBN 0–88192–019–3

Printed and bound in Great Britain

Contents

Colour Plates

Preface

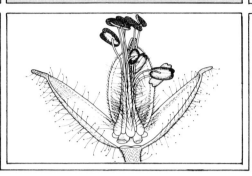

The expression 'hardy geraniums' is the favoured one in horticultural circles for distinguishing *Geranium* of the botanists from *Pelargonium*, and it therefore forms the title of this book, but within its covers they are usually referred to as cranesbills. The title calls for a small apology, in that I have included some species that can stand only a few degrees of frost.

There is a mere handful of different cranesbills in general cultivation in British gardens, yet the number of species, cultivars, etc. that is available is considerable. There are many gardeners who, having, I suppose, become aware of the range of variation which the genus displays, become enthusiasts for them, and eagerly seek them out to embellish their gardens or even simply to amass a collection for the satisfaction of exploring the beauty expressed in their apparently endless variations on a theme. It is to assist these enthusiasts along their way, and to encourage others to join them, that this book has been written. For, sadly, the cranesbills have been poorly treated in the great encyclopedic works, and the only works entirely devoted to them in English that I know of are a handful of booklets and articles. These contain much useful information based on personal knowledge of the plants, but cannot claim to provide accounts which are both up to date and comprehensive. Nothing has yet appeared which will permit confident identification of cultivated cranesbills. I have tried to fill that gap, attempting to make the

process one which can be accomplished by the amateur, while at the same time providing a book to which the professional botanist will turn when he needs to.

In connection with my work as taxonomist at the University Botanic Garden, Cambridge, I have, during the last 15 years, been making the acquaintance of an ever-widening circle of cranesbills. During this period there has been an upsurge of interest in them in the horticultural world: there has been a trial of *Geranium* in the Garden of the Royal Horticultural Society at Wisley; the Hardy Plant Society has formed a *Geranium* group; and the British Pelargonium and Geranium Society has established a Geraniaceae Group, devoted to the study of all members of that family other than the more advanced hybrids of *Pelargonium*, which is the principal concern of the parent Society. The time now seems ripe for me to share my knowledge in a more formal and universal way than I have done hitherto, and although I came to know the cranesbills in the course of botanical duty, I am urged on by my delight in them as garden plants.

The conditions of my employment in Cambridge University helped in several ways to make the writing of this book possible. I have at my disposal the combined resources of the University and Departmental Libraries and had an entitlement to Study Leave, which I took for two terms in 1983. My colleagues in the Botany School and University Botanic Garden willingly undertook to cover my teaching responsibilities in those two terms, and my colleagues at the Garden, chiefly the Director at the time, Dr S.M. Walters, and Assistant Taxonomist, Mr C.J. King, have absorbed for nine months many duties that would normally have fallen to me in two terms and three vacations. The Secretary to the Director of the Garden, Mrs Anne James, has ably and patiently typed the manuscript and Miss J.A. Hulyer has photographed the leaf-silhouettes. The managers of the Cory Fund of Cambridge University made a grant to assist me to travel to gardens in England and Scotland in 1983.

I am deeply aware of my good fortune in all these respects and deeply grateful to all the people mentioned.

Equally essential to the writing of this book has been the generosity of many plantsmen, gardeners and garden curators who have given me plants, shared their knowledge and in many cases given their hospitality, and I have pleasure in offering hearty thanks to them. Their names, or the names of the gardens for which they work, are mentioned in the book as sources of plants or information, and I hope they will accept this collective acknowledgement.

The writing of this book was not long foreseen. It was, therefore, only possible to write on the basis of my purely British experience of *Geranium,* which itself could be boosted only by a few short trips within this country while I was writing. I have usually, therefore, been explicit about where my knowledge comes from, and where it is applicable. I have, in fact, been helped with information from abroad by the following: Dr A. Kress, of the Botanic Garden, München-Nymphenburg, Mr T. Nottle, of Stirling, South Australia, Mrs R. Parer of Kentfield, California and the International Geranium Society, and Mr W.R. Sykes of the DSIR, Christchurch, New Zealand. I am also grateful to the following horticulturists who are not otherwise mentioned: Dr D.K. Davies, Mrs Eleanor Fisher, Mr R. Hope-Simpson (Lakeland Horticultural Society, Windermere, Cumbria), Mr J.J. Hornyold-Strickland (Sizergh Castle, Cumbria), Miss B. Hudson, Mrs Jean Llewellyn, Mr G. Moon (Wallington, Northumberland; National Trust), Mrs H. Rakusen, Mr G.G. Stewart (Branklyn Garden, National Trust for Scotland).

In addition I am indebted to Dr R.K. Brummitt (Kew), Dr H.M. Burdet (Geneva) and Mr A.O. Chater (British Museum, Natural History) for advice on nomenclature and help with the literature, to Drs R.J. Gornall (Leicester), V.A. Matthews (Edinburgh) and A.C. Leslie (Wisley) for testing my keys and providing many valuable comments, to Mr M.J.E. Coode (Kew) for help with the Latin descriptions, to Professor D.A. Webb (Dublin) for some ideas used in the glossary, to the authorities of the Kew Herbarium for facilities and of the Conservatoire Botanique de Genève for a loan of herbarium specimens, to the Council of the Linnean Society of London for permission to use figures published in the Botanical Journal of the Linnean Society in 1973 and 1984, to Dr S.M. Walters for reading the first draft of the early chapters and encouraging me to continue with the project and, especially, Mr Graham Thomas, who is many times mentioned as a source of plants, but who also generously undertook to read several chapters, including Chapter 9, and who furnished many valuable comments. I further thank Frances Hibberd for the care she has taken in meeting my requirements for line-drawings, Clive King for help in typing and checking the proofs, and Jo Hemmings and other staff at Croom Helm for their amiable collaboration with me. I thank my wife, Elizabeth, for her interest and support and for criticising parts of the text, helping to select photographs and generously giving much time to work on the typescript and proofs

The photographs for colour plates 4 and 36 were taken by the late F.T.N. Elborn, the rest by myself. The following line-drawings are by Frances Hibberd: 4.5, 4.6, 4.7, 5.1–5.5, 9.9, 9.15, 9.26, 9.27, 9.33, 9.48, 9.69, 9.72, 9.74–9.76, 9.91, 9.100 and 9.108.

·CHAPTER 1·
History

THE SCOPE OF THE BOOK

This book deals only with those plants covered by the scientific name *Geranium*. However, 'geranium', as a word in the English language, applies to the group which botanists call *Pelargonium*. This anomaly is a source of frequent bewilderment to the layman and it stems from changes in botanical classification, as will be explained in a moment. The plants included in this book are those species of *Geranium* which are in cultivation at the present time in the British Isles, together with their named variants and their hybrids. Because *nearly* all *Geranium* species have some ornamental value the enthusiast is liable to try any that can be obtained, and this means that a few species of minimal garden value are in circulation and need to be included. Several species are native to the British Isles and among these too are some weedy species; they have also been included as they are liable to be encountered in gardens even though their presence is unintended by the owner. Finally, a few species that are not in cultivation but whose names are in circulation, misapplied to other species, are briefly dealt with for the purpose of clarification, as well as a few others that are likely to be introduced or have been (one hopes temporarily) lost.

GERANIUM, PELARGONIUM AND *ERODIUM*: THE NAMES

Geranium belongs to the botanical family Geraniaceae. Botanists differ in their opinion as to what genera should be included in this family, but the present tendency, which I support, is to restrict it to the five genera: *Geranium, Pelargonium, Erodium, Monsonia* and *Sarcocaulon*. In all of them there is a narrow beak-like structure at the top of the fruit and this has inspired the naming of the first three genera after birds. *Geranium* comes from Greek *geranion*, a diminutive form of *geranos*, a crane. *Geranion* has been in use for members of the family since the time of Dioscorides in the first century AD. By analogy, *Pelargonium* was coined from the Greek *pelargos*, a stork, and *Erodium* from *erodios*, a heron. However, vernacular usage does not correspond with these derivations because, although *Geranium* is called cranesbill, it is *Erodium* that we call storksbill.

The confusion between *Geranium* and *Pelargonium* arose as follows. *Pelargonium* was first proposed as a group separable from *Geranium* by Joannis Burman in his book *Rariorum africanorum plantarum* (1738–9). But Linnaeus, in his *Species Plantarum* (1753), which we take as the starting point for the nomenclature of flowering plants, did not accept *Pelargonium* as distinct from *Geranium*. So all the species we now place in *Pelargonium* were called by him *Geranium*, in which he also included the plants we now call *Erodium*. There was a considerable influx of southern African plants to Europe in the eighteenth century and the pelargoniums were sufficiently numerous and striking to catch the public's attention. In view of Linnaeus' reputation and the importance of his publications, they were inevitably called *Geranium*.

It was the French magistrate and distinguished amateur botanist Charles-Louis L'Héritier de Brutelle who asserted that *Pelargonium* ought to be recognised as a separate genus and he now carried the botanical world with him. L'Héritier's work achieved publication in William Aiton's *Hortus Kewensis* (1789), where also his new genus *Erodium* was published. This, alas, was too late to change the public's notions, and the more popular kinds of *Pelargonium* are still known as geraniums.

PUBLICATIONS ON *GERANIUM*

There has only been one world monograph of *Geranium* — that of R. Knuth (1912), published in the series *Das Pflanzenreich* and forming part of a treatment of the whole family Geraniaceae. A dip into the introduction to this work, or the account of the Geraniaceae in Hegi's *Illustrierte Flora von Mittel-Europa* (Gams, 1923–4), will show that a great deal has been written about *Geranium* — on its morphology, anatomy and physiology — and that it is nearly all in German, like these two great works in which one may trace the references. More recently, bibliographies of both *Geranium* and Geraniaceae have been published by Robertson (1972).

For taxonomic accounts of *Geranium* we must look first to two early attempts to cover all plants, Linnaeus' *Species Plantarum* (1753) (*Geranium* on pp. 676–83) and A.P. De Candolle's *Prodromus Systematis Naturalis Regni Vegetabilis* vol. 1 (1824) (*Geranium* on pp. 639–44). After these, and apart from Knuth's monograph, we have to rely mainly on regional monographs and floras (the works in which all the plants of a country or region are described). In *Species Plantarum* there were 15 species of what we now call *Geranium*, while in the *Prodromus* there were 66. Knuth included 260-odd species and many more have been described since. Not all of these are really distinct species. Noteworthy regional monographs are one for Mexico and Central America by Moore (1943), one for Australasia by Carolin (1964), one for the perennials of North America by Jones and Jones (1943), one for East Africa by

Kokwaro (1971) and one for Malesia by Veldkamp & Moerman (1978), but not all of these are of much importance for the horticulturist. In addition there is a revision of The Tuberosum Group by Davis (1970).

Knuth's monograph, although quite essential for the researcher, is in some ways defective. Knuth failed to classify the species satisfactorily, which means that many closely related species are described far apart in the text. In his key to the sections one may have to decide simultaneously between as many as 13 different possibilities, and the keys to species of the various sections contain frequent contradictions. Added to all this is the fact that the keys and descriptions are in Latin. Knuth's species-descriptions are, however, usually good.

Nearly all modern floras provide quite effectively for the identification of their included species of *Geranium*.

In the horticultural literature, the principal sources of information are the encyclopedias. Of the five great English-language encyclopedias, the three earlier ones, Nicholson's *Dictionary of Gardening* (1884–7), Bailey's *Standard Cyclopedia of Horticulture* (1914–17) and Chittenden's *Royal Horticultural Society Dictionary of Gardening* (1951), are better than the two later ones, *Hortus Third* (Bailey Hortorium, 1976) and Everett's *New York Botanical Garden Encyclopedia of Horticulture*, vol. 5 (1981). All contain quite a number of errors (not all of them the fault of the compilers) but *Hortus Third* fails more frequently in characterisation than its predecessors as does the *New York Encyclopedia* which also includes at least one misidentified photograph.

The report of the trial of *Geranium* in the Royal Horticultural Society's Garden at Wisley, Surrey, mentioned in the Preface, appears in *The Garden*, vol. 103, Proceedings, pp. 67–71 (1978).

Several authors have tried to help the horticulturist and plantsman by means of fairly cheaply produced leaflets. The first of these was the late Walter Ingwersen's *The Genus Geranium* (1946), issued as leaflet no. 19 by the nursery firm of W.E. Th. Ingwersen Ltd. It is 31 pages long and contains a wealth of observation from personal experience. More recent publications on similar lines are *Geraniums* by Mr Melvyn Crann, Harlow Car Publication no. 1 (Northern Horticultural Society, Harlow Car Gardens, Harrogate) (1982), *Hardy Geraniums*, compiled by Mr Dennis Thompson of Seattle (1982) and *Growing*

Geraniums and Pelargoniums in Australia and New Zealand (Llewellyn, Hudson & Morrison, 1981). *Geranium Family, Species Check List, edn 3, part 2, Geranium (1984)*, compiled by R.T.F. Clifton, is published by the British Pelargonium and Geranium Society (BPGS), and the same society has published a descriptive list of species and cultivars of *Geranium* by Mr Clifton with the title *Hardy Geraniums (Cranesbills) Today* (1979). A list of names of cultivated species, hybrids and a few cultivars is also included in *A Guide to Cranesbills* (Geranium) which I wrote in 1977 and which is sold at the University Botanic Garden, Cambridge, though also available from the Geraniaceae Group of the BPGS. Other contributions which should be noted are an article by Mrs Joy Forty (1980) entitled 'A survey of hardy Geraniums in cultivation', to which there is a supplement (Forty, 1981), an article by Mr Graham Thomas (1960) on 'Geraniums for ground cover', and the sections on *Geranium* in two other works by this author, *The Modern Florilegium* (1958) and the book that developed from this pamphlet, *Perennial Garden Plants* (1982). Despite their age, the writings of E.A. Bowles on *Geranium* (e.g. Bowles, 1914 and 1921) are outstandingly useful.

THE NATURAL OCCURRENCE OF *GERANIUM*

Whereas *Pelargonium* is essentially a genus of warm-temperate conditions, with very few species being hardy in Britain, *Geranium* is equally characteristic of cool-temperate conditions, and very few are tender in Britain. As aridity is rare in the cool-temperate parts of the world, so most cranesbills are adapted to well-watered soils. The great majority of the species, therefore, come from the temperate northern part of Eurasia and its more southerly mountain regions, and from the temperate and mountainous parts of North and South America. But practically everywhere that suitable climates are to be found *Geranium* will be found too, including South Africa, the Arabian peninsula, the Indian peninsula, Taiwan, Indonesia, New Guinea and the Hawaiian Islands. In addition it is found in Australia (including Tasmania), New Zealand, the Azores, Canary Islands and Madeira. In the warmer parts of these regions annual species become more prevalent, as in the Mediterranean Region, East Tropical Africa, the Arabian peninsula and the southern part of Iran. In these areas annuals will usually pass the summer as seeds and grow through the winter. Also in the Mediterranean Region and Southwest Asia there are perennial species with more or less well-developed tubers and these become dormant in summer. Depending on the severity of the winters to which they are subjected the summer-dormant species begin growth either in the autumn or in the spring, and in the latter case they may have a very short growing season.

The great majority of perennial species of *Geranium* range from 30 to 120cm in height and grow in grassland and tall-herb communities such as meadows, roadsides and woodland margins, and in open woodland or low scrub (which is often an indication of rocky ground with little topsoil). Alpine species, which are usually less than 30cm tall, and always bear most of their foliage much below that height, are quite uncommon. In Europe they are represented only by the *G. cinereum* group. Several alpines exist in the eastern Himalayas and the mountains of West China, East Tropical Africa and Central America, and in the northern Andes. It is in the last-named area that the alpine growth habit is at its most extreme.

The *Geranium* species of oceanic islands are specialised in two different ways: those of the North Atlantic islands are giant rosette herbs, with large leaves, whereas those of the Hawaiian Islands are bushy in habit and have small leaves with simplified shapes and, sometimes, veining.

THE INTRODUCTION OF CRANESBILLS INTO CULTIVATION

No one seems to have established when cranesbills were first cultivated and it seems unlikely that they ever will. The species that probably has the longest recorded history is *G. robertianum*, Herb Robert. This is because, of all European species, it is the one that has been most used for medicinal purposes. In mediaeval Latin it was called Herba Roberti, and the English form, 'herbe Robert' was already in use in the thirteenth century (Grigson, 1955). Gams (1923–4) states that Saint Robert or Ruprecht is said to have taught its use in medicine, but Gams suspects that all the names for *G. robertianum* which are based on Robert or Ruprecht represent corruptions of 'herba rubra'. Grigson, however, suggests that the German name Ruprechtskraut refers to Knecht Ruprecht, a mythical servant who will protect the house if well treated (a German 'Robin Goodfellow'). Grigson shows that the species has an unusually large number of common names, so for whatever reason or reasons, it is a plant that has long attracted people's attention, and the history of the names still in use is, therefore, unlikely to be unravelled. As it is such a common plant, readily appearing around the house (at least in rural conditions) (Grigson 1955) it is unlikely that it was deliberately cultivated, and if it was encouraged it would have been in order to maintain a supply for medicinal use. According to Gams it is, or was, used for treatment of conjunctivitis, nosebleed, rashes, bruises, all kinds of swellings, tooth-ache, fever, gout and afflictions of the kidneys, lungs and genitalia. Today, when little use is made of medicinal herbs, and ornament is the only reason for growing cranesbills, *G. robertianum* is tolerated, rather than cultivated (except for one or two of its variations).

Naturally enough, the longer a plant has been in cultivation, the less likely we are to have a record of when it was first introduced. Nobody can know when the first Briton placed a piece of Meadow Cranesbill (*G. pratense*), one of our finest wild flowers, in his garden simply for the joy of having it close at hand — and there are two other British natives of real garden value to which the same applies: *G. sanguineum* and *G. sylvaticum*.

It was in the late eighteenth century and the nineteenth century that authors began to seek out the earliest dates of cultivation of our garden plants, and a typical example of a publication in which such dates are given is J.C. Loudon's *Hortus Britannicus* (1830, 2nd edn 1832). In the latter there are 24 *Geranium* species which, I allow, have some garden value, and dates of their first recorded cultivation are given for 21 of these. Two fall into the sixteenth century, two into the seventeenth and six into the eighteenth. The four earliest are *G. macrorrhizum* (1576), which must have been grown for its herbal value, *G. tuberosum* (1596), *G. versicolor* (syn. *G. striatum*) (1629) and *G. argenteum* (1699). Two others which must have come in before the eighteenth century are *G. pyrenaicum*, which has

become well naturalised in Britain, and *G. phaeum* (Mourning Widow). All these are European. Of the six eighteenth-century introductions, four are European, one South African and one North American. But even by 1832 Loudon was able to record eleven nineteenth-century introductions, five from South-east Europe and the Caucasus, three from North and East Asia and three from the Himalayas. A trickle of new species has continued to come in from these regions right up to the present, for example, *G. shikokianum* from Japan and *G. peloponnesiacum* from Greece about 1970 and *G. linearilobum* from Central Asia in 1980 (their collectors were, respectively, Kenneth Beckett, Richard Gorer and Ray Hunter). The one really productive area that had not been touched by the time of *Hortus Britannicus* was South-west China. The plants from this area began to come in at the beginning of this century, through the expeditions of William Purdom, George Forrest and E.H. Wilson. Surprisingly, few species from this rich area are at present in cultivation in the West. However, a stream of tours and expeditions is now going to China and we may expect fresh introductions and reintroductions from there. Indeed, one species not in cultivation, *G. yunnanense*, was brought back by the Scottish Botanical Expedition to China in 1981 (the plant which some people know as *G. yunnanense* has turned out to be *G. pogonanthum*).

The Andean region has so far contributed nothing to our stock of garden cranesbills. I suspect that this is in the first place due to the difficulty of finding plants with ripe seed attached. However, even if seeds were imported it would probably be found that *Geranium* shares with other Andean alpines their notorious difficulty of cultivation.

Species which are probably garden-worthy still remain to be introduced from China and elsewhere. Apart from this there are botanically named subspecies and varieties which may be horticulturally distinct and there is always the possibility of selecting from the wild new colour variants or improvements — from the garden point of view — in habit.

The horticultural history of *Geranium* also includes the origin of garden hybrids, but this subject is dealt with in Chapter 7.

·CHAPTER 2·
Cranesbills as Garden Plants

USES AND CULTIVATION

There are many books on various aspects of gardening which mention *Geranium*. In scanning some of these I have been surprised at the plant heights and flower sizes quoted for some species, not because they are too large but because they seem too small. Let the reader not take the details in such books too literally! In my preface I mentioned that very few cranesbills are generally cultivated. My impressions as to which these are have been confirmed by this survey: they are *G. ibericum* × *G. platypetalum* (=*G.×magnificum*), *G. endressii* and its hybrids with *G. versicolor*, *G. macrorrhizum*, *G. sanguineum* and its var. *striatum*, and *G. himalayense*, together with its hybrid with *G. pratense*: 'Johnson's Blue'. Naturally these are among the more adaptable members of the genus but even so each one has its most appropriate niche in the garden and they will be mentioned again in the course of this chapter.

I have not come across any mention of cranesbills being particular as to the acidity or alkalinity of the soil (pH) in which they grow. However, the plants that grow naturally on limestones, such as *G. pratense* and *G. sanguineum*, will be the better ones to try if one is gardening on soils over limestone and, if they are dry, especially *G. sanguineum*. *G. wallichianum* is variously said to need a moist soil and to tolerate dry shade, and *G. soboliferum* seems to need both full sun and continual moisture at the roots. *G. palustre* actually grows on ditch-banks in nature but grows quite well in light dry

Cambridge flower beds. The alpines of the *G. cinereum* group are happy with plenty of grit and chippings in their soil, and some of the dwarfs are known or presumed to live in scree in the wild, and are probably best in scree conditions in the garden too: these are *G. pylzowianum*, *G. orientalitibeticum*, *G. farreri* and *G. stapfianum*.

Almost all cranesbills except the alpines will do well in light shade; many, but not all, will also tolerate full sun. Their range of uses in the garden is, therefore, considerable. In the herbaceous border *G. pratense* is the tallest and its pale-flowered cultivars, such as 'Silver Queen', and the doubles are all valuable; flowering is mainly in July and is reasonably prolonged. Its hybrid, 'Johnson's Blue' is less tall and, being sterile, goes on for longer but eventually becomes straggly. The king of the cranesbills is surely *G. ibericum* × *G. platypetalum* (= *G. ×magnificum*), less tall than *pratense*, and earlier, with a brief concentrated display of purplish-veined violet flowers; it too is sterile and I have never seen a repeat flowering, though the leaves colour well in autumn. Near the front of the border the slightly creeping (some say invasive) *G. himalayense* throws up its great blue flowers above a mass of foliage in June, and then again later, sporadically until October. Early in the season the more modest performances of the *G. phaeum* group, with generally sombre flowers, and *G. macrorrhizum*, in its various colour forms, may be appreciated in the border. *G. psilostemon* 'Bressingham Flair' is also a good border plant, being a little more compact and floriferous than the typical form, and though the flowers are rich pink with a dark centre, they are less fiercely coloured than in the latter. When *Geranium* is grown in the border, it may be found worthwhile to cut off the inflorescences when the end of flowering approaches. In many cases (but not that of *G. ×magnificum*) this will encourage a second flowering. Most species and hybrids suitable for the border throw up a fresh crop of basal leaves just as flowering ends, which will cover any stubs left after tidying-up.

Many of the slightly smaller species can be used not only for the front of the border, but for patios, terraces and wall-gardens. Examples are *G. wallichianum* (favoured in its unique white-centred blue form: 'Buxton's Variety'), *G. endressii*, bright pink but with an unusual salmon-pink cultivar in 'Wargrave Pink', *G. sanguineum*, naturally rather a fierce red but available in softer tones, and flesh-coloured in its var. *striatum*, *G. renardii*, with shallowly lobed, sage-textured leaves and bluish white petals netted with violet, two dwarf relatives of *G. macrorrhizum* — *G. dalmaticum* and *G. cataractarum* — and the long-lasting sterile hybrids between *G. endressii* and *G. traversii* (*G. ×riversleaianum* 'Russell Prichard' and 'Mavis Simpson'). One of the larger plants for this sort of situation is a relative newcomer: *G.* 'Ann Folkard' (*G. procurrens × G. psilostemon*), with black-centred rich reddish-purple flowers with a velvety texture, the strength of colour aptly set off by a freckling of gold in the younger leaves. It is sterile and flowers indefinitely, forming a mound of foliage on intertwined stems. For warm corners with protection from wind, and where height is acceptable, *G. rubescens*, *G. palmatum* and *G. canariense* may be tried.

As mentioned, most cranesbills are happy in light shade. For medium shade, of those already mentioned, the following should be suitable: *G. endressii*, *G. versicolor*, the hybrids between them (= *G. ×oxonianum*), the *G. phaeum* group, *G. macrorrhizum* (Plate 1) and *G. psilostemon*. There are many more, for example, *G. gracile*, *G. lambertii*, *G. nodosum*, *G. sinense* and *G. sylvaticum*. The shade of trees, especially isolated specimens, is often dry shade, and according to Paterson (1981) the following accept dry shade: *G. macrorrhizum*, *G. nodosum*, *G. psilostemon* and *G. wallichianum*. Most 'wild gardens' are more or less shady, and cranesbills are an essential ingredient of wild gardens and woodland gardens. In the latter, where shrubs are grown in

beds, they make a charming ground-cover (as at Sizergh Castle in Cumbria). It is here that such plants as *G. robertianum* and even the tiny-flowered *G. lucidum* also have a role.

The need for ground-cover is likely to make itself felt in either sun or shade, and the following cranesbills are suitable for ground-cover in sun or at least light shade (the names are in order of decreasing stature): *G. ibericum × G. platypetalum* (= *G. ×magnificum*), *G. macrorrhizum*, *G. endressii × G. versicolor* (= *G. ×oxonianum*; especially 'Claridge Druce'), the parents of the preceding, *G. himalayense*, *G. wlassovianum*, *G. procurrens*, *G. dalmaticum × G. macrorrhizum* (= *G. ×cantabrigiense*), *G. dalmaticum* and *G. endressii × G. traversii*: 'Russell Prichard' (= *G. ×riversleaianum*). Of these, *G. versicolor* and its hybrids and *G. macrorrhizum* and its hybrids normally keep their leaves through the winter. *G. macrorrhizum* and its hybrids and *G. himalayense* creep underground.

An important factor in the choice of species for ground-cover is ease of propagation, and of the plants mentioned in the two preceding paragraphs *G. lambertii* and *G. wlassovianum* are possibly less acceptable in this respect than the others.

The leaves of most species of *Geranium* turn brilliant red when dying (as mentioned above for *G. ×magnificum* and in Chapter 9 for some other species). This possibility is worth bearing in mind when choosing plants for ground-cover.

Of the cranesbills suitable for the rock garden, some have been mentioned already in connection with soils. In the *G. cinereum* group there are a number of valuable hybrids, of which 'Ballerina' perhaps qualifies to be included in the list of cranesbills in common cultivation. There are many others suitable for rock garden use, such as *G. dalmaticum*, *G. cataractarum*, *G. polyanthes*, *G. glaberrimum*, *G. schiedeanum* and, moving slightly up the scale of size, *G. pogonanthum* and *G. clarkei* 'Kashmir White' (the last is invasive on some soils). Other possibilities for the rock garden are the summer-dormant kinds: *G. tuberosum*, *G. malviflorum*, *G. peloponnesiacum* and *G. libani*, though the last three are well above the 'alpines' in stature, and I think they would do well against a warm wall. Another tuberous species, *G. macrostylum*, although quite pretty, has proved itself a pest in some East Anglian gardens.

Of the annual and biennial species, *G. robertianum* is the one most used and its shade-tolerance has already been mentioned. Those who actually grow it usually possess the cultivar 'Album' which has white or pinkish-white petals, and much red and brown pigment in the sepals and elsewhere; 'Celtic White' is quite devoid of these colourings and being dwarf is better suited to exposed situations. *G. brutium,* from South Europe, is a really showy annual, although the flowers are an ordinary shade of bright pink.

The following summaries give details of those species which are distinctive in time of flowering, height and colour. The finer detail of the range of habit, form and texture of leaf and form and colour of flower cannot be shown in lists but will emerge from the descriptions and illustrations (Chapter 9). Ideas for underplanting particular roses with particular cranesbills, or for combining the latter attractively with other flowers, are given by Thomas (1960 and 1982). Cranesbills are also strongly featured in Berrisford (1963), Johnson (1937) and Thomas (1977).

Early and Late

Most cranesbills begin to flower in June or early July. Lists of those beginning to flower earlier (May or even late April) or later (mid-July onwards) are as follows:

Earlier	*Later*
albiflorum (12)	krameri (40)
erianthum (21)	lambertii (23)
eriostemon (some forms) (20)	pogonanthum (31)
libani (75)	procurrens (25)
linearilobum (67)	rubifolium (27)
macrorrhizum (89)	sinense (28)
macrostylum (66)	soboliferum (39)
maculatum (54)	thunbergii (47)
malviflorum (68)	wallichianum (most forms)
peloponnesiacum (74)	(22)
phaeum (100)	
phaeum × reflexum (101)	
reflexum (102)	
rivulare (10)	
sylvaticum (9)	
tuberosum (65)	Numbering of species in Chapter 9 is shown in ( )

Tall and Short

Lists of taller and shorter species are given below. Some trailing or scrambling species may be less than 25cm or more than 50cm high,

according to the availability of support. A list of these is supplied as well. Annuals and biennials are omitted from these lists.

Tall	*Short*
(usually more than 50cm — about 2 ft)	(usually less than 25cm — about 1 ft)
maculatum (54)	argenteum (104)
maderense (99)	argenteum × cinereum (105)
nervosum (some forms) (58)	cinereum (106–10)
palmatum (98)	dalmaticum (91)
phaeum (some forms) (100)	dalmaticum × macrorrhizum (90)
pratense (some forms) (16)	endressii × sessiliflorum (4)
psilostemon (13)	endressii × traversii (3)
rubescens (96)	farreri (33)
	glaberrimum (88)
Extensively Trailing or Scrambling	incanum (53)
albanum (83)	macrostylum (66)
asphodeloides subsp. asphodeloides (63a)	nepalense (48)
lambertii (23)	orientalitibeticum (44)
lambertii × procurrens (24)	polyanthes (79)
procurrens (25)	pylzowianum (43)
procurrens × psilostemon (14)	schiedeanum (62)
	sessiliflorum (52)
	sessiliflorum × traversii (51)
	sibiricum (49)
	stapfianum (38)
Numbering of species in Chapter 9 is shown in ( )	thunbergii (47)
	traversii (50)

'Red, White and Blue'

The majority of *Geranium* species are some shade of pink or purplish blue. Below are given lists of plants with deeper purplish red flowers, white flowers and blue flowers (these always lean towards violet). By no means all cranesbills do fit into these groups, some having different shades, or varying patterns and combinations of colours. Some small-flowered species are omitted.

Purplish Red

argenteum × cinereum:
'Gypsy' (105b)
biuncinatum (dark eye) (82)
cinereum var. subcaulescens (dark eye) (110)
endressii × traversii: 'Russell Prichard' (3)
incanum (53)
kishtvariense (26)
macrorrhizum 'Bevan's Var.' (89)
ocellatum (dark eye) (81)
palustre (34)
phaeum var. phaeum × reflexum (101)
procurrens (dark eye) (25)
procurrens × psilostemon (dark eye) (14)
psilostemon (dark eye) (13)
sanguineum (45)
stapfianum (38)

White

albiflorum (12)

asphodeloides (some forms) (63)

cinereum var. cinereum 'Album' (106)

clarkei 'Kashmir White' (18)

dalmaticum 'Album' (pink sepals) (91)

dalmaticum × macrorrhizum: 'Biokovo' (pink sepals) (90)

lambertii 'Swansdown' (crimson eye) (23)

macrorrhizum 'Album' (pink sepals) (89)

phaeum 'Album' (100)

pratense 'Galactic' (16)

pratense 'Plenum Album' (16)

pyrenaicum forma albiflorum (84)

refractum (some forms) (30)

richardsonii (61)

rivulare (10)

robertianum 'Album' (brown sepals) (95)

robertianum 'Celtic White' (95)

sanguineum 'Album' (45)

sessiliflorum (52)

sylvaticum forma albiflorum (9)

sylvaticum 'Album' (9)

thunbergii (some forms) (47)

Blue

erianthum (21)

gymnocaulon (72)

himalayense (19)

himalayense × pratense (17)

libani (75)

malviflorum (some forms) (68)

peloponnesiacum (74)

platypetalum (69)

pratense (16)

Numbering of species in Chapter 9 is shown in ( )

North and South

Where summers are cooler, or rainfall is higher, the majority of the larger-growing species of *Geranium* are likely to flourish better than in the hotter south-east of England. I observed long ago that some of the more popular species grow well in the railway station gardens of Inverness-shire and I am told by Mr Alan Bremner that some, at least, grow well in the Orkney Isles, where *G. pratense* has escaped from cultivation into the wild. Mr Jack Drake, of Aviemore, Inverness-shire, has experience with the lower-growing species and hybrids and finds that many grow well, including *G. sanguineum* forms and the *G. cinereum* group. It is probably about this latitude, however, that noticeable limitations on what can be grown compared with southern England begin to make themselves felt. *G. wallichianum* has been a failure at Aviemore though I have seen it at the University Botanic Garden of Aberdeen. Mr Drake finds that *G. dalmaticum* only flowers well at Aviemore if grown on the sunny side of a wall, and *G. himalayense* does not produce enough flowers to make it worth growing.

Although most species are in fact hardy in at least the greater part of the British Isles, a few are marginally hardy or slightly tender and in the colder parts of the country these species will be impossible, or will be lost intermittently. Plants in these categories are *G. traversii* and its hybrids, *G. incanum, G. palmatum* and perhaps *G. polyanthes*.

I suspect there is nowhere in the inhabited parts of the British Isles where some *Geranium* species cannot be grown, and it seems that over a considerable part of this area climatic variation does not noticeably limit the possibilities.

Outside the British Isles

Most of the inland parts of the British Isles come into Hardiness Zone H4 of the *European Garden Flora* (Walters *et al.*, 1984), with a mean winter minimum of −5°C to −10°C; the extreme minimum in the British Isles is around −20° C. As most *Geranium* species are considered generally hardy in the British Isles they will survive at least this minimum. This places them in Hardiness Zone 4 of the United States Department of Agriculture, in which temperatures down to −18° C may be expected for up to a week at a time. Many will survive a lower minimum: *Geranium* species native to the United States and Canada, eastern Europe and most of North Asia, together with many from the Himalayas and West China will be among these hardier plants. In any case, conditions for the plants are ameliorated if there is a good cover of snow.

Species which do not always survive the winter in inland Britain are *G. incanum, G. traversii* (and also its hybrids), *G. palmatum, G. canariense* and *G. maderense*. These will only be reasonably safe in Zone H5 for Europe (mean winter minimum down to −5° C) or Zone 6 in North America, except perhaps *G. maderense*, which can probably survive −5° C if hardened off progressively but would not survive the coldest winters experienced in this zone. A few other species, among them *G. polyanthes*, are suspected of not being very hardy in Britain.

Most *Geranium* species are certain to be winter-hardy in the lowlands of the cooler parts of Australia and New Zealand. In the parts of these countries (and the USA) where frost is rare, summers are likely to be too hot or too dry, or both (unless lack of frost is due to oceanic westerly winds). I give below a list of species mentioned for California, the warmer parts of New Zealand, and for Australia (Sydney, New South Wales, and Stirling, South Australia) by my correspondents in these areas as being at least reasonably easy to grow.

G. cinereum 'Ballerina' (107)
G. dalmaticum (91)
G. incanum (53)
G. macrorrhizum (89)
G. maculatum (54)
G. pratense (16)
G. sanguineum (45)
G. thunbergii (47)

It will be noticed that these include some of the species that are not fully winter-hardy in Britain, together with *G. sanguineum* which grows in hot dry situations, and some Mediterranean species. Mr Trevor Nottle, of Stirling, South Australia, where winter temperature is rarely below 0° C, and summer temperature goes to 34-38° C, has succeeded with a much wider range of *Geranium* species and hybrids, in some cases using the shade of a wall or an insulating layer of cobbles.

PROPAGATION

Almost all perennial *Geranium* species can be propagated easily by division of the rootstock. In a few the rootstock tends to grow above-ground, producing branches that do not readily root, and for these the use of seed may be as good or better; examples are *G. cataractarum* and *G. glaberrimum*. Members of the *G. cinereum* group have a similar habit but as they cross so freely, stem-cuttings should be tried or, if these do not root readily, root cuttings taken in autumn. As explained in Chapter 4, the branching, short-lived, above-ground stems of *Geranium* are really inflorescences and in most species they cannot be rooted. In a few, however, there is no rosette and nearly all the foliage leaves are borne on these flowering stems, which are more persistent than is the rule. Examples are *G. sanguineum*, *G. incanum* and *G. wallichianum*; the stems of these can be rooted. As *G. incanum* is not quite hardy in most of Britain and *G. wallichianum* is difficult to move, propagation by cuttings may be a useful method. *G. procurrens* is most unusual in that its flowering stems run along the ground and take root. Plenty of new plants can be obtained in this way. However, its hybrid, *G. 'Ann Folkard'*, does not root itself readily.

Seed of *Geranium* is not difficult to collect provided one looks for those fruits in which the rostrum is turning brown but has not yet exploded. In most cases the seeds need a few months of after-ripening before germination is possible. Even then, germination may be prolonged, and the main flush may not take place until spring. A very few species may be reluctant to germinate at all. The seeds of the blue-flowered biennial, *G. bohemicum*, mostly germinate after fires. Occasionally, at the Cambridge Botanic Garden, we light a small bonfire at the site where we grow this species, and soon afterwards there is a new crop of seedlings.

To check for any special requirements as to use or propagation, the reader should see the account of the species concerned.

DISEASES AND PESTS

Geranium is relatively disease-free. *G. canariense* occasionally seems to carry a virus causing distortion of the flowers, and this may be transferred to such related plants as *G. rubescens* and *G. maderense*. Affected plants should be destroyed and new stock grown from seed; any deformed plants in the progeny should be destroyed also. Some species may serve as hosts for white-fly and aphides but infestations of plants out of doors are not usually serious. The thick rootstocks and frequently thick roots provide an ideal habitat for the larvae of crane-flies (Tipulids), the yellow-underwing moth and certain beetles such as the vine weevil (*Otiorrhynchus sulcatus*) (Clifton, 1979). These may seriously weaken plants in pots or may even kill them. Infested pots should be tipped out and the insects removed. Wilted or snipped-off leaves and poor growth are the symptoms. For plants in the open one should take the precaution of establishing a number of separate plants as soon as possible after acquisition. Another pest which I have observed is a small caterpillar which lives on the undersides of the leaves and eats numerous elliptical holes in them. I have no remedy for this.

ROYAL HORTICULTURAL SOCIETY AWARDS TO *GERANIUM*

Most of these awards arose out of the trial at Wisley, 1973–6 (see *The Garden,* vol. 103, Proceedings, pp. 67–71, 1978). The awards are: AGM, Award of Garden Merit (which marks plants of outstanding excellence for garden use) and, in order of decreasing distinction, FCC, first-class certificate; AM, award of merit; HC, highly commended. The names of plants are as printed in the above-cited reference or in Synge and Platt (1962) (AGM only). In parentheses I give the parentage, or what I believe to be the correct name, or the name to be adopted in this book. Any problems connected with the following names are discussed in Chapter 9.

AM	'Ballerina' (*G. cinereum* 'Ballerina')
AM	*dalmaticum*
AM	'Farrer's Pink' (*Journ. Royal Horticultural Society*, 50, 1, 1925) (*G. farreri*)
AM	*himalayense* 'Birch Double' (*himalayense* 'Plenum')
AM	*himalayense* 'Gravetye'
HC	*himalayense* 'Irish Blue'
AGM	*ibericum* (almost certainly *G.* ×*magnificum* which was not distinguished when the award was given)
HC	*ibericum*
FCC	'Johnson's Blue' (*G. himalayense* × *G. pratense*)
AM	*macrorrhizum*
AM	×*magnificum* (*ibericum* ×*platypetalum*) (see also *ibericum*)
AM	*pratense album* (*G. pratense* 'Galactic')
AM	*pratense* 'Caeruleum Plenum' (*G. pratense* 'Plenum Caeruleum')
HC	*pratense* 'Kashmir Purple' (*G. clarkei* 'Kashmir Purple')
AM	*pratense* 'Kashmir White' (*G. clarkei* 'Kashmir White')
AM	*pratense* 'Mrs Kendall Clark'
HC	*pratense* 'Silver Queen'
FCC	*psilostemon*
AM	'Rose Clair' (*G.* ×*oxonianum* 'Rose Clair')

FCC	'Russell Prichard' (*G.* ×*riversleaianum* 'Russell Prichard')
HC	*sanguineum*
AM	*sanguineum* 'Album'
FCC	*sanguineum* 'Jubilee Pink'
AGM	*sanguineum* var. *lancastriense* (*G. sanguineum* var. *striatum*)
AM	*sanguineum* var. *lancastriense* (*G. sanguineum* var. *striatum*)
AM	*sanguineum* var. *lancastriense* 'Splendens' (cultivar epithet probably illegitimate) (*G. sanguineum* var. *striatum* 'Splendens')
HC	*sanguineum* 'Shepherd's Warning'
AM	*cinereum* subsp. *subcaulescens* var. *subcaulescens* (*G. cinereum* var. *subcaulescens*)
AM	*sylvaticum album* (*G. sylvaticum* 'Album')
FCC	*wallichianum* 'Shirley Blue' (*Journ. Royal Horticultural Society*, 12, cxxiv, 1890)
AGM	*wallichianum* 'Buxton's Variety'
AM	'Walter Ingwersen' (*G. renardii* 'Walter Ingwersen')
AM	'Wargrave Pink' (*G. endressii* 'Wargrave Pink')

SOURCES

For the less common kinds of *Geranium* the best sources are probably the specialist societies, though non-specialist horticultural societies which distribute seed may be helpful. Many of the specialist societies are more concerned with *Pelargonium* than *Geranium*. Below are given names and addresses of suitable societies in various countries, and names and addresses of a few commercial suppliers or, where possible, particulars of guides to suppliers. Some of the information is taken from Llewellyn, Hudson & Morrison (1981) and much has been supplied by helpful correspondents overseas.

Australia
Australian Geranium Society
    The Science Centre, 35–43 Clarence Street, Sydney, NSW 2000 *and* 210 Porter Street, Templestowe, Victoria 3106
Canberra Geranium and Fuchsia Society
    25 Savage Street, Campbell, ACT 2601
South Australia Geranium and Pelargonium Society Inc. 244 Young Street, Unley, South Australia 5061

West Australian Geranium Society
25 Kirwan Street, Floreat, Western Australia 6014

Canada
Canadian Geranium and Pelargonium Society
4124 Hoskins Road, North Vancouver, BC, V7K 2P5

Germany (Federal Republic)
Gesellschaft der Staudenfreunde e.V.
Justinus-Kerner-Strasse 11, 7250 Leonberg (seed-list)
Deutsche Gartenbaugesellschaft
Ubierstrasse 30, 5300 Bonn 2
Zentralverband des Deutsches Gartenbaues
Godesberger Allee 142–148, 5300 Bonn 2
(the last two have available lists of German nurserymen, arranged either alphabetically by name or geographically in numerical order of postal code)

Great Britain — Societies
The Royal Horticultural Society
Vincent Square, London SW1P 2PE (seed-list)
The Hardy Plant Society
Secretary: Miss B. White, 10 St Barnabas Road, Emmer Green, Caversham, Reading, Berkshire RG4 8RA
The British Pelargonium and Geranium Society
Hon. Membership Secretary: Mr L.A. Davey, 2/108 Rosendale Road, London SE21 8LF (ask about the Geraniaceae Group)
The Alpine Garden Society
Lye End Link, St John's, Woking, Surrey GU21 1SW (seed-list)
The Scottish Rock Garden Society
Hon. Subscription Secretary: Mrs E.R. Law, Kippielaw Farm, Haddington, East Lothian EH14 4PY (seed-list)
The Western Counties Pelargonium and Geranium Society
Flat 3, 29 Castle Road, Clevedon, Avon BS21 7DA
National Council for the Conservation of Plants and Gardens
See next section, 'Conservation'

Great Britain — Sources: refer to
The Hardy Plant Directory, Silver Jubilee Edition, 1982 (from the Hardy Plant Society; see above)
Green pages (Crichton & Crawford, 1979)
Forty (1980)

The Netherlands
Nederlandse Pelargonium en Geranium Vereniging
Hollands End 89, 1244 NP Ankeveen

New Zealand
Canterbury Alpine Garden Society
84 Tomes Road, Papanui, Christchurch

Republic of South Africa
South African Geranium and Pelargonium Society
P.O. Box 55342, Northlands, Johannesburg 2116

USA — Societies
International Geranium Society
Membership Secretary: Mr Bill McKilligan, 1442 North Gordon, Hollywood, California 90028
American Rock Garden Society
Secretary: Mr Norman Singer, SR66 Box 114, Norfolk Road, Sandisfield, Mass. 01255
American Horticultural Society
Box 0105, Mount Vernon, Virginia 22121

USA — Sources
Far North Gardens, 16785 Harrison, Livonia, Michigan 48154
(commercial seed supplier)

Refer to
Gardening by Mail, from Mailorder Association of Nurserymen Inc.,
210 Cartwright Rd., Massapequa Park, NY 11762

CONSERVATION

Only a few species of *Geranium* are thought to be endangered in nature. Some in Hawaii are under threat from habitat destruction, and *G. maderense* in Madeira is, as far as is known, extremely rare, but it lives in rather inaccessible terrain, and the extent of its occurrence may not be fully known. It is widely cultivated and its survival in gardens is certainly assured. *G. endressii*, endemic to the Pyrenees, is possibly endangered.

Apart from this, enthusiasts for *Geranium* will want to know that worthwhile species and cultivars are not lost to cultivation. In the United

Kingdom it is a function of The National Council for the Conservation of Plants and Gardens (NCCPG) to try to prevent this, by identifying plants that are at present rare in cultivation and encouraging their propagation and distribution. This is being effected by the establishment of national reference collections and the way this is done is outlined by Stungo (1982). Holders of collections under this scheme may charge for material supplied to applicants and may limit the quantity supplied. It is hoped that, though some plants have become rare because of the inability of nurseries to maintain stocks in the face of commercial pressures and the ever-expanding range of plants available, some nurseries may now be stimulated by the activities of the NCCPG to provide commercial outlets for some of the rare plants which the national reference collections contain. The reference collection of *Geranium* is at the University Botanic Garden, Cambridge CB2 1JF. Membership of the NCCPG is open to the public and the Council is organized into local groups, of which a list is to be found in the Newsletter of the NCCPG, no. 2, Spring 1983. The central office is at the Royal Horticultural Society's Garden, Wisley, Woking, Surrey GU23 6QB.

·CHAPTER 3·
Nomenclature

Classification consists of putting objects into groups. In biological classification — but not only in biological classification — similar individuals are placed in groups and similar groups are arranged into higher groups, and so on. The process continues upwards, forming a hierarchy embracing, in the case of a biological classification, all living things. The groups at the different levels are called categories; for example, 'species', 'genus' and 'family' are categories. Each category is said to have a rank; thus a genus has a lower rank than a family but a higher rank than a species. The two words 'family' and 'variety' are commonly used in a loose sense by laymen in talking about plants and animals, and it is important to remember that in biology these words are used for particular categories with their own definite ranks. Note that 'species' is the same in the singular and plural and that the plural of 'genus' is 'genera'.

Nomenclature is the process of putting names to the various groups which one wishes to recognise at the various ranks. Named groups are called 'taxa', singular 'taxon'. Nomenclature makes classification explicit, and as classifications vary, so names change. Thus, what for Linnaeus was *Geranium* became for L'Héritier *Geranium*, *Pelargonium* and *Erodium*. Similarly, what for Boissier was *Geranium crenophilum* became for Bornmüller *Geranium asphodeloides* subspecies *crenophilum*; where Rydberg saw a distinct species, *G. strigosum*, and Royle another, *G. lindleyanum*, most botanists nowadays see only *G. nervosum* and *G. robertianum* respectively. On the other hand, although

Knuth took a similar view of *G. canariense*, equating it with *G. anemonifolium*, which was first described from Madeira, those who have seen the Madeiran plant and its Canarian counterpart in the living state have no doubt that the two are distinct species. The freedom to reclassify is essential in order that we may take into account new knowledge, and to annul the excesses or rectify the faults of observation of our predecessors. But whatever the facts at our disposal, the use we make of them in producing a classification is the result of a series of personal decisions. Sometimes we feel we have to annul the excesses and rectify the faults even of our contemporaries! Contemporary classifications can and do differ, and the bystander who has not time to make his own detailed studies must make some more or less arbitrary decision which of them to follow. The process of classification is called taxonomy, and the changes of name, and of the sense of names, mentioned in this paragraph are taxonomic changes. Taxonomy is never correct or incorrect, it is merely more or less reasonable or acceptable.

A kind of mistake which deserves separate mention is the misapplication of names. For example, cultivated plants from Kingdon Ward's collection, no. 22796, from Burma, were at first thought by me and other botanists to be *Geranium yunnanense*. Now, however, I am sure they are *G. pogonanthum*. This error can quite easily be corrected by re-labelling the specimens which exist in a few great herbaria, but it will probably persist in the naming of the plants in cultivation for a very long time. Although in this

21

case (professional) botanists were implicated in the original misapplication of the name, it is a kind of error that is easily made by the amateur botanist or horticulturist in attempting his own identifications, or even by the gardener who lets his labels become switched when sowing his seeds or some time thereafter. Misapplied names are not synonyms and are not shown as such in this book.

The application of scientific names of plants is regulated by the *International Code of Botanical Nomenclature* (Voss, *et al.*, 1983). This states that for a name to be acceptable it must meet certain conditions of publication ('effective publication'), so as to make sure it is available to the botanical public, and certain conditions for 'valid publication', so that others may verify how the name is to be applied. The two most important conditions for valid publication are that the name be accompanied by or related to an effectively published description, and that a 'type' (usually a 'type-specimen') be indicated. Within this framework the principle of priority is maintained. Thus, the earliest name which fulfils all the conditions laid down is the correct one (i.e. nomenclaturally correct).

Priority does, however, imply a starting point, and for most plants this is the publication date of Linnaeus' *Species Plantarum* in 1753; in that work binary names (two-word names, see next paragraph) for species were first consistently adopted. There is no doubt that we must have a Code, but a code should, ideally, be unchanging. Unfortunately, so much plant nomenclature was already in existence by the time people started to frame rules that there was no alternative to trying to legalise the best practice of the time. So the Code has evolved over a long time, incorporating many changes in an attempt to take care of previously unforeseen contingencies as well as being subject to occasional major changes of policy. Although the intention of the *International Code of Botanical Nomenclature* is to promote stability, name-changes for 'nomenclatural' reasons (i.e. non-taxonomic reasons) do take place, and they have four main causes: (1) a previously overlooked prior name is discovered; (2) the Code is changed; (3) a long-used name is for the first time examined in the light of the Code and found to infringe the rules; and (4) an author infringes the rules embodied in the Code in force at the time of writing; this may happen

through more or less blatant disregard for the Code or by an honest failure to interpret the rules correctly. Similar to (1) is the case where fresh information comes to light about the precise dates of publication of two names for the same plant, whereby their priority is reversed. Names overthrown for any of the reasons given above become synonyms of the correct name.

The name of a species consists of two words, the generic name (written with a capital initial letter) and the specific epithet (written with a small initial letter). Sometimes it is felt necessary taxonomically to divide a species, and the three principal categories of lower rank used for this purpose are, in order of descending rank, subspecies ('subsp.' or 'ssp.'), variety ('var.') and forma ('f'). (However, when the English word 'form' is used in this book it means a variant of unspecified rank.) When a plant in one of these so-called 'infra-specific' categories is named the term denoting the category must always be included, as was done in the example above of *G. asphodeloides* subsp. *crenophilum*.

The species of a genus may be arranged in groups of lower rank than genus; several categories are available for this purpose, those used in this book being subgenus ('subg.'), section ('sect.') and subsection ('subsect.'). Here too, the term denoting the category must be included in the name, for example *Geranium* sect. *Tuberosa*. The epithet of a subdivision of a genus always has a capital initial letter.

Hybrids are of great importance in horticulture, and they may be referred to by the use of a hybrid formula, thus: *G. ibericum* × *G. platypetalum*. It is convenient, however, to have names for hybrids, and the name *G.* ×*magnificum* has been provided for this particular hybrid. Such names are in Latin form and fall under the regulations of the *International Code of Botanical Nomenclature*. They are part of the corpus of botanical nomenclature, which means that they must conform to all the rules, and that a name for a hybrid cannot be the same as the name of a non-hybrid group (for example, a species) of the same rank. All this means that after a new hybrid has arisen, its naming must await the decision of someone conversant with the rules to get on with the job of describing it in Latin and publishing it in a suitable place. However, this delay may be avoided by the use of cultivar names (see below).

When different individuals from the same two

parent species are crossed the progeny are likely to be different. Some hybrids are fertile, and when they are self-fertilised, crossed with their sisters, or crossed back to their parents, a burst of much more extreme variation is usually released. Nevertheless, the formula, or the name of the interspecific hybrid, covers all individuals which are known or reasonably believed to be descended from the crossing of the two named parent species. This does not mean, however, that such variation has to go unrecognised, as will be explained shortly.

The exact meaning of the word 'hybrid' depends on the context. A hybrid can be the result of a cross between any two individuals which differ genetically. To make matters more precise we can talk about an interspecific hybrid, for example. If we refer to a hybrid between *Geranium ibericum* and *G. platypetalum* it probably means we are talking about a single individual (of an interspecific hybrid). If we say '*Geranium* ×*magnificum* is a hybrid between *G. ibericum* and *G. platypetalum*' we are talking about all the individuals which might ever arise from the crossing of the two named parent species. However, in the 1983 edition of the *International Code of Botanical Nomenclature* (Voss *et al.*, 1983) a new term for such an assemblage of individuals was introduced, namely 'nothospecies' (literally 'hybrid-species'). Similarly, it will be possible to refer, for example, to 'nothosubspecies' or, in general, 'nothotaxa'.

The use of authors' names after plant names is best explained by quoting directly from the *International Code of Botanical Nomenclature*, thus: 'For the indication of the name of a taxon to be accurate and complete, and in order that the date may be readily verified, it is necessary to cite the name of the author(s) who first validly published the name concerned . . .' The need for such accuracy and completeness is most obvious in instances where the same name has been published for two different species. For example, Knuth (1912) included in his monograph both *Geranium platypetalum* Fischer & Meyer, and *G. platypetalum* Franchet. This, naturally enough, is not allowed by the Code. Knuth apparently spotted the mistake at the last moment and in the addenda at the end of the monograph he supplied a fresh name, *G. sinense* Knuth, as a replacement for *G. platypetalum* Franchet which is the later of the two identical names ('homonyms'). A similar case is provided by the name *G. grandiflorum* Edgeworth. Before Edgeworth described this Himalayan plant which has become so well known in gardens, the same name had been used for different plants by several authors, of whom the earliest was Linnaeus. Linnaeus' *G. grandiflorum* is not even a member of the family Geraniaceae so it will never be used for a *Geranium* again: nevertheless the rules say that the later homonyms may not be used. The author citation for our cranesbill is, therefore, *G. grandiflorum* Edgeworth not Linnaeus. That this name infringed the rules was first noticed by Hylander; he dealt with the matter by seeking an independently published name for the same plant, and he found *G. meeboldii* Briquet. He therefore stated (Hylander, 1960) that this was the correct name for *G. grandiflorum* Edgeworth. However, some time later Schönbeck-Temesy (1970) took the view that *G. himalayense* Klotzsch also applied to the same plant and, as it was of earlier date, it should therefore be adopted. The problem with this name is that there is no type specimen and the original description and illustration are very incomplete. Knuth (1912) had considered it to be a synonym of *G. pratense*. However, on the evidence available, I support Schönbeck-Temesy's view, so *G. himalayense* is the name adopted in this book.

Frequently the reader will encounter double author citations, that is, a name or names within parentheses and another name or other names outside them, thus (taking a plant name already mentioned): *G. asphodeloides* N.L. Burman subsp. *crenophilum* (Boissier) Bornmüller. This reflects the fact that Boissier described the plant as a species and Bornmüller regarded it as a subspecies (that is, he changed its rank downwards). Such double citations are required also for upward changes of rank and for 'sideways' movements, for example the transfer of a subspecies out of one species and into another (see also Appendix I).

The kind of variation which is found among individuals arising from the crossing of two named species (or other taxa) is dealt with — in the case of cultivated plants — by the *International Code of Nomenclature for Cultivated plants* (Brickell *et al.*, 1980). As far as this book is concerned, the only category in this code which we need to use is that of 'cultivar'. The definition of cultivar can vary according to the nature of the plants concerned. Thus for annuals and biennials it is normally a sexually reproducing group in which certain specified characters are maintained from generation to generation. In woody plants and perennial herbs a cultivar is normally a clone and there is not much point in trying to apply cultivar nomenclature unless the clones are distinguishable. However, there are cases in *Geranium* where perennials which vary within narrow limits when grown from seed are treated as cultivars (examples are *G.* ×*oxonianum* 'Claridge Druce' and *G. wallichianum* 'Buxton's Variety'). As is shown by the second of these examples, cultivar nomenclature is applicable not only to the results of hybridisation but also to variants of species (or indeed taxa of other ranks) which may arise in cultivation or are brought into cultivation from the wild. Like the botanical code, the code for cultivated plants adopts the principle of priority and lays down certain requirements for the publication of names and the ways in which names are to be formed. Cultivar epithets must be names in common language unless they were published before 1 January 1959 (in which case they may be in Latin) or unless they were published in conformity with the botanical code for plants which are now considered to be cultivars. In all cases they must be typographically distinguished from botanical names and this is normally done by giving them capital initial letters, by placing single quotation marks around them and by not printing them in italics. The cultivar epithet has to be attached to what is called a 'collective name' and this is most often a botanical name in the rank of genus or below. In *Geranium* the collective name is nearly always that of a species or interspecific hybrid (nothospecies) or is a hybrid formula (in which case it is a good idea to place a colon between the formula and the cultivar epithet). Typical examples of cultivar names appear in the preceding paragraph. Attachment of the cultivar epithet to the generic name is seen in *Geranium* 'Russell Prichard', a hybrid of which the parents have long been in doubt.

The freedom to attach a cultivar epithet to a collective name in any of the above forms means that when a new hybrid arises it may be named as a cultivar even if there is no Latin name for the hybrid as such. The conditions for valid publication laid down by the code for cultivated plants are easier to meet than those in the botanical code, and anyone who studies the *International Code of Nomenclature for Cultivated Plants* carefully should be able to carry out valid publication of new cultivar names.

I have deliberately kept this chapter very brief because more detailed explanations of the rules of nomenclature are readily available elsewhere. The most complete coverage is in Jeffrey (1977). Accounts directed especially at the horticulturist are those of McClintock (1980) and Rowley (1980; chapter entitled 'How plants are named'). The practice of taxonomy is described by Jeffrey (1982).

·CHAPTER 4·
Structure &
Terminology

THE CONSTRUCTION OF THE
GERANIUM PLANT

Introduction

Those aspects of the structure of the *Geranium* plant most relevant to its identification are described here. The description of the structure does not attempt to cover every variation, and exceptions to some of the statements will easily be discovered by anyone deeply involved with cranesbills. Many of these will be accounted for in the individual species-descriptions.

It is necessary to read the whole of this chapter to prepare oneself to use the later parts of the book. A pocket lens with a magnification of about eight times is necessary for looking at hairs on the plant and the sculpture of the ripe carpels.

Terms and expressions which are defined here are italicised. Definitions of other technical terms used here will be found in the glossary.

Roots and Stems

The plant consists essentially of roots, a vegetative stem and flowering stem. The difference between the two types of stem is best understood by considering one of the overwintering annual species such as *Geranium robertianum* in the early stages of flowering. The plant will be found to have a *rosette* of leaves crowded on to a much abbreviated rooted stem (Figure 4.1). From the axils of the uppermost leaves arises a group of radiating flowering branches. Each of these begins with an internode which bears a pair of *opposite* leaves at the top. Between the bases of these leaves (that is, in their axils) arises a pair of branches and between these a pair of flowers. The branches behave in exactly the same way as the first group of branches (Figure 4.4). Indefinite continuation of this system of forking would double the number of branches at every node, producing a dense and tangled branch system and probable overcrowding of leaves and flowers. However, in *G. robertianum* possible congestion is often reduced by inequality in thickness and length of the branches of a pair; this inequality increases upwards until the stage is reached at which one branch remains as a dormant bud. In some perennial

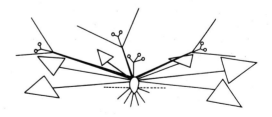

Figure 4.1 Diagram of a rosette-forming annual *Geranium* plant. The short central stem produces many leaves crowded into a rosette; these leaves are shown as triangles. Flowering stems grow out from the axils of the upper rosette-leaves; each internode terminates in a pair of leaves (not shown), two axillary branches and a cymule. The central stem bears a three-flowered cymule (see p. 27).

species there are only a few forking nodes and the leaves diminish in size very rapidly, becoming mere *bracts,* with a simplified outline.

An alternative way for annual species to develop is by the production of a few extended internodes below the group of radiating branches (Figure 4.2). In some annual species, such as *G. ocellatum,* there is no rosette and no visible differentiation into the two types of stem described above.

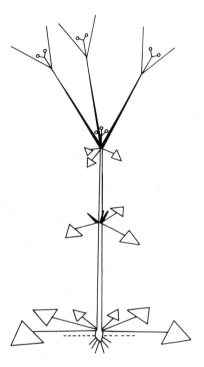

Figure 4.2 Diagrammatic representation of a rosette-forming annual *Geranium* plant which produces an elongated central stem from which the flowering branches arise

Although the forking stems potentially bear a pair of flowers at every node, those at the first node, or the first few nodes, are often suppressed. Nevertheless, it seems that the forking stems are in fact the flowering stems, being essentially different in their behaviour and shorter life span from the first-formed, rosette-bearing stems. However, I shall, in this book use the term *inflorescence* for that part of the branching system which bears flowers, that is, omitting those nodes in which the potential flowers do not develop.

In perennial species the roots sent out by the

initially-formed, rosette-bearing stem often pull it into an oblique or horizontal attitude. The stem continues to grow in length, and it goes on producing leaves after the emission of the flowering stems (Figure 4.3). Then, when it is ready to flower again, more flowering stems appear in the axils of some of the newer leaves. The rooted stem forms the *rootstock,* which is often woody. This usually grows slowly, with very short internodes, but with longer internodes it can vary to become a stout rhizome or tuber or, in extreme cases, a far-creeping underground stolon. In some perennial species, for example *G. sanguineum* and *G. wallichianum,* there are so few leaves on the rootstock that one cannot talk of a rosette and most of the foliage is borne on the flowering stems.

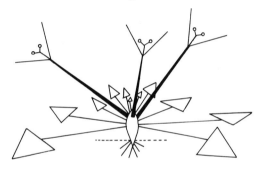

Figure 4.3 Diagrammatic representation of a perennial rosette-forming *Geranium* of compact growth. The short central stem continues to grow after the flowering stems have developed, producing more leaves and eventually more flowering stems (not shown); it usually becomes horizontal or oblique

There are several ways in which the basic plan of branching in *Geranium* is modified. Sometimes the internode of one member of each pair of branches is suppressed (Figure 4.4); this is not tantamount to the suppression of that shoot, for the pair of leaves which should be produced at the top of the internode unfolds and rests against the preceding leaf. From its axils arise one normal shoot and one with a suppressed internode, and so on. Some species produce single-leaved nodes and in this book the leaves so borne are described as *solitary;* at such nodes there may be one branch or two, or one branch and a flower-pair.

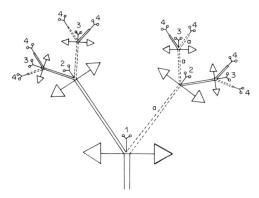

Figure 4.4 Basic plan of *Geranium* inflorescence. Leaves and lateral branches are omitted after the third level of branching. The system is capable of indefinite continuation; in its natural condition it is three-dimensional. Internodes shown by dashed lines may be suppressed

The production of flowers in pairs is characteristic of *Geranium*. The two flower-stalks (*pedicels*) arise at the top of a common stalk, the *peduncle*, where there are four *bracteoles* (lesser bracts). The two-flowered unit is referred to as a *cymule*. Some species occasionally or consistently produce one-flowered cymules. In *G. sanguineum* these always have a peduncle, whereas in *G. sibiricum* the peduncle is sometimes suppressed, and the flower is then borne on a stalk with no joint and no bracteoles. Occasionally, three-flowered cymules may be seen.

The type of inflorescence seen in *G. robertianum* may be described as *diffuse*, for the shoot has a prolonged development, producing a succession of flower-pairs over a long period. Flowering finally ceases when neither of the two axillary buds flanking a cymule grows out. In diffuse inflorescences, the leaves become very gradually reduced in size and complexity of lobing. Contrasted with the diffuse inflorescence is the *dense* type. This makes a striking display of flowers over a relatively short period. Various modifications may contribute to this. Where there is suppression of internodes, as described above, some of the flower-pairs are inevitably brought closer together; if the later ones become increasingly advanced in their development they flower in quick succession and before they can be smothered by the growth of the shoots which did not have suppressed internodes. In more normal systems a similar advance in the timing of flowers at later nodes,

combined with a rapid decrease of leaf-size and internode-length, can also give rise to a dense inflorescence. The end of flowering in dense inflorescences may result from the non-growth of an axillary bud but sometimes cymules take the place of ordinary branches. In some species the peduncles of the later cymules, and apparently some of the internodes supporting them, are suppressed. We then find a cluster of un-jointed flower-stalks (pedicels) arising from a single point, producing an *umbel-like* grouping (this happens in *G. erianthum*).

Flowers and Fruits

The flower structure in *Geranium* is very uniform (Figure 4.5). There are five sepals, five petals, 10 stamens in two whorls and five carpels. The sepals always have a projecting point (the *mucro*) at the tip. The petals are variously shaped and may or may not have an apical notch. In a few cases the petal is divisible into a stalk (or *claw*) and a blade (Figure 4.5 B,C). The stamens in the outer whorl are placed opposite the petals. At the base of each inner stamen is a swollen gland, the *nectary*. These can be exposed to view by detaching the sepals and petals, and each will usually be found to be encased in a glistening drop of nectar. The five carpels are joined to a central column but not to each other; they are topped by a common style, which is thickened at the base and divided at the top into five stigmatic branches with the receptive (stigmatic) surface on the inner side (the branches are referred to as *stigmas* in this book). The five carpel-chambers each contain two ovules, of which only one normally develops into a seed. The fruit is dry when ripe.

When the flower has opened the anthers of the five outer stamens soon burst. Later (perhaps the next day) the other five burst. After this (often after another day's delay) the stigmas, which have hitherto remained straight and pressed against each other (Figure 4.5), curl back and are for the first time receptive to pollen (Figure 9.69D). The flower therefore has definite *male and female stages*. However, this applies only to the larger-flowered species which are adapted to cross-pollination by insects. In small-flowered species the inner anthers may burst only an hour or two later than the outer, and the stigmas spread at about the same time as the flower opens. Such flowers are mainly self-pollinated, though they retain the potentiality for being cross-pollinated.

After fertilisation there is a rapid growth in length of the thickened base of the style to form the *rostrum* (Figure 4.6A). The seeds are dispersed by the explosive break-up of the rostrum as it dries out: five horny strips (the *awns*) — one for each carpel — suddenly peel away from the bottom upwards, leaving behind a *central column* (Figure 4.6B). Before this happens, each carpel is gently freed from the lower part of the central column and then remains attached only to the lower end of its awn. Thus, when the awns move the carpels move. The genus is sharply divided into three groups according to the manner in which the seeds are despatched; the details will be found in Chapter 5. The separated carpels derived from a fruit which splits up as in *Geranium* are called *mericarps*.

DESCRIPTIVE CONVENTIONS

The following conventions have been adopted for the description of plants in Chapter 9 and for use in the keys in Chapter 8.

Dimensions. An unqualified measurement always refers to length.

The Leaf. In all our species the leaf is palmate and stipules are present. The primary segments are called *divisions*. Each division is usually *lobed* and the lobes bear *teeth*. If the cutting of the divisions is very uniform it is considered that they have teeth but no lobes. In a few species the lobes have no teeth. The ways of reckoning the length and breadth of lobes are shown in Figure 4.7. It will be seen that the width of a division includes the lobes and the width of a lobe includes the teeth. When counting the teeth on a lobe the tip of the lobe should be ignored.

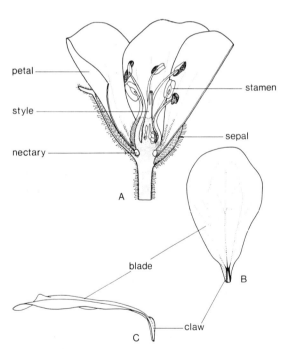

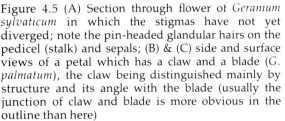

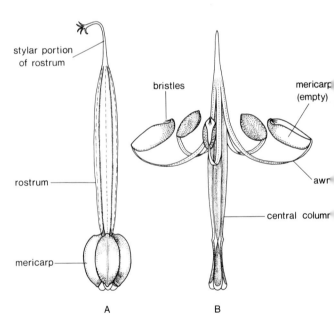

Figure 4.5 (A) Section through flower of *Geranium sylvaticum* in which the stigmas have not yet diverged; note the pin-headed glandular hairs on the pedicel (stalk) and sepals; (B) & (C) side and surface views of a petal which has a claw and a blade (*G. palmatum*), the claw being distinguished mainly by structure and its angle with the blade (usually the junction of claw and blade is more obvious in the outline than here)

Figure 4.6 The parts of the fruit of *Geranium*: (A) when nearly mature; (B) after discharge. This is a seed-ejecting type with retention of the seed in the pre-explosive interval by a tuft of bristles (see Chapter 5)

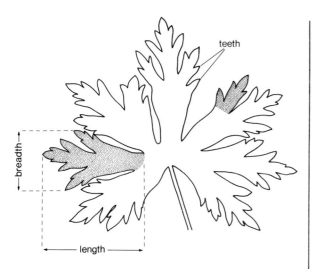

Figure 4.7 Leaf-blade of *Geranium* with a *division* shaded on the left and a *lobe* shaded on the right

Where the lobes are very narrow they are not contiguously arranged on the division, and the same applies to narrow teeth on the lobes (Figure 9.57). When this is the case the width of the divisions (defined as above) is irrelevant; what is significant is the width of the portions of the divisions lying between successive pairs of lobes. The same applies to parts of lobes between successive pairs of teeth. These widths are not likely to differ much within the leaf. In this case *all* these parts are referred to as *segments*. (The use of the terms division, lobe, tooth and segment as explained here is standardised in this way only in this book.)

Each leaf-division has a broadest point somewhere above the base. If it is at the apex, the latter has a more or less cut-off or rounded appearance and the overall outline of the leaf will be rather even, and rounded, kidney-shaped or weakly angled (Figures 9.8 and 9.47 show examples). More usually the broadest point is below the apex and the division is then tapered in both directions. The nearer the widest point is to the apex the more briefly and abruptly is the division tapered beyond its widest point.

A consequence of having the broadest point at or near the apex is that the lobes are apical; in fact they have a palmate arrangement, to the extent that this is possible in a relatively narrow organ. Other arrangements of the lobes occur when the widest point is some way down from the apex. Occasionally, but usually only when the lobing extends down the sides of the division below the widest point, the lobing is pinnate. Most commonly, however, the lobing is confined to the portion beyond the widest part and is of an intermediate type: *palmato-pinnate* (as in Figure 4.7).

Leaf-size. This is measured by width which is usually indicated approximately as a range based on units of 5 or 10cm, e.g.

not more than 5cm
between 5 and 10cm
between 10 and 20cm
more than 20cm.

Size is given for the largest leaves, which are usually the basal (rosette) leaves or the lower stem leaves. If the largest leaves are usually on the borderline between two ranges the size is given as 'about 10cm' (etc., as the case may be). As leaf-size is very flexible, allowance has to be made for exceptional sizes resulting from exceptional growing conditions. Most gardeners will probably find that my measurements for leaf-size are usually on the low side.

Hairs. The only parts of a *Geranium* plant which never seem to have hairs are the anthers, the stigmatic surfaces and the seed-coats. Descriptions of the hair-covering are therefore sometimes omitted. The hair-distribution on petals or stamens will, in fact, almost always be mentioned, because it is more or less characteristic for the species. *Glandular hairs* are those with a rounded, usually spherically swollen and often red tip (Figure 4.5A). Hairs without this are called *eglandular*. Examination with a strong lens will often show that a *Geranium* plant is beset with very tiny glandular hairs. These are not usually mentioned in the descriptions, and if glandular hairs are mentioned one should look for sizeable ones, similar in size to the pointed eglandular hairs which will usually also be present.

Flower Posture. The posture of the flower bud is not very important, although there are exceptions to the usual nodding posture. The commonest posture of the open flower is upwardly inclined. There are also some species in which the flower is held strictly erect, but distinguishing between these classes will not be necessary for identification within this book. In some species the flowers are approximately horizontal (good examples are *G. pratense* and *G. farreri*), which means that the petals are vertical. To avoid confusion, therefore, this condition will be indicated by the phrase *'floral axis horizontal'*. A distinction will also sometimes be made between *inverted* flowers, which face vertically downwards, and *nodding* flowers, which have the floral axis below the horizontal but not vertical. When the fruit is ripe it is always upright. In the interval between flowering and the ripening of the fruit the posture of the pedicels and of the immature fruit is important. When the posture of the immature fruit differs from that of its pedicel, the pedicel is bent under the fruit.

Sepal-length. This is always given without including the mucro. The collective term for the sepals of one flower, *calyx*, is sometimes used but not where length is under consideration. At fruiting-time the sepals are always larger than at flowering-time; the sepal-length given covers both stages unless the increase is conspicuous.

Petal-size. This may be given in millimetres or treated like leaf-size, on a scale of three different length ranges (or their borderline areas) thus:

not more than 8mm

8–16mm

more than 16mm.

The apex of the petal may or may not have a central notch. As an aberration, often temporary, there may be a number of unequal narrow incisions, obscuring the true shape. For notched petals, the length given is the overall length.

Flower-colour. A range of flower colours from a not-quite true blue to a deep pinkish red occurs in *Geranium*. The description of shades in this range is subjective because people's perception of them differs. However, for me most shades appear to fall to one side or other of a line which divides blue from pink and pinkish red, and I shall endeavour to indicate this distinction in my descriptions. On the borderline is violet, and a *Geranium* which is on this borderline is *G. sylvaticum* in its prevalent form. Sometimes the colour is somewhat greyed, and the greyed hues are represented by a range from bluish lilac (in some forms of *G. phaeum*) to dark maroon (in *G. sinense*). Where an exact description of colour is necessary, as is especially the case in characterising cultivars, colour-chart readings are given. Where possible the *Royal Horticultural Society Colour Chart* (1966) has been used (it is referred to as RHSCC). Sometimes it has been necessary to refer to the *Horticultural Colour Chart* (HCC) (Wilson, 1939 and 1942). Both of these have cross-references to other charts. The cross-references in RHSCC to HCC were obtained using a standardised light source. Under the conditions in which I work, however, I get different matchings between the two charts and have here recorded my own readings.

Anther-colour. When this is pale the lines along which the anthers burst are often the most strongly coloured part. These lines are called the edges of the anthers, though they form their edges only after bursting.

Length of Stamens, Style and Rostrum. Stamen-length will usually be given in comparison with sepal-length. If it lies between $2/3$ and $1\frac{1}{3}$ times the length of the sepal (excluding the mucro) it is unremarkable and may not be mentioned. Stamens are usually measurable until the fruit is nearly ripe, but there is a slight increase in their length during the flowering period and immediately after petal-fall. *Style-length* is usually about the same as stamen-length and, as with stamens, if it is not mentioned it can be assumed that the style attains between $2/3$ and $1\frac{1}{3}$ times the length of the sepals. However, its length will sometimes be given in millimetres, taken from the base of the ovary (young carpels) to the base of the stigmas. The *rostrum* is at its full length when the fruit is ripe and slightly before. It is measured from the top of the mericarps to the base of the stigmas. It thus includes the slender tip which formed the style (or most of it) at flowering time. The length of this *stylar portion* is usually stated in the descriptions, though sometimes it cannot be determined because the rostrum is too gradually tapered.

Carpels and Seeds. In order to avoid confusion between a seed and a detached mericarp with a seed inside, please see Chapter 5. The fruit-discharge types, described there, are indicated in Chapter 9 for all species. The term 'mericarp' will be applied in this book to the ripe seed-containing part of the carpel, although technically it is probable that the awn is part of the carpel.

·CHAPTER 5·
Classification

THE DIFFERENCE BETWEEN *GERANIUM* AND RELATED GENERA

Of the four other genera in the family Geraniaceae, perhaps the most similar to *Geranium* is *Monsonia*. Its leaves are simple and in some cases palmately lobed, the cymules are sometimes two-flowered and the flowers are radially symmetric. The number of stamens, however, is 15, not 10. Another genus, *Sarcocaulon*, also has radially symmetric flowers and 15 stamens, but the flowers are solitary; it is a desert plant with succulent stems and reduced leaves. In *Erodium* the leaves may be simple, lobed or pinnate, the inflorescence is often umbel-like and the flowers are slightly irregular (bilaterally symmetric); the five inner stamens are normal but the five outer, opposite the petals, are without anthers. *Pelargonium* is similar to *Erodium* in its great range of leaf-shapes and in usually having the flowers in umbels. The flower is usually rather strongly irregular (bilaterally symmetric) and the number of stamens with anthers ranges from seven to two. All species of *Pelargonium* also have a narrow and often long nectarial tube running back from the flower along the upper side of the pedicel.

All four of the genera related to *Geranium* are alike in the way the ripe fruit breaks up: each mericarp, complete with awn, is thrown clear by a small explosion resulting from the release of tension built up in the rostrum during drying out (Figure 5.1). The seed remains in the meri-carp. In *Monsonia* and *Erodium* the awn is either plumed for wind-dispersal, or it is coiled and apparently able to drive the mericarp body into the ground (Figure 5.1, left). The awn of *Sarcocaulon* is plumed. That of *Pelargonium* is also plumed, but it is helically twisted as well (Figure 5.1, right).

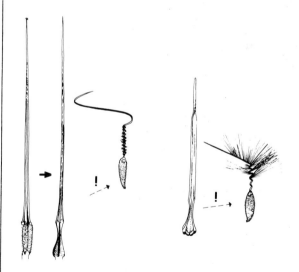

Figure 5.1 Left: fruit of *Erodium* before and after discharge, with one separated mericarp. Right: central column of fruit of *Pelargonium* after discharge, with one separated mericarp

CLASSIFICATION OF *GERANIUM* SPECIES

There are three different ways in which the fruit breaks up in *Geranium* and this provides a convenient basis for dividing the genus into three subgenera.

One method of break-up of the fruit is that just described: the mericarp with the seed inside and the awn attached comes away from the central column, being thrown a short distance by the explosion (Figure 5.2). The awn becomes coiled but is not plumed. I have called this type of discharge the *Erodium-type*, though in fact the awn coils more or less at right angles to the mericarp and not in line with it as it does in *Erodium*. Species of *Geranium* with this type of fruit-discharge are placed in subgenus *Erodioideae*.

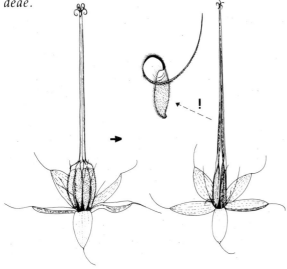

Figure 5.2 Fruit of *Geranium* subgenus *Erodioideae* with 'Erodium-type' discharge. Left: in pre-explosive interval. Right: after discharge (one detached mericarp with awn shown). After discharge the central column is naked

The second method is termed *carpel-projection*, for the mericarp without the awn is thrown off to a distance of a few feet, and the awn simply drops away at the moment of discharge (Figure 5.3). Species with this type of discharge constitute the subgenus *Robertium* which, as its name suggests, includes *G. robertianum* (Herb Robert).

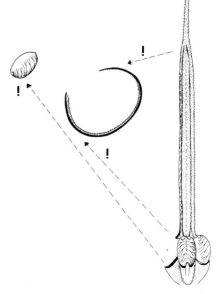

Figure 5.3 Fruit of *Geranium* subgenus *Robertium* with 'carpel-projection' discharge. The fruit is shown partly in the pre-explosive interval but with one awn and mericarp separated. After discharge the central column is naked

The third method is called *seed-ejection*, because on discharge the awn curls back and the seed is thrown out of the mericarp (Figure 4.6). The mechanism is very like that of a Roman ballista, but it is upside-down compared with that. Species with seed-ejection are placed in subgenus *Geranium*.

It will be recalled from the description of the fruit in Chapter 4 that before discharge the mericarps separate from the central column so that each is then attached only to its awn. The mericarps of subgenus *Geranium* have to have a hole big enough to let the seed out, and the elevation of the mericarp just before discharge could permit the seed to fall out prematurely if there were no arrangements to prevent it. There are in fact three different ways of doing this, and subgenus *Geranium* is split into three according to the method of seed-retention in the pre-explosive interval. The commonest method is to have a cluster of stiff hairs at the lower end of the carpel-orifice; these can bend under the pressure from the seed when the mericarp changes direction as its awn curls up during the explosion (Figure 4.6). These bristles are always borne on a horny tubercle which projects a short distance below the lower end of the mericarp; they are attached along its sides and change direction at the beginning of the pre-explosive interval so as to support the seed. Species with this arrangement are placed in section *Geranium*.

The second kind of arrangement for seed-retention is a flexible prong on the lower edge of the orifice of the mericarp, in a position corresponding to that of the bristles in the previously-described type. The prong has the same texture as the rest of the mericarp wall and it functions in the same way as the bristles. The prong is cut out from the mericarp wall by the specially curved line of cleavage, which leaves a distinctively shaped residue attached to the central column (Figure 5.4). Species with this type of seed-retention constitute the section *Dissecta*.

The third arrangement is quite different from the others, in that retention is achieved by a twist at the point where the mericarp joins the awn, bringing the open side of the mericarp into a sideways-facing position (Figure 5.5). This in itself must reduce the likelihood of the seed's dropping out but additional security is provided by the persistent stamen-filaments, every other one of which bars a carpel-orifice. In all species with this type of retention the mericarp and awn drop away at the end of the explosion, immediately after the seed has been ejected. Thus the familiar candelabrum-like appearance of the discharged cranesbill fruit is in fact restricted to subgenus *Geranium*, sections *Geranium* and *Dissecta*. Species with the twist-method of seed-retention belong to section *Tuberosa*, which contains The *G. tuberosum* Group and The *G. platypetalum* Group.

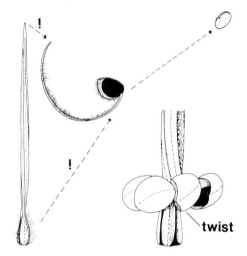

Figure 5.5 Fruit of *Geranium* subgenus *Geranium* section *Tuberosa* with 'seed-ejection' discharge. Retention of the seed in the pre-explosive interval is due to twisting of the mericarps in the pre-explosive interval (right) and is assisted by the stamens (not shown). After discharge the central column is naked (left, on a smaller scale)

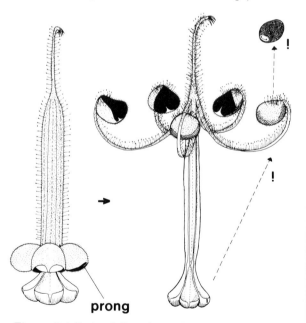

Figure 5.4 Fruit of *Geranium* subgenus *Geranium* section *Dissecta* with 'seed-ejection' discharge. Retention of the seed in the pre-explosive interval is by a prong. The carpels remain attached to the central column by their awns after discharge. The true trajectory of the seed is obliquely upwards

All the different fruit-types described so far are quite easily observed and they can be of considerable assistance in identification. The fruits (and seeds) of the European and Caucasian species of *Geranium* have been excellently illustrated by Tokarski (1972). The classification based on them (Yeo, 1984b) is quite different from that of Knuth (1912) who put most of the annuals together and relied considerably on the type of rootstock to classify the perennials.

Among the sections of subgenus *Geranium*,

there is evident correlation of characters with that of fruit-type in section *Tuberosa*. Section *Dissecta*, however, is too small for such correlation to be apparent and section *Geranium* too large.

Various groups of correlated characters, including some from the fruit, can be used to divide up the two smaller subgenera. Thus subgenus *Erodioideae* comprises The *G. phaeum* Group — section *Erodioideae* — and The *G. cinereum* Group — section *Subacaulia*, while subgenus *Robertium* is here divided into eight sections. The characters of the sections of these two subgenera are outlined in Chapter 9, where the species are dealt with in systematic order. This is preferable to alphabetical order as it has the effect of putting similar species near each other and separating dissimilar species. Similarity, of course, is a subjective concept, but systematic botany takes into account as many characters as possible in order to determine overall similarity. The nature of plant variation is such that occasionally plants with pronounced differences in inconspicuous characters look superficially alike. Examples of pairs of species which look similar, but differ in their type of fruit-discharge, are *Geranium phaeum* and *G. sinense*, and *G. nodosum* and *G. gracile*. A modicum of application should suffice to convince the doubtful reader of the basic dissimilarity of the members of these pairs.

The hierarchical classification outlined so far is set out below, with indications of the approximate numbers of species in the sections, and the name of one well-known species included in each. The subgenera are placed in order of size (number of included species).

Geranium Linnaeus

Subgenus *Geranium*
  Section *Geranium*: 250–300 species (*G. pratense*)
  Section *Dissecta* Yeo: 3 species (*G. asphodeloides*)
  Section *Tuberosa* Reiche: 20 or 21 species (*G. platypetalum*)
Subgenus *Robertium* Picard
  Section *Polyantha* Reiche: 6 species (*G. polyanthes*)
  Section *Trilopha* Yeo: 5 or 6 species (*G. trilophum*)
  Section *Divaricata* Rouy & Foucaud: 2 species (*G. albanum*)
  Section *Batrachioides* W.D.J. Koch: 4 or 5 species (*G. pyrenaicum*)
  Section *Unguiculata* Reiche: 5 species (*G. macrorrhizum*)
  Section *Lucida* Knuth: 1 species (*G. lucidum*)
  Section *Ruberta* Dumortier: 4 species (*G. robertianum*)
  Section *Anemonifolia* Knuth: 2 species (*G. palmatum*)
Subgenus *Erodioideae* Yeo
  Section *Erodioideae* Picard: 3 species (*G. phaeum*)
  Section *Subacaulia* Reiche: 6–12 species (species-limits are difficult to decide in this group) (*G. cinereum*)

This statement reveals the big snag with this classification — the existence of 250 or more species in section *Geranium*. This needs to be divided up into smaller groups but at present I do not see how such groups can be defined. In Chapter 9, therefore, I have not used the botanical categories of subsection or series for section *Geranium*, but have arranged the species as best I can in informally named groups. Within these groups there are certainly some species that I believe are closely related, but I am not sure that every species is rightly placed with its near relatives. Even more difficult than forming these groups is the problem of their sequence; there is very little to go on here, and it will be evident that geographical distribution has played some part in determining the sequence I have adopted in Chapter 9.

·CHAPTER 6·
Structure in Relation to Function

The relation of structure to function on the level of the organ or the whole plant has been subject to relatively little scientific investigation. These notes are therefore necessarily largely conjectural, but they should serve to show that the variations found within a genus of plants have their functions. This will perhaps add another dimension of interest to the making of a collection of *Geranium* species in cultivation.

ROOTS AND ROOTSTOCKS

Many species of *Geranium* produce remarkably thick roots which penetrate deeply into the soil. These are often accompanied by finer roots near the surface. Little is known about the way *Geranium* roots exploit the soil, however. The rootstock is made up of the permanent stem and the roots it bears. The compact type of rootstock is usually associated with plants which produce plenty of basal leaves and have erect self-supporting stems. These rootstocks hold water and nutrients during the unfavourable season, which may be summer or winter. Such plants are *G. sylvaticum*, *G. pratense*, *G. maculatum*, *G. oreganum* and *G. platypetalum*, which grow in stable soils. Especially if summer is the unfavourable season the rootstock may be tuberous, as in *G. peloponnesiacum* and, even more so, in the related Tuberosum Group. Some species in the latter group have invaded cultivated land and their tubers then function also as organs of dispersal. A stout, slow-growing rootstock which develops on the surface is found in *G. phaeum*, producing a mass of rhizomes reminiscent of those of the Bearded Iris (*Iris germanica*). They probably get winter protection from snow in their natural habitat and their function might be to swamp competition or to allow slow migration away from exhausted soil. The woody rootstock of the North American *G. nervosum* perhaps suits it to the dry shade of pine woods where it often grows.

European examples of species with farcreeping rhizomes or stolons are *G. macrorrhizum* and *G. dalmaticum*. These tend to grow on cliffs, and their rhizomes presumably help them to spread along crevices and into cracks. Some of the Chinese high mountain species (*G. stapfianum*, *G. pylzowianum*, *G. orientalitibeticum*) have slender rhizomes which seem to be related to growing in turf affected by frost-heaving or to scree conditions.

An interesting contrast in rootstocks is presented by two closely related species from Kashmir, *G. rubifolium*, which is almost tuberous, and *G. kishtvariense*, which has rather slender rapidly-spreading underground stolons. To what differences of habitat these variations are related we do not yet know.

ABOVE-GROUND HABIT

Plants of medium or large stature with little or no ability to spread underground fall into two main types above ground. Some produce a strong flush of basal leaves in the spring and then erect flowering stems. Examples are *G. sylvaticum*, *G. pratense* (Figures 9.9 and 9.17) and many others. Others produce few or no rosette leaves and have stems which are not self-supporting (Figure 9.30). In our gardens they may trail on the ground, but if we let them grow among other plants we see what is probably their natural habit: they scramble up through small shrubs or keep pace with other herbaceous perennials which give them support. Thus these two growth habits are apparently two ways of dealing with competition. In the first case the basal leaves compete by shading adjacent plants; in the second the plant is always climbing up to the light and producing new leaves favourably placed to receive it. The first type of habit is compatible with having a dense inflorescence of many flowers produced in a short time, whereas the second is not, and all species with this habit have diffuse inflorescences. Sometimes, as in *G. albanum,* the scrambling growth-habit is combined with the production of abundant basal leaves.

What seems to be a rather different habit is that seen in *G. sanguineum* and, perhaps less markedly, in *G. dahuricum* and *G. yesoense.* Here the plant often finds itself without support and its thin but stiff branches diverge at wide angles so that a bushy growth with numerous contact-points with the soil is formed. If other, taller plants are available, however, these species can scramble through them. There are bulbous thickenings (*pulvini*) at the nodes of the stems and the bases of the leaf-stalks. These can alter the angles between internodes and between leaf and stem, an adaptation which is useful if the supporting structures shift.

LEAVES AND HAIRS

Little is known about the ways in which the varied attributes of the leaves function, but there is a clear correlation between leaf-type and habitat. The shadier the habitat the more likely is the leaf of *Geranium* to have shallow divisions and lobes and numerous small teeth; the texture tends to be wrinkled, the colour yellowish and the hairiness moderate (Figures 9.33 and 9.82). At the other extreme are plants of dry places usually with darker green leaves which have very narrow leaf segments. Examples are *G. sanguineum* (Figure 9.50), the Mexican *G. schiedeanum* (Figure 9.65) and the South African *G. incanum* (Figure 9.57), the last two of which have the leaf-edges recurved and the channelled undersides of the segments more or less filled up with hairs.

Alpines, and many annuals, have small leaves with the divisions broadest at or near the apex and terminally lobed, so that the overall outline of the leaf is a nearly smooth curve (Figures 9.52 and 9.8). Some members of the *G. cinereum* group, with leaves of this kind, have a silvery covering of appressed hairs, whose reflective properties may protect the leaf from excessive heating.

Plants of moderately sunny habitats have leaves intermediate in lobing, texture and hairiness (e.g. Figure 9.61).

The hairs which clothe the leaves, and vary in density in approximate agreement with the exposure of the plants to sun, are eglandular. Some species also have glandular hairs. These are almost always more abundant on the upper parts of the plant and are more often found on stems and sepals than on the leaves. They usually make the plant sticky to the touch and may, therefore, be a protection against infestation by aphides and an impediment to access by ants, which often encourage and protect aphides. Most lowland species of *Geranium* have glandular hairs, whereas most alpine species lack them, probably because such small insect pests are less important in the alpine climate.

INFLORESCENCES

Most annual species have relatively small flowers which, as mentioned in Chapter 4, are essentially adapted to self-pollination. They do not make a big display individually, and there would seem to be no point in their being massed into dense inflorescences if insect-pollination is relatively unimportant.

Among large-flowered species we have seen how the trailing and climbing growth-habit restricts its possessors to a diffuse type of inflorescence. Dense inflorescences are found in the self-supporting species (examples are *G. pratense* (Plates 9 and 10), *G. sylvaticum, G. maculatum, G. erianthum* and *G. palmatum*). Whether the density of the inflorescence is primarily adapted to attracting insects effectively or is related to some other aspect of the plant's life which perhaps demands concentrated seed-maturation is not known.

The posture of the unripe fruits and their pedicels shows interesting variations (Figures 9.9, 9.15, and 9.17). These are probably concerned with keeping the unripe fruits away from open flowers, the method varying according to the form of the inflorescence and the posture of the open flowers.

FLOWERS

The life of the flower has four stages: bud, open flower, unripe fruit, ripe fruit. Buds are often nodding, and the mucros of the sepals in many cases probably act as 'drip-tips', helping to discharge rainwater from the surface.

The open flower is involved in several functions: it has to present pollen for removal by pollinators or, in self-pollinating species, for transfer to the stigmas; it has to receive pollen on its stigmas; if it is insect-pollinated it has to attract insects and reward them so that they will visit a succession of flowers; it then also has to ensure that they make the right movements to carry out pollination; and it has to prevent insects which are too small to cause pollination from stealing the reward. The attraction is provided by the petals, which in many species have coloured marks which either increase the attractiveness of the flower to the insect or act as guide-marks, signalling the centre of the flower where the nectar is. In a few species of *Geranium* with inconspicuous guide-marks, photography with ultra-violet filters has shown distinct patterns of ultra-violet absorption in the flower. As insects can see ultra-violet light, these UV-free areas look different to them. Therefore, it may be expected that further investigation will show that the number of species with insect-visible guide-marks is much greater than the number with human-visible guide-marks. At present we know little of the significance of the different flower colours and their patterns in *Geranium*.

The reward offered by *Geranium* is always nectar, and at least some of even the very small-flowered species produce it. The pollen is usually accessible and much must be taken by the bees which are the principal pollinators of *Geranium*. They could either take it directly or stow it in their pollen baskets after grooming themselves between flower-visits. Thus the floral economy has to allow for the diversion of some pollen from its proper function.

Certainly there are some specialisations in pollination as between the different species of *Geranium*, and these involve not only petal colour but the colours of other floral parts. In addition flower size and shape (i.e. hollow, flat or convex), posture (from erect to inverted) and the size, position and curvature of the stamens and stigmas are all involved. The petals and stamens bear hairs; here again there is doubt about the exact functions of the different arrangements, but obvious possibilities are to improve the foothold for pollinators or to influence the directions from which they probe the flowers, and to exclude very small insects from the nectaries.

We may now look at some examples of these adaptive types. Bumble-bees are large and have moderately to extremely long tongues. In general, the plants most conspicuously adapted to them have long tubular flowers (for example Labiatae and some Boraginaceae) or petals formed into long nectar spurs, as in *Aquilegia*, columbine. These possibilities are not open to *Geranium* but it has been noted that bumble-bees are more ready than some other insects to cling upside-down to flowers. Hence, some *Geranium* species with a strong adaptation to bumble-bees have a horizontal or nodding floral axis and long stamens held near the centre of the flower on which the bees alight. Examples are *G. pratense* (Plates 8 and 9) and *G. erianthum* (Plates 13 and 14). More strongly nodding flowers, flat or convex, are found in *G. phaeum* and *G. reflexum* (Plate 38). The sombre colouring of *G. phaeum* var. *phaeum* suggests, by analogy with similarly coloured flowers in other families, that these flowers are wasp-pollinated. However, the flowers are produced very early, when only queen wasps are available, and they seem readily to attract bees. The extremely similar but unrelated *G. sinense* (Plate 18), from China, flowers later and really does attract wasps, though in England in some years great numbers of hoverflies visit it. Both types of insect cling to the stamens. It is interesting to note that the floral hairs in *G. sinense* are rudimentary and the nectaries are fused into a prominent ring around the flower. As wasps have very short and relatively broad tongues these floral characteristics would seem to be adapted to their needs.

The above-mentioned nodding flowers with centrally positioned stamens usually have white or pale and translucent petal bases. This gives the flower a pale centre which is sometimes strikingly illuminated from behind by the sun, as in *G. phaeum* var. *phaeum*.

When the flower is pendent but has diverging

stamens, as in *G. lambertii, G. pogonanthum* and *G. yunnanense,* it seems probable that the pollinators alight on the petals.

The opposite extreme from these types is found in the pink-flowered *G. nervosum* and *G. fremontii* of North America (Plate 22). Here the flower is strictly upright and the stamens with rather long anthers curve outwards near their tips. Bees, often the shorter-tongued species of bumble-bee, walk round the flower on the petals, contacting the anthers with their backs. When the flower reaches the female stage, long curving stigmas stand at the level formerly occupied by the anthers.

Some *Geranium* species have found a way of demanding a long reach by the insect's tongue and so specialising more exclusively on the long-tongued insects. In *G. dalmaticum* and *G. macrorrhizum* there is a bladdery calyx, clawed petals and a narrow throat (Plate 34). The stamens and style are curved downwards and are used as an alighting place by bumble-bees. A further refinement is found in *G. robertianum* and its allies. Each petal claw bears a channelled ridge which fits against a stamen filament. The claws are flanged on either side of the ridge in such a way that two neighbouring petals form a narrow passage leading to the nectary situated between their points of attachment. The visiting insect has to probe each in turn. Bumble-bees and the long-tongued hoverfly, *Rhingia,* visit *G. robertianum.* This species is rather anomalous in possessing such an arrangement because the stigmas are receptive when the flower opens and self-pollination readily occurs. Among the allied species with this construction is *G. palmatum,* in which the nectar passages have a slit-like instead of a circular entrance. I suspect this suits the flowers to butterflies. The related *G. maderense* has slightly less slit-like entrances, upright instead of horizontal flowers, and over-arching stamens, suggesting that it may be visited by rather small bees which are touched on their backs by the anthers and stigmas.

It is only in this group that slight zygomorphy (bilateral symmetry) of the flowers occurs, being evident in *G. dalmaticum, G. macrorrhizum* and *G. palmatum.*

Though greatly outnumbered in individuals by honey-bees and bumble-bees, there are numerous species of solitary bees of varying sizes which may provide pollinators for many of the species of *Geranium* which are without extreme specialisations of floral form and colour. On the mixed collection of *Geranium* plants that I grow together in pots at Cambridge the mason bee, *Osmia rufa,* is sometimes common; it has a long tongue but visits the different species readily.

A final possible specialisation of *Geranium* flower is towards beetle-pollination. This is generally more important in warm conditions. When I collected *G. richardsonii* in Colorado several beetles came out of the flowers, which are unusual in being white and in having a great quantity of hair on the upper surface of the petals (Plate 23). Whether such features can be related to beetle-pollination remains to be seen.

At the stage of the immature fruit the sepals usually close over the developing carpels and diverge again when the fruit is ripe, thereby making way for the operation of the explosive discharge mechanism.

When the fruit is ripe it assumes an upright position, regardless of its posture during development. *Geranium* must be classed as a heavy-seeded genus, and the role of its discharge mechanism is presumably simply to get the seeds clear of the parent plant. Long-distance dispersal must then be left to chance.

A possible exception to this rule is found in *G. robertianum* and *G. purpureum.* In these species each mericarp, when shot off, trails 'tangle-strands' (see p. 153), by which it frequently gets caught up on surrounding vegetation. A possible function for this is to assist consumption by browsing mammals which would, if the seeds are resistant to the animals' digestive enzymes, cause dispersal over longer distances. It is perhaps significant that *G. robertianum* is a woodland plant with an enormous distribution from West Europe to China and Japan. Plants with fruits or seeds dispersed by animals (usually externally) are particularly prevalent in woodland.

The remarkable inflexed wings on the fruits of *G. trilophum* and *G. biuncinatum* suggest adaptation to wind-dispersal, but *G. biuncinatum* also has a pair of hooks on each mericarp which is probably an arrangement for adhesion to the fur of animals, in which case this species has both 'belt and braces'. The small rounded fruits of the little weed, *G. molle,* if tipped out on to a table, roll about as if with a life of their own. This probably helps them to find a crevice in the soil before they come to rest after discharge.

·CHAPTER 7·
Chromosome
Numbers & Hybrids

CHROMOSOME NUMBERS

Chromosome numbers sometimes give indications of relationships and the possibilities for hybridisation, and they may govern the outcome of hybridisation if it occurs. However, chromosome number is only one of several factors that can determine whether a cross-pollination leads to the formation of a viable hybrid, and whether such a hybrid is in some degree fertile. Nevertheless, one can say that hybridisation is less likely to take place if the chromosome numbers of the parents are unequal than if they are equal, and that hybrids between parents differing in chromosome number are usually more or less completely sterile. A knowledge of chromosome numbers is, therefore, helpful background to a survey of hybrids or for any programme of deliberate hybridisation.

The known diploid (2n) chromosome numbers of *Geranium* are listed below (sometimes the haploid condition was observed; in these cases the count has been doubled). References to the sources of most of this information are in Yeo (1984b, Table 2). It should be mentioned that mistakes are sometimes made in counting chromosomes. The chromosomes of *Geranium* are relatively small and do not stain well, and some erroneous counts appear to have been published, though in fact it is rarely possible to prove that an error has been made. Because most species of plants have a single characteristic chromosome number, the finding of a number different from one already reported

needs to be particularly well substantiated. In the following paragraphs the reader will perhaps distinguish my reactions of credence, neutrality or doubt towards reports of different numbers in the same species. Erroneous reports can also arise from misidentification, which can easily be cleared up if voucher specimens are kept, something which has frequently been neglected in the past.

Subgenus *Geranium*, section *Geranium*, most commonly shows 28 chromosomes — a number found so far in over 30 species from Europe, Continental Asia, Japan and New Zealand (*G. traversii*). Tetraploids, that is, species with exactly double this number (56), are rare: the following are reported: *G. sessiliflorum* (probably of Australasian rather than South American origin); the related *G. hyperacrion*, from New Guinea; and *G. wlassovianum* from North and East Asia. Another species from New Guinea, *G. niuginiense*, has 36 chromosomes, a number also found in subgenus *Robertium* but not known elsewhere in subgenus *Geranium*. A record of 56 chromosomes is also available for *G. palustre* but there are three records of 28 for this species. A higher multiple of 28, namely 84 (hexaploid), also exists in this section, having been found repeatedly in *G. sanguineum*, for which, however, there is also one count of approximately 56.

The number 26, found also in two sections of subgenus *Robertium*, is found in section *Geranium* of subgenus *Geranium*. It has been reported twice for the perennial *G. endressii*, for which 28 has also been reported, and it is the only number reported for *G. rotundifolium*, in which it has been found several times.

The tetraploid number corresponding to 26, namely 52, is found in the only two known North American annuals and in six perennials ranging from Canada to Venezuela. The only other number reported in North America is 28 for *G. erianthum*, a species of the far North-west which also occurs in North-east Asia.

Counts of 24 have been published for two species, *G. pratense* and *G. sylvaticum*, which usually have 28. These should be regarded with caution.

The only other chromosome number known in this section is 18, found repeatedly in the annual species, *G. columbinum*.

In section *Dissecta* of subgenus *Geranium*, the number 28 shows up again, in *G. asphodeloides*, which is, however, the most variable in chromosome number of all *Geranium* species, showing also 30, 26 and 24. *G. asphodeloides* is perennial or biennial. The related annual species, *G. dissectum*, has 22 chromosomes.

Finally, we come to section *Tuberosa* in this subgenus. Here, 28 is the number known for two species of The *G. tuberosum* Group, and two of The *G. platypetalum* Group, namely, *G. platypetalum* itself and *G. gymnocaulon*. However, the investigator of the latter also found 56 chromosomes in the same species. *G. ibericum* has 56 chromosomes. Reports of 42 in *G. platypetalum* are based on the misidentification of *G.* ×*magnificum*, a sterile hybrid between *G. platypetalum* and *G. ibericum*. There are two annual or biennial species in this group, *G. bohemicum* with 28 and *G. lanuginosum* with 48 chromosomes.

Subgenus *Robertium* is by far the most diverse in chromosome number.

From section *Polyantha* only the solitary cultivated species, *G. polyanthes*, has been counted: it has 28 chromosomes.

In section *Trilopha* there is an old count of 50 for *G. favosum* and a recent one of 56 for *G. ocellatum* of West African origin.

In section *Divaricata* the perennial species *G. albanum* has 28 and there are recent counts of both 26 and 28 for the annual species *G. divaricatum*.

In section *Batrachioides* there are several reports of both 26 and 28 for the perennial *G. pyrenaicum* and of 26 for both the annuals, *G. molle* and *G. pusillum*. The solitary report of 34 for the latter is believed to be an error.

In section *Unguiculata*, *G. glaberrimum* has 30

chromosomes, *G. cataractarum* 36 (reported for both South Spanish and North-west African plants), and *G. dalmaticum* and *G. macrorrhizum* both have 46. For the latter there is a count of 87–93, but there are several of 46.

Section *Lucida* contains only *G. lucidum*, for which both 20 and 40 have been counted more than once and 60 once.

In section *Ruberta*, *G. purpureum* has 32, *G. robertianum* has 64, and *G. rubescens* and *G. canariense* have 128. Reports of 32, 54 and 56 for *G. robertianum* are in need of substantiation.

The two species of section *Anemonifolia*, *G. palmatum* (syn. *G. anemonifolium*) and *G. maderense*, both have 68 chromosomes. The report of 128 for the former arose from an editorial error; it really refers to *G. canariense*.

In subgenus *Erodioideae*, section *Erodioideae*, all three species have 28 chromosomes. The number 14 has been reported twice for *G. phaeum*, but in an incidental manner and not in the affirmative way that one requires for a number that is known in no other species and is at variance with three independent counts of 28. In section *Subacaulia*, 28 has been reported for *G. argenteum*, *G. cinereum* var. *cinereum* and *G. cinereum* var. *subcaulescens*, as well as for *G. cinereum* subsp. *nanum* (refuting an earlier count of 26).

To summarise: a diploid number of 28 is found in all sections of subgenera *Erodioideae* and *Geranium*, and in three sections of subgenus *Robertium*; multiples of this number are rare but involve one additional section of subgenus *Robertium*; of the five annuals in subgenus *Geranium*, three have numbers below 28; all species confined to the Americas, whether annual or perennial, have 52 chromosomes, as far as is known; chromosome number is highly variable in subgenus *Robertium*.

CHROMOSOME DOUBLING AND THE ORIGIN OF NEW SPECIES

Species whose chromosome number is an exact multiple of some other number found in the genus (polyploids) have already been mentioned. The way this comes about is usually as follows. A hybrid is formed between two species with the same chromosome number. The parents are sufficiently distantly related that their chromosomes, when brought together in the hybrid, do not form pairs at reduction division (meiosis), the process in which the sex cells are formed. (It is a simplification to say that the products of meiosis are sex cells, but full details are unnecessary here.) If the chromosomes do not pair the sex cells do not receive a complete and correct set of chromosomes. They are then either inviable or give rise, after taking part in fertilisation, to inviable embryos. The hybrid is, accordingly, sterile. Then, by one of a number of methods, an individual containing a double set of chromosomes, a complete set from each of the two original parent species, arises from the hybrid. When this individual comes to form sex cells every chromosome finds a suitable partner, and the plant produces progeny. These will be similar to the original hybrid but will probably show a little more variation than did either parent, but nothing like as much as the progeny of an initially fertile hybrid. If they succeed in the struggle for existence a new species will have come into existence instantaneously. This fertile tetraploid is genetically isolated from its parents because, if it crosses with them, the progeny will have an odd number of chromosome sets (it will be a triploid) and will be sterile. This is the probable origin of *Geranium* species such as *G. ibericum* and *G. wlassovianum* with 56 chromosomes instead of the usual 28. The sterility of the triploid back-cross is due to the fact that only half the chromosomes derived from the tetraploid hybrid can find partners at meiosis. Exactly this situation is found in the sterile garden hybrid, *G. ×magnificum*; it has 42 chromosomes, and at meiosis in the anthers, approximately 14 pairs of chromosomes and 14 odd chromosomes can be seen. On grounds of its external characters it was inferred that this hybrid was a cross between *G. ibericum* (56) and *G. platypetalum* (28). The observations on chromosome behaviour in the hybrid suggest that one of the progenitors of *G. ibericum* was *G. platypetalum* or something closely related to it. If the chromosome set of *G. ×magnificum* was doubled we should have a plant with 84 chromosomes. This might or might not be fertile depending on whether there was preferential pairing among the *platypetalum* chromosomes and the *platypetalum*-like chromosomes derived from *G. ibericum*. If pairing can take place among

chromosome sets of different origin, the chromosomes can join up to form groups of three and four and this leads to incorrect segregation and sterility. However, a tetraploid might cross with a distantly related diploid, and if the triploid resulting doubled its chromosome number we might expect the hexaploid to be fertile. There is one *Geranium* with 84 chromosomes, namely *G. sanguineum*. Always with polyploids one is tempted to speculate on their likely origin, and we have seen that there is evidence of involvement of *G. platypetalum* in the origin of *G. ibericum*. There might have been three species involved in the origin of *G. sanguineum*, but I can offer no suggestions as to what they were. Possibly its ancestors no longer survive. These considerations cast suspicion on the report of about 56 chromosomes for *G. sanguineum*, mentioned earlier.

The situation found in *G. ibericum* is also found in *G. robertianum* (64 chromosomes) in relation to *G. purpureum* (32). There presumably is or was another species with 32 chromosomes that joined up with *G. purpureum* to make *G. robertianum*. There is, however, unpublished evidence for the idea that *G. canariense* and *G. rubescens* (each with 128 chromosomes) arose on different occasions by the doubling of the chromosomes of *G. robertianum*, and not by the involvement of a further species. This process is less likely to lead to the development of a new species than the one where a hybrid arises first, and is less common.

The origin of new species by hybridisation followed by chromosome doubling can take place with any combination of parental chromosome numbers. It has already been indicated that it can happen when a diploid and a tetraploid cross. It can also happen with numbers which are neither equal nor multiples of the same number. *Geranium maderense* and *G. palmatum* have 68 chromosomes, which is rather puzzling in view of the occurrence of 64 in the related *G. robertianum*. When it became known that *G. cataractarum* had 36 chromosomes I noticed that 68 could be got by summing 36 and 32. Accordingly *G. maderense* was crossed with *G. cataractarum* and *G. purpureum*. The first of these crosses produced a hybrid, in the meiosis of which approximately 18 chromosome-pairs were formed. *G. maderense* is thus probably of hybrid origin, one of the parents being *G. cataractarum*.

THE KNOWN HYBRIDS OF *GERANIUM*

The known *Geranium* hybrids have arisen partly by chance and partly as a result of deliberate crossing. Most of the chance crosses have arisen in gardens, and very few in nature. Not all of them are horticulturally important, and most of those that are have arisen by chance. Of the deliberate crosses, some that have been made in the *G. cinereum* group have had horticultural improvement as their objective; otherwise, deliberate crossing seems to have been done only by a handful of research workers. These efforts were not made with horticulture in mind and have resulted in few, if any, plants of garden value. The most concentrated pieces of artificial hybridisation have been those by Dahlgren (1923, 1925) with *G. bohemicum* and *G. lanuginosum*; by the staff of The John Innes Horticultural Institute in the 1920s and 1930s (Sansome, 1936) with *G. endressii* and *G. versicolor*; and by Dr Helen Kiefer when she was a research student with me, working mainly on members of subgenus *Robertium* (unpublished).

The horticulturally valuable hybrids are dealt with in Chapter 9, but as no full list of *Geranium* hybrids has appeared since Knuth's monograph (1912) I am taking the opportunity to give one here. The list is alphabetical and the hybrid formulae are alphabetically composed; chromosome numbers are given where known. Binomials are given where available; those in parentheses are illegitimate later homonyms or not validly published, and should not be used (they are included for comparison with Knuth's list and so that their unacceptability may be known).

Between Subgenera Geranium and Robertium
pratense × *robertianum*, 28 × 64, STERILE

A single plant of this was reported by Drabble and Drabble (1908); it bore two dissimilar flowers, one more like that of *G. pratense*, and the other more like that of *G. robertianum*; no material was preserved. The plant was found in Lathkildale, Derbyshire, England. It is a highly improbable cross.

Between Subgenera Geranium and Erodioideae
phaeum × *sylvaticum*, 28 × 28 (*G.* ×*zermattense* Gams, not validly published)

This is listed by Gams (1923–4), having been reported in Cantons Valais and Graubunden, Switzerland, but considered by him to be very doubtful.

Within Subgenus Geranium: Between Sections Dissecta and Tuberosa
asphodeloides × *bohemicum*, 24–30 × 28, = *G.* ×*decipiens* Haussknecht, STERILE

Found in Greece, growing with the parents (Knuth, 1912). Although the seeds were considered to be sterile they were sufficiently developed for the surface pitting to be observed. The difference between the seed-discharge arrangements of the parents suggests that they are too distantly related to be able to form even such imperfect seeds, and that the identification of the hybrid might be wrong.

Within Subgenus Geranium, Section Geranium
bicknellii × *carolinianum*, 52 × 52, STERILE

One plant found on the Geranium Display Bed in Cambridge Botanic Garden in 1980. Both parents are annuals and so was the hybrid, but dried specimens were made before it died.

bicknellii or *carolinianum* × *endressii*, 52 × 26 or 28, STERILE

One plant, as preceding, 1981. The plant was transferred to a greenhouse and despite careful study it was not possible to decide which of the two North American annual species, *bicknellii* and *carolinianum*, was the parent; possibly the preceding hybrid produced good pollen and acted as one parent, in which case this is a triple hybrid.

clarkei × *collinum*, ? × 28, STERILE

Found on the Research Plot, University Botanic Garden, Cambridge, 1978.

clarkei × *himalayense*, STERILE

This appeared on the Research Plot, University Botanic Garden, Cambridge, in 1978.

clarkei × *pratense*, ? × 28, partly STERILE

A plant of this was raised at Cambridge in 1975 by Dr Kiefer, using the white-flowered form of *G. clarkei*. When grown in a greenhouse in 1980 it produced no seed under open pollination or when selfed from the few perfect stamens it produced; when grown in the open in 1981 it produced a scattering of ripe carpels under open pollination and some of these contained apparently good seeds. On the Research Plot at Cambridge a hybrid was found in 1978 that appeared to be G. *clarkei* crossed with the "Nepal Form" of G. *pratense*, or perhaps with a hybrid between the "Nepal" and "European Forms". This also produced a scattering of apparently good seeds under open pollination out of doors.

collinum × *dahuricum*, 28 × ?, = G. ×*bergianum* Lundström

Described by Lundström (1914) from plants growing in the University Botanic Garden, Stockholm.

collinum × *dahuricum* × *pratense*, 28 × ? × 28

Lundström (1914) thought some of the plants growing in the Stockholm Botanic Garden were this triple hybrid. Lundström did not indicate G. *collinum* as a parent of these two hybrids, but named G. *londesii* which he considered to be a distinct species, a view not shared by either previous or subsequent authors, who have regarded it as a synonym of G. *collinum*.

collinum × *pratense*, 28 × 28, FERTILE

Reported in the Stockholm Botanic Garden by Lundström (1914), who found it to be very variable. Seen by me in University Botanic Garden, Lund, Sweden, in 1977, where it was also variable. One plant, believed to be of this hybrid, was found by me on the Research Plot, University Botanic Garden, Cambridge, in 1981; at the time it was found, just at the beginning of flowering, the stamens were abortive.

dahuricum × *pratense*, ? × 28, apparently FERTILE

Found by Lundström in the Stockholm Botanic Garden in 1912–13 (Lundström, 1914). The herbarium specimens showed that it had been there since 1885.

delavayi × *sinense*, ? × 28

In South-west China, where these two species are native, intermediates are frequently found, suggesting that natural hybridisation occurs commonly.

endressii × *sessiliflorum*, 26 or 28 × 56, STERILE

A self-sown seedling of this was found in 1978 by the Rev. O.G. Folkard in his garden at Sleaford, England, and a root was later sent to Cambridge for study. The brown-tinged leaves show that G. *sessiliflorum* 'Nigricans' was one of the

parents. (See below, under G. *sessiliflorum* × G. *traversii*, for discussion of chromosome number of the former.)

endressii × *traversii*, 26 or 28 × 28, = G. ×*riversleaianum* Yeo, STERILE

This appears to be the parentage of the well-known cultivar 'Russell Prichard' which has intensely magenta flowers, unlike those of either parent. A similar plant was raised by Mr Jan Stephens of Tring, England (Stephens, 1967), together with one with light pink flowers; they were called, respectively, 'Chapel End Red' and 'Chapel End Pink'. Dried specimens of the latter have been preserved at Cambridge. Another pink-flowered plant of this type has arisen at Kew and been named 'Mavis Simpson'.

endressii × *versicolor*, 26 or 28 × 28, = G. ×*oxonianum* Yeo, FERTILE

This occurs readily in gardens where both parents are grown, and has been found in England in places where both species are naturalised. However, most wild populations of this hybrid in Britain have probably originated as such from gardens (McClintock in Stace, 1975). Some cultivars have been named. The cross and back-crosses were also made deliberately at The John Innes Horticultural Institute (Sansome, 1936).

himalayense × *pratense*,? × 28, STERILE

The cultivar 'Johnson's Blue' has long been suspected of being an example of this cross, and I am sure it is. Dr Kiefer made the cross at Cambridge in 1975, producing a plant quite a lot different from 'Johnson's Blue'. On the Research Plot at Cambridge a plant has appeared which seems to be G. *himalayense* crossed with the "Nepal Form" of G. *pratense* (see Chapter 9). My stock of 'Johnson's Blue', surrounded by several stocks belonging to the G. *pratense* group, once yielded a good seed from which I raised another sterile plant.

lambertii × *procurrens*

A single seedling appeared in the garden of Miss Elizabeth Strangman, Washfield Nursery, Hawkhurst, Kent, England, about 1981.

pratense × *sylvaticum*, 28 × 28, STERILE

A plant diagnosed as this by me has been sent to Cambridge by Mr R.D. Nutt; it has white flowers with pale lilac veining.

potentilloides × *sessiliflorum*, ? × 56

On the Kosciusko plateau in New South Wales there appears to be extensive crossing between *G. potentilloides* var. *abditum* and *G. sessiliflorum* subsp. *brevicaule*; one specimen has been found which agrees exactly with a first generation hybrid between these taxa raised by Carolin (Carolin, 1964, p. 340). Probably the same two species hybridise in New Zealand (ibid., p. 356).

procurrens × *psilostemon*, STERILE

A plant of this was raised by the Rev. O.G. Folkard from seed collected from *G. procurrens* growing near to *G. psilostemon* in his garden at Sleaford, England. *G. procurrens* was at the time newly described, and Mr Folkard's plant was misidentified as *G. collinum* (Folkard, 1974). Mr Folkard's identification of the male parent is consistent with the characters of the hybrid, as I have confirmed on a plant growing at Cambridge.

rivulare × *sylvaticum*, 28 × 28 (*G.* ×*besseanum* Gams, not validly published)

This is listed by Gams (1923–4). It was found near Riddes in Canton Valais, Switzerland.

sessiliflorum × *traversii*, 56 × 28, FERTILE or STERILE

I saw this hybrid in the Royal Botanic Gardens, Kew, in 1971, and it appeared to be fertile. In 1980 I saw a hybrid swarm of it in Mr Alan Bloom's garden at Bressingham Hall, Norfolk. The fertility of this hybrid casts doubt on the chromosome counts, which have been made only once for each of the parent species. In 1981 I was given a plant with this parentage by Mr K.A. Beckett, but this has little or no fertility.

Within Subgenus Geranium, Section Dissecta
asphodeloides subsp. *asphodeloides* × subsp. *crenophilum*, 24–30 × ?, FERTILE

This cross between two rather distinct subspecies occurred on the Geranium Display Bed at the Cambridge Botanic Garden in 1980. Subspecies *asphodeloides* was represented by both pink- and white-flowered plants, and both colours were represented among the hybrids, which were quite numerous. Three of each colour were removed and kept growing elsewhere in the Garden.

Within Subgenus Geranium, Section Tuberosa
bohemicum × *lanuginosum*, 28 × 48, STERILE

This cross was made deliberately by Dahlgren (1923, 1925) in both directions, and the plants obtained were variegated with chlorophyll-deficient areas. Some progeny grew to maturity and proved to be sterile. Chlorophyll deficiency in the seedlings was more severe when *G. bohemicum* was the female parent and as a result a smaller proportion survived to maturity.

ibericum × *platypetalum*, 56 × 28, = *G.* ×*magnificum* Hylander, STERILE

Identified in cultivation and provided with a name by Hylander (1961). Its origin is unknown but it presumably arose in cultivation; there are three clones in cultivation in Britain (see Chapter 9). It has 42 chromosomes.

platypetalum × *renardii*, 28 × ?

Stated to occur naturally in two places in Transcaucasia (Bobrov, 1949). Knuth (1912) suspected that it was a form of *G. platypetalum*, though the description by Woronow which he quotes gives reasonable support for the identification.

Within Subgenus Robertium: Between Sections Anemonifolia and Ruberta
maderense × *robertianum*, 68 × 64, STERILE
Raised by Dr Kiefer at Cambridge in 1974.

Within Subgenus Robertium: Between Sections Anemonifolia and Unguiculata
cataractarum × *maderense*, 36 × 68, STERILE
Raised at Cambridge in the 1970s, once by me and once by Dr Kiefer.

Within Subgenus Robertium: Between Sections Lucida and Ruberta
lucidum × *robertianum*, 20, 40 or 60 × 64 (*G.* ×*hybridum* F.A. Lees, not Linnaeus), STERILE

Twice reported by F.A. Lees (see McClintock in Stace, 1975), a knowledgeable but eccentric and probably unreliable English naturalist of the nineteenth century.

Within Subgenus Robertium, Section Anemonifolia
maderense × *palmatum*, 68 × 68, FERTILE
Raised by me in 1967 and by Dr Kiefer in 1974.

Within Subgenus Robertium, Section Batrachioides

molle × pusillum, 26 × 26 (*G. ×oenense* Murray, not validly published)

molle × pyrenaicum, 26 × 26 or 28 (*G. ×luganese* Schröter, not validly published)

pusillum × pyrenaicum, 26 × 26 or 28 (*G. ×hybridum* Haussknecht, not Linnaeus), STERILE

All three of these hybrids were listed by Knuth (1912), who cast doubt on the report of the first, saying it would be difficult to recognise. All the occurrences were natural, the first in Austria, the second in Switzerland and the third in Germany.

Within Subgenus Robertium, Section Ruberta

purpureum × robertianum, 32 × 64, STERILE

canariense × rubescens, 128 × 128, FERTILE

robertianum × rubescens, 64 × 128, STERILE

All three of these hybrids were raised at Cambridge by Dr Kiefer in the 1970s. In addition the first was raised by Professor H.G. Baker at Leeds in the 1940s and by Mr P.M. Benoit some time later (see McClintock in Stace, 1975). These latter workers considered their hybrids to be indistinguishable from *G. robertianum*, except in their sterility. However, one of Dr Kiefer's plants which I examined and preserved, and some which I raised in 1979, were clearly intermediate between the parents in floral characters, and they were slender in habit, perhaps more so than either parent. The fertile hybrid between *G. canariense* and *G. rubescens* was also raised in California by Professor Baker in the 1970s.

Within Subgenus Robertium, Section Unguiculata

dalmaticum × macrorrhizum, 46 × 46, = *G. ×cantabrigiense* Yeo, STERILE

Raised in Cambridge by Dr Kiefer, about 1974, and about the same time found in a natural habitat in Yugoslavia by a German horticulturist, Mr Hans Simon, who gave it the cultivar name 'Biokovo', after the district where it was found.

Within Subgenus Erodioideae, Section Erodioideae

phaeum × reflexum, 28 × 28, = *G. ×monacense* Harz, apparently partly FERTILE

Has arisen in gardens, probably repeatedly; in fact it appears that different colour forms owe their existence to the participation of both *G. phaeum* var. *phaeum* and *G. phaeum* var. *lividum* in the formation of the hybrids.

Within Subgenus Erodioideae, Section Subacaulia

argenteum × cinereum var. *cinereum*, 28 × 28, = *G. ×lindavicum* Knuth (*G. ×intermedium* Knuth, not Colla), FERTILE

argenteum × cinereum var. *subcaulescens*, 28 × 28, = *G. ×lindavicum*, nearly STERILE

cinereum var. *cinereum × var. subcaulescens*, 28 × 28, nearly STERILE

These three hybrids have arisen repeatedly in cultivation and some of the plants are of horticultural value, outstanding being a clone of the third in the list, called 'Ballerina'.

COMMENTS ON THE HYBRIDS

There are a few cases in this list of evidently closely related species producing fertile hybrids, and in fact it is not difficult to believe that the parents of each of the fertile ones are closely related. Perhaps the least obviously alike are *G. collinum* and *G. pratense*. Rather surprisingly, some evidently closely related species have produced hybrids which are sterile, namely *G. pusillum* and *G. pyrenaicum*, *G. dalmaticum* and *G. macrorrhizum*, and *G. bicknellii* and *G. carolinianum*. Where the chromosome number is markedly different, hybrids between even closely related species may be expected to be sterile. *G. himalayense* forms a sterile hybrid with *G. pratense* though it is more similar to *G. pratense* than is *G. collinum*, and it would not be surprising if it turned out to have 56 chromosomes. Crosses between morphologically rather distinct, and geographically remote, species sometimes occur, as in *G. procurrens* (Himalayas) × *G. psilostemon* (E. Turkey, S. Caucasus) and in *G. endressii* (Pyrenees) × *G. traversii* (New Zealand). Crosses between distantly related species in subgenus *Geranium* do not seem to have been attempted artificially, so we do not know whether they take place with ease or not. The cross *G. endressii × G. traversii* must be regarded as an expression of the evident readiness of *G. endressii* to hybridise — a trait known to plant breeders as 'combining ability'.

Dr Helen Kiefer, in her hybridisation experiments at Cambridge with species of subgenus *Robertium*, found that in all reciprocal pollinations the response was highly unequal, and in all cases where progeny arose they were obtained by crossing in one direction only. It would be interesting to try reciprocal crossing with G. endressii and other species of subgenus Geranium.

A peculiarity of the stamens of some sterile hybrids of Geranium is the varying extent of their development, even in the same plant at different times. I have seen this in G. ×magnificum and in hybrids of the G. pratense group. The most extreme indication of male-sterility is severe, early abortion of the anthers and drastic reduction in the length of the filaments. A less extreme manifestation is expressed in normal or slightly shortened filaments, and normal-sized but mustard-coloured anthers which do not open. Then sometimes one finds superficially normal anthers which burst to produce normal-sized pollen grains of a normal blue colour. Microscopic examination of these reveals that they are empty.

As the last four sections of subgenus Robertium are comparatively closely related, the occurrence of intersectional hybrids among them is not surprising. Nevertheless, McClintock (in Stace, 1975) points out that G. lucidum and G. robertianum commonly occur together, yet no observer other than F.A. Lees has reported the hybrid between them. The one intersectional cross reported within subgenus Geranium is inherently more improbable still because the sections here are more fundamentally different. The intersubgeneric crosses, G. pratense × G. robertianum and G. phaeum × G. sylvaticum, seem highly improbable. However, we should keep an open mind on these reports, and field botanists and horticulturists should look out for hybrids. Anybody who finds one should take all possible steps to obtain evidence, preferably by collecting a portion of the plant and carefully pressing it, by taking measurements of floral parts while still fresh, and by photographing it.

One final incongruity in the list of hybrids, the apparent fertility of G. sessiliflorum × G. traversii in the light of the dissimilarity of the parental chromosome numbers, has already been mentioned. It can only be supposed that one of the counts is wrong, or that one of the parents exists in more than one chromosome-race.

RAISING NEW HYBRIDS

Controlled crossing of Geranium is not at all difficult, though it is much less hazardous if a greenhouse is available. As the anthers mature before the stigmas (Chapter 4), it is easy to remove them with fine scissors or fine forceps before the stigmas are receptive. A lens should be used to inspect the flower after this operation to make sure no pollen has been scattered. If only a few grains have been scattered it will be worth while trying to remove them. The flower is then covered with a small translucent envelope which can be secured with one or two paper-clips. A day or two later the bag is removed, and if the stigmas are spreading they are touched with a freshly opened anther from the intended male parent. The bag is then replaced and it has to stay in position until after the fruit is ripe to prevent the loss of the seeds. Paper bags will not last out of doors unless one is exceptionally lucky with the weather. If hybridising has to be done in the open it may be possible to enclose the flowers in plastic tubing with gauze over the top for ventilation and wadding round the flower-stalk. The tubing would have to be wired to a stick. An excellent brief guide to plant-breeding is that of Lawrence (1948). Careful written records of attempts at crossing should always be kept; not only will they guard against lapses of memory but, even if the object is to produce interesting new plants for the garden, the records will have scientific value.

The garden value of some of the existing Geranium hybrids gives one optimism that more good garden plants might be obtained by deliberate breeding efforts.

Up to now there seems to be insufficient evidence as to what crosses are likely to succeed. Some undoubtedly closely related species cross rather readily, and crossing species belonging to subgenus Geranium which are placed near one another in Chapter 9 would be an interesting test of my classification. On the other hand, as the parents of some hybrids in this subgenus seem to be rather distantly related it would seem to be worth trying to hybridise any species whose desirable qualities might combine well.

·CHAPTER 8·
Identification

This book is mainly about identification and readers are most strongly urged to try to identify specimens for themselves. However, for one reason or another, the would-be identifier may from time to time fail to arrive at a convincing identification, and may then need outside help, hence the two sections of this chapter.

GETTING IT DONE FOR YOU

Experts, professional and otherwise, are usually willing to identify specimens submitted in good condition. Specimens to be sent fresh should be sealed into a polythene bag as soon as they are cut. Polythene transmits oxygen and carbon dioxide but not water or water-vapour. Excess water in a polythene bag merely sets up rot, and no water should be added unless the specimen is collected in hot sunshine when the sparsest possible sprinkling of water should be added, or you can breathe into the bag before sealing it. If the journey to the expert is likely to take more than two days it is better to make a pressed specimen. This also has the advantage that if the expert is away from base, the specimen will not have deteriorated by the time he gets back.

If you do not have a plant press, place the specimen in the middle of 12–20 thicknesses of newspaper and cover with a pile of books. Change the newspaper after 24 hours and again later if conditions are cool and humid. Some *Geranium* species are slightly succulent and take unusually long to dry. Dry specimens are for the most part quite stiff.

The specimen should include a good length of stem and basal leaves if available, and unripe and ripe fruit if possible. If the dimensions of the plant seem to require it, cut the top off and place it in the press as an additional layer with extra paper. If the branching is prolific, discard some of the branches. If the leaves are complex in outline, detach one or two from the plant and flatten them carefully before closing the press. Allow a few petals to lie detached in the press and include one or two flowers from which two or three sepals and petals have been removed from one side so as to expose the stamens. Take a note of any leaf-markings and the colour of sepals, petals, stamens and stigmas.

DOING IT YOURSELF

Gardeners will normally have fresh specimens to hand but there is no reason why they should not work from specimens they have pressed themselves (see above). Please do not rush to identify an unknown plant the moment the first flower opens. A delay of a week or two will see the immature fruits in being, and four or five weeks will give you a ripe fruit, making available many more useful characters. Some species may finish flowering before the first fruits are ripe, in which case dried specimens of the flowers will be needed.

It is necessary to read chapters 4 and 5 before embarking on identifications. Those with little or no botanical experience are advised to take one or two species the names of which they know, and see if they can get the right answer using one or other of the keys, before starting on an unknown specimen. Keys get easier to use the more you use them.

Two keys are provided, a multi-access and a dichotomous key. The multi-access key makes minimal use of the characters of the ripe fruit. The dichotomous key (which is broken up into sections) makes full use of fruit characters. If you have ripe fruit the dichotomous key may be preferable because more than one third of the species fall into the smaller groups with relatively short keys. If fruit is not fully developed identification with the dichotomous key may still be attempted, following the list of hints given at the beginning of the key. In any case the sculpture of the fruit, mentioned in couplet 3 of the dichotomous key to groups, is visible some time before the fruit is ripe. Although in most species fruit-discharge is explosive, resulting in the disappearance of the seeds or the carpels, it is usually possible to find some fruits which are just ripe and which can be induced to explode and of which the discharge-products can be collected. For this purpose, look for rostra which are drying out and turning brown. Do not forget that the keys cover only the species and hybrids which I have decided to include in the book.

Plants with Double Flowers

These cannot be identified with the keys but they are known in only five species (or hybrids), as numbered in Chapter 9:

2. *G.* ×*oxonianum* (double-flowered forms also have the petals narrow, strap-shaped)
16. *G. pratense*
17. *G. himalayense*
45. *G. sanguineum*

How to Use the Multi-access Key

For each of the eleven characters listed below write down an alphabetic formula by choosing the letter of the character-state corresponding to your plant (write the letters in groups, as in the key beginning on p. 49, to make it easier to read the formula). If a character-state is not observable, write alternative formulae with all possible states for the group concerned. Plants that have been in flower for some time without showing any development of the fruit may be sterile hybrids and for these blanks should be

left in the formula for the last three characters. For technical terms see Chapters 4 and 5 and the Glossary. Trace the formula in the alphabetically arranged list, turn up the species indicated (Chapter 9) and check the description (the short one, if provided, will usually show whether you are right or not). If a species has two formulae differing in only one character, so that the formulae would be adjacent in the list, the two states of the character are shown one above the other, thus $\frac{O}{P}$. If two species have the same formula it will be necessary to check both; if more than two species have the same formula there is a reference to the diagnostic notes given at the end of the key (before using these it is essential to understand the terms 'division', 'lobe' and 'tooth' as applied to the leaves; see Chapter 4, especially Figure 4.7). If the key has clearly failed, go through the list of characters again looking for borderline cases and prepare alternative formulae for any that you find. This type of key requires you to answer most of the necessary questions about your specimen as a first step, whereas a forking (dichotomous) key requires attention to the plant and the key alternately throughout the entire process of identification. If the answers to some questions are uncertain it is easier to try alternative possibilities with this key than with a dichotomous key, which acts like a maze in these circumstances.

Characters and character-states used in the multi-access key

CHARACTER 1	NOTES
A. Main leaves with deepest incisions not reaching more than ⅔ of the way to the top of the leaf-stalk	1. Main leaves are the basal leaves (if any) and/or lower stem-leaves
B. Main leaves with deepest incisions reaching more than ⅔ of the way to the top of the leaf-stalk but not all the way	
C. Main leaves with deepest incisions reaching top of leaf-stalk	
CHARACTER 2	2. See Note 1
D. Divisions of main leaves broadest at or very close to apex, lobes apical	

E. Divisions of main leaves broadest well below apex, lobing pinnate or palmato-pinnate

CHARACTER 3
F. Glandular hairs present, at least on upper parts
G. Glandular hairs not present

CHARACTER 4
H. Floral axis above the horizontal (flowers erect or upwardly inclined)
I. Floral axis horizontal or below the horizontal (flowers directed horizontally or nodding)

CHARACTER 5
J. Sepal mucro not more than $\frac{1}{8}$ length of sepal
K. Sepal mucro more than $\frac{1}{8}$ length of sepal

CHARACTER 6
L. Petals not over 8mm long
M. Petals over 8mm but not over 16mm long
N. Petals over 16mm long

CHARACTER 7
O. Petals with a distinct central apical notch
P. Petals feebly or not at all notched at apex

CHARACTER 8
Q. Petal base without hairs on central part of front surface
R. Petal base with hairs on central part of front surface

8. The petal base usually has lateral hair-tufts which may extend onto

3. Check pedicels, sepals, mericarps and base of rostrum
4. Ignore very small hairs, difficult to see at 8 × magnification

5. Length of sepal does not include mucro. The ratio can usually be judged by eye

6. Include length of claw if any

7. As an aberration the petals may have a number of narrow incisions; if so, try 'P'

surface; look for surface hairs between the tufts or a continuous hair tract right across petal; in *G. macrorrhizum* the hairless part may be restricted to the central channel, overhung by hairs on the ridges of the claw

CHARACTER 9
S. Immature fruit horizontal or drooping
T. Immature fruit upwardly inclined or erect

CHARACTER 10
U. Rostrum with stylar portion not more than 4mm, sometimes none
V. Rostrum with stylar portion more than 4mm

CHARACTER 11
W. Mericarps with a pattern of raised ribs, at least at the top, or with crests
X. Mericarps without a pattern of raised ribs, without crests

9. This can be observed as soon as obvious development of the rostrum has begun; the *ripe* fruit is always upright and ripeness is first shown by the browning of the rostrum

10. This character can be observed long before the fruit is ripe or on ripe fruit if not broken; in a few species it may not be possible to use this character because the transition from thick rostrum to thin stylar portion is too indefinite

11. Specimens qualifying as 'X' may have one or two conspicuous but thin and scarcely raised transverse veins near top

The multi-access key

ADF HJLO RTUX	8. rotundifolium
ADF HJLP QTUW	94. lucidum
	80. trilophum (b)
ADF HJLP QTVW	94. lucidum
ADF HJMO QTUW	79. polyanthes
	86. brutium
ADF HJMO QTUX	84. pyrenaicum
ADF HJMO QTVW	83. albanum
ADF HJMP QTUW	82. biuncinatum
ADF HKLO QTUX	57. carolinianum
ADF HKMO QTUW	79. polyanthes
ADF HKMP QTUW	81. ocellatum
	82. biuncinatum
ADF HKMP QTUX	63. asphodeloides
ADF IJNO QT $\frac{U}{V}$ X	73. renardii
ADF IKN $\frac{O}{P}$ QTVX	69. platypetalum
ADG HJLO QTUX	87. molle

ADG HJLO QTUW	85. pusillum	BDF IKNP R---	90. ×cantabrigiense
ADG HJMO QTVW	83. albanum	BDG HJLO QTUX	87. molle
ADG HJMO RTU $\frac{W}{X}$	108. cinerum var. obtusilobum	BDG HJLO QTUW	85. pusillum
		BDG HJMO QTUX	38. stapfianum
ADG HJMP $\frac{Q}{R}$ TUX	50. traversii var. elegans	BDG HJMO RTUW	See diagnostic notes
ADG HKLP $\frac{Q}{R}$ TUX	52. sessiliflorum subsp. novae-zelandiae	BDG HJMO RTUX	36. donianum
		BDG HJMP QTUW	110. cinereum var. subcaulescens
ADG HKMP $\frac{Q}{R}$ TUX	51. sessiliflorum × traversii	BDG HJMP RTUW	104. argenteum
		BDG HJMP RTUX	36. donianum
ADG IJNO QT $\frac{U}{V}$ X	73. renardii	BDG HJNO QTUX	38. stapfianum
ADG IJNP RTUX	23. lambertii	BDG HJNO RTUW	105. × lindavicum
AEF HJLP QTUW	80. trilophum (b)		107. cinereum 'Ballerina'
AEF HJMP QTUW	82. biuncinatum		
AEF HJNO QTUX	74. peloponnesiacum	BDG HJNO RTUX	36. donianum
		BDG HJNP QTUW	109. cinereum var. palmatipartitum
AEF HJNP RTUX	25. procurrens		
AEF HKLP RTUX	47. thunbergii	BDG HJNP QTVW	88. glaberrimum
AEF HKMP QTUX	81. ocellatum	BDG HJNP RTUX	See diagnostic notes
	82. biuncinatum		
AEF HKMP RSUX	27. rubifolium	BDG HKMO RTUW	104. argenteum
AEF HKMP RTUX	47. thunbergii		106. cinereum var. cinereum
AEF HKNO QTUX	78. gracile		
AEF HKNP RSUX	26. kishtvariense	BDG HKMP RTUW	106. cinereum var. cinereum
	27. rubifolium		
AEF IKMP QTVW	89. macrorrhizum	BDG HKMP RTUX	41. dahuricum
AEF IKMP QTVX	20. eriostemon		34. palustre
	21. erianthum	BDG HKNP RTUX	34. palustre
AEF IKNP QTVW	89. macrorrhizum	BDG IJMP RSVX	33. farreri
AEF IKNP QTVX	21. erianthum	BEF HJMP RTUW	100. phaeum
AEG HJ $\frac{M}{N}$ P R---	3. ×riversleaianum	BEF HJMP RTUX	25. procurrens
AEG HKMO R---	4. endressii × sessiliflorum	BEF HJMP RTVX	58. nervosum
		BEF HJNP RTUX	25. procurrens
AEG HK $\frac{M}{N}$ P R---	3. ×riversleaianum		58. nervosum
	4. endressii × sessiliflorum	BEF HJNP RTVX	58. nervosum
		BEF HKLO RSUX	12. albiflorum
AEG HKNO RSUX	6. nodosum	BEF HKLO RTUX	56. bicknellii
AEG HKNO RTUX	22. wallichianum		11. pseudosibiricum
AEG HKNO RTVX	5. versicolor	BEF HKLP QTUW	80. trilophum (a)
AEG HKNP RTUX	22. wallichianum	BEF HKLP RTUX	11. pseudosibiricum
AWG IJNO QTUX	75. libani		47. thunbergii
AEG IJNO RTUX	23. lambertii	BEF HKMO QTUX	76. bohemicum
BDF HJMO QTUX	79. polyanthes		77. lanuginosum
BDF HJNO RTUX	60. fremontii	BEF HKMO RSUX	12. albiflorum
BDF HJNP QTVW	88. glaberrimum	BEF HKMP QTUW	81. ocellatum
BDF HJNP RTUX	60. fremontii	BEF HKMP QTUX	62. schiedeanum
BDF HKLO QTUX	57. carolinianum	BEF HKMP RTUX	See diagnostic notes
	64. dissectum		
BDF HKMO QTUW	79. polyanthes	BEF HKMP RTVX	58. nervosum
BDF HKMP QTUW	81. ocellatum	BEF HKNO QT $\frac{U}{V}$ X	See diagnostic notes
BDF HKMP QTUX	63. asphodeloides		
BDF IKNP RTVW	91. dalmaticum		

BEF HKNO RTUX   1. endressii
    2. ×oxonianum
BEF HKNP QSVX   18. clarkei
BEF HKNP QTUX   See diagnostic notes

BEF HKNP QTVC   15. collinum
BEF HKNP R---   14. procurrens
    × psilostemon
BEF HKNP RTUX   See diagnostic notes

BEF HKNP RTVX   58. nervosum
    59. viscosissimum
BEF IJMP QSUW   101. ×monacense
    102. reflexum
BEF IJMP QSUX   29. delavayi
BEF IJMP QSVX   29. delavayi
    30. refractum
BEF IJMP Q$\frac{S}{T}$UW   101. ×monacense
BEF IJMP RTUW   100. phaeum
BEF IJNP QSVX   19. himalayense
BEF IKMP QSUX   28. sinense
BEF IKMP QSVX   28. sinense
    30. refractum
BEF IKMP QTUW   103. aristatum
BEF IKMP QTVW   89. macrorrhizum
BEF IKMP QTVX   20. eriostemon
    21. erianthum
BEF IKMP RSVX   30. refractum
BEF IKNP QSVX   16. pratense
    17. himalayense ×
    pratense
BEF IKNP QTVW   89. macrorrhizum
BEF IKNP QTVX   70. ibericum subsp.
    jubatum
    21. erianthum
BEG HJMO RTUX   45. sanguineum
BEG HJMP RTUW   100. phaeum
BEG HJMP RTUX   40. krameri
    45. sanguineum
BEG HJNP QTUX   39. soboliferum
BEG HJNP RTUX   35. wlassovianum
    39. soboliferum
BEG HKLO QTUX   49. sibiricum
BEG HKLO RSUX   12. albiflorum
BEG HKLO RTUX   11. pseudosibiricum
    48. nepalense
BEG HKLP QTUX   49. sibiricum
BEG HKLP RTUX   11. pseudosibiricum
    48. nepalense
BEG HKMO QTUX   46. columbinum
BEG HKMO RSUX   7. rectum
    12. albiflorum

BEG HKMO RTUX   See diagnostic notes

BEG HKMP QTUX   46. columbinum
BEG HKMP RTUX   See diagnostic notes

BEG HKNO QTVX   70. ibericum subsp.
    ibericum
BEG HKNO RSUX   7. rectum
BEG HKNO RTUX   See diagnostic notes

BEG HKNO RTVX   5. versicolor
BEG HKNO QTUX   37. shikokianum
BEG HKNP QTUX   54. maculatum
BEG HKNP QTVX   15. collinum
BEG HKNP RTUX   See diagnostic notes

BEG IJMP Q$\frac{S}{T}$UW   101. ×monacense
    102. reflexum
BEG IJMP RSVX   32. yunnanense
BEG IJMP RTUW   100. phaeum
BEG IJNO QTUX   75. libani
BEG IJNP RSVX   32. yunnanense
BEG IKMP RSVX   31. pogonanthum
BEG IKNO QTUX   72. gymnocaulon
CEF HJMO QTUX   53a. magniflorum
CEF HJMP QTVX   92. cataractarum
CEF HJNP Q---   93. cataractarum
    × maderense
CEF HJNP QTVW   99. maderense
CEF HJ$\frac{L}{M}$O QTUX   66. macrostylum
CEF HKMP QTVW   95. robertianum
CEF HKNP QTVW   96. rubescens
CEF IJNP QSVW   97. canariense
CEF IKNP QSVW   98. palmatum
CEG HKMO QTUX   65. tuberosum
    67. linearilobum
CEG HKMO RTUX   53. incanum
CEG HKNO QTUX   65. tuberosum
    68. malviflorum
CEG HKNO QTVX   68. malviflorum
CEG HKNO RTUX   53. incanum

Diagnostic notes for multi-access key (stop when you reach a description that fits the specimen) specimen)
BDG HJMO RTUW   1. Leaves silvery-silky, divisions 3-lobed to beyond the middle, 104. *argenteum* or 105. × *lindavicum*
    2. Leaves greyish,

not silky, divisions 3-lobed for ¹/₅–¹/₃ of their length, 106. *cinereum* var. *cinereum*

3. Leaves slightly silky, divisions lobed for less than ½ but more than ⅓ of their length, 105. × *lindavicum*

BDG HJNP RTUX
1. Rootstock not composed of small tubers joined by lengths of slender rhizome, 36. *donianum*
2. Leaves conspicuously marbled; stigmas 3–6mm, 44. *orientalitibeticum*
3. Leaves not or scarcely marbled; stigmas less than 3mm, 43. *pylzowianum*

BEF HKMP RTUX
1. Sides of leaf-divisions with lobes and teeth extending nearly to base and far below broadest part of division, 9. *sylvaticum*
2. Flowers funnel-shaped, 10. *rivulare*
3. Erect; petals notched, pink; stigmas 4–6mm, 58. *nervosum*
4. Erect; petals not notched, white or nearly so; stigmas 3–4mm, 61. *richardsonii*
5. Sprawling; petals not more than 10.5 mm, 47. *thunbergii*
6. Sprawling; petals 15–16mm, 62. *schiedeanum*

BEF HKNO QTX
1. Flowering period short, April–May; petals rather pale blue, 74. *peloponnesiacum*
2. Flowering period short, June–July; petals deep blue or purple, 71. × *magnificum*
3. Flowering period long, June onwards; flowers funnel-shaped; petals pink, 78. *gracile*

BEF HKNP QTUX
1. Petals magenta with blackish base, 13. *psilostemon*
2. Erect; flowers about 30mm in diameter, partly in umbel-like clusters, 54. *maculatum*
3. Erect; flowers more than 40mm in diameter, not in umbel-like clusters, 55. *oreganum*
4. Sprawling; sepal mucro not more than 1.5mm, 62. *schiedeanum*

BEF HKNP RTUX
1. Erect; petals notched, pink, 58. *nervosum*
2. Erect; petals not notched, white or nearly so, 61. *richardsonii*
3. Sprawling; petals bluish lilac, 62. *schiedeanum*

BEG HKMO RTUX
1. Cymules 1-flowered; petals more than 12mm, 45. *sanguineum*
2. Cymules 2-flowered; petals more than 12mm, 7. *rectum*
3. Petals less than 10mm, 48. *nepalense*

BEG HKMP RTUX
1. Cymules 1-flowered, petals not less than 12mm, 45. *sanguineum*
2. Erect; sides of leaf-divisions with lobes and teeth extending nearly to base, and far below broadest part of division, 9. *sylvaticum*
3. Sprawling; petals brilliant purplish pink, 34. *palustre*
4. Sprawling; leaf-lobes 2–3 times as long as broad, 42. *yesoense*
5. Sprawling or erect; petals less than 10mm, 48. *nepalense*

BEG HKNO RTUX
1. Cymules 1-flowered, 45. *sanguineum*
2. Flowers saucer-shaped; anthers and stigmas

blackish, 22. *wallichianum*
3. Flowers funnel-shaped;
anthers and stigmas
not blackish, 7. *rectum*

BEG HKNP RTUX   1. Cymules 1-flowered,
45. *sanguineum*
2. Leaf-divisions deep,
deeply cut, 42. *yesoense*
3. Anthers and stigmas
blackish, 22. *wallichianum*
4. Petals brilliant purplish
pink; stigmas up to 3mm,
34. *palustre*
5. Petals not brilliantly
coloured; stigmas more
than 3.5mm, 35. *wlas-
sovianum*

How to use the dichotomous key

The key is broken up into sections; the first
section is a key to groups. Each number in the
left-hand margin is linked with two descriptions
(a couplet) of some character of the plant, let-
tered 'a' and 'b'. Start with couplet '1' and decide
whether your plant corresponds with 'a' or 'b'.
The next step is indicated in the right-hand
margin. If there is a number, go to the couplet of
that number; if a group is mentioned, go to the
group indicated and proceed in the same way. In
the groups you either go to another couplet or
arrive at the name of a species or other taxon,
numbered as in Chapter 9. In the latter case,
verify your identification with the description
in Chapter 9, as with the multi-access key.

What to do if the characters of the fruit are not available

If the fruit is unripe or fails to develop but the
plant will not key out in Group A it may be
possible to arrive at an identification with the
aid of the following hints.

(1) If the flowers are more or less nodding and
have widely spreading or reflexed petals and
the pedicels of immature fruits are not erect
consider Group C and Group G, couplet 6
onwards.
(2) If the petals have a clearly defined claw the
plant will probably be found in Group D.

(3) If the stamens are twice or more as long as
the sepals go to Group D.
(4) If the flower is funnel-shaped but without
sharply defined or strongly keeled petal-
claws go to Group G or species 78. *G. gracile*.
(5) If the leaf-blades are divided to the base
(incisions reaching leaf-stalk) try Groups D
and E before G.
(6) If the anthers are scarlet before they burst go
to Group D.
(7) If the petals are blue with feathered veins
and are notched at the apex go to Group E.
(8) If the plant is an annual not fulfilling condition (7) try Groups D and F.
(9) If none of these conditions holds the plant is
most likely to be a member of Group G and
although this has the longest key it is probably best to try this first.

The dichotomous key

KEY TO GROUPS

1a. Sterile hybrid, not developing fruit, or if
doing so, not developing seed
                        Group A, p. 54
  b. Not a sterile hybrid, usually developing
fruit and seeds   2

2a. Fruit-discharge mechanism inoperative,
carpels shed when ripe or after a long delay,
not thrown off; rostrum remaining thin
                        Group B, p. 54
  b. Fruit forcibly disrupted at maturity; rostrum
soon thick   3

3a. Mericarps thrown off with the seed inside,
frequently prominently sculptured   4
  b. Seeds ejected from mericarps, the latter
often remaining attached by the awn to the
rostrum; mericarps not sculptured   5

4a. Mericarps thrown off with awn (which
becomes coiled) attached (Figure 5.1)
                        Group C, p. 54
  b. Mericarps separating from the awn at the
moment of explosion, awns falling to the
ground (Figure 5.3)   Group D, p. 55

5a. Mericarp without a seed-retaining structure
at lower end of orifice, falling after discharge
(Figure 5.5)   Group E, p. 56
  b. Mericarp with a prong or tuft of bristles at

lower end of orifice for temporary retention of seed in pre-explosive interval, nearly always remaining attached to rostrum after discharge   6

6a. Mericarp with a prong at lower end of orifice, usually bent so as to be inside the chamber after the seed has been expelled (Figure 5.4); rare   Group F, p. 57
  b. Mericarp with a tuft of bristles seated on a horny tubercle at lower end of orifice (Figure 4.6B); common   Group G, p. 57

GROUP A

1a. Petals purplish red with a black base (16–22mm long)   *14. procurrens × psilostemon*
  b. Petals otherwise coloured   2

2a. Petals with a blackish violet base and veins on a nearly white ground
                              24. lambertii × procurrens
  b. Petals otherwise coloured   3

3a. Petals essentially blue, 22–25mm   4
  b. Petals not blue, not more than 18mm   5

4a. Petals not notched
                              17. himalayense × pratense
  b. Petals notched   *71. × magnificum*

5a. Calyx bladdery   *90. × cantabrigiense*
  b. Calyx not bladdery   6

6a. Leaf-blades divided to the base
                              93. cataractarum × maderense
  b. Leaf-blades not divided to the base   7

7a. Plant erect, usually more than 25cm high; petals reflexed or recurved *101. × monacense*
  b. Plant trailing, usually less than 25cm high; petals not reflexed or recurved   8

8a. Leaf-blades at base of plant between 5 and 10cm wide; petals 14–17mm
                              3. × riversleaianum
  b. Leaf-blades not more than 5cm wide; petals about 10mm   *4. endressii × sessiliflorum*

GROUP B

1a. Flowers more than 20mm in diameter; plant perennial   *83. albanum*
  b. Flowers 10mm in diameter or less; plant annual   *G. divaricatum* (see p. 144)

GROUP C

1a. Usually more than 30cm in height; floral axis below the horizontal; petals widely spreading (flower flat) or reflexed   2
  b. Usually less than 30cm in height; flowers more or less erect, saucer-shaped or bowl-shaped   5

2a. Sepal mucro more than half as long as sepal body   *103. aristatum*
  b. Sepal mucro much less than half as long as sepal body   3

3a. Petals nearly as wide as long or wider, widely spreading; (filaments with long hairs)   *100. phaeum*
  b. Petals about ²/₃ as wide as long or less, evidently reflexed just above the base   4

4a. Petals plum-purple to lilac-pink, about ²/₃ as wide as long (detach them for examination); filaments with long spreading glistening hairs on lower half
                              101. × monacense
  b. Petals bright rose-pink, about ½ as wide as long; filaments with only very fine hairs on the edges at the base   *102. reflexum*

5a. Leaf-blades divided nearly to the base, silvery-silky; (petals pale pink to white)
                              104. argenteum
  b. Leaf-blades divided as far as ⅚ or less; slightly or not at all silky; (petals variously coloured)   6

6a. Ground-colour of petals white or nearly so
                                                        7
  b. Ground-colour of petals strongly purple or reddish   8

7a. Leaf-blades greyish green, scarcely hairy; petals strongly net-veined or completely white *106. cinereum* var. *cinereum* (see also *105.* × *lindavicum (a)*)

b. Leaf-blades light green, velvety above, woolly beneath; petals faintly tinged pink, darker veins not netted
108. cinereum var. *obtusilobum*

8a. Petals intensely coloured, deep purplish pink or more or less magenta, often with a black basal spot; anthers and stigmas blackish *110. cinereum* var. *subcaulescens*

b. Petals not intense purplish pink or magenta; anthers and stigmas purplish 9

9a. Petals purplish with a close network of dark red veins 10

b. Petals not conspicuously and darkly net-veined 11

10a. Ground-colour of petals whitish or dull purplish *107. cinereum* 'Ballerina', etc.

b. Ground-colour of petals bright red
105. × *lindavicum* (b)

11a. Lobes of leaf-blades acute; flowers with a large white centre
109. cinereum var. *palmatipartitum*

b. Lobes of leaf-blades often obtuse; flowers not usually white-centred
105. × *lindavicum* (b)

GROUP D

1a. Leaf-blades divided to the base 2
b. Leaf-blades not divided as far as the base 8

2a. Stamens about twice as long as sepals 3
b. Stamens not nearly twice as long as sepals 4

3a. Central division of leaf-blade wedge-shaped, not stalked *97. canariense*
b. Central division of leaf-blade constricted into a distinct stalk *98. palmatum*

4a. Leaf-blades mostly much more than 20cm wide, readily reaching 40cm in width; petals 13–18mm wide with claw only 2.5mm *99. maderense*
b. Leaf-blades not much more than 20cm wide, if that; petals not more than 13mm wide with claw 5mm long or more 5

5a. Flowers 11–16mm in diameter; detached mericarps with long hair-like fibres attached at top *95. robertianum*
b. Flowers 17mm in diameter or more; detached mericarps without long hair-like fibres attached at top 6

6a. Biennial; sepal mucro $\frac{1}{4}$–$\frac{1}{3}$ as long as sepal body *96. rubescens*
b. Perennial; sepal mucro $\frac{1}{8}$–$\frac{1}{6}$ as long as sepal body 7

7a. Leaf-blades up to about 10cm wide; flowers 17–19mm in diameter *92. cataractarum*
b. Leaf-blades 10–20cm wide or more; flowers 30mm in diameter
93. cataractarum × *maderense*

8a. Stamens nearly twice as long as sepals or more 9
b. Stamens much less than twice as long as sepals 12

9a. Calyx not bladdery; flowers upwardly inclined; stamens and style straight
88. glaberrimum
b. Calyx bladdery; floral axis horizontal; stamens and style sinuous 10

10a. Blades of lower leaves less than 5cm wide *91. dalmaticum*
b. Blades of lower leaves more than 5cm wide (sometimes less in no. 90) 11

11a. Some of the lower leaves more than 10cm wide; fruit developing and seed normally ripening *89. macrorrhizum*
b. Lower leaves not more than about 7cm wide; fruit sometimes not enlarging; seed not ripening *90.* × *cantabrigiense*

12a. Most of the flowers in dense umbel-like clusters; (perennial) *79. polyanthes*
b. Most of the flowers forming a diffuse inflorescence; (perennial, biennial or annual) 13

13a. Most of the flowers on each plant cleistogamous (without petals and producing fruit without ever opening) 14
b. None of the flowers cleistogamous 16

14a. Mericarp with a saw-edged wing on each side which is inrolled so that the two rows of teeth are directed towards each other 15
 b. Mericarp without wings, transversely ribbed *81. ocellatum*

15a. Mericarp with two hooks at the top *82. biuncinatum*
 b. Mericarp without hooks *80. trilophum*

16a. Plant glossy and fleshy; sepals with deep keels and cross-ribs; petals clawed *94. lucidum*
 b. Plant with dull hairy surface, not fleshy; sepals only ordinarily ribbed; petals not clawed 17

17a. Mericarp hairy, not extensively ribbed 18
 b. Mericarp hairless, closely ribbed 19

18a. Perennial; flowers 12–18mm in diameter *84. pyrenaicum*
 b. Annual, often overwintering; flowers about 6mm in diameter *85. pusillum*

19a. Petals 8–12.5mm *86. brutium*
 b. Petals 4–6mm *87. molle*

GROUP E

1a. Blades of main leaves divided to the base 2
 b. Blades of main leaves not divided to the base 5

2a. Sepals 7–9mm; petals 16–22mm, bluish; stylar portion of rostrum 3–5mm *68. malviflorum*
 b. Sepals 4–7mm; petals 8–17mm, pinkish; stylar portion of rostrum less than 3mm 3

3a. Upper parts of plant freely clothed with glandular hairs *66. macrostylum*
 b. Plant without conspicuous glandular hairs 4

4a. Basal leaves with divisions lobed from just below the middle and beyond, or with few lobes, or with both these conditions; lateral divisions of basal leaves joined for ⅙ –¼ of their length *67. linearilobum*

 b. Basal leaves with divisions lobed for most of their length, lobes numerous; lateral divisions free or nearly so except for outermost pair on each side which may be joined for up to ⅙ of their length *65. tuberosum*

5a. Flowers funnel-shaped; petals pink *68. gracile*
 b. Flowers not funnel-shaped; petals not pink 6

6a. Leaves sage-textured, greyish; petals whitish with strong violet-blue veins *73. renardii*
 b. Leaves not sage-textured and greyish, though sometimes wrinkled; petals blue 7

7a. Sprawling annuals or biennials with diffuse inflorescences; flowers not more than 23mm in diameter 8
 b. Erect perennials wth dense inflorescences; flowers 28mm or more in diameter 9

8a. Biennial; petals about 9–11 × 8–9mm, ground-colour not whitish at base; seeds mottled in light and dark brown *76. bohemicum*
 b. Annual; petals about 8–9 × 6–7mm, ground-colour nearly white at base; seeds uniformly brown *77. lanuginosum*

9a. Basal leaves scarcely angled in outline, divided about half way to the base, their divisions broadest near the apex, palmately lobed (lobes apical) *69. platypetalum*
 b. Basal leaves distinctly angled in outline, divided as far as ⅔ or more, their divisions broadest well below the apex, palmato-pinnately lobed (lobes on the sides) 10

10a. Plant with conspicuous glandular hairs on upper parts 11
 b. Plant without conspicuous glandular hairs 13

11a. Basal leaves with sides of divisions lobed and toothed nearly to the base; plant flowering in June, leafy all summer; stylar portion of rostrum 4–7mm 12
 b. Basal leaves with sides of divisions not lobed and toothed below the widest part;

plant flowering in May, leaves disappearing in summer; stylar portion of rostrum 2–3mm   74. *peloponnesiacum*

12a. A sterile hybrid, never producing good seeds   71. ×*magnificum*
  b. A naturally-occurring fertile plant *ibericum* subsp. *jubatum* (see under no. 70)

13a. Plant flowering in May, leaves disappearing in summer   75. *libani*
  b. Plant flowering in June or later, leafy all summer   14

14a. Noticeably hairy plant with wrinkled leaves and upwardly inclined flowers 40–48mm in diameter
          70. *ibericum* subsp. *ibericum*
  b. Inconspicuously hairy plant with unwrinkled leaves and horizontal floral axis; flowers about 35mm in diameter
          72. *gymnocaulon*

GROUP F

1a. Petals between 8 and 16mm
          63. *asphodeloides*
  b. Petals not more than 8mm   64. *dissectum*

GROUP G

1a. Annuals, easily pulled up complete with root system   2
  b. Perennials, usually breaking from the root system when pulled up   5

2a. Immature fruits erect on reflexed pedicels 3
  b. Immature fruits erect on erect pedicels   4

3a. Leaf-blades divided nearly to base; sepals 6–8mm, enlarging to 8–9mm
          46. *columbinum*
  b. Leaf-blades not divided nearly to base; sepals 3.5–5mm   8. *rotundifolium*

4a. One fruiting pedicel in each cymule twice as long as sepals or more; rostrum with stylar portion 2–3mm   56. *bicknellii*
  b. Fruiting pedicels at most 1½ times as long as sepals; rostrum with stylar portion about 1.5mm   57. *carolinianum*

5a. Flowers nodding or inverted   6
  b. Flowers not nodding   12

6a. Tips of filaments, anthers and stigmas blackish; stigmas 5–6mm   23. *lambertii*
  b. Tips of filaments, anthers and stigmas paler though sometimes rather dark red or the anthers inky blue; stigmas not more than 4.5mm   7

7a. Upper part of plant with coarse dense entirely purple glandular hairs 30. *refractum*
  b. Glandular hairs of upper part of plant colourless or sometimes red-tipped, dense to sparse or sometimes absent   8

8a. Petals with very few hairs on edges at base, none on surface; nectary forming a ring all round the flower; (petals blackish)
          28. *sinense*
  b. Petals with numerous hairs on the edge at base; nectaries five, separate; (petals rarely blackish)   9

9a. Flowers light violet-blue, mostly in dense umbel-like clusters; immature fruits erect, standing above the currently open flowers
          20. *eriostemon*
  b. Flowers not violet-blue, in 2-flowered cymules; immature fruits nodding   10

10a. Filaments almost without hairs
          29. *delavayi*
  b. Filaments profusely hairy at base   11

11a. Petals not more than 1⅓ times as long as broad, forming a bowl-shaped or saucer-shaped flower   32. *yunnanense*
  b. Petals about twice as long as wide, curling backwards gently between the sepals
          31. *pogonanthum*

12a. Sprawling or trailing plants with small, usually pale flowers (petals 10.5mm or less) dispersed amongst the leaves   13
  b. Plants not with this combination of characters; petals usually more than 10.5mm   18

13a. Anthers violet-blue   14
  b. Anthers pale pink, cream or whitish, sometimes with blue edges   16

14a. Flowers 12–15mm in diameter; some glandular hairs present on sepals, rostrum,

mericarps and, sometimes, pedicels
47. *thunbergii*

b. Flowers 9–12mm in diameter; plant without glandular hairs 15

15a. Leaf-divisions short, broad, rather abruptly tapered; cymules 2-flowered or a mixture of 1-flowered and 2-flowered
48. *nepalense*

b. Leaf-divisions long, narrow, gradually tapered; cymules 1-flowered 49. *sibiricum*

16a. Flowers about 10mm in diameter, white, scarcely raised above the foliage
52. *sessiliflorum* subsp. *novaezelandiae*

b. Flowers about 15mm in diameter, white or pink, conspicuous 17

17a. Divisions of leaf-blades broadest near the middle; cymules both 1-flowered and 2-flowered 4. *endressii* × *sessiliflorum*

b. Divisions of leaf-blades broadest near the apex; cymules 1-flowered
51. *sessiliflorum* × *traversii*

18a. Rootstock a system of tubers up to 10 × 6mm interlinked by lengths of slender stolon (underground rhizome); (plant usually small, inflorescence few-flowered) 19

b. Rootstock not so constructed; (plant stature variable) 20

19a. Leaves marbled, tips of teeth and lobes more or less obtuse; flowers purplish pink with a cup-shaped white centre; stigmas 3–6mm 44. *orientalitibeticum*

b. Leaves not marbled, tips of teeth and lobes more or less acute; flowers deep rose-pink, trumpet-shaped, with petals white only at extreme base; stigmas less than 3mm
43. *pylzowianum*

20a. Flowers funnel-shaped or trumpet-shaped (view them from the side) 21

b. Flowers not funnel-shaped or trumpet-shaped 30

21a. Pedicels of immature fruits spreading just above or below the horizontal 22

b. Pedicels of immature fruits erect 25

22a. Divisions of leaf-blades toothed but not lobed 6. *nodosum*

b. Divisions of leaf-blades clearly lobed as well as toothed 23

23a. Rosette-leaves numerous at flowering time; one pedicel in each pair usually shorter than sepals; petals white or pale lilac, less than 12mm 12. *albiflorum*

b. Rosette-leaves few or none at flowering time; pedicels usually 1½–4 times as long as sepals; petals pink, usually 16mm or more 24

24a. Plant bushy; leaves not wrinkled; stigmas 4.5mm 37. *shikokianum*

b. Plant erect; leaves wrinkled; stigmas 2.5–3.5mm 7. *rectum*

25a. Lobes of main leaf-blades mostly 2–4 times as long as broad; blades not usually divided less than ⁴/₅ and often nearly to base 26

b. Lobes of main leaf-blades not more than about 1½ times as long as broad; blades not usually divided beyond ⁴/₅, occasionally to ⁵/₆ 27

26a. Main leaves with divisions broadest near middle; inflorescence dense; flowers white 10. *rivulare*

b. Main leaves with divisions broadest at or near apex; inflorescence diffuse; flowers deep reddish purple or magenta
36. *donianum*

27a. Petals net-veined 28

b. Petals not net-veined 29

28a. Ground-colour of petals white; flowers usually 25–30mm in diameter 5. *versicolor*

b. Ground-colour of petals pink; flowers usually more than 30mm in diameter, or petals aberrant, linear 2. × *oxonianum*

29a. Plant hoary on account of its dense clothing of appressed hairs 3. × *riversleaianum*

b. Plant without a hoary hair-clothing
1. *endressii* and 2. × *oxonianum*

30a. Petals not more than 8mm; (flowers held well above leaves in a loose, much-branched inflorescence; blue or lilac)

b. Petals more than 8mm   *11. pseudosibiricum*   31

31a. Cymules all 1-flowered; flowers not in umbel-like clusters   32
  b. Cymules all or mostly 2-flowered or flowers in umbel-like clusters   33

32a. Divisions of leaf-blades deeply cut with more or less spear-like lobes and, sometimes, teeth   *45. sanguineum*
  b. Divisions of leaf-blades shallowly cut with lobes broader than long and with small teeth   *50. traversii* var. *elegans*

33a. Flowers partly in umbel-like clusters   34
  b. Flowers not in umbel-like clusters   37

34a. Floral axis horizontal; stamens appressed to style; petals bluish   35
  b. Floral axis more or less erect; stamens curving away from style; petals pink   36

35a. Eglandular hairs of lower or middle part of stem spreading   *20. eriostemon*
  b. Eglandular hairs of lower or middle part of stem appressed   *21. erianthum*

36a. Sepal mucro 2–3.5mm; petals without hairs all across front surface at base; pedicels of immature fruits erect   *54. maculatum*
  b. Sepal mucro 1–1.5mm; petals with hairs all across front surface at base; pedicels of immature fruits reflexed   *59. viscosissimum*

37a. Floral axis approximately horizontal   38
  b. Floral axis upwardly inclined or vertically erect   42

38a. Dwarf alpine plants up to about 25cm; leaf-lobes and divisions not very narrow   39
  b. Plants usually more than 30cm tall, if smaller then with very narrow leaf-lobes and divisions   40

39a. Leaf-divisions tapered towards apex; petals blue; immature fruits reflexed on reflexed pedicels   *16c. regelii*
  b. Leaf-divisions broadest at apex; petals pale pink; immature fruits spreading or lying on the ground   *33. farreri*

40a. Sterile hybrid, fruit scarcely developing   *17. himalayense* × *pratense*
  b. Fertile, fruits developing freely (on reflexed pedicels)   41

41a. Main leaves divided as far as ⁴/₅ or less; rootstock more or less creeping underground; inflorescence diffuse; flowers 40–60mm in diameter   *19. himalayense*
  b. Main leaves divided as far as ⁶/₇ or more; rootstock compact, not creeping; inflorescence dense; flowers 35–45mm in diameter   *16. pratense*

42a. Petals purplish red with a black spot at the base   43
  b. Petals otherwise coloured   45

43a. Bushy plant with gold-tinged leaves; sterile hybrid with no development of fruit   *14. procurrens* × *psilostemon*
  b. Tall erect plant or low trailing plant; fruit developing freely   44

44a. Tall erect plant to 80cm or more; petal colour brilliant   *13. psilostemon*
  b. Low trailing plant; stems rooting at nodes; petal colour rather dull   *25. procurrens*

45a. Immature fruits spreading or nodding (on spreading or reflexed pedicels)   46
  b. Immature fruits erect (on erect or reflexed pedicels)   49

46a. Stylar portion of rostrum 7–8mm; petals bluish violet, 22–29mm   *18. clarkei*
  b. Stylar portion of rostrum absent or up to 1.5mm; petals pink or pinkish purple, about 14–21mm   47

47a. Petals whitish with a blackish violet base and heavy veins of the same colour   *24. lambertii* × *procurrens*
  b. Petals purple   48

48a. Plant sprawling, spreading rapidly by slender underground stolons; stigmas and tips of stamens blackish; rostrum with no stylar portion   *26. kishtvariense*
  b. Plant erect, with a compact, almost tuberous, rootstock; stigmas reddish, tips of stamens purplish; rostrum with a stylar portion 1–1.5mm   *27. rubifolium*

49a. Leaf-segments not more than 2mm wide   *53. incanum*

b. Leaf-segments, at least of the main leaves, more than 2mm wide   50

50a. All stipules completely united in pairs (without free tips); stigmas and tips of stamens blackish or dark violet; (stigmas 5.5–7mm)   *22. wallichianum*

b. Stipules free or some of them incompletely united in pairs (free at tips); stigmas and tips of stamens not blackish or dark violet   51

51a. Petals without hairs all across front at base   52

b. Petals with hairs all across front at base   55

52a. Dwarf alpine plant with slender underground stolons; petals deep pink with red base, notched at apex; sepals reddish   *38. stapfianum*

b. Plant without the above combination of characters   53

53a. Low-growing plant with leaf-lobes and teeth strongly divergent; leaf-segments whitish-hairy beneath; stigmas 3.5–4mm; rostrum with stylar portion not more than 1mm   *62. schiedeanum*

b. Erect or bushy plant with leaf-lobes and teeth weakly divergent; leaf-segments not whitish-hairy beneath; stigmas not more than 3mm; rostrum with stylar portion 3–5mm   54

54a. Petals about 23mm, nearly as broad as long; immature fruits erect on erect pedicels   *55. oreganum*

b. Petals not more than 20mm, 1¼–2 times as long as broad; immature fruits erect on more or less reflexed pedicels *15. collinum*

55a. Plant with glandular hairs   56

b. Plant without glandular hairs   59

56a. Divisions of main leaves with lobes and teeth extending down the sides nearly to base; inflorescence dense; stigmas 2–3mm; (pedicels erect)   *9. sylvaticum*

b. Divisions of main leaves with lobes and teeth extending down the sides only to the middle or just beyond; inflorescence diffuse; stigmas 3–6mm; (pedicels usually spreading or reflexed)   57

57a. Petals white or pale lilac, not notched, 12–18mm; stigmas 3–4mm   *61. richardsonii*

b. Petals pink, 13–22mm, more or less notched; stigmas 4–6mm   58

58a. Flowering stems usually clustered, branching from near the ground, profusely branched; stem-leaves numerous   *60. fremontii*

b. Flowering stems usually solitary, branching high up, not profusely; stem-leaves few   *58. nervosum*

59a. Pedicels of immature fruits erect   60

b. Pedicels of immature fruits spreading or reflexed   61

60a. Stigmas 2–3mm; leaf-divisions broad   *9. sylvaticum*

b. Stigmas 5–6mm; leaf-divisions narrow   *39. soboliferum*

61a. Divisions of lower stem-leaves with longest lateral lobes 2 or more times as long as broad   62

b. Divisions of lower stem-leaves with longest lateral lobes not more than 1½ times as long as broad   63

62a. Divisions of main leaves broadest just below apex   *41. dahuricum*

b. Divisions of main leaves broadest just above middle   *42. yesoense*

63a. Petals brilliant deep magenta; stigmas 2.5–3mm   *34. palustre*

b. Petals pink or purple; stigmas 3.5–5.5mm 64

64a. Petals not more than 16mm, 1⅓ times as long as broad, with hairs on front surface extending above basal tuft over basal ⅓ or ½; stylar portion of rostrum about 1.5mm   *40. krameri*

b. Petals 17–22mm, more than 1½ times as long as broad, with hairs on front surface confined to basal tuft; stylar portion of rostrum 2–3mm *35. wlassovianum*

·CHAPTER 9·
The Cultivated Cranesbills

Introduction and Explanations

The standard treatment for each species in this chapter includes a summary description and a full botanical description. The first gives the full range of flower colours, whereas the second gives only the typical colour, provided any variations are covered in descriptions of varieties, cultivars, etc.

The range of material on which the descriptions are based varies widely, and some allowance must be made for this. The emphasis, however, has been on plants that are in cultivation.

Important information contained in the descriptions of the subdivisions of the genus (see Chapter 5) and of the informal groups is repeated in the species-descriptions except in the cases of section *Tuberosa* and of groups represented by only one species.

Synonyms which are current in horticultural circles are given in parentheses after the current name at the beginning of each description. Other synonyms are given when it seems useful to do so. Misapplied names (see Chapter 3) are not shown as synonyms but are dealt with in the discussion sections and, like the synonyms, can be traced in the index.

Terminology, conventions and abbreviated references to colour charts cited as RHSCC and HCC are explained in the second part of Chapter 4. In the present chapter I use place-names to indicate certain important British gardens, thus 'Cambridge' means the University Botanic Garden, Cambridge, 'Edinburgh' the Royal Botanic Garden, Edinburgh, 'Kew' the Royal Botanic Gardens, Kew, London and 'Wisley' the Garden of the Royal Horticultural Society, Wisley, near Woking, Surrey. 'The Wisley Trial' means the trial held at Wisley for horticultural evaluation of *Geranium* in the years 1973–6. 'The Report of the Wisley Trial' means the report in *Proceedings of the Royal Horticultural Society, 103*, 67–71 (1978) (in library copies the proceedings are usually bound with *The Garden* (formerly *Journal of the Royal Horticultural Society*) for the same year, which has the same volume number).

The Illustrations

The silhouettes or line-drawings of leaves show the basal leaves or lower stem-leaves unless otherwise indicated. In all cranesbills there is variation according to the part of the plant on which the leaves are borne and the climatic conditions under which they unfolded, as well as variation between plants on account of their varying genetic constitutions; the illustrations on their own should therefore not be relied upon for identification, but used for confirmation.

Most specimens illustrated were cultivated at the University Botanic Garden, Cambridge. For these the caption gives the donor and date of donation, if known ('B. G.' means 'botanic garden'). A few specimens were obtained from other gardens and for these the name of the grower appears, preceded by 'cult.', and followed by the date of collection of the specimen. Collecting-numbers and collector's names (when differing from the name of the donor) are given in parentheses after the locality. Captions to colour plates omit some of this information but include the month in which the photograph was taken and the place (if other than Cambridge).

Classification and Arrangement of Species

The following list shows at a glance how the species treated in this chapter are grouped. A more condensed presentation of the classification of the genus *Geranium* is given in Chapter 5.

Geranium Linnaeus
Subgenus I Geranium
Section Geranium, The
Sylvaticum Section

The Endressii Group

1. G. endressii Gay
2. G. × oxonianum Yeo (G. endressii × G. versicolor)
3. G. × riversleaianum Yeo (G. endressii × G. traversii)
4. G. endressii Gay × G. sessiliflorum Cavanilles
5. G. versicolor Linnaeus
6. G. nodosum Linnaeus
7. G. rectum Trautvetter

The Rotundifolium Group

8. G. rotundifolium Linnaeus

The Sylvaticum Group

9. G. sylvaticum Linnaeus
10. G. rivulare Villars
11. G. pseudosibiricum J. Mayer
12. G. albiflorum Ledebour
13. G. psilostemon Ledebour
14. G. procurrens Yeo × G. psilostemon Ledebour

The Collinum Group

15. G. collinum Willdenow

The Pratense Group

16. G. pratense Linnaeus
    and (a) G. transbaicalicum (b) "Nepal Form" (c) G. regelii Nevski
17. G. himalayense Klotzsch × G. pratense Linnaeus
18. G. clarkei Yeo
19. G. himalayense Klotzsch

The Erianthum Group

20. G. eriostemon De Candolle
21. G. erianthum De Candolle

The Wallichianum Group

22. G. wallichianum D. Don
23. G. lambertii Sweet
24. G. lambertii Sweet × G. procurrens Yeo
25. G. procurrens Yeo
26. G. kishtvariense Knuth
27. G. rubifolium Lindley

The Refractum Group

28. G. sinense Knuth
29. G. delavayi Franchet
30. G. refractum Edgeworth & J.D. Hooker
31. G. pogonanthum Franchet
32. G. yunnanense Franchet

The Farreri Group

33. G. farreri Stapf

The Palustre Group

34. G. palustre Linnaeus
35. G. wlassovianum Link
36. G. donianum Sweet
37. G. shikokianum Matsumura

The Stapfianum Group

38. G. stapfianum Handel-Mazzetti

The Krameri Group

39. G. soboliferum Komarov
40. G. krameri Franchet & Savatier
41. G. dahuricum De Candolle
42. G. yesoense Franchet & Savatier

The Pylzowianum Group

43. G. pylzowianum Maximowicz
44. G. orientalitibeticum Knuth

The Sanguineum Group

45. G. sanguineum Linnaeus

The Columbinum Group

46. G. columbinum Linnaeus

The Sibiricum Group

47. G. thunbergii Lindley & Paxton
48. G. nepalense Sweet
49. G. sibiricum Linnaeus

The Sessiliflorum Group

50. G. traversii J.D. Hooker var. elegans Cockayne
51. G. sessiliflorum Cavanilles subsp. novaezelandiae Carolin × G. traversii J.D. Hooker var. elegans Cockayne
52. G. sessiliflorum Cavanilles subsp. novaezelandiae Carolin

The Incanum Group

53. G. incanum N.L. Burman
    and (a) G. magniflorum Knuth

The Maculatum Group

54. G. maculatum Linnaeus
55. G. oreganum Howell
56. G. bicknellii Britton
57. G. carolinianum Linnaeus

The Fremontii Group

58. G. nervosum Rydberg
59. G. viscosissimum Fischer & Meyer
60. G. fremontii Gray

The Richardsonii Group

61. G. richardsonii Fischer & Trautvetter

The Bellum Group

62. G. schiedeanum Schlechtendal

Section Dissecta Yeo, The Dissectum Section

63. G. asphodeloides N.L. Burman
64. G. dissectum Linnaeus

Section Tuberosa Reiche, The Tuberosum Section

Subsection Tuberosa, The Tuberosum Group

65. G. tuberosum Linnaeus
66. G. macrostylum Boissier
67. G. linearilobum De Candolle
68. G. malviflorum Boissier & Reuter

Subsection Mediterranea Knuth, The Platypetalum Group

69. G. platypetalum Fischer & Meyer
70. G. ibericum Cavanilles subsp. ibericum
71. G. ×magnificum Hylander (G. ibericum × G. platypetalum)
72. G. gymnocaulon De Candolle
73. G. renardii Trautvetter
74. G. peloponnesiacum Boissier
75. G. libani Davis
76. G. bohemicum Linnaeus
77. G. lanuginosum Lamarck
78. G. gracile Nordmann

Subgenus II Robertium Picard

Section Polyantha Reiche, The Polyanthes Group

79. G. polyanthes Edgeworth & J.D. Hooker

Section Trilopha Yeo, The Trilophum Group

80. G. trilophum Boissier
81. G. ocellatum Cambessèdes
82. G. biuncinatum Kokwaro

Section Divaricata Rouy & Foucaud, The Albanum Group

83. G. albanum Bieberstein

Section Batrachioides W.D.J. Koch, The Pyrenaicum Group

84. G. pyrenaicum N.L. Burman

85. G. pusillum Linnaeus
86. G. brutium Gasparrini
87. G. molle Linnaeus

Section Unguiculata Reiche, The Macrorrhizum Group

88. G. glaberrimum Boissier & Heldreich
89. G. macrorrhizum Linnaeus
90. G. × cantabrigiense Yeo (G. dalmaticum × G. macrorrhizum)
91. G. dalmaticum (Beck) Rechinger
92. G. cataractarum Cosson

Section Unguiculata × Section Anemonifolia

93. G. cataractarum Cosson × G. maderense Yeo

Section Lucida Knuth, G. lucidum

94. G. lucidum Linnaeus

Section Ruberta Dumortier, The Robertianum Group

95. G. robertianum Linnaeus
96. G. rubescens Yeo
97. G. canariense Reuter

Section Anemonifolia Knuth, The Palmatum Group

98. G. palmatum Cavanilles
99. G. maderense Yeo

Subgenus III Erodioideae Yeo

Section Erodioideae Picard, The Phaeum Group

100. G. phaeum Linnaeus
101. G. ×monacense Harz (G. phaeum × G. reflexum)
102. G. reflexum Linnaeus
103. G. aristatum Freyn

Section Subacaulia Reiche, The Cinereum Group

104. G. argenteum Linnaeus
105. G. ×lindavicum Knuth (G. argenteum × G. cinereum)
106. G. cinereum Cavanilles var. cinereum
107. G. cinereum Cavanilles 'Ballerina', etc. (var. cinereum × var. subcaulescens)
108. G. cinereum Cavanilles var. obtusilobum (Bornmüller) Yeo
109. G. cinereum Cavanilles var. palmatipartitum Knuth
110. G. cinereum Cavanilles var. subcaulescens (De Candolle) Knuth

The Descriptions

Subgenus I Geranium

Plants annual or perennial. Fruit discharge by seed-ejection: each carpel has a hole big enough to allow the seed to escape, which it does during the explosive recurvature of the awn. The carpel does not separate from the awn. The awn may or may not remain attached to the central column of the rostrum. Mericarps not sculptured.

Section Geranium, The Sylvaticum Section

Plants annual or perennial. Retention of seed in mericarp during the pre-explosive interval by bristles attached to a horny tubercle at the lower end of the mericarp. Awn remaining attached to central column of rostrum after discharge.

This section forms the major part of the subgenus and is world-wide in distribution. The species dealt with here are assigned to 22 informally named groups.

The Endressii Group

Perennials with compact or creeping rootstock. Leaves with diamond-shaped or elliptic divisions. Stipules slender-pointed. Flowers erect, funnel-shaped, with more or less notched petals which are hairy across front at base. Immature fruits and their pedicels erect, spreading or reflexed.

Four species from S. Europe and W. Asia, all cultivated. (Three hybrids of 1. G. endressii are also described here though two involve members of other groups.)

1. G. endressii Gay (Figure 9.1)
Rather small perennial with moderately deeply cut, pointed leaf-divisions and bright pink or salmon-pink upright funnel-shaped flowers, 30–37mm in diameter, with notched petals. Border, woodland, ground-cover. Leafy in winter. June to September.

Plant with extensive elongated rhizomes on or just below the surface, and stems usually 25–50cm tall. Blades of basal leaves between 5 and 10cm wide, light green, wrinkled, divided as far as $^4/_5$–$^5/_6$ into 5; divisions gently tapered both ways from about the middle, palmato-pinnately lobed about half-way to the midrib, the lobes 1–1½ times as long as broad, usually with 2 or 3 teeth. Teeth and tips of lobes acute. Lowest one or two stem-leaves solitary. Stem-leaves gradually diminishing in size and length of stalk upwards, changing little in shape. Plant conspicuously hairy, some of the hairs on the sepals, and sometimes also pedicels and peduncles, glandular. Inflorescence rather dense. Pedicels up to 2½ times as long as sepals. Flowers erect, funnel-shaped. Sepals 7–9mm; mucro 1–2mm. Petals more than 16mm, about twice as long as broad, more or less notched at apex, broadest above the middle, bright deep pink, becoming darker and redder with age; base and lower parts of veins colourless, trans-lucent; apical parts of veins slightly darker than ground-colour and slightly netted; base with hairs extending across front surface and on margins, hardly tufted. Stamens about $^2/_3$ as long as sepals to nearly equalling them; filaments curving outwards at tips, white, tinged with pink, hairy in the lower half; anthers yellow or purplish. Stigmas 2.5–3.5mm, pink or reddish, bristly on the backs. Immature fruits and their pedicels erect. Rostrum 18–21mm, including stylar portion 2.5–3mm, with dense minute hairs and sparse longer bristles. Meri-carps 3.5mm. Discharge: seed-ejection (bristles).

Western half of Basses Pyrénées, mainly in France but just extending into Spain. Naturalised further north.

Figure 9.1 G. *endressii*, Mrs O. Vaughan, 1975, coll. Britain: Devon (naturalised), × $^2/_3$

A strongly colonising evergreen perennial, tolerating shade or sun. The bright pink flowers are colourful for a long period; E.A. Bowles (1914) described the colour as 'raspberry-ice pink' to which A.T. Johnson (1937) added 'chalky', the chalkiness being imparted by a silvery sheen. The petal colour intensifies with age and becomes slightly redder. Thus the colour progresses from HCC Mallow Purple, slightly paler than 630/1, through Cyclamen Purple 30/2 to Rhodamine Purple 29/2 and, in the withering flower, Fuchsia Purple, between 28/2 and 28/1. (HCC 30/2 approximates to RHSCC Red-Purple Group 74C and HCC 28/1–2 is near Red-Purple Group 67B and C: the other shades cannot be approximated in RHSCC.)

G. *endressii* differs from 78. G. *gracile* in the jagged edges of the leaf-divisions, in fruit-discharge type and in many less conspicuous characters; for differences from 5. G. *versicolor* see that species. It is a notably promiscuous hybridiser. It is easily propagated by separation of the rhizomes.

G. *endressii* 'Wargrave Pink' ('Wargrave') has petals of a light salmon-pink, (RHSCC Red Group 55B), though a little bluer at the ex-treme edge in young flowers; towards the tips a slightly darker network of veins is visible. The petals change colour with age only slightly. Petals distinctly notched. Stigmas scarcely 2.5mm long. It grows to about twice the height of G. *endressii* when in the sun. The compact rootstock and the height suggest that this may be a cross with G. *versicolor* (i.e. belongs to 2. G. ×*oxonianum*) but in most details the plant is so like G. *endressii* that I retain it as a cultivar of that species. 'War-grave Pink' was introduced by Waterer, Sons & Crisp in 1930, having been found in their nursery by their foreman, Mr G.W. Wright (Clifton, 1979).

HYBRIDS. G. *endressii* has formed a number of hybrids spontaneously (see Chapter 7), namely with 56. G. *bicknellii* or 57. G. *carolinianum* (sterile), with 5. G. *versicolor* (= 2. G. ×*oxonianum*), with 50. G. *traversii* (sterile; = 3. G. ×*riversleaianum*) and with 52. G. *sessiliflorum* (sterile; = 4. G. 'Kate').

2. G. ×oxonianum Yeo (Figure 9.2, Plate 2)
Leafy perennial, up to about 80cm, combining in various ways the characters of 1. G. *endressii* and 5. G. *versicolor*, and usually recognisable by the funnel-shaped flowers, up to 40mm in dia-

meter, and the pink petals with darker net-veining, notched at the apex. Border, woodland, ground-cover. June onwards.

Figure 9.2 *G. × oxonianum* 'Claridge Druce', G.S. Thomas, 1974 × ²/₃

Generally taller than either parent. Leaf-blades between 5 and 20cm wide, sometimes brown-blotched, more or less wrinkled; divisions usually with the more solid outline, greater relative breadth and abrupt tapering of *G. versicolor* but lobing a little deeper and coarser, as in *G. endressii*. Flowers (at least in the named cultivars) larger than in either parent, with sepals to 11mm and petals to 26mm long and 15mm wide, in some cases more than half as wide as long. Plants with aberrant narrow petals sometimes occurring. Petals usually pink with a network of dark veins but sometimes without the latter. Rostrum to 27mm, its stylar portion 3–4mm. Discharge: seed-ejection (bristles).

A fertile hybrid between 1. *G. endressii* and 5. *G. versicolor*. Has escaped into the wild in Britain in the absence of the parents.

This hybrid arises readily when the parents are grown together. Being fertile it is able to produce a great range of variants, most of which will never deserve naming. Some have, however, been named, one of them being 'Claridge Druce', a specimen of which has been designated as the type of the nothospecies (hybrid) *G. ×oxonianum*. This cultivar 'was named in memory of the noted botanist who discovered it' in 1960 by Mr Graham Thomas and the curator of

the University Botanic Garden, Oxford, Mr G.W. Robinson, when the former was on a visit to Oxford (Thomas, 1970, 1976). The cultivars should normally be propagated by division.

In those cultivars which have normal petals that are not heavily veined (i.e. excluding 'Claridge Druce') the veining shows up more strongly when the light falls in such a way as to bring out the silvery sheen on the surface, against which they make a contrast.

G. ×oxonianum 'Armitageae' (*G. endressii* var. *armitageae* Turrill) is distinguished by having petals 16–17 × 4–4.5mm; they are 'deep rosy pink'. When describing it, Turrill did not rule out the possibility that this was *G. endressii* × *G. versicolor*, and as the basal leaves are outside the range of *G. endressii* in shape, and the rostrum lacks large hairs, I believe this is what it is. In other characters it agrees better with *G. endressii*. There is at Cambridge a dried specimen culvitated there 'ex Armitage', gathered on 16 October 1932 by (Professor) W.T. Stearn and confirmed as to its identity by Dr W.B. Turrill in March 1933. The plant was originally described from material cultivated by Miss E. Armitage, Dadnor Garden, Herefordshire. See also *G. ×oxonianum* 'Thurstonianum'.

G. ×oxonianum 'A.T. Johnson' (*G. endressii* 'A.T. Johnson's Var.') is one of two cultivars presented by A.T. Johnson to the firm of Ingwersen which were named, described and distributed by the latter (the other one is 'Rose Clair'). The descriptions of them given by Ingwersen (1946) clearly relate them to the first two of three described by Johnson (1937, p. 179). 'A.T. Johnson' was said to be dwarfer than typical *G. endressii*, similar to it in foliage, and with 'the blossoms . . . a beautiful shade of silvery-pink'. It would seem from this that it should not have the salmon tint of 'Rose Clair' and should therefore be bluer. However, plants with salmon-pink petals (HCC 23/2 or 23/3, RHSCC Red Group 55B or the very similar Red-Purple Group 62A) are in circulation under the name 'A.T. Johnson' and one was submitted to the Wisley Trial under that name. It may be doubted whether the true 'A.T. Johnson' is still in cultivation.

G. ×oxonianum 'Claridge Druce' (Figure 9.2) is a very vigorous and rather tall, strongly hairy plant with dark, slightly glossy foliage, large trumpet-shaped flowers, the petals of which are lightly notched, up to 26 × 14mm and rosy pink in colour: HCC Petunia Purple 32/2, RHSCC Purple-Violet Group 90C, with a strong network of darker veins, fading to unveined white in the basal ⅕–¼. Thomas (1982) states that it seems to come true from seed. In fact, plants show some variation, but many are so similar that it is certainly necessary to accept that 'Claridge Druce' is a name not restricted to one clone, but applicable to any clone having approximately the characters given above.

G. ×oxonianum 'Rose Clair' (G. endressii 'Rose Clair') was described by Ingwersen (1946) as indistinguishable from 'A.T. Johnson' (q.v.) in habit and freedom and continuity of flowering, but with flowers 'a shade of clear rose-salmon with just the faintest trace of veining'. The plant to which an Award of Merit was made in the Wisley Trial had petals RHSCC Red-Purple Group 66C–67D, a tint that is hardly suggestive of salmon-pink and much bluer than the salmon tint of G. endressii 'Wargrave Pink'. Although this makes it seem probable that this plant is not the original 'Rose Clair' it is best to let it retain the name unless an indisputably authentic but different 'Rose Clair' should come to light.

G. ×oxonianum 'Thurstonianum' (G. endressii var. thurstonianum Turrill) has aberrant flowers with extremely narrow, strap-shaped purple petals and the stamens more or less petaloid (i.e. like the abnormal petals). For discussion and further references (going back to Bowles, 1914), see McClintock in Stace (1975). Plants vary as to presence or absence of leaf-blotching and in leaf-shape and pedicellength; the petal width also varies, and when it lies between about 3 and 6mm netted veins are clearly visible showing that a failure of lateral expansion has made the veins crowded, thereby causing the colour to seem dark. This is another instance where it is inappropriate to limit the cultivar name to a single clone.

G. ×oxonianum 'Winscombe' (Plate 2) is near G. endressii but is distinguished by a greater change in petal colour during the life of the flower, from nearly white to moderately deep pink. The petals are noticeably net-veined when old. Colour chart readings are, for youngest flowers, HCC Rhodamine Pink 527/2, for older flowers, HCC Persian Rose 628/2,

and finally HCC 628/1 and 628 (the first three of these approximate to RHSCC Red-Purple Group 62C, 73C and 68B respectively). 'Winscombe' was found in a cottage garden, presumably in the village of Winscombe, Somerset, by the late Mrs Margery Fish.

3. G. ×riversleaianum Yeo (Figure 9.3, Plate 3)
Trailing hoary perennials; leaves angular with divisions more or less tapered to the tip; flowers pink to deep magenta, 20–32mm in diameter, with faintly notched petals; sterile. Rock garden, ground-cover. June onwards.

Plant with a short stout rootstock. Blades of basal leaves between 5 and 10cm wide, divided as far as ⅔ or ¾ into 7; divisions tapered both ways from above the middle, rather abruptly so to the tip, mostly lobed for about ⅓ of their length, the lobes about as long as broad, few-toothed; teeth and tips of lobes obtuse or acute. Lower stem-leaves paired or solitary, upper paired, stalked, reduced in size gradually upwards. Flowering stems forming a diffuse inflorescence, ascending or trailing, up to 1m long. Whole plant covered in rather short more or less appressed hairs, enhancing the naturally greyish component in the colour of the leaves. Cymules 2-flowered. Flowers more or less erect, widely funnel-shaped. Sepals 6–7mm; mucro 1mm or less. Petals 14–17mm, slightly longer than broad, lightly notched at apex, light pink, with faint darker unbranched veins, to deep magenta, with obscure darker feathering; base slightly hairy on front surface and margins. Filaments shorter than sepals, white or nearly so, hairy; anthers yellow or purplish, usually empty and failing to burst. Stigmas 2–3.5mm, pink to crimson, outer surfaces with few or many bristles. Rostrum and carpels not developing.

Hybrids between 1. G. endressii and 50. G. traversii.

This hybrid seems to arise fairly easily when the parents occur together in gardens, despite the fact that G. endressii is Pyrenean and G. traversii comes from Chatham Island, off New Zealand. It makes extensive, abundantly flowering carpets which die back to the rootstock in winter. Thomas (1977) says 'Russell Prichard' is not reliably hardy except in our warmer counties, but Ingwersen (1946) found it hardy in the Weald of Sussex; in my experience the rootstock benefits by division and replanting every few years. The petal colour may fade slightly with age, unlike that of 2. *G. ×oxonianum*, which intensifies. The name is explained below under 'Russell Prichard'.

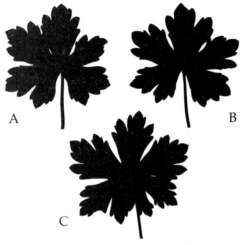

Figure 9.3 *G × riversleaianum*: (A) & (B) 'Russell Prichard', G.S. Thomas, 1974; (C) 'Mavis Simpson', G.S. Thomas, 1981 × ²/₃

G. ×riversleaianum 'Chapel End Pink' was raised by Mr Jan Stephens (see Stephens, 1967) and has 'shell-pink' flowers 2.5cm in diameter. There are dried specimens, dated 1967, in the Herbarium of the University Botanic Garden, Cambridge. It has more bluntly toothed and greyer leaves than 'Russell Prichard'. The stigmas have very few bristles on the back, despite their copious presence in both parents.

G. ×riversleaianum 'Chapel End Red', is a sister to the preceding (q.v.), with crimson flowers 'rather paler and brighter than the colour of the "Russell Prichard" flower'.

G. ×riversleaianum 'Mavis Simpson' (Figure 9.3 C) has the leaf-divisions and lobes broader in relation to their length than those of 'Chapel End Pink' and 'Russell Prichard', and in spring faint brown blotches are present in the notches; petals light pink ('shell-pink'): darkest parts of darkest flowers HCC Phlox Purple 632/2 (in RHSCC this is between Red-Purple Group 73B and 75A–B but is remote from both), pale towards middle and base, becoming paler with age, their surface with a silvery sheen and the dark purple veins conspicuous, slightly feathered; anthers pale

yellow; stigmas crimson. The plant was found at Kew and named after one of the staff there (Clifton, 1982). The brown blotches on the leaves suggest that this may be a triple hybrid, *G. ×oxonianum × G. traversii*, but Mr Brian Halliwell, of Kew, tells me that *G. traversii* var. *elegans* and *G. endressii* were growing near the spot where it was found.

G. ×riversleaianum 'Russell Prichard' (Figures 9.3A & B, Plate 3) has flowers fully 3cm in diameter, of a rich magenta, and sharply toothed leaf-divisions. The flower colour is much more intense than in either parent and this, apparently, has led to the supposition that the plant is *G. sanguineum × G. traversii*. It is named after a member of the family which owned the now defunct Riverslea Nursery in Hampshire (see Appendix II).

4. *G. endressii* Gay × *G. sessiliflorum* Cavanilles: 'Kate' (Figure 9.4)

A dwarf, trailing perennial with small bronzy leaves in which the central division is the largest, and blush-pink flowers 15mm in diameter; petals lightly notched; sterile. Rock garden, ground-cover. June onwards.

Rootstock compact. Leaf-blades dark bronzy green, those of the basal leaves not more than 5cm wide, divided as far as about ²/₃ into 5; divisions broadly diamond-shaped or broadly elliptic, the middle one much the largest, all shortly tapered both ways from beyond the middle, lobed for about ¼ of their length or less; lobes ½ as long as broad, with an occasional tooth; teeth and tips of lobes more or less obtuse. Lower stem-leaves like the basal, upper usually divided into 3, the divisions sparsely lobed, acute, often with curved margins, all usually in unequal pairs. Stems and leaf-stalks with dense appressed hairs, these sparser on upper surfaces of leaves; sepals and lower surfaces of leaves with spreading bristly hairs. Stems mostly forking regularly but unequally, forming a trailing inflorescence up to 35cm long. Cymules with one or two flowers. Flowers funnel-shaped. Sepals 5–6mm, flushed with brown; mucro 1.5mm. Petals about 10 × 6.5mm, nearly triangular with a usually lightly notched apex, apical half pale pink with dark, slightly forked veins, basal half translucent white, revealing the green colour of the sepals; base with a few hairs on the front surface and the margins. Stamens about ²/₃ as long as sepals; filaments strongly enlarged below, white, hairy; anthers pale pink, apparently abortive. Stigmas about 1mm, pale buff, with bristles pressed to outer surface. Rostrum and carpels not developing.

Figure 9.4 *G. endressii* × *G. sessiliflorum*: 'Kate', O.G. Folkard, 1979 × ²/₃

This pretty hybrid appeared in the garden of the Rev. O.G. Folkard at Sleaford, Lincolnshire, and was sent to Cambridge in 1979. Mr Folkard named it after his daughter and suggested the above parentage which seems to be correct. Clifton (1979) lists it as 'Kate Folkard'. The bronzy colouring of the leaves indicates that the dark bronze-leaved form of *G. sessiliflorum* was involved; the full hybrid formula for the cultivar is therefore *G. endressii* × *G. sessiliflorum* subsp. *novae-zelandiae* 'Nigricans' (nos. 1. and 52. respectively in this book). It is propagated by division.

5. *G. versicolor* Linnaeus (*G. striatum* Linnaeus) (Figure 9.5, Plate 4)

Rather low-growing perennial with blotched leaves, shallowly cut and broadly pointed leaf-divisions and strongly net-veined white trumpet-shaped flowers, 25–30mm in diameter, with clearly notched petals. Rock garden, woodland, ground-cover. Leafy in winter. May to October.

Plant with a rather compact rootstock, with stems up to 60cm in length but spreading so that the plant is usually low and bushy. Blades of basal leaves between 5 and 20cm wide, usually brown-blotched between the divisions, divided as far as ²/₃ or ⁴/₅ into 5; divisions abruptly tapered both ways from about the middle, palmato-pinnately lobed about ⅓ of the way to the midrib; lobes as long as broad or less, with 1–3 teeth. Teeth and tips of lobes obtuse or acute. Stem-leaves paired, gradually diminishing in size and length of stalk upwards, changing little in shape. Plant covered with bristly hairs, sometimes densely, but in any case

sparsely on peduncles and pedicels. Inflorescence diffuse. Pedicels up to about 1½ times as long as sepals but one of each pair nearly always shorter than sepals. Flowers erect, trumpet-shaped. Sepals 7–9mm, erect but not appressed to petal-bases, recurved at tips, with a few long hairs; mucro about 1.5mm. Petals slightly more than 16mm, twice as long as broad, notched, broadest near apex, erect at base, spreading above and recurved at tips, white with a close network of fine magenta-coloured veins which fades in age; base thinly hairy on margins and front surface, the hairs not tufted. Stamens slightly longer than sepals; filaments white with pink tips, sparsely hairy to beyond the middle; anthers bluish. Stigmas 3.5mm, red with whitish receptive surface, not bristly. Immature fruits and their pedicels erect. Rostrum about 18mm, including stylar portion about 6mm, with dense minute hairs and no bristles. Mericarps 3.5mm. Discharge: seed-ejection (bristles).

Figure 9.5 *G. versicolor*, × ²/₃

Central and S. Italy, Sicily, southern part of Balkan Peninsula (including Greece, Yugoslavia and Albania).

This species is attractive in its unusual net-veined flowers and its crop of fresh-looking leaves held through the winter. Plants vary in their density of hair-covering and obtuseness of leaf-teeth. As well as differing from 1. *G. endressii* in the obvious characters of the leaves and petals, *G. versicolor* differs also in the much more compact rootstock, the sparseness of the hairs on the peduncles, pedicels and calyx, the absence of large glandular hairs on these parts (not always present in *G. endressii*, however), lack of long hairs on the rostrum, the shorter pedicels and longer stamens (other floral parts are remarkably similar in size). This list may assist in the diagnosis of hybrids. In the dried state *G. versicolor* may resemble 78. *G. gracile*; that, however, has glandular hairs, smaller sepals, a different fruit-discharge type and other differences.

HYBRIDS. Produces a fertile hybrid with 1. *G. endressii* (= 2. *G. ×oxonianum*).

6. G. nodosum Linnaeus (Figure 9.6)

Perennial with swellings above the nodes of the stems and bright green leaves with 3 or 5 elliptic or lanceolate divisions, which are toothed but scarcely lobed; flowers about 2.5–3cm in diameter, erect, funnel-shaped, in a diffuse inflorescence, with bright purplish pink slightly veiny and distinctly notched petals. Young fruits horizontal. Woodland and wild garden. June to October.

Plant with elongated rhizomes on or just below the surface, and stems usually 20–50cm tall. Blades of basal leaves between 5 and 20cm wide, bright green and slightly glossy above, glossy beneath, divided as far as about $^2/_3$ into 5; divisions more or less elliptic with gradually tapered tips, scarcely lobed, unevenly toothed except at base, the basal pair widely splayed; teeth and tips of divisions acute. Stem-leaves paired, decreasing gradually in size and length of stalk upwards, mostly with 3 lanceolate divisions, the upper nearly stalkless. Inflorescence unequally forked, diffuse. Stems, leaf-stalks and sepals with more or less numerous small appressed hairs; leaf-blades with scattered larger spreading hairs. Flowers erect. Sepals 8–9mm; mucro 1.5–2mm. Petals more than 16mm, twice as long as broad or more, wedge-shaped, broadest near the deeply notched apex, bright purplish pink or tending to violet with carmine veins at base, which are slightly branched above; base with rather numerous hairs across front surface and on margins. Stamens longer than sepals; filaments white, hairy for $^2/_3$ of their length; anthers blue. Styles red. Stigmas about 2mm, red, hairless. Immature fruits and their pedicels horizontal or slightly nodding.

Rostrum about 22mm, including stylar portion about 3mm, with minute hairs only. Mericarps 3.5mm. Discharge: seed-ejection (bristles).

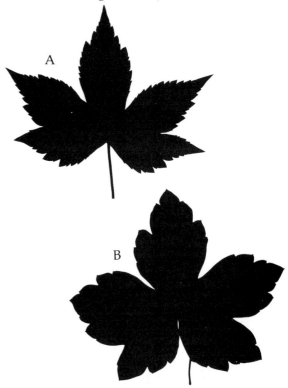

Figure 9.6 *G. nodosum:* (A) origin unknown; (B) W. Ingwersen, 1976, × $^2/_3$ (difference partly genetic, partly environmental)

Central France to Pyrenees, C. Italy, C. Yugoslavia.

G. nodosum grows naturally in mountain woods, and is an attractive subject for the woodland and wild garden, mainly on account of its glossy leaves with virtually unlobed but saw-edged divisions. It differs from 78. *G. gracile* in fruit-discharge type, absence of glandular hairs, posture of immature fruit, etc. It is easily propagated by seed or by division.

7. G. rectum Trautvetter (Figure 9.7)

Perennial with sharply toothed and lobed leaf-divisions, a very diffuse inflorescence and bright pink, funnel-shaped or trumpet-shaped flowers about 25mm in diameter, with slightly veiny, more or less notched petals. Woodland. June to October.

Rootstock thick, compact. Basal leaves on flowering shoots few or none. Leaves like those of 1. *G. endressii* or similar but with shorter and broader divisions, lobes and teeth, sometimes slightly marbled. Hair-clothing like that of 6. *G. nodosum.* Inflorescence very diffuse. Pedicels mostly 1½–4 times as long as sepals. Sepals 7–8mm; mucro 1.5mm. Petals about 16mm, twice as long as broad or less, broadest above the middle, rounded or distinctly notched at apex, bright rose-pink with white base and dark crimson, scarcely branched veins; base hairy across front and on margins. Stamens longer than sepals; filaments white, hairy to beyond the middle; anthers whitish with blue margins. Stigmas 2.5–3.5mm, pink to crimson. Immature fruits erect or deflexed on pedicels spreading just above the horizontal. Rostrum about 20mm, including stylar portion 2–3mm. Mericarps 4.5mm. Discharge: seed-ejection (bristles).

Figure 9.7 *G rectum:* (A) Mrs J. Forty, 1973 (probably from USSR); (B) Moscow Acad. Sci. B.G., 1980 × ²/₃

Soviet Central Asia (Tian Shan and Dzungaria/Tarbagatai), Chinese Turkestan, N.W. Himalayas.

A plant of little horticultural interest with leaves more or less like those of 1. *G. endressii* in shape, with hair-clothing sparse and very like that of 6. *G. nodosum,* and with floral details very similar to those of the latter. It differs from both species in its compact rootstock and long pedicels. The variation noted in the description reflects a rather pronounced divergence between two stocks grown at Cambridge which, nevertheless, clearly belong to the same species. It is propagated by seed or by division of the rootstock.

The Rotundifolium Group

Only one species.

8. *G. rotundifolium* Linnaeus (Figure 9.8)
Annual with blades of lower leaves less than 5 or up to 10cm wide, rounded in outline, divided nearly as far as half into 7 or 9; divisions lobed for ⅓ of their length; lobes sparsely toothed; lobes and teeth obtuse; notches marked with a small crimson spot; stipules and bracteoles crimson; stem-leaves paired, stalked, the upper with acute lobes and teeth; glandular hairs present on most parts of the plant. Sepals about 3.5–5mm, nearly erect, with a very short mucro. Petals up to about 7 × 3mm, erect with spreading tips, wedge-shaped, almost clawed, weakly notched at apex, terminal ⅓ pink, otherwise white; base with a few small hairs on front surface and margins. Anthers bluish. Style evident, about 1.5mm long; style and outer surfaces of stigmas hairy. Immature fruits erect on sharply reflexed pedicels. Rostrum 13–14mm, including stylar portion 2.5mm. Discharge: seed-ejection (bristles).

Figure 9.8 *G. retundifolium,* × ²/₃

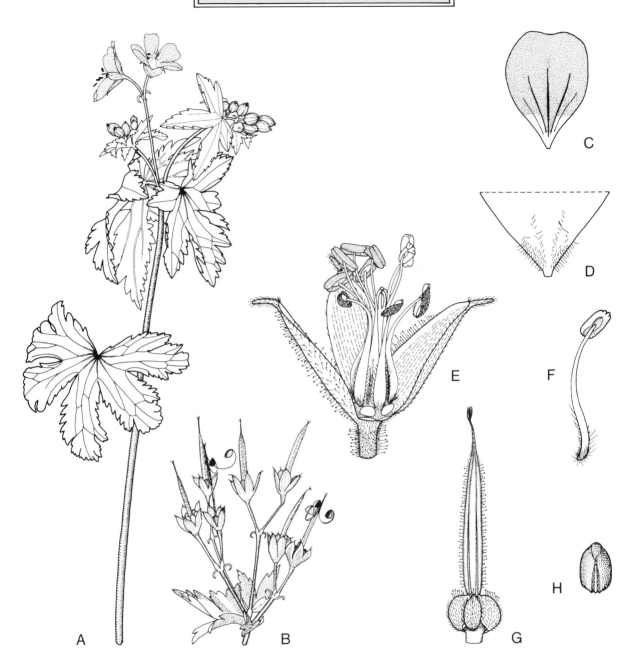

Europe, Asia, N. Africa.

A weed, sometimes troublesome, overwinter-ing or flowering in the season of germination, normally found in tilled ground. Easily distin-guished from 85. *G. pusillum* and 87. *G. molle* by the abundant glandular hairs and the fruit type. From *G. molle* it differs also in the scarcely notched petals with erect base and from *G. pusil-lum* in the larger, bright pink petals.

Figure 9.9 *G. sylvaticum* (Miss M. McC. Webster, 1965, coll. Britain: E. Scotland). (A) shoot beginning to flower, × ²/₃ ; (B) portion of inflorescence with mature and immature fruit, × ²/₃ ; (C) petal, with pigmenta-tion, × 2; (D) base of front surface of petal, × 4; (E) flower in male stage with petals and two sepals removed, × 4; (F) stamen of outer whorl, seen from back, × 4; (G) ripe fruit, × 2; (H) seed, × 4

On the supposition that the erect, slightly notched petals and distinctly developed style are vestiges retained from a larger-flowered ancestor I have concluded that this species may be related to The Endressii Group. Glandular hairs, surface hairs on the petals and hairy stigmas also occur in that group, but not deflexed pedicels with upturned tips.

The Sylvaticum Group

Perennials with a compact rootstock. Leaves generally with rather broad, freely lobed and toothed divisions. Flowers more or less erect. Sepals rather small in relation to the size of the petals and the mericarps.

Six species of Europe and N. and W. Asia are placed in this group. They are linked by groups of characters, very few of which hold for all species. Five species are treated here, together with a hybrid involving a species from outside the group.

9. *G. sylvaticum* Linnaeus (Figures 9.9 & 9.10) Medium-sized perennial with rather deeply divided leaves with the divisions profusely lobed and toothed nearly to the base, flowers 22–30mm in diameter, borne in a dense inflorescence, and usually violet-blue with a white centre but also pink or white, and with immature fruits erect on erect pedicels. Sun or light shade or in the wild garden. May and June.

Plant erect, 30–70cm tall, with compact rootstock. Basal leaves 10–20cm wide or more, divided as far as $^4/_5$ or more into 7 or 9; divisions tapered both ways from a point above the middle, rather solid in outline, with lobing and toothing continued down the sides nearly to the base; lobes up to twice as long as broad, with up to 4 teeth. Teeth and tips of lobes acute. Lowest one or two stem leaves solitary. Length of leaf-stalks diminishing rapidly upwards so that upper leaves are almost stalkless. Upper stems, peduncles, pedicels, sepals and rostrum usually with glandular hairs. Inflorescence dense. Flowers numerous, erect, saucer-shaped. Sepals 5–7mm; mucro about $^1/_5$ as long as sepal. Petals slightly less than 16mm, not more than 1½ times as long as broad, rounded or slightly notched at apex, usually purplish violet with white base; base with hairs all across front surface. Filaments divergent, arched outwards in female

stage of flower, pinkish; anthers bluish. Stigmas 2–3mm, purplish. Immature fruits and their pedicels erect. Rostrum 17–21mm, including stylar portion 1.5–2.5mm. Mericarps about 4mm. Discharge: seed-ejection (bristles).

Most of Europe; N. Turkey.

Figure 9.10 *G. sylvaticum*, Miss M. McC. Webster, 1965, coll. Britain: E. Scotland, × ½

G. sylvaticum is common in meadows in the mountains of southern Europe; further North and East it occurs down to sea level. It is native in Britain, being common from Yorkshire northwards to about the Great Glen in Scotland. It may be found not only in meadows but on roadsides, in stream gullies and in lightly shaded situations. It is a reasonably showy plant for the garden in early summer. There is a very effective mass-planting of it under hazel at Sissinghurst Castle, Kent.

In North-east Europe pink and white flowers become more prevalent as one goes North, so that populations with all three colours, or pink and white, or white only, may be found. Pink-flowered, and probably white-flowered, forms occur occasionally elsewhere in the range of the species. In addition, a totally anthocyanin-free form is cultivated in Britain. This is without the pink colouring in the sepals, stamens and stigmas which is present in white-flowered plants usually found in nature, and it has paler green leaves than usual. These and other variants are listed below.

G. sylvaticum forma *albiflorum* A.G. Blytt is the naturally-occurring white-petalled variant mentioned above (not the same as *G. albiflorum* Ledebour).

G. sylvaticum 'Album' is the pale-leaved, anthocyanin-free, white-flowered cultivar, which comes true from seed.

G. sylvaticum var. *alpestre* Domin & Podpera (*G. alpestre* Schur, not Chaix) has no glandular hairs and has purplish pink petals; it is endemic to the Carpathian mountains; plants growing at Cambridge, obtained as seed named *G. alpestre* from the Botanic Garden of Lvov, Ukraine, have a dense hoary hair-covering on the upper stems but also an admixture of glandular hairs; although thus differing from the description of the variety, they also have thicker leaves than western European plants of *G. sylvaticum* in general, as does a plant from the north side of the Caucasus (Rix 2533), also in cultivation.

G. sylvaticum 'Angulatum' (*G. angulatum* Curtis) is the same in its petal colour as *G. sylvaticum* var. *wanneri* but the petals are large and broad, and slightly notched. When it was described in 1792 no indication of its occurrence in the wild was given and I therefore treat it as a cultivar; it was still in cultivation in 1914 (Bowles, 1914) and may perhaps still be so, but I have not seen it. Bowles confirmed the large petal-size, saying the flower was the size of a four-shilling piece which, I understand, was about 4cm in diameter. The epithet *angulatum* refers to the angled stems.

G. sylvaticum 'Mayflower' is claimed to be an improved clone; it has flowers of a specially good rich violet-blue, the white centres of which are small; it was introduced by Alan Bloom about 1972.

G. sylvaticum forma *roseum* Murray is the naturally-occuring pink-petalled variant; a particularly beautiful pink-flowered plant has been introduced to cultivation from the Swiss Alps by Mr A.W.A. Baker, but it has not yet received a cultivar name.

G. sylvaticum var. *wanneri* Briquet has pale rose-pink petals with bright rose veins. The original dried specimens, which I have seen, have the sepal mucro half as long as the sepal or nearly so. They were collected from Mont Billiat and a few other localities in the Genevan alps and the original collection was reported to be constant in cultivation. The specimens do not resemble *G. rivulare*, although Briquet said they did. The plant at present grown under this name in Britain (seen by me at Edinburgh in 1983) does not have particularly long sepal mucros; the darker veins on the petals are feathered and looped. (See also *G. angulatum*.)

HYBRID. 16. *G. pratense* × *G. sylvaticum*: a plant submitted to the Wisley Trial and later presented to Cambridge by Mr R.D. Nutt appears to be this hybrid. It has leaves similar to those of *G. sylvaticum* but with slightly deeper teeth, and very crowded, upwardly inclined flowers with rather short peduncles and often almost no pedicels. The petals are white with a pale lilac network (not typical of either parent) and have hairs all across the front surface at the base which is drawn out into a point to a greater extent than in either supposed parent. The fruits do not develop.

10. G. rivulare Villars (*G. aconitifolium* L'Héritier; *G. sylvaticum* Linnaeus subsp. *rivulare* (Villars) Rouy) (Figure 9.11, Plate 5)
Compact perennial with deeply divided and narrowly lobed leaves, and medium-sized, erect, funnel-shaped flowers 15–25mm in diameter, borne in a dense inflorescence; petals white with violet veins. Sun or light shade. May and June.

Erect perennial, 20–45cm, with compact rootstock. Basal leaves between 5 and 20cm wide, divided nearly to the base into 7 or 9; divisions tapered both ways from near the middle, broken in outline; lobes 2–4 times as long as broad, sometimes with several teeth which may be bent outwards and/or widely separated from one another. Lowest one or two stem-leaves solitary.

Stem-leaves, and some of the basal, differing much from those of *G. sylvaticum* in having the divisions deeply cut into long, narrow, sometimes spreading, almost toothless lobes. Tips of lobes and teeth acute. Length of leaf-stalks diminishing rapidly upwards so that the upper leaves are almost stalkless. Plant without glandular hairs except on the mericarps and lower part of rostrum. Inflorescence dense. Flowers fairly numerous, erect, funnel-shaped. Sepals about 5–7mm; mucro about ¹/₆ as long as sepal. Petals slightly less than 16mm, more than 1½ times as long as broad, white with fine violet veins extending nearly to tip; base with hairs all across front surface. Stamens with white filaments and violet anthers. Stigmas about 2mm, deep pink. Stylar portion of rostrum about 2mm. Immature fruits and their pedicels erect. Mericarps about 4mm, bearing long glandular hairs. Discharge: seed-ejection (bristles).

Figure 9.11 *G. rivulare*: (A) J. Stephens, 1960; (B) W.J.N. Warner, 1966, × ½

West and centre of the European Alps.

Grows in poor alpine meadows, dwarf-shrub heaths and woods of Larch and Arolla Pine.

A tidily growing, rather inconspicuous plant, not without a modest — though short-lived — charm when in flower. It is not particular about its cultural conditions, despite its name.

The similarity of *G. rivulare* to 9. *G. sylvaticum*, under which it is placed as a subspecies in *Flora Europaea* (Webb & Ferguson, 1968), lies mainly in the habit, with a rather regular dense inflorescence of many erect flowers borne on pedicels which remain erect after flowering, and in the presence of hairs across the width of the upper surface of the petal-base. *G. rivulare* has a more obvious resemblance to *G. caeruleatum* Schur, the latter differing in its violet-blue flowers and the absence of glandular hairs on the fruit; it is treated as *G. sylvaticum* Linnaeus subsp. *caeruleatum* (Schur) Webb & Ferguson in *Flora Europaea*. I have not seen it in cultivation.

11. G. pseudosibiricum J. Mayer (*G. sylvaticum* Linnaeus subsp. *pseudosibiricum* (J. Mayer) Webb & Ferguson)
Similar in leaf and habit to 10. *G. rivulare* but probably with smaller leaves on average and with a looser inflorescence of usually tiny blue or lilac flowers (petals not more than 8mm and sepals less than 5mm.) The upper stems may or may not have glandular hairs. Discharge: seed-ejection (bristles).

Ural Mountains and Siberia.

Grows in similar habitats to those of 9. *G. sylvaticum*.

Like 10. *G. rivulare*, this species is also treated as a subspecies of 9. *G. sylvaticum* in *Flora Europaea*. I am not aware that it is in cultivation in West European gardens but its name is sometimes misapplied to Siberian forms of 16. *G. pratense*, a species with a much larger flower and horizontal floral axis. It resembles 49. *G. sibiricum* in the small size of its flowers and to some extent in leaf-shape but is entirely different in habit.

12. G. albiflorum Ledebour (Figure 9.12)
A low perennial, with the stems, leaf-edges and sepals purplish brown; leaves rather like those of 9. *G. sylvaticum*. Inflorescence loose. Petals less than 8mm or sometimes more, white with violet veins, notched. May and June, and usually again later.

Perennial, with the stems usually inclined,

20–60cm, with compact rootstock. Basal leaves between 5 and 20cm wide, divided as far as ⁴/₅ or slightly more into 7; divisions tapered both ways from a point above the middle, rather solid in outline; lobes not more than twice as long as broad, with 1–3 teeth; tips of lobes and teeth rather blunt or acute. Upper leaves sometimes with more space between the divisions, and fewer teeth on the lobes, more or less stalked. Stems and leaf-margins purplish brown. Branches diverging rather widely. Glandular hairs absent or sometimes present on peduncles and pedicels. Inflorescence diffuse. One pedicel of each pair often shorter than sepals. Flowers rather few, upwardly inclined, widely funnel-shaped. Sepals about 4.5mm, flushed with purplish brown; mucro between 0.5 and 1mm. Petals less than 8mm or sometimes more, more than 1½ times as long as broad, notched at apex, white or pale lilac with violet veins; base with hairs all across front surface. Stigmas between 1.5 and 2mm, pale pink. Immature fruits and their pedicels slightly nodding. Rostrum about 18mm including stylar portion about 2mm. Mericarps just under 4mm. Discharge: seed-ejection (bristles).

Figure 9.12 *G. albiflorum*, Moscow Acad. Sci. B.G., 1979, × ½

North and Central Asia and north-eastern part of European Russia.

Grows in similar habitats to those of 10. *G. rivulare*.

I have grown a group of plants of this species in pots since 1979, when I received the seed from the Botanic Garden of the Academy of Sciences, Moscow, and my description is based mainly on these. They make delicate, attractively coloured plants but are not showy. My characterisation of them as low-growing is based on these pot-grown plants; further horticultural evaluation depends on their being planted out.

G. albiflorum has basal leaves rather like those of 9. *G. sylvaticum* but less profusely toothed, and petals like those of 10. *G. rivulare* but smaller. The brown tinting of stems and leaves, the loose branching, notched petals and the slightly nodding immature fruits are distinctive.

13. G. psilostemon Ledebour (*G. armenum* Boissier; *G. backhousianum* Regel (Figure 9.13, Plate 6)
Tall perennial with very large basal leaves and a rather loose inflorescence of flowers about 35mm in diameter, bright magenta with a black centre and black veins. Border, wild garden, sun or shade. June–August.

Erect perennial, 80–120cm tall, with compact rootstock. Blades of basal leaves more than 20cm wide, divided as far as ⁴/₅ into 7; divisions tapered both ways from beyond the middle; lobes slightly longer than broad, with several teeth, some of them deep. Teeth and tips of lobes acute. Stem-leaves paired, mostly with 5 divisions, diminishing gradually in size and length of stalk upwards. Leaf-blades sparsely hairy; upper stems, peduncles and pedicels with dense short hairs and longer glandular hairs; hairs of sepals and rostrum mostly glandular. Inflorescence erect, diffuse. Flowers erect, shallowly bowl-shaped. Sepals 8–9mm; mucro about 3mm. Petals about 18mm long and nearly as wide, rounded or lightly notched at apex; base with a few hairs at either edge. Filaments divergent towards their tips, mainly blackish but with pale dilations on either side at base; anthers blackish. Stigmas 2.5–3mm, dark red-purple. Immature fruits erect on more or less reflexed pedicels. Rostrum 27–30mm, including stylar portion about 3mm. Mericarps 5mm. Discharge: seed-ejection (bristles).

Figure 9.13 *G. psilostemon*, John Innes Hort. Inst., 1922, × ⅓

N.E. Turkey, S.W. Caucasus Region.

A stately plant best grown in broken shade against a dark background; the sunlit flowers will then appear intensely luminous. The stems usually need support. Its first sign of life in spring is the production of crimson stipular sheaths; it ends its season of growth with fine autumn colour. Propagated by division and seeds.

G. psilostemon 'Bressingham Flair' (Plate 6) is less tall-growing and has rather less intensely coloured petals which are somewhat crumpled and lightly notched; it was introduced by Bloom's Nurseries, Diss, Norfolk, in 1973.

HYBRID. Has crossed with 25. *G. procurrens* (see 14. *G. procurrens* × *G. psilostemon:* 'Ann Folkard' which is sterile).

14. G. procurrens Yeo × **G. psilostemon** Ledebour: **'Ann Folkard'** (Figure 9.14, Plate 7)
Perennial with a mound of golden-green foliage borne on a tangled mass of stems, surmounted by dusky-purple black-centred flowers 35–40mm in diameter, with velvety-looking petals. Border, sun. June to October.

Plant with compact rootstock, making bushy growth up to about 50cm high. Blades of lowest leaves between 5 and 20cm wide, divided as far as ¾ into 5 or 7, surface flushed with gold away from the edges; divisions tapered both ways from about the middle, pinnately lobed; lobes about as long as broad, with several teeth. Teeth and tips of lobes acute. Stem-leaves paired,

gradually diminishing upwards in size and length of leaf-stalk, changing little in shape. Plant moderately hairy except for upper surfaces of leaves which are nearly hairless; glandular hairs present in addition to eglandular on stems, leaf-stalks, peduncles, pedicels and sepals. Lower leaf-pairs usually subtending two branches, upper subtending one branch and one peduncle. Flowers erect, saucer-shaped. Sepals 9mm, tinged and veined with red; mucro 1.5–2mm. Petals 16–22mm long and ¾ as wide, rich purple, shot with bluish, giving a velvety appearance, and with a black area at the base running out into numerous feathered black veins; base with a few hairs on front surface and a rather feeble tuft at either side. Filaments black, fringed with long white hairs; anthers red, apparently barren. Ovary densely white-hairy. Style and stigmas black; stigmas about 4mm. Rostrum and mericarps not developed.

Figure 9.14 *G. procurrens* × *G. psilostemon:* 'Ann Folkard', O.G. *Folkard*, 1975, × ½

Raised from seed gathered from *G. procurrens* by the Rev. O.G. Folkard about 1973 in his garden at Sleaford, Lincolnshire. Botanically this is rather a surprising hybrid: both parents have purplish, black-centred flowers, but otherwise they have nothing much in common, and they are widely separated geographically (Nepal and Caucasus). What is not surprising is that it is sterile. Horticulturally I consider it a stunning

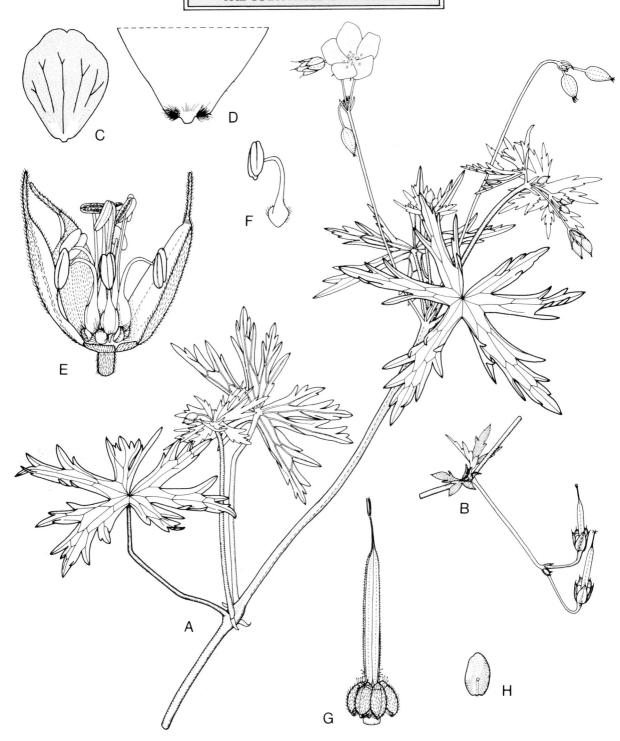

Figure 9.15 *G. collinum* (P.H. Davis, 1955, coll. Turkey: Van Prov., no. 23804). (A) shoot beginning to flower, × ²/₃ ; (B) cymule with immature fruit, × ²/₃ ; (C) petal, with pigmentation, × 2; (D) base of front surface of petal (the occurrence of hairs between the tufts is most unusual in this species), × 4; (E) flower in male stage with petals and two sepals removed, × 4 ; (F) stamen of outer whorl, seen from back, × 4; (G) ripe fruit in pre-explosive interval, × 2; (H) seed, × 4

plant. It is propagated by division of the rootstock.

The Collinum Group

Perennials with compact rootstock and diffuse habit. Stipules of basal leaves long, slender, acute. Leaf-divisions more or less pinnately lobed with lobes more than twice as long as broad, sharply toothed. Flowers about 25–30mm in diameter, saucer-shaped; petals without hairs across front surface at base. Style well-developed.

One widespread species, *G. collinum*, in S.E. Europe and W. and C. Asia; other species have been segregated from *G. collinum* in C. Asia but I have not formed definite opinions about their distinctness.

15. *G. collinum* Willdenow (Figures 9.15 & 9.16) Bushy perennial with sharply toothed leaves and diffuse habit, producing saucer-shaped pink flowers 25–30mm in diameter over a long period; petals rounded, weakly veiny. Border, wild garden, sun. June to September.

Rootstock compact, producing very thick roots. Young leaves in spring often yellowish and flushed with pink. Blades of basal leaves between 5 and 20cm wide, divided as far as $^4/_5$–$^5/_6$ into 7; divisions tapered both ways from well above the middle, palmato-pinnately lobed for nearly $^1/_2$ their length; lobes rather far apart, some of them 2–3 times as long as broad, with few to several teeth; teeth up to about $2^1/_2$ times as long as broad. Teeth and tips of lobes acute or rarely obtusish. Stipules of basal leaves up to 3cm, narrow, tapered to a fine point. Stem-leaves paired, decreasing gradually in size and length of stalk upwards, lobing becoming more pinnate and leaf outline less rounded, more angular, uppermost greatly reduced and nearly stalkless. Plant generally covered with small appressed hairs but undersides of leaves with larger more spreading hairs; glandular hairs often present on upper peduncles, pedicels, sepal-bases and rostra. Inflorescence diffuse, branches usually paired and unequal. Peduncles mostly 4–14cm. Pedicels mostly 1.5–3.5cm. Sepals 7–12mm, gradually tapered at apex; mucro usually 2–3mm, occasionally shorter. Petals 13–20mm, broadest above the middle, about $1^1/_4$–2 times as long as broad, rounded at

apex, usually medium pink, sometimes paler or darker, sometimes with red simple or feathered veins; base with a dense tuft of white hairs at either side and above this a fringe of hairs, but without hairs extending across front surface. Filaments abruptly widened at base, lilac or pink at tips, finely fringed with hairs in lower part; anthers yellowish or pinkish, usually appearing greyish after opening. Nectaries topped with a tuft of hairs. Stigmas 1.5–2.5mm, pinkish or reddish. Immature fruits erect on

Figure 9.16 *G. collinum*: (A) C.D. Brickell, 1980, coll. Iran: Elburz Mts; (B) P.H. Davis, 1955, coll. Turkey: Van Prov. (23804); (C) J. Stephens, 1966, coll. Iran: Marand (Furse 9091), × ½

more or less reflexed pedicels. Rostrum 20–27mm including the distinct stylar portion 4–5mm long. Mericarps about 3–4mm. Discharge: seed-ejection (bristles).

S.E. Europe, C. and E. Turkey, W. and C. Asia, extending to Siberia and N.W. Himalayas.

A widespread and somewhat variable species, usually easily recognised by its bushy habit, medium-sized pink flowers and sharply toothed leaves slightly recalling those of 16. *G. pratense* but with fewer, coarser teeth and lobes. It is not of great garden value but is fairly frequently included in the collections of expeditions. In nature it often grows in damp meadows but it grows well in dry conditions in British gardens. It has virtually no superficial resemblance to *G. pratense* but it forms fertile hybrids with it and has strong resemblance in floral details: the rounded petals, the hairs over the nectaries, the enlarged stamen-bases, the distinct style and rather short stigmas. It is distinguished from 42. *G. yesoense* by the tuft of hairs over the nectaries and the lack of hairs across the front surface of the petal-bases; there are also differences in the leaves.

HYBRIDS. *G. collinum* crosses in gardens with 16. *G. pratense* to give fertile hybrids; it has produced a sterile hybrid with 18. *G. clarkei* at Cambridge. Its hybrid with 41. *G. dahuricum* (*G. ×bergianum* Lundström) was found in the Stockholm Botanic Garden (See Chapter 7; Lundström referred to it as *G. londesii* Link).

The Pratense Group

Perennials with a compact or creeping rootstock. Inflorescence usually with glandular hairs. Flowers large; floral axis usually horizontal; petals blue or pink, not notched; petals without hairs across front surface at base; style long; immature fruits and their pedicels downwardly inclined or reflexed; pedicels short or very short in relation to sepals.

An uncertain number of species in C. Asia and N.W. Himalayas, and one, *G. pratense*, occurring from W. Europe to W. China.

16. *G. pratense* Linnaeus (Figure 9.17 & 9.18)
More or less tall perennial with rather finely cut leaves; inflorescence dense; flowers 35–45mm in diameter, saucer-shaped, with horizontal axis; petals not notched, blue to white; style long; immature fruits and their pedicels reflexed. Border, wild garden, sun or light shade. June to July and often again.

Rootstock compact, about 2cm thick. Plant usually about 75cm tall but up to 130cm. Blades of basal leaves often more than 20cm wide, divided as far as $^6/_7$–$^9/_{10}$ into 7 or 9, sometimes broader than long; divisions tapered both ways from above the middle, pinnately lobed, rather open in outline; lobes mostly 2–3 times as long as broad, curving outwards, with several teeth, usually very unequal in number on the two sides. Teeth and tips of lobes acute or obtusish. Stipules of basal leaves up to about 3cm, narrow, tapered to a fine point. Stem-leaves paired, decreasing gradually in size and length of stalk upwards, their divisions tapered from about the middle, those of the middle leaves often with the terminal part more or less evenly and deeply cut into toothless lobes. Upper surfaces of leaves with small appressed hairs; lower surface with similar or more divergent hairs on the veins; stems and leaf-stalks with larger reflexed hairs diverging weakly or strongly; upper part of inflorescence with dense glandular hairs. Flowering stems bearing peduncles only in the upper part, these becoming very short or suppressed at high nodes, forming a dense inflorescence. Peduncles mostly 2–10cm. Pedicels short, one or both in each cymule shorter than the sepals. Floral axis horizontal. Sepals 7–12mm, usually tapered at apex, forming a slightly bladdery calyx after flowering; mucro 1.5–3.5mm. Petals 16–24 x 13–20mm, only slightly longer than broad, rounded at apex, deep violet-blue or campanula-blue, varying to white, usually white at extreme base, with translucent, sometimes pinkish, veins; base with a dense tuft of hairs on either side and a fine fringe above this, but without hairs extending across front surface. Stamens slightly longer than sepals; filaments abruptly widened at base, more or less deep pink, finely fringed with hairs in lower part; anthers dark violet or blue-black. Nectaries topped with a tuft of hairs. Stigmas 2–2.5mm, greenish, tinged with pink, or brownish, dull purple or crimson. Immature fruits reflexed on reflexed pedicels. Rostrum 23–29mm including the distinct stylar portion 7 or 8mm long. Mericarps 4.5–5mm. Discharge: seed-ejection (bristles).

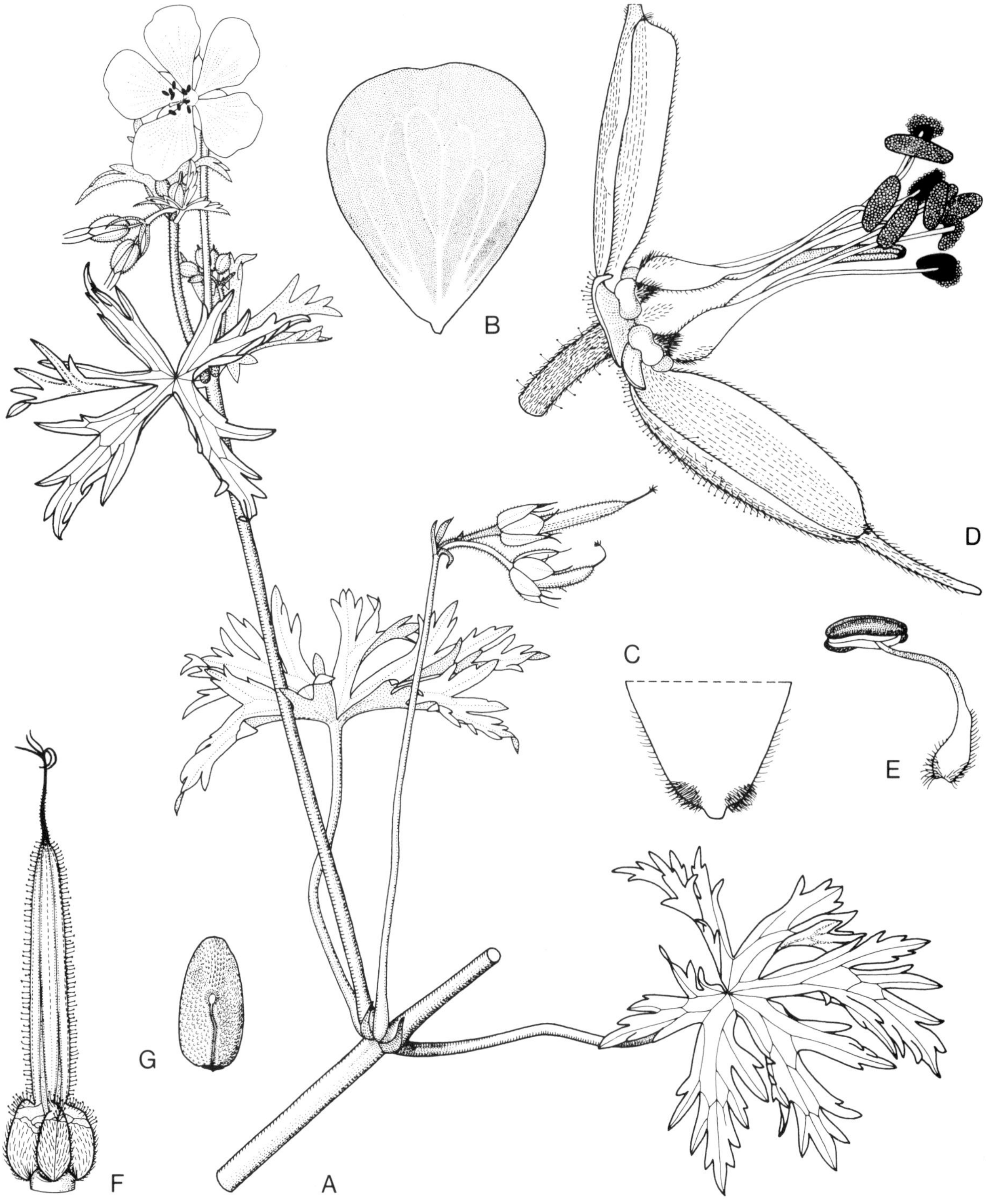

Figure 9.17 *G. pratense* "European Form" (Halle B.G., 1974, coll. E. Germany: Röblingen See). (A) portion of shoot beginning to flower, × 2/3 , (immature fruit is normally distinctly nodding); (B) petal, with pigmentation, × 2; (C) base of front surface of petal, × 4; (D) flower in male stage with petals and three sepals removed, × 4; (E) stamen of outer whorl, seen from back, × 4; (F) ripe fruit, × 2; (G) seed, × 4

Figure 9.18 *G. pratense*, "European Form", P.F. Yeo, 1966, coll. Britain: Somerset, × ½

The above description refers to plants from Europe and the Altai Mountains of C. Asia, possibly W. and E. Siberia and W. China.

In England this species, Meadow Cranesbill, occurs in great abundance on the carboniferous and Jurassic limestones, on chalk in the southwest and more sparsely on clay in East Anglia, and it usually grows on roadsides. In Europe, where it is widespread, it often grows in meadows and is not confined to calcareous soils. It readily establishes colonies outside its native range, and has done so in east North America. As a colonist it is usually found near houses. It does not grow naturally in shade.

The plants covered by the above description may conveniently be referred to as the "European Form" despite the inclusion of plants from the Altai Region of the USSR. The latter, when grown in Cambridge, become dormant in autumn in the normal way but their dormancy is easily broken by mild weather; the leaves that then come up are usually frosted sooner or later and the damage may even be severe enough to prevent flowering at the normal time. Apart from such plants *G. pratense* is easily grown and may be propagated by division or seed. Not only is it one of Britain's finest wild flowers but it is a lovely garden plant, valuable especially in herbaceous borders and making its main effect in June, July and sometimes August. The petals of a typical British form of wild origin gave a colour chart reading near RHSCC Violet-Blue Group 93C (actually HCC Hyacinth Blue 40/1, becoming Methyl Violet 39/1); readings for the

Altai plants taken with HCC and matched by me with RHSCC are Violet-Blue Group 90D, 91A and 92A, i.e. less blue.

The species as a whole extends outside the area already indicated, into the Caucasus, Soviet Central Asia (i.e. south-west of W. Siberia) and thence into the Himalayas. There seem to be considerable taxonomic difficulties in these areas but certain more or less well-marked forms are dealt with separately below, as is the special form from the region of Lake Baikal.

First, however, I deal with the variants of the "European Form". It may be mentioned that pale-flowered or white-flowered plants are not infrequent in nature. For all double-flowered cultivars I have placed 'Plenum' as the first word of the cultivar epithet, following Thomas (1976, 1982).

G. pratense forma *albiflorum* Opiz is the botanical name for white-flowered plants and need not be reserved for plants which are strictly anthocyanin-free. It may be used for white-flowered plants growing wild or brought into cultivation from the wild (see also *G. pratense* 'Galactic').

G. pratense 'Bicolor' is a synonym of 'Striatum'.

G. pratense 'Galactic' is a name here proposed for an anthocyanin-free plant grown at Cambridge, having been received from Mrs Joy Forty in 1971; in a dry situation it grows to about 75cm in height and has a flat-topped inflorescence; the flowers are 40–48mm in diameter with overlapping petals which sometimes have a hint of a notch (there are dried specimens in the Herbarium of the University Botanic Garden, dated 3 July 1973 and 30 June 1978). It is probably the same as the plant which received an Award of Merit at Wisley Trial as "*G. pratense album*". That had dark green leaves to 16cm wide, light yellowish-green stems 90–105cm tall, and freely produced flowers 35mm in diameter with the petals slightly notched and slightly overlapping, white with translucent veins. Ingwersen's (1946) description of *G. pratense* var. *album* ('a very fine pure albino with large milk-white flowers') suggests the same plant, and I have chosen the cultivar epithet to reflect this emphasis on milky whiteness. Ingwersen was probably unaware of the botanically validly published name *G. pratense* var. *album* Weston, which is best treated as a synonym of *G. pratense* forma *albiflorum* (see above), as the description reads merely 'with white flowers'.

G. *pratense* 'Kashmir Purple' and 'Kashmir White' do not represent the "European Form" and are now treated as a separate species, 18. G. *clarkei*.

G. *pratense* 'Mrs Kendall Clark' has a flower-colour which Ingwersen (1946) found 'not easy to describe. The nearest we can get to it is pearl-grey flushed with softest rose.' The Report of the Wisley Trial gives the colour as RHSCC Violet-Blue Group 91A (a moderately pale colour) with white veining (which would make it seem paler), and the height as 75cm. Mr Alan Bloom and Mrs Joy Forty grow (or have grown) this veiny-petalled plant (Plate 9) as 'Mrs Kendall Clark' but Mr Graham Thomas tells me that the true 'Mrs Kendall Clark' was not in the Wisley Trial, and in this he is supported by the discordance of the descriptions here quoted.

G. *pratense* 'Plenum Album' is a double white with rather small flowers. Ingwersen (1946) states that the flowers deteriorate noticeably in old clumps.

G. *pratense* 'Plenum Caeruleum' (Plate 10) has rather small light lavender-blue double flowers tinged with lilac (RHSCC Violet-Blue Group 94B), loosely petalled according to Thomas (1982). It was misdescribed in the Report of the Wisley Trial. The flower-form is less regular than in 'Plenum Violaceum'.

G. *pratense* 'Plenum Violaceum' has rather small rich deep violet-blue (RHSCC Violet Group 87–89) double flowers tinged with purple (RHSCC Violet Group 86B) in the centre and petals 'arranged in a cup-formation' so that 'each flower is an exquisite rosette' (Thomas, 1976, 1982). Flowering in July.

G. *pratense* 'Purpureum Plenum' is probably the same as the preceding.

G. *pratense* 'Silver Queen' was raised by A.T. Johnson and is a tall plant with large 'silver-blue' flowers (Ingwersen, 1946). The Wisley Trial Report gives its height as 130cm and the flower-colour as white with a slight tinge of very pale violet.

G. *pratense* 'Striatum' ('Bicolor') has white petals spotted and streaked with violet-blue in varying intensities and to very varying extents. At least a proportion of the seedlings come true (Ingwersen, 1946).

The following are rather distinct regional variants of G. *pratense*.

16a. G. transbaicalicum Sergievskaya (Figure 9.19, Plate 8)

Plants about 25cm tall, slender, with darkly pigmented stems. Basal leaf-stalks more or less prostrate. Blades of basal leaves often less than 20cm wide with numerous narrow lobes and teeth; basal and stem-leaves edged with red or brown, the segments more or less channelled; petals often a darker tint of the colour usual in G. *pratense*.

Figure 9.19 G. *pratense* ("G. *transbaicalicum*"): (A) Yakutsk Acad. Sci. B.G., 1973; (B) Moscow Acad. Sci. B.G., 1975, × ½

Siberia, in the regions to E. and W. of Lake Baikal.

Two samples with such low growth and finely cut leaves are growing at Cambridge, having been received from the Botanic Gardens of the Academy of Sciences in Moscow in 1975 and Yakutsk in 1973 respectively. In the former, named G. *transbaicalicum*, the leaf-divisions are freely pinnately lobed with the lobes spaced out along a narrow central portion, starting just above the base. This is a most distinctive and attractive plant. In the latter the divisions are less narrow, are palmato-pinnately lobed, starting just below the middle, and the lobes and teeth are correspondingly broader. In some plants of the Yakutsk stock there is a slight chlorophyll deficiency giving a golden tinge to the centres of the leaf-divisions.

Apart from these I have grown plants from seed obtained from the American Rock Garden Society in 1972 which approach the others in their relatively delicate foliage, and sometimes gold-tinged leaves, but are not as extreme and they grow up to about 50cm in height. The existence of this series of plants progressively more like the "European Form" of *G. pratense* makes me reluctant to accept *G. transbaicalicum* as deserving specific rank. All these stocks break their dormancy too early in Britain; the attractive Moscow one would be suitable for rock gardens in parts of Europe with a continental climate.

16b. *G. pratense* Linnaeus "Nepal Form" (lacks a formal scientific name) (Figure 9.20)
Differs from "European Form" in the following points: blades of basal leaves often less than 20cm wide, with 7 divisions; all leaves with divisions rather abruptly tapered both ways from about the middle, with a much more solid outline because the lobes and teeth are broader and, though more or less acute, abruptly tapered; paired branches more unequal and the upper internodes of the inflorescence longer, so that rather elongated and one-sided shoots are formed.

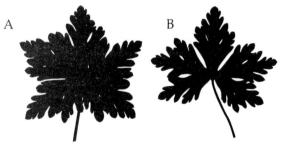

Figure 9.20 *G. pratense*, "Nepal Form": (A) J. Stephens, 1968; (B) Wisley Garden, 1971, × ½

W. and C. Nepal, Kashmir, perhaps N.E. Afghanistan.

Two stocks of the "Nepal Form" are grown at Cambridge. One was received from Mr Jan Stephens in 1968; it has softly hairy leaves with pale marbling on the upper surface; the petals

are flushed with a purple tinge in the lower half but fade to white at the base. The other I found growing at Wisley in 1971; the leaves are not marbled and they have a coarser hair-covering; the petal colour is rather intense but white at the extreme base; the petal-veins are purple for about ²/₃ the length of the petal; it never has many flowers out at once and is of little garden value. A colour chart reading on the Stephens stock was redder than for the European form at equivalent of RHSCC Violet Group 86C–D, becoming Purple-Violet Group 82B–C.

At first glance the "Nepal Form" might not be recognised as *G. pratense* because the leaves are so different, but the blue flowers with horizontal axis, the minor floral details and the reflexed immature fruits with bladdery calyx are essentially those of *G. pratense*.

16c. *G. regelii* Nevski
A dwarf alpine with blades of basal leaves not more than 10cm wide, their lobing and toothing broad, much simplified; inflorescence small and few-flowered; flowers like those of *G. pratense*.

Soviet Central Asia, N.E. Afghanistan, N. Pakistan.

This is not known to be in cultivation; if it retained its dwarf habit it would be a desirable plant to grow. The flowers are so like those of *G. pratense* that it seems doubtful whether it should be treated as a distinct species.

HYBRIDS. *G. pratense* has formed fertile hybrids with 15. *G. collinum* and 41. *G. dahuricum* and sterile or nearly sterile hybrids with 19. *G. himalayense* (see no. 17), 18. *G. clarkei*, and 9. *G. sylvaticum*; the improbable hybrid *G. pratense* × 95. *G. robertianum* has been reported but not substantiated (see Chapter 7).

17. *G. himalayense* Klotzsch × ***G. pratense*** Linnaeus: **'Johnson's Blue'** (Figure 9.21)
A somewhat creeping perennial with leafy stems to about 70cm; leaves with rather narrow divisions, lobes and teeth; flowers about 50mm in diameter, held well above foliage, blue. Border, sun. June onwards.

Perennial, spreading moderately by underground rhizomes. Blades of basal leaves between 5 and 20cm wide, divided as far as ³/₄–⁷/₈ into 7; divisions tapered both ways from about the middle with short, spreading lobes and small teeth. Teeth and tips of lobes more or less acute. Stem-leaves divided as far as $^7/_8$ into 7, the divisions deeply cut into acute, sharply toothed lobes about 1½ times as long as broad, changing upwards very gradually. Hair-clothing like that of 16. *G. pratense*. Stems forking rather regularly, producing a loose but profuse inflorescence. Peduncles usually 3–10cm; pedicels ½ to twice as long as sepals. Floral axis horizontal. Sepals 7–9mm, with a purplish stain at base; mucro 1–2mm. Petals about 25 × 17mm, similar to those of 16. *G. pratense*, deep campanula-blue, paler and pinker towards base with translucent and almost colourless veins. Stamens like those of 16. *G. pratense* but often with brown anthers which do not open. Stigmas about 3mm. Rostrum up to about 28mm, with stylar portion about 9mm. Seeds not developing.

Figure 9.21 *G. himalayense* × *G. pratense*: 'Johnson's Blue', G.F. Clark, 1971, *ex* Knightshayes Garden *per* D. Wright, × ½

The plant bearing the cultivar name 'Johnson's Blue' is evidently a hybrid between 16. *G. pratense* and 19. *G. himalayense*. It seems to have appeared about 1950 among plants raised by Mr B. Ruys, of Dedemsvaart in Holland, from seed of *G. pratense* sent from Mr A.T. Johnson, of Tyn-y-Groes, North Wales, who had selected an improved strain of that species (Thomas, 1976; Johnson, 1937). Thomas (1958) proposed the name 'Arthur Johnson' for the plant which had already acquired the epithet 'A.T. Johnson's Variety', and he did so because the latter contra-

vened the International Code of Nomenclature for Cultivated Plants (Thomas, 1960). However, by 1960, the name 'Johnson's Blue' was already in circulation (Thomas, 1960) and it has now ousted 'Arthur Johnson'.

'Johnson's Blue' is a fairly exact intermediate between the putative parents. As these differ rather strongly in habit the hybrid is also distinctive in this respect. Although much taller than *G. himalayense* its stems are never as massive as those of well-grown *G. pratense* and it is comparatively graceful. It flowers persistently because it is unable to set seed, but with the continual branching of the inflorescence it eventually becomes untidy. Despite this it is a really valuable and deservedly popular garden plant. The Report of the Wisley Trial gives the flower colour as Violet-Blue Group 94B tinged with Violet-Blue Group 94A, flushed towards base of petal with Purple Group 77A; the principal colour is thus bluer than that of *G. pratense* and about as blue as *G. himalayense*.

In 1975 Dr Helen Kiefer crossed *G. pratense* "European Form" with *G. himalayense* 'Gravetye' at Cambridge and raised two seedlings. These have petals of a deeper colour than 'Johnson's Blue', abruptly fading to white at the base. I have not yet judged their garden value. Evidently, with numerous clones of *G. himalayense* in cultivation, and diverse forms of *G. pratense*, there are possibilities for raising further distinct and perhaps valuable hybrids.

18. *G. clarkei* Yeo (Figure 9.22)
Rhizomatous perennial up to about 50cm tall. Blades of basal leaves deeply divided, the divisions with numerous, deep, few-toothed or entire lobes. Inflorescence looser than in *G. pratense* with longer pedicels. Flowers upwardly inclined, 42–48mm in diameter, purplish violet or white with lilac-pink veins. Border, sun. June onwards.

Perennial with moderately stout rootstock and creeping underground rhizomes. Blades of basal leaves between 5 and 15cm wide, divided nearly to the base into 7; divisions tapered both ways from about the middle, deeply pinnately lobed; lobes mostly 2–3 times as long as broad with one or two teeth. Teeth and tips of lobes acute. Peduncles mostly 1.5–8cm. Both pedicels about as long as calyx or longer. Flowers upwardly inclined, less shallow than in 16. *G. pratense*.

Sepals 11–13mm; mucro 1.5–2.5mm. Petals 22–29 x 18–22mm, purplish violet, or white with lilac-pink veins. Stamens shorter than sepals. Immature fruits slightly nodding on spreading or slightly nodding pedicels. All other details are as in 16. *G. pratense*. Discharge: seed-ejection (bristles).

Kashmir.

Figure 9.22 *G. clarkei*, J. Stephens, 1969, as *G. bergianum*, × ¹/₂

This species occurs naturally at altitudes from 7,000 to 14,000 ft (2,100 to 4,200m). It was brought to my notice by Mr Jan Stephens when, in 1968, he gave me the violet-flowered form under the name *G. bergianum* and the white as *G. rectum*, under which names they had been growing at Kew. I sought specimens in herbaria and matched these plants with many specimens from Kashmir (two of them actually labelled *G. rectum*). Because of their obvious relationship with 16. *G. pratense* they were, at the Wisley Trial, 1973–6, treated as cultivars of that species, and named respectively 'Kashmir Purple' and 'Kashmir White'. (*G. ×bergianum* Lundström is 15. *G. collinum* × 41. *G. dahuricum*).

In habit this species is very different from *G. pratense*, being of lower growth, producing a carpet of basal leaves, and having a more diffuse inflorescence, although still with abundant flowers. Some growers find its spread by means of rhizomes too invasive. I have named this species after C.B. Clarke (see Appendix II for a full English description and additional discussion of its relationships).

Material assigned to the two cultivars below is very uniform. More precise characterisations of them will depend on comparison with further stocks of wild origin.

G. clarkei 'Kashmir Purple' (*G. pratense* 'Kashmir Purple') has the petal-colour RHSCC Purple-Violet Group near 82B–C, becoming 81A (less blue than *G. pratense* "Nepal Form" and still less blue than *G. pratense* "European Form"). This plant appears to come true from seed.

G. clarkei 'Kashmir White' (*G. pratense* 'Kashmir White') (Plate 11) is rather less vigorous than the purple variant and has white petals with pale lilac-pink veins which appear greyish at a distance. Miss Elizabeth Strangman has raised plants from seed and found a proportion of them to be purple-flowered, even though 'Kashmir Purple' was not growing in the same garden.

HYBRIDS. A sterile hybrid with 15. *G. collinum* and another with 17. *G. himalayense* have appeared at Cambridge. Dr Helen Kiefer produced a hybrid at Cambridge with 16. *G. pratense* ("European Form") using the white-flowered *G. clarkei*; this was nearly sterile as was a spontaneous hybrid between this species and what was probably 16. *G. pratense* "Nepal Form".

19. G. himalayense Klotzsch (*G. grandiflorum* Edgeworth, not Linnaeus; *G. meeboldii* Briquet) (Figures 9.23 & 9.24, Plate 12)
A carpeting plant with angularly cut leaves and long-stalked deep blue flowers generally 40–60mm in diameter. Border, ground-cover, sun or partial shade. June, sometimes continuing to October.

Perennial spreading by underground rhizomes. Blades of basal leaves between 5 and 20cm wide, divided as far as ³/₄ or ⁴/₅ into 7; divisions shortly tapered both ways from about the middle, rather solid in outline, 3-lobed at the apex; lobes about as broad as long, usually somewhat spreading, sometimes strongly so, with a few teeth. Teeth and tips of lobes obtuse or obtusish. Stipules rather narrow, acute, up to 2cm long. Stem-leaves paired, gradually diminishing in size and length of stalk upwards and becoming slightly more broken in outline and more sharply toothed. Plant rather uniformly covered in small more or less appressed hairs, those of the undersides of the leaves sometimes longer and more spreading; glandular hairs present on upper stems, calyces and rostra.

Stems slender, forking regularly, forming a diffuse inflorescence. Peduncles mostly 4–18cm long. Pedicels short, one in each cymule usually no longer than the calyx. Floral axis horizontal (rarely upwardly inclined). Flowers saucershaped. Sepals 8–12mm, often stained with purplish at base; mucro 0.5–1.5mm. Petals 20–31 × 18–25mm, 1⅓ times as long as broad to nearly equal in length and breadth, rounded at apex, deep campanula-blue, often flushed with pinkish near base and white at extreme base; base with a short dense tuft of hairs at either side and a fringe above this, but without hairs all across front surface. Filaments usually tinged with pink, abruptly enlarged at base, which is fringed with fine hairs; anthers dark blue. Stigmas 2–3.5mm, pink to purplish. Immature fruits reflexed on reflexed pedicels. Rostrum 27–30mm, including stylar portion 7–10mm. Mericarps 4.5–5mm. Discharge: seed-ejection (bristles).

Figure 9.23 *G. himalayense*, Alan Bloom, 1956, one division separated, × ½

Himalayas from N.E. Afghanistan to C. Nepal; USSR (Pamir Region).

This is the largest-flowered of all species of *Geranium* and is a fine garden plant, with a long flowering season and good ground-covering (and weed-smothering) ability. Colour-chart readings are bluer than those of 16. *G. pratense*, around RHSCC Violet-Blue Group 94B (HCC Hyacinth Blue 40/1–2 to Lobelia Blue 41/1–2). It occurs with various leaf-shapes and flower-sizes; one with broad leaf-lobes is distributed

by Bloom's Nurseries, Diss, Norfolk, and is perhaps the same as the subject of H.G. Moon's painting in 'Flora and Sylva', vol. 1, opposite p. 54, 1903), though that portrait was thought by Johnson (1937) to represent 'Gravetye'. A plant with upwardly inclined flowers was noted in 1983 at the Northern Horticultural Society's Garden, Harlow Car, Harrogate, Yorkshire.

Floral and fruit details are closely similar to those of *G. pratense*, making clear the rather close relationship of these two species.

G. himalayense 'Gravetye' (Plate 12) has smaller foliage with sharper and narrower lobes and teeth than other stocks and is slightly lower-growing; it has larger flowers with a stronger purplish flush in the centre, a disadvantage in the eyes of some. I have received two clones under the name *G. grandiflorum* var. *alpinum* (Figure 9.24), to both of which the above description applies, and I do not know whether it is feasible to restrict the name 'Gravetye' to one; if it is, it should be used for the clone which received an Award of Merit in the Wisley Trial and was submitted by Messrs. Ingwersen. The principal colour of its flowers is RHSCC Violet-Blue Group 94B. (The name *G. grandiflorum* Edgeworth var. *alpinum* (Regel) Knuth has been commonly misapplied to this plant; in its original sense it is a synonym of 16c. *G. regelii*.)

G. himalayense 'Irish Blue' has flowers 35mm in diameter and paler than usual (RHSCC 94C), a difference which makes them look less blue, and with a still larger central purplish area than in 'Gravetye'; the petals are faintly notched at the apex. The plant was found by Mr Graham Thomas in Eire about 1947 (Clifton, 1979). A plant with the same flower-colour is grown at Edinburgh under a collector's number which I have investigated and found to be erroneous; possibly it is this same clone.

G. himalayense 'Plenum' ('Birch Double') has purplish double flowers not more than 35mm in diameter with narrow petals sometimes lobed on the surface and with a second calyx inside the outer petals. The petals are purplish pink (RHSCC Purple-Violet Group 80A) with blue shades (Violet Group 86C) and darker veins (colour-chart readings from Wisley Trial Report). The leaves are small with short, relatively rounded, divisions, lobes and teeth. The plant is much less vigorous than single-flowered stocks. Records of this plant go back to 1928 (Clifton, 1979), but the name 'Birch Double' (referring to Ingwersen's Birch Farm Nursery) was introduced in the Report of the Wisley Trial. However, as Ingwersen's themselves are still using the epithet 'Plenum' there seems to be no case for adopting the later name.

HYBRIDS A sterile hybrid with 18. *G. clarkei* has occurred spontaneously at Cambridge. For *G. himalayense* × *G. pratense* see no. 17 and notes thereunder.

The Erianthum Group

Perennials with few solitary lower stem-leaves, few paired upper stem-leaves and very dense, partly umbel-like inflorescences. Floral axis horizontal or nodding. Flowers flat. Petals not notched, without hairs across front surface at base. Stamens appressed to the style, filaments moderately enlarged at base and covered with long spreading or recurved hairs in lower part. Immature fruits erect.

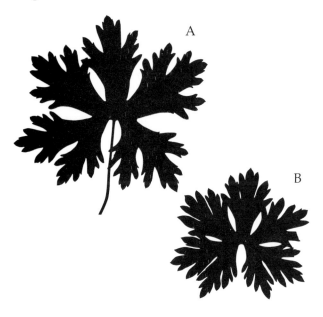

Figure 9.24 *G. himalayense*, 2 clones received as *G. grandiflorum alpinum*, either of which might be 'Gravetye': (A) J.E. Raven, 1976; (B) J. Stephens, 1969, × ½

Three species of N.E. Asia (one extending into N.W. America). Two are cultivated; the third is unnamed.

20. *G. eriostemon* De Candolle (*G. platyanthum* Duthie) (Figure 9.25)

Strongly hairy perennial with pale green, sometimes wrinkled leaf-blades which are cut half-way or slightly more into broad shallowly lobed divisions, and very crowded horizontal or nodding pale violet flowers which are 25–32mm in diameter and flat or nearly so; stamens appressed to the style, dark-tipped; fruits erect, held above the flowers. Woodland and wild garden. April, May or June, often flowering again.

Plant usually 30–50cm tall, with a thick, compact rootstock. Blades of basal leaves between 5 and 20cm wide, sometimes more, divided as far as ½ or ³/₅ into 5 or 7, upper surface light green, sometimes wrinkled, sometimes narrowly red-edged; divisions shortly tapered to the apex from above the middle, hardly tapered towards the base, shallowly 3-lobed at apex with toothed lobes or merely unevenly toothed. Teeth and tips of lobes very short but more or less acute. Stem-leaves similar, few, with 3 or 5 divisions which are less abruptly tapered at the tip, lowest few solitary, others paired; length of stalks decreasing upwards rapidly. Plant covered with coarse, more or less spreading, eglandular hairs, with an admixture of glandular hairs throughout or in upper parts. Inflorescence very dense, with a large proportion of the flowers in umbel-like clusters, though some of the suppressed peduncles may develop during the maturation of the fruit. Floral axis horizontal or strongly nodding. Flowers flat or nearly so. Sepals 7–9.5mm, flushed with brownish red, widely spreading; mucro 0.5–1mm. Petals not more than 16mm, nearly as broad as long, rounded or shallowly and irregularly lobed at apex, flat except for waved margins, widely spreading, rather light violet-blue fading to white at base; base with a dense tuft of hairs on either side and a fringe beyond this, but without hairs across front surface (many on the back). Filaments appressed to the style, moderately enlarged at base, enlargement white, remainder blackish purple, basal half covered with long coarse spreading hairs with recurved tips; anthers dull bluish. Style 8.5–10.5mm, mostly hairless. Stigmas 1.5–3mm, greenish to dull red. Immature fruits erect on erect pedicels, standing above the currently open flowers. Rostrum 22–28mm, including stylar portion 5–6mm. Mericarps 3.5–4mm, nearly black. Discharge: seed-ejection (bristles).

N.E. Asia from E. Siberia eastwards, E. Tibet and W. China, Korea, Japan.

G. eriostemon is a rather thick-set plant, described unmistakably by A.T. Johnson (1937) in the following words: 'with leaves like a hollyhock that colour well in autumn and a stature of over two feet (it) crests this massive pyramid with down-turned blooms the size of a shilling (22.5mm in diameter) in cool violet'. He said it came to him as *G. sinense,* which he rightly thought it was not. I first met it at Wisley in 1971 as "*G. chinense*". It is curious that it should be so misnamed, as it was introduced into cultivation as *G. platyanthum* Duthie, described in 1906 on the basis of E.H. Wilson's nos. 1948 and 3298 from, respectively, Western Hubei (Hupeh) and Sichuan, China. It was listed in Messrs Veitch's 'Novelties for 1906'. Duthie did not compare *G. platyanthum* with *G. eriostemon* but Knuth (1912) placed it (I am sure correctly) in the synonymy of the latter without comment. In nature *G. eriostemon* grows in woodland habitats and mountain meadows.

Figure 9.25 *G. eriostemon*, Mrs J. Forty, 1972, × ½

At Cambridge I have grown the Wisley plant, and one from Mrs Joy Forty, together with plants raised from seed under the name *G. erianthum* (see no. 21) from the Botanic Garden of the Academy of Sciences, Vladivostok, on the Soviet Pacific Coast. The last differs slightly from the first two in the shape and relative sizes of the leaf-divisions, in flowering first in April or May rather than in June, and in having the floral axis horizontal rather than nodding. *G. eriostemon* is easily propagated by division of the roostock or from seed.

The short, shallowly lobed leaf-divisions and spreading hairs on the lower stems and undersides of the veins of the lower leaves are the best characters for distinguishing *G. eriostemon* from 21. *G. erianthum*. However, most (perhaps all) plants occurring in Japan belong to:

G. eriostemon var. *reinii* (Franchet & Savatier) Maximowicz which has the leaf-divisions and lobes more elongated and thus more like those of *G. erianthum,* though still with shallow teeth.

G. eriostemon var. *reinii* forma *onoei* (Franchet & Savatier) Hara is described as dwarfer, with more deeply coloured flowers and coming from alpine habitats.

21. G. erianthum De Candolle (Figures 9.26 & 9.27, Plates 13 & 14)
Plant similar to 20. *G. eriostemon* but lower stems with eglandular hairs not spreading, and with more deeply divided and more acutely and profusely lobed and toothed leaves; flowers 27–37mm in diameter, often veiny, with horizontal axis. Border, wild garden, sun or partial shade. May to June and often once or twice again.

Similar to 20. *G. eriostemon* in habit, flowers and fruits, differing as follows: blades of basal leaves divided as far as $^2/_3$–$^4/_5$ into 7 or 9; divisions tapered both ways from the middle, overlapping their neighbours (even the basal pair), freely lobed; lobes about as long as broad with rather numerous teeth; teeth and tips of lobes acute; upper leaves like lower but with 5 or 7 narrower divisions; eglandular hairs of the stem fine and appressed, those of undersides of leaf-veins directed forwards; floral axis horizontal; petals from less than 16mm to considerably more, nearly triangular, light to deep violet-blue, darkly veined, veins sometimes feathered. Stylar portion of rostrum 6–7mm. Discharge: seed-ejection (bristles).

E. Siberia, Kuril Isles and Sakhalin Island, Japan, Alaska, Aleutian Isles, Canada (N. British Columbia).

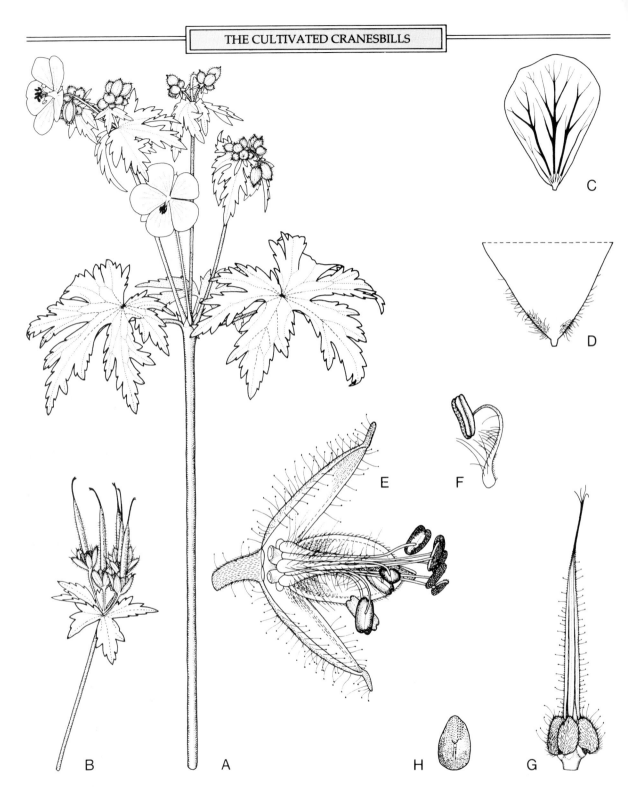

Figure 9.26 *G. erianthum* (Moscow Acad. Sci. B.G., 1973). (A) shoot beginning to flower, × ²/₃ ; (B) portion of inflorescence with immature fruit, × ²/₃ ; (C) petal, showing pigmentation of veins, × 2; (D) base of front surface of petal, × 4; (E) flower in male stage with petals and two sepals removed, × 4; (F) stamen of outer whorl, seen from back, × 4; (F) stamen of outer whorl, seen from back, × 4; (G) ripe fruit in pre-explosive interval, × 2; (H) seed, × 4

Figure 9.27 *G. erianthum*, Uppsala B.G., 1973, *ex* Sapporo B.G., × ½

A showier plant than *G. eriostemon*, like it in producing good autumn colour in the foliage, but probably more tolerant of full sun. Easily the finest stock at Cambridge, with vigorous growth and large deep blue flowers, came from the University Botanic Garden of Uppsala, Sweden. They received it from Sapporo Botanic Garden, Japan, incorrectly named *G. eriostemon* forma *onoei*. An attractive form with smaller, paler, more veiny petals, has been received from the Botanic Garden of the Academy of Sciences in Moscow. The most distinctive form received at Cambridge is from the Botanic Garden of the Academy of Sciences in Vladivostok, on the Soviet Pacific Coast, incorrectly named *G. maximowiczii*. It not only has the palest petals of any I have seen in this species, with the strongest veining which is bluish and smudgy, but it is low in stature and the leaves are darker green and firmer in texture (Plate 14).

The Wallichianum Group

Leaves divided as far as ¾ or less into 3 or 5; basal rosettes scarcely developed, stems usually trailing or scrambling. Petals with hairs all across front surface at base. Style very short, about ²/₃ as long as sepals. Stigmas very long (4mm or more).

I have assembled five Himalayan species which are in cultivation to make up this group. The little-known Chinese species, *G. christensenianum* Handel-Mazzetti, probably belongs with them.

22. G. wallichianum D. Don (Figure 9.28, Plate 15)
Variable perennial with no rosette-leaves, trailing stems with leaves divided into 5, and conspicuous blunt stipules, all united in pairs for the whole of their length; flowers 27–36mm in diameter, purplish pink to blue, usually with a more or less circular white centre, with slightly notched petals and blackish stamens and stigmas. Rock garden, patio, shrubbery. July to October.

Rootstock stout. Stems sometimes erect when young, otherwise trailing or scrambling. Blades of main leaves between 5 and 15cm wide, more or less wrinkled and marbled on upper surface, divided as far as ²/₃ or ¾ into 5 or sometimes 3; divisions abruptly or gently tapered both ways from about the middle, often with a slender tip, shallowly or very shallowly lobed; lobes toothed. Teeth and tips of lobes acute. Leaves paired, the 4 stipules of a pair joined to make two, broadly ovate, obtuse, conspicuous; branches occasionally paired but many nodes with only one branch or a branch and a cymule. Hair-clothing variable, eglandular. Inflorescence diffuse, leafy. Peduncles 3–14cm. Pedicels mostly 2–6 times as long as sepals. Flowers upwardly inclined, saucer-shaped or nearly flat. Sepals 6–9mm, the base and the lower parts of the veins purplish; mucro 1.5–3.5mm. Petals 16–17 × 13–16mm, approximately heart-shaped or triangular, more or less notched at apex, rather deep pink or purplish pink, marked with dark, simple or feathered veins, especially on the back, and with a fairly sharply marked basal white area, usually ¼–½ as long as petal; base with a dense tuft of hairs at either side and usually a belt of erect hairs on front surface between them. Stamens ²/₃ as long as or equalling sepals; filaments curving outwards, blackish to red-purple at tip with whitish flanges forming the basal enlargement, or almost entirely blackish, lower part fringed with fine hairs, base with a more or less distinct tuft; anthers black. Style 5–6mm. Stigmas 5.5–7mm, black to dark red-purple, sometimes with minute hairs on outer surface. Immature fruits erect on deflexed pedicels. Rostrum 22–32mm, including stylar portion 1–2 mm. Mericarps 4–5mm, unusually widely open at base. Discharge: seed-ejection (bristles).

Himalayas from N.E. Afghanistan to Kashmir.

Figure 9.28 *G. wallichianum*: (A) J. Stephens, 1968; (B) 'Buxton's Variety', G.W.T. White, 1973, × ⅔

A very variable species, always distinguishable by its very large fused stipules. The extremes of variation mentioned above in, for example, extent of white on petals, length of mucro and length of rostrum, are represented in different plants, not in the same one. The trailing habit makes *G. wallichianum* suitable for retaining-walls and patios provided the plants are cool and moist at the roots, but it is also happy scrambling upwards through dwarf shrubs. The plant forms a deep taproot and there are no rosette-bearing shoots, which makes it difficult to divide; it is therefore usually propagated by seed. The individual flowers of most stocks are beautiful but in general *G. wallichianum* is not of great garden merit, except in 'Buxton's Variety', which is quite outstanding.

G. wallichianum 'Buxton's Variety' ('Buxton's Blue') (Figure 9.28B, Plate 16) has compact, closely creeping growth, small marbled leaves with very short and shallowly lobed divisions, medium campanula-blue flowers, delicately veined and with a very large white centre. To indicate its value, I cannot do better than quote Thomas (1976): 'It is a pearl

beyond price, producing a non-stop display from the end of June onwards of lovely Spode-blue flowers with large white centres and dark stamens over a luxuriantly leafed plant.' The name commemorates E.C. Buxton of Bettws-y-Coed, in whose garden it appeared about 1920 (Clifton, 1979). The selection of Nemophila-blue forms and the elimination of other colours was, however, described earlier by Wolley Dod (1903) and Clifton (1979) points out that a plant called 'Shirley Blue' received an RHS award in 1890. Wolley Dod noted that as the weather gets cooler in autumn the flowers become bluer. The plant we have today is distinctive in its vegetative parts, as I have indicated above, even though it is propagated by seed.

23. *G. lambertii* Sweet (*G. grevilleanum* Wallich; *G. chumbiense* Knuth) (Figure 9.29)
Trailing and scrambling perennial with leaves divided into 5 and nodding or inverted flowers 30–35mm in diameter, either pale pink, or virtually white, then usually with a dull crimson stain at the base of each petal; stamens, at least at the tips, blackish, very hairy in the lower half; stigmas black. Wild garden, ground-cover, partial shade. July, August.

Plant with very few basal leaves. Blades of main leaves between 5 and 15cm wide, somewhat wrinkled above, divided just beyond half-way into 5; divisions broad, tapered both ways from well above the middle, the tips therefore very abruptly tapered, 3-lobed; lobes about as long as broad or rather less, toothed. Teeth and tips of lobes acute. Leaves paired, the upper similar to the lower or with slightly narrower divisions with the lobes curved outwards. Stipules 10–15mm, ovate, acute, not united. Plant moderately hairy; glandular hairs usually present at the base of the calyx and on the rostrum. Branches usually paired and unequal, sometimes solitary in the inflorescence. Inflorescence diffuse. Peduncles mostly 5–15cm. Pedicels 1–3 times as long as sepals. Flowers with horizontal axis or, more usually, nodding or inverted, saucer-shaped or shallowly bowl-shaped. Sepals 9–11mm, broad, purplish at base; mucro 1–2mm. Petals about 20mm long and nearly as broad, broadest near the rounded apex, more or less strongly narrowed at the base, pale pink or white and then usually with a crimson stain at the base running out somewhat into the veins (white petals may turn faint lilac on drying); base with a dense tuft of hairs on either side and some spread across front surface. Stamens about as long as sepals; filaments curving outwards, dull crimson at the base which is only gradually enlarged, black at the tips, covered densely at the base with spreading white hairs, more sparsely so above, hairless in the upper ¼; anthers black. Style 6–8mm. Stigmas 5–6mm, black, with bristly hairs on the outside, at least at the base. Immature fruits erect on reflexed pedicels. Mericarps 5mm. Mature rostrum 26–30mm, including stylar portion about 4mm. Discharge: seed-ejection (bristles).

Himalayas from C. Nepal to Bhutan and adjacent parts of Tibet; reports of occurrence from further West are probably erroneous.

The pink form of this species, which is the one described by Sweet, is an attractive carpeter. The white form usually has a crimson stain at the base of each petal ('Swansdown' see below), but I have seen it without; it has flatter, more strongly inverted flowers than the pink. The species seems to like growing up through small shrubs. I have not been able to arrange for this in the Cambridge Botanic Garden (where the white form is grown), and when unsupported and in the open it hardly blooms, producing a few flowers and then going back to leaf-production. However, G. lambertii does not seem to give problems elsewhere in East Anglia. G. candicans Knuth, a name often misapplied to the white

form of G. lambertii, is a white-flowered form of 32. G. yunnanense, not in cultivation (Yeo, 1983). Edgeworth and Hooker (1874) noted the occurrence in Sikkim of a very pale form (probably white in life) with a purplish eye. When writing about 25. G. procurrens (Yeo, 1973) I incorrectly assumed this was a misinterpretation of C.B. Clarke's notes on a specimen of that species.

? 'candidum' from Bressingham

G. lambertii 'Swansdown' is the name published by Clifton (1979) for the white form with deep rose or crimson centre (RHSCC about 53A); veins of petals faintly pink; bases of the stamens the same colour as the petal-bases; leaves moss-green, marbled in lighter and darker shades. Comes true from seed.

HYBRID. G. lambertii × G. procurrens is described below.

24. G. lambertii Sweet × G. procurrens Yeo
Stems reddish, trailing and scrambling but not rooting, with long internodes. Leaves intermediate between those of 23. G. lambertii and 25. G. procurrens, with long stalks and slightly marbled blades. Peduncles long. Flowers upwardly inclined, flatter than in G. lambertii, intermediate in size between those of the parents; petals with dark violet base and heavy dark violet veins running out from it on a nearly white, violet-tinged, ground. Stamens and stigmas dark. Mid-July onwards.

A single plant of this hybrid appeared in the garden of Miss Elizabeth Strangman, Washfield Nursery, Hawkhurst, Kent, about 1981. It occurred at a place where both the parent species grew. In the colour of the flowers it represents a novelty in *Geranium*.

25. G. procurrens Yeo (Figures 9.30 & 9.31)
Stems red, trailing for long distances and rooting; leaf-divisions 5, lobed about half-way to the midrib; flowers more or less erect, 25–35mm in diameter, dull pinkish purple with black centre; petals not overlapping; stamens and stigmas black. Wild garden, ground-cover, preferably in shade. July to October or November.

Plant with few basal leaves and trailing stems extending to 1m or more in a season's growth, rooting at the nodes. Blades of earlier leaves of the season between 5 and 10cm wide, divided as far as ²/₃ into 5 or rarely 7, upper surface slightly

Figure 9.29 G. lambertii, Leeds B.G., 1980, × ²/₃

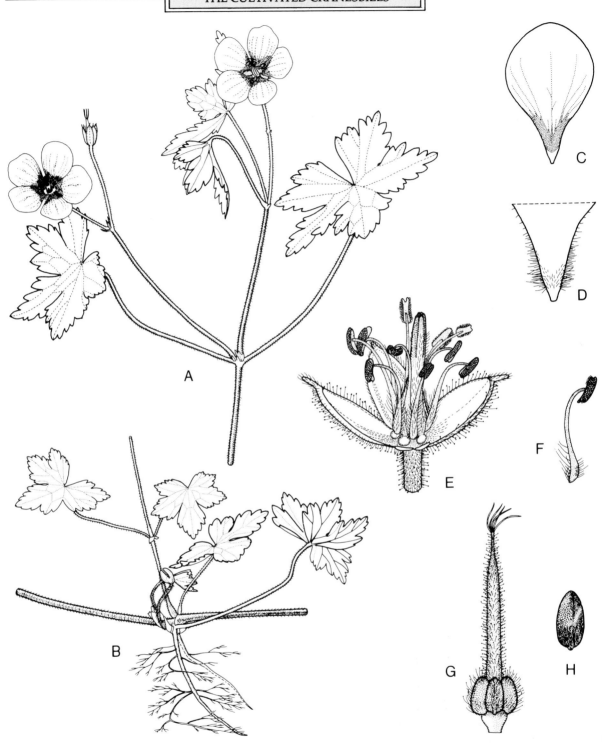

Figure 9.30 *G. procurrens* (Wisley Garden, 1971, *ex* O.G. Folkard). (A) portion of flowering shoot, × ²/₃ , (B) portion of trailing shoot formed early in season, with roots at node, × ²/₃ ; (C) petal, showing dark pigmentation, × 2; (D) base of front surface of petal, × 4; (E) flower in male stage with petals and two sepals removed, × 4; (F) stamen of outer whorl, seen obliquely from back, × 4; (G) mature fruit, × 2; (H) seed, × 4

wrinkled and faintly marbled; divisions tapered both ways from above the middle or near the tip, apex 3-lobed; lobes as long as broad or less, toothless or with one or two teeth. Teeth and tips of lobes obtuse or acute. Leaves paired, some of their stipules free, some united in pairs for part of their length, acute; divisions of upper leaves narrower than those of the lower and with a more broken outline. Plant moderately hairy; glandular hairs present on upper parts including leaf-stalks, sepals and rostra. Inflorescence very diffuse. Peduncles mostly 5–8cm. Pedicels 3–5 times as long as sepals. Sepals 6–9mm, reddish at base; mucro 1mm or less. Petals 16–18 × 8.5–12mm, enlarging noticeably with age, rather dull deep pinkish purple with V-shaped black area at base and black veins; base with a dense tuft of hairs on each side running out into an extensive fringe and with hairs all across front surface between the tufts. Stamens about as long as sepals, black; filaments not enlarged at base, with relatively sparse long white bristly hairs at base. Style about 5.5mm. Stigmas 4–4.5mm, black, with some bristly hairs on the outside at the base. Immature fruits erect on erect pedicels. Rostrum about 18mm, including stylar portion about 1.5mm. Mericarps about 4mm, black with black hairs. Discharge: seed-ejection (bristles).

Himalayas (E. Nepal, Sikkim).

The history of this plant has been told by Yeo (1973). Specimens were collected in the 1840s but were generally thought to be *G. lambertii* (for which the name *G. grevilleanum* was in use). It was cultivated at Kew in 1931 and may have lingered on, little known, in some gardens.

Figure 9.31 *G. procurrens*, Wisley Garden, 1971, *ex* O.G. Folkard, × ²/₃

However, it was again introduced by Dr G.A.C. Herklots in 1967, and after that it rapidly became widely distributed in British gardens. On its re-introduction it was unfortunately misidentified as 15. *G. collinum*. Its trailing habit and late production of slightly sombre flowers makes it a somewhat specialised plant for gardens. Its runners die off in autumn leaving behind young rooted plants. Propagation is therefore easy. I have never seen a seedling of this species.

HYBRIDS. Its hybrid with 13. *G. psilostemon* has proved to be an outstanding garden plant (no. 14). A hybrid with 23. *G. lambertii* has occurred spontaneously (see no. 24).

26. *G. kishtvariense* Knuth (Figure 9.32, Plate 17) Rhizomatous plant with bushy growth, bright green wrinkled leaves with 3 or 5 serrated divisions, swollen nodes and leaf-stalk bases; flowers nearly 40mm in diameter, of a rich royal purple; petals with a V-shaped white patch at base, finely veined; stigmas and tips of stamens blackish red. Immature fruits reflexed. Woodland and semi-shade. June to September.

Perennial with extensively creeping, rather slender, underground stolons. Blades of basal leaves (often not produced on flowering shoots) and lower stem-leaves mostly 4–9cm wide, bright green, wrinkled, divided as far as about ²/₃ into 5; divisions tapered both ways from about the middle, moderately wide, rather shallowly lobed; lobes broader than long, with one or several teeth. Teeth and tips of lobes finely acute. Lowest leaves solitary, others paired, gradually changing upwards to a 3-lobed condition, with predominance of the middle lobe. Stems slender, with internodes of very variable length, producing bushy growth; nodes and bases of leaf-stalks swollen. Stipules free or joined in pairs. Plant with rather bristly more or less appressed hairs and with glandular hairs on upper parts including sepals and rostra. Peduncles mostly 3–6cm. Pedicels about 1½–4 times as long as sepals. Flowers upwardly inclined. Sepals 7–9mm, purple at base; mucro 2–3mm. Petals about 21 × 17mm, broadest above the middle, rounded at apex, deep pinkish purple with fine, slightly feathered, purple veins and a V-shaped white area at the base; base with a dense tuft of short hairs near each margin, a fringe on the margin, and rather dense hairs on front surface between the tufts.

Stamens about ²/₃ as long as sepals; filaments white and strongly enlarged at base, blackish red and curving outwards at apex, with a tuft of hairs at extreme base and hairs on back and margins of the enlarged part, minutely fringed above this to about half their height; anthers blackish. Style about 5mm. Stigmas about 4.5mm, blackish red, finely bristly on the outside. Immature fruits reflexed on reflexed pedicels. Rostrum 17–18mm, without a stylar portion. Mericarps about 3.5mm. Discharge: seed-ejection (bristles).

Figure 9.32 G. *kishtvariense*, C.R. Lancaster, 1980, coll. India: Gulmarg, Kashmir (159), × ½

Kashmir.

The introduction of this species into cultivation is due to Mr Roy Lancaster, who collected the plant described above in 1978 (no. L. 159) on the perimeter track, Gulmarg, near Srinagar, and another plant (not seen by me) at the upper edge of the forest between Gulmarg and Khillanmarg (L. 177). It has finely formed flowers of a splendid colour (RHSCC Purple Group near 78, between A and B; HCC Petunia Purple 32/1, approaching 32/2 in age); botanically it is distinctive in its rhizomes, swollen nodes, very short stamens, more or less obliterated style and reflexed immature fruits. In some characters it recalls 7. G. *rectum* but it more strongly resembles 27. G. *rubifolium*. It is easily increased by division.

There has been some difficulty in deciding whether Mr Lancaster's L. 159 belongs to a species already named. Before L. 159 was introduced I already knew of the same plant from specimens in the Kew Herbarium collected at Gulmarg and from a colour photograph taken by Mr O. Polunin at Apharwat, and I considered

that it was related to 7. G. *rectum*. On comparing L. 159 in cultivation with the subsequently acquired G. *rubifolium* (no. 27), I became aware of the extraordinary similarity of the two species, except in their completely different underground parts, and the corresponding difference in the number of stems produced.

G. *kishtvariense* was described by Knuth eleven years after the publication of his monograph; no comparison with any other species was offered, beyond the statement that the type specimen had originally been named G. *rectum*. Nevertheless, the description agrees rather well with the little-known G. *rubifolium* Lindley and I supposed G. *kishtvariense* to be a synonym of that, its publication arising out of Knuth's inadequate knowledge of G. *rubifolium* (which can be inferred from the monograph (Knuth, 1912)). On seeing the resemblance of L. 159 to G. *rubifolium* I had to reconsider the identity of G. *kishtvariense*. The type of the latter (Schlagintweit 3777) was burnt in Berlin in 1945 and the description only contains one character which is decisive: 'perennial with a rhizome'. In fact, Knuth used the word 'rhizome' also when the rootstock is compact but he usually makes this clear. Thus he says (Knuth, 1912) that the rhizomes and stems of G. *rubifolium* are like those of G. *wallichianum* and then says that the latter has a short vertical rootstock ('caudex'). The unqualified inclusion of the phrase quoted must, on any normal interpretation, rule out the possibility that the description of G. *kishtvariense* applies to G. *rubifolium* and it renders it appropriate for the species represented by L. 159.

Figure 9.33 G. *rubifolium*, S.K. Raina, 1981, coll. India: Duchsum, Kashmir, × ½

1   *Geranium macrorrhizum* in the rose garden, Sizergh Castle, Cumbria (National Trust); June

2   *G.* × *oxonianum* 'Winscombe', cult. R.P. Dales, Sussex, 1983; July

3   *G.* × *riversleaianum* 'Russell Prichard', G.S. Thomas, 1974; September

4   *G. versicolor*, September

5   *G. rivulare*, J. Stephens, 1960; May

6   *G. psilostemon* 'Bressingham Flair', cult. Alan Bloom, 1974; June

7 *G. procurrens* × *G. psilostemon*: 'Ann Folkard',
   O.G. Folkard, 1975; July

8 *G. pratense* : variant known as *G. transbaicalicum*,
   Yakutsk Acad. Sci. B.G., 1973; July

9 *G. pratense*, cultivar known, apparently incorrectly,
   as 'Mrs Kendall Clark'; cult. Mrs J. Forty, Surrey,
   1981; June

10 *G. pratense* 'Plenum Caeruleum', cult. R.P. Dales,
   Sussex, 1983; July

11 *G. clarkei* 'Kashmir White', J. Stephens, 1968; June

12 *G. himalayense*, probably 'Gravetye', J.E. Raven, 1970; June

13 *G. erianthum*, Uppsala B.G., 1978; May

14 *G. erianthum*, pale veiny form, Vladivostok B.G., 1971; August

15 *G. wallichianum*, Mrs J. Forty, 1974; July

16 *G. wallichianum*, near 'Buxton's Variety', cult. Harlow Car Gardens, 1982; August

17 *G. kishtvariense*, C.R. Lancaster, 1980, coll. Kashmir; July

18   *G. sinense,* J. Stephens, 1968; July

19   *G. orientalitibeticum,* foliage, H.E. Guinness, 1960; May

20   *G. sanguineum* var. *striatum,* cult. Sizergh Castle, Cumbria (National Trust), 1983; June

21   *G. stapfianum*, J. Stephens, 1969; May

22   *G. fremontii*, H.E. Moore, 1973, coll. Colorado; June

23   *G. richardsonii*, Yeo, 1973, coll. Colorado; June

24   *G. asphodeloides* subsp. *asphodeloides*, white form, E.M. Rix, 1971, coll. in Turkey by C.R. Fraser-Jenkins; June

25   *G. malviflorum*, J. Stephens, 1966; May

26   *G. ibericum*, June

27 *G. × magnificum*, Clone'C'. cult. Mrs J. Forty, 1983; June

28 *G. renardii*, T. Watson, 1955; May

29 *G. peloponnesiacum*, Wisley Garden. 1971, coll.
R. Gorer in Greece; May

30 *G. polyanthes*, Mrs B.C. Rogers, 1960; July

31   *G. biuncinatum*, Kew B.G., 1981, coll. in Yemen by
      J.R.I. Wood, 1982; March (greenhouse)

32   *G. albanum*, J. Stephens, 1968; June

33   *G. glaberrimum*, G.G. Guittonneau, 1976, coll. Turkey; May (greenhouse)

34 *G. × cantabrigiense,* Miss H.E.M. Kiefer,1974; June   35 *G. dalmaticum,* cult. P.F. Yeo, 1980; June

36 *G. cataractarum,* R.C. Barneby, 1970, coll. S. Spain; April (greenhouse)

37   *G. maderense*, March (greenhouse)

38 Upper row: left, *G. phaeum* var. *phaeum*, Dresden B.G.; middle, *G. reflexum*, Marburg B.G.; right, *G. phaeum* var. *lividum*, B. Wurzell. Lower row: left, *G. × monacense* nothovar. *monacense*, G.S. Thomas; right, *G. × monacense* nothovar. *anglicum*, R.P. Dales; May

39 *G. aristatum*, Kew B.G., 1976; June

40 *G. × lindavicum* 'Gypsy', cult. Mrs J. Forty, Surrey, 1983; June

41 *G. cinereum* var. *cinereum*, Spetchley Park Gardens, 1960; June

42 *G. cinereum* 'Ballerina', R.F. Hunter, 1972; June

43 *G. cinereum* var. *subcaulescens*, Alan Bloom, 1957; June

44 *G. cinereum* var. *subcaulescens* 'Splendens', Wisley Gardens, 1976; June

27. G. rubifolium Lindley (Figure 9.33)
Perennial with compact rootstock, erect stems, bright green wrinkled leaves divided about half-way or as far as ²/₃ into 3 or 5 broad serrated divisions, and swollen nodes; flowers about 25–30mm in diameter; petals purplish violet or violet with V-shaped white patch at base, finely veined; stigmas reddish to blackish. Rock garden, perhaps partial shade. June to September.

Rootstock compact with swollen roots. Vegetative parts similar to those of 26. *G. kishtvariense* but main leaves mostly 5–14cm wide, with scarcely lobed divisions which are very broad on the lower leaves but distinctly elongated on the upper; the flowers differ in the slightly smaller sepals with mucro about 1–1.5mm, smaller petals, 14–18mm long, purplish violet or violet in colour with faintly notched apex, filaments about as long as sepals, usually merely purplish pink at tips, anthers greyish violet to blackish, and sometimes reddish stigmas; the rostrum has a distinct stylar portion 1–1.5mm long, and the mericarps are about 4.5mm long. Discharge: seed-ejection (bristles).

Kashmir.

The characters given above for distinguishing the above-ground parts of *G. rubifolium* from those of *G. kishtvariense* apply only to the plants known to me in cultivation. A survey of specimens in the Kew Herbarium suggests that the floral differences are inconstant.

This species was described from plants raised in the garden of the Horticultural Society of London in 1839, from seed sent by J.F. Royle from the Himalayas. Lindley, when describing it, stated that 'it should be planted in light soil, or on rock work, as it is soon destroyed by the wet in winter'. In fact it seems soon to have died out. However, I raised plants from seed sent in 1981 by Dr S.K. Raina, collected at Duchsum in Kashmir. Their growth was at first sluggish and intermittent, but several plants grew well and flowered in 1983. In most of my plants the petal colour is RHSCC Purple Violet Group 80B–81B, but in one they switched to Violet Group 84A during the 1983 growing season and later reverted to the original colour; in this plant the upper parts of the stamens are dark whereas in the purple-petalled plants they may be dark or pale.

The Refractum Group

Perennials with a thick compact rootstock. Basal rosettes present. Lower leaves usually divided beyond ¾; divisions 5 or 7. Some of the stipules usually united in pairs. Inflorescence diffuse. Flowers nodding or fully inverted. Pollen usually yellow (unknown in *G. delavayi*). Style more than 7mm long. Stigmas 4.5mm or less. Immature fruits reflexed on more or less reflexed pedicels.

Five species of the Himalayas, S.W. China and N. Burma. All are dealt with here although only three of them are in cultivation at present.

28. G. sinense Knuth (*G. platypetalum* Franchet, not Fischer & Meyer) (Figure 9.34, Plate 18)
Late-flowering perennial with inverted flowers less than 2cm in diameter; petals reflexed, blackish maroon with a coral-pink base; stamens crimson, appressed to the style; immature fruits reflexed. Woodland. July, August.

Perennial with a thick compact rootstock. Blades of basal leaves between 5 and 20cm wide, rich green, slightly glossy and slightly marbled, divided as far as ¾–⅞ into 7, the central pair of incisions noticeably longer than the others; divisions rather elongated, tapered both ways from above the middle, lobed or merely unequally toothed, the untoothed sides straight; lobes usually broader than long. Teeth and tips of lobes rounded in profile but usually more or less acute. Stem-leaves partly solitary, partly paired, with widely splayed basal divisions, gradually diminishing in size upwards, lower sometimes larger than the basal, with 5 or 7 divisions, upper with 3, and with abruptly shorter stalks; lobes and teeth acute; stipules conspicuous, brown, pointed, those of paired leaves united in pairs for part or most of their length. Glandular hairs present in the inflorescence but not on the rostrum. Inflorescence diffuse. Peduncles mostly 1.5–6cm but some of the upper suppressed. Pedicels mostly 2–3 times as long as sepals. Flowers inverted. Sepals 5.5–7.5mm, reflexed, green with reddish base; mucro about 0.75–1.5mm. Petals 9–10 × 6mm, broadest slightly above the middle, rounded but with irregular lobes at apex, sharply reflexed just above the base, slightly more spreading at tips where appressed to sepals, blackish maroon with a dull pink base, the basal half of which is fleshy and translucent; base with a handful of hairs on each margin and sometimes on front surface. Nectary one, forming a ring round the flower with a recess for the attachment of each petal, greenish. Stamens about $1\frac{1}{3}$ times as long as sepals; filaments appressed to the style, deep red with a pale base, feebly and evenly enlarged towards the base and hairless or with scattered bristly hairs in the lower half; anthers blackish. Style about 9mm. Stigmas 1.5–2mm, dark red. Immature fruits reflexed on spreading or reflexed pedicels. Rostrum 18–22mm, including stylar portion about 4mm. Mericarps about 3.5mm. Discharge: seed-ejection (bristles).

Figure 9.34 *G. sinense*, Oxford B.G., 1971, × ½

S.W. China (Yunnan, Sichuan).

The flowers of *G. sinense* are objects of curiosity which only reveal their beauty on close examination. It is thus something of a connoisseur's plant, and as such its praises have been sung both by Johnson (1937) and Ingwersen (1946) (in both cases as *G. delavayi*). It is a rather uniform species, usually grown under the name of its variable close ally, 29. *G. delavayi*. The nectary in the form of a ring round the flower is unique in the genus, as far as I know. The freely accessible nectar attracts wasps and in some years great numbers of hoverflies of the *Syrphus balteatus* group. Propagation is by division of the rootstock or by seed.

This species and *G. delavayi* show a strong resemblance in their flowers to members of the *G. phaeum* Group (nos. 100–103) from Europe, but the difference in fruit-discharge mechanism shows that this is the result of convergent evolution.

HYBRIDS. In S.W. China many intermediates between *G. sinense* and 29. *G. delavayi* have been collected, suggesting that natural hybridisation is occurring.

29. G. delavayi Franchet (*G. forrestii* Knuth; *G. kariense* Knuth)
Similar to 28. *G. sinense* but with broader, more or less overlapping leaf-divisions, hairier petals, usually (but not always) of paler colour, and separate nectaries. Probably not in cultivation.

Other differences from *G. sinense* are as follows: leaf-divisions more distinctly lobed, all incisions more or less closed; blades of stem-leaves not larger than those of basal leaves, decreasing in size abruptly after the first 2 or 3 nodes but their stalks decreasing gradually in length; sepals 6–9mm with shorter mucro; base of petal with a dense tuft of (usually straight) hairs on either edge; filaments with a small basal tuft of hairs; nectaries 5, separate; mericarps 5mm. Variable characters are glandular hairs (sometimes absent), petal size and shape (8–12 or rarely to 14mm long and $1\frac{1}{4}$–$1\frac{1}{2}$ or rarely to $3\frac{1}{2}$ times as long as broad), petal colour (blackish red to pale pink or rarely white, whitish at base, sometimes with a dark band above the whitish base), and hairs on petal-base between the lateral tufts (often absent). Discharge: seed-ejection (bristles).

S.W. China (Yunnan, Sichuan).

The name of this plant has been commonly applied in gardens to *G. sinense*, probably as a result of misidentification of the field-collections from which the seed came. Typically, it differs from *G. sinense* in leaf-shape, petal-colour and in the separate nectaries. It is variable in floral details. It seems never to have become established in cultivation. It differs from 31. *G. pogonanthum* to some extent in leaf-shape and in the less hairy reflexed rather than recurved petals, less hairy stamens and the darker filaments which are longer in relation to the sepals.

HYBRIDS. See under 28. *G. sinense*.

30. G. refractum Edgeworth & J.D. Hooker (*G. melanandrum* Franchet)
Perennial with deeply divided leaves with teeth and lobes turned outwards, rather blunt, and inverted or nodding white or pink flowers with

narrow, reflexed, petals, borne in an inflorescence covered with conspicuous, wholly purple, glandular hairs. Not in cultivation.

Rootstock compact. Blades of basal leaves between 5 and 10cm wide, often marbled, divided as far as $^5/_6$ or $^9/_{10}$ into 5; divisions broadest near the apex, palmato-pinnately lobed, middle one often relatively short; lobes mostly 1–2½ times as long as broad, with 1–3 teeth. Teeth and tips of lobes usually curved outwards, more or less obtuse. Stem-leaves gradually decreasing in size upwards, mostly stalked. Large glandular hairs, with the stalk and the head purple, present on the upper leaves and in the inflorescence but not on the rostrum. Inflorescence sparse. Flowers reflexed. Sepals usually 8–10mm, flushed with purple and with a dark purple base. Petals mostly 12–16mm long and 2–3 times as long as broad, reflexed just above the base, rounded at apex, white, pale pink or, rarely, red-purple; base with a dense tuft of silvery crisped hairs on either side,

similar hairs sometimes spread across front surface. Filaments 11–14mm, appressed to the style, rather evenly enlarged towards base, reddish purple at tips and pale at base, or uniformly pink, usually with fine hairs on lower part; anthers blue-black. Style 7.5–12mm. Stigmas usually 2–3mm, pink to purplish red. Immature fruits reflexed on reflexed pedicels. Rostrum 15–22mm, including stylar portion 5–8mm. Mericarps 3.5–4mm. Discharge: seed-ejection (bristles).

Himalayas (Nepal to Bhutan), N. Burma, S.W. China (Yunnan, Sichuan).

It is rather strange that this widespread species is not in cultivation, a fact which suggests it may be difficult to grow. Among the species with nodding flowers and reflexed petals it is immediately distinguished by the coarse, wholly purple, glandular hairs. It was originally described from the Himalayas, where the flowers are white, whereas Chinese plants, usually pink-flowered, were given another name, *G. melanandrum*. However, the Edinburgh botanist W. Edgar Evans recognised that *G. melanandrum* was a synonym of *G. refractum* and E.H. Wilson named all his Chinese specimens of this species *G. refractum*.

31. G. pogonanthum Franchet (Figure 9.35)
Perennial with a compact rootstock and marbled leaves with sharply toothed and deeply lobed divisions; flowers inverted, about 25–35mm in diameter; petals pink, rather narrow, gently recurved, conspicuously bearded; filaments crimson, divergent at the tips; anthers blackish. Rock garden, wild garden, sun or shade. July to September.

Rootstock thick and compact. Blades of basal leaves between 5 and 10cm wide or occasionally more, marbled above, divided as far as $^2/_3$ or $^9/_{10}$ into 5 or 7; divisions tapered both ways from above the middle, palmato-pinnately lobed, the untoothed sides straight or slightly concave; lobes prominently toothed. Teeth and tips of lobes acute. Stem-leaves paired, decreasing gradually in size and length of stalk upwards, the upper relatively long-stalked. Stipules acute, some of them fused in pairs. Glandular hairs sometimes present on upper parts of plant, but not the rostrum, colourless or with only the head reddish. Branches paired or the upper solitary.

A

B

Figure 9.35 *G. pogonanthum*: (A) Wisley Garden, 1971; (B) Edinburgh B.G., 1973, both coll. Burma: Mt Victoria (Kingdon Ward 22796), × $^2/_3$

Inflorescence diffuse. Peduncles mostly 4–8cm. Pedicels 1½–3 times as long as sepals. Sepals 7–10mm, purple at base; mucro 1–1.5mm or sometimes to 2mm. Petals 8–16mm or sometimes to 20mm, usually about twice as long as broad, rounded at apex, widely spreading from the base and recurved between the sepals towards the tip, pink or purple or nearly white; base with a dense tuft of long, somewhat wavy, white hairs on each side and longer, less dense hairs across the front surface. Stamens slightly longer than sepals; filaments 8–10mm, curving outwards at the tips, feebly but evenly enlarged towards base, purplish red with paler base, the lower ⅓–²/₃ covered with long spreading hairs; anthers blue-black. Style 8–11mm. Stigmas 2.5–4mm. Immature fruits reflexed on reflexed pedicels. Rostrum 18–23mm, including stylar portion about 6mm. Mericarps 3.5–4.5mm Discharge: seed-ejection (bristles).

S.W. China (Yunnan, Sichuan), W. Central and N. Burma.

This species was introduced into cultivation by F. Kingdon Ward after his last expedition, which was to Mount Victoria, in West Central Burma, in 1956. The collecting number was 22796, but there was also a seed number: U Maung Gale (local collector) 5897. Ward noted 'petals reflexed like a Martagon lily's, the nodding pink flowers also suggest a miniature *Nomocharis* at first sight'. It is a graceful plant with beautiful and unique flowers and is now quite widely grown. It is tolerant of various conditions but does not thrive in open ground at Cambridge. It makes a very thick rootstock which becomes built up above soil level and if the plants show signs of ailing this should be divided up and the pieces replanted. It is also easily raised from seed.

After its introduction it was identified, I believe at Kew, as *G. yunnanense* and I later published a detailed description of it under that name (Yeo, 1975). However, as explained elsewhere (Yeo, 1983), I have since then reviewed a large amount of herbarium material from S.W. China, and have learnt to distinguish this plant from 32. *G. yunnanense*. Although it was described in 1889, I have discovered only a single specimen identified with it since then, and that identifcation was mistaken.

G. delavayi (no. 29) sometimes resembles *G.*

pogonanthum: distinctions are given under the former species.

32. G. yunnanense Franchet (*G. candicans* Knuth, not of gardens) (Figure 9.36)
Perennial with a compact rootstock, marbled and rather bluntly toothed and lobed leaves with a diffuse, few-flowered inflorescence; flowers 25–35mm in diameter, nodding or almost fully inverted, bowl-shaped, with rather broad pink petals, pale filaments diverging from the base and blackish anthers. June, July.

Rootstock thick and compact. Blades of basal leaves between 5 and 10cm wide, marbled above, divided as far as ⁴/₅ or ⁶/₇ into 5; divisions tapered both ways from above the middle, palmato-pinnately lobed; lobes 1–2 times as long as broad, few-toothed. Teeth and tips of lobes more or less acute. Stipules acute, the middle ones sometimes united in pairs. Glandular hairs absent or sparsely present on undersides of leaves. Inflorescence diffuse, usually with fewer flowers than in 31. *G. pogonanthum*. Flowers nodding to almost inverted, shallowly bowl-shaped. Sepals 10–12mm; mucro 1–1.5mm. Petals 15–20mm long and not more than 1⅓ times as long as broad, rounded at apex, divergent, usually pink; base with a dense tuft of straight hairs on either side of hairs across front surface. Filaments 11–15mm, slightly divergent at base, more so at tips, feebly but evenly enlarged towards base, white or greenish at base, pink or purplish tips, with long spreading hairs; anthers blue-black. Style 5–14mm. Stigmas 2.5–4.5mm. Immature fruits

Figure 9.36 *G. yunnanense*, Edinburgh B.G. (no. 812574/0611), 1981, coll. China: Yunnan Prov., × ²/₃ (the separation of the lateral lobes from the middle one is not characteristic)

nodding on spreading or reflexed pedicels. Rostrum 15mm (stylar portion 2–3mm) or up to 23mm. Mericarps 3–4mm. Discharge: seed-ejection (bristles).

S.W. China (Yunnan), N. Burma.

Although it has often been collected I have no evidence that *G. yunnanense* was cultivated until the 1981 Scottish Botanical Expedition to China brought it back. A plant was kindly presented by the Royal Botanic Garden, Edinburgh, to Cambridge that year and it flowered there in 1982 (Yeo, 1983). *G. yunnanense* differs from 31. *G. pogonanthum* in having more sparsely and less acutely lobed and toothed leaves, fewer, larger bowl-shaped flowers with broad, non-recurved petals, and more divergent stamens. The individual flowers are beautiful but the garden value of *G. yunnanense* is still unknown. The plant cultivated has rather short styles, style-length being a character in which the species is unusually variable.

The name *G. candicans* is a synonym of *G. yunnanense*; it refers to a white-flowered form of it which occurs rather rarely. However, in gardens the name has been misapplied to 24. *G. lambertii*.

The Farreri Group

Plant dwarf, without tubers or stolons. Hairs eglandular. Floral axis horizontal. Petals with hair-tufts on margins at base and a small tuft on front surface. Filaments enlarged at base. Stamens slightly diverging when functional. Style long; stigmas short. Immature fruits lying on the ground or more or less horizontal.

One species from W. China.

G. farreri seems to have no close relationships with other dwarf alpine species in its geographical area. The pink petals with hairs on the

Figure 9.37 *G. farreri*, Uppsala B.G., 1969, × 2/3

front surface at the base and the contrasted blue-black anthers on slightly divergent filaments agree with *G. yunnanense*. Connections with The Palustre and Krameri Groups seem to be totally ruled out by the pollination system of *G. farreri* which involves a long style, short stigmas and weakly divergent stamens which are probably used as an alighting place (as in 16. *G. pratense*).

33. *G. farreri* Stapf (Figure 9.37)
Dwarf alpine plant with shallowly lobed leaf-divisions, reddish stems, leaf-stalks and leaf-margins, and flowers about 30–35mm in diameter with horizontal axis; petals and filaments very pale pink; anthers blue-black. Alpine house, rock garden. Late May, June.

Perennial with small rootstock which apparently splits up, each crown usually with a tap-root thicker than the other roots. Plant to about 12cm high with stems, leaf-stalks and margins of leaves more or less red. Blades of basal leaves not more than 5cm wide, rounded or kidney-shaped in outline, faintly marbled on upper surface, divided as far as ¾ or ⁵/₆ into 7; divisions broadest near the apex where they are 3-lobed for about ¼–⅓ of their length; lobes as broad as long or broader, with an occasional tooth. Teeth acute, tips of lobes obtuse or acutish. Stem-leaves paired, those of a pair often unequal, their divisions somewhat tapered from above the middle, decreasing in size gradually upwards. Hairs eglandular. Stem usually oblique or sprawling with short lower internodes, so that most of the foliage, including the long-stalked basal leaves, is at about the same level. Branches solitary or paired. Peduncles mostly 2–4cm and pedicels about 2½ times as long as sepals, holding the flowers well above the leaves. Sepals 7–9mm; mucro 0.5–1mm. Petals 13–15 × 10–15mm, abruptly expanded at the base into a short broad claw, with a rounded blade and crinkled margin, very pale pink; base with a dense tuft of hairs on either side and a fringe beyond this, and a small tuft in middle on the front surface, not connected with the lateral tufts. Filaments 9–11mm, slightly diverging, distinctly enlarged at the extreme base, white with a pink tinge at tips, with a few small mainly marginal hairs at base; anthers blue-black. Style 10–13mm, pink, hairless. Stigmas 1.5mm, pinkish. Immature fruits lying on the ground or spreading horizontally on deflexed pedicels attached to horizontal peduncles. Rostrum about 23mm, including stylar portion 7–9mm. Mericarps 3.5–4mm. Discharge: seed-ejection (bristles).

W. China (Gansu).

Farrer (1917) found this plant at 12,000 feet (3,600m) and above on the Red Ridge of the Min-Shan in Western Kansu (Gansu), but he states that Purdom had collected it there before him. According to Stapf (1926) the effective introduction of the species to cultivation was by seed mixed with seed of G. pylzowianum under Farrer's number F. 170, and consequently plants were, at first, grown under that name. Much more persistently it has been known as G. napuligerum Franchet, with which it was tentatively identified when the species received an Award of Merit of the Royal Horticultural Society in May 1924 (Journ. R.H.S., 50, page 1, 1925). The identity of the plant can be ascertained from the photograph in Gardeners' Chronicle, 75, 333 (1924). I have encountered no evidence that G. napuligerum has ever been in cultivation. The only wild-collected herbarium specimen of G. farreri that I have seen is Joseph Rock's no. 13184, from the T'ao River Basin, which lies on the north-east flank of the Min-Shan with valleys running towards the crest of the latter.

G. farreri is by far the most charming of all alpine species of Geranium. Farrer (1917, p. 172) is irresistibly quotable: 'all the wide wilderness of shingle and scree was tufted and carpet-bedded with this new treasure. No other plant or flower was there at all; the Geranium fills the whole stage with its profusion of large and very pale pink flowers springing all over the close and matted tufts that ramify through the shingle . . . [there was a] crowded dance of its faintly flushing blossoms, silvery in the cold pale air that day.'

I am not certain how the rootstock splits up but it is probably as follows: a tap-rooted rosette produces another rosette from the side and this develops its own taproot; then, perhaps, the connection of the rosettes decays and perhaps also the roots have some contractile power. The drawing in Stapf (1926) is consistent with this suggestion. The plant has no power of spreading by rhizomes. When grown in pots G. farreri seems to benefit from frequent re-potting.

For the relationships of G. farreri, see above under The Farreri Group.

The Palustre Group

Perennials of bushy habit. Main leaves divided about as far as ⁵/₆ or less into 5 or 7, their lobes not more than 1½ times as long as broad. Hairs eglandular. Pedicels 1½ times as long as sepals or more. Petals pink to purple, with or without hairs on front surface between basal tufts; without hairs more extensively scattered over front surface. Filaments enlarged at base, with or without a tuft of hairs above each nectary. Style more or less distinctly shorter than sepals. Stigmas 2.5–5.5mm. Immature fruits erect on spreading or reflexed pedicels.

This group is tentatively assembled for the purpose of this book and consists of four species, one East European, one Himalayan and two East Asian. At least the latter seem very closely related to The Krameri Group (p. 103). The Palustre Group is distinguished from the latter mainly by the absence of hairs over an extensive area of the front surface of the petal-base. Both groups have the styles rather short in relation to the sepals and the stigmas long in relation to the size of the flower.

34. G. palustre Linnaeus (Figure 9.38)
A low bushy perennial with bright green coarsely lobed and toothed leaves; flowers about 30–35mm in diameter, in a diffuse inflorescence; petals deep magenta, not overlapping, rounded at apex. Border, wild garden. June to August.

Perennial with a stout, compact rootstock; bushy, reaching about 40cm. Blades of basal leaves between 5 and 10cm wide, thickish, rather smooth above, often glossy beneath, divided as far as ²/₃ or ⁵/₆ into 7; divisions tapered both ways from the middle or above, occasionally broadest near apex and sometimes nearly parallel-sided, coarsely pinnately lobed; lobes about as broad as long, with 1–3 teeth. Teeth and tips of lobes obtuse or acute, usually with strongly curved margins. Stem-leaves paired, numerous, decreasing in size upwards gradually, with 3 or 5 divisions. Plant covered with rather bristly eglandular hairs, those of upper surfaces of leaves and those of the sepals and pedicels appressed, the latter reflexed, others more or less spreading. Stems and branches thin; branches mostly paired, forming a diffuse inflorescence of long duration. Peduncles 2–7cm. Pedicels 2½–4 times as long as sepals. Flowers widely trumpet-shaped. Sepals 6.5–8mm; mucro about 1mm. Petals 16–18 × 9–10mm, about 1½ to nearly 2 times as long as broad, broadest near the top, evenly tapered to the base, rounded at apex, brilliant deep magenta with very dark purplish, slightly feathered veins, white at extreme base; base with rather coarse loose hairs on margins and all across front surface. Filaments with a narrowly triangular enlargement at base, coloured like the petals but paler at base, or mainly pale and tinged with pink at tips, lower part with bristly hairs on the margins; anthers violet or cream, becoming violet. Nectaries not topped by hair-tufts. Style about 6mm. Stigmas 2.5–3mm, flesh-coloured to dark red. Immature fruits erect on deflexed pedicels. Rostrum about 17mm, including stylar portion about 2.5mm. Mericarps about 3.5mm. Discharge: seed-ejection (bristles).

Figure 9.38 *G. palustre*, Halle B.G., 1974, coll. Germany: Harz, × ½

East and C. Europe (with only scattered occurrences W. of the Rhine Valley).

In nature *G. palustre* is often associated with ditches and small river valleys but it also grows in drier situations in scrub and on wood margins. In the garden it tolerates dry soil and full sun. The flowers are brilliantly but rather harshly coloured, and the plant lacks distinction of habit.

35. *G. wlassovianum* Link (Figure 9.39)
Bushy perennial with softly greyish-hairy leaves, rather shallowly but sharply cut, and dusky magenta-purple or sometimes pink,

heavily veined flowers in a diffuse inflorescence; petals rounded at apex. Wild garden, sun or partial shade. July, August.

Rootstock stout, compact. Plant growing to about 30cm in height. All leaves relatively short-stalked, blades often flushed with brown above, the basal few, their blades mostly 5–15cm wide, divided as far as ²/₃–⁵/₆ into 7; divisions broadest at the middle or above, shortly tapered to the apex, only slightly tapered below the widest point, palmato-pinnately lobed for about ¼ of their length; lobes mostly broader than long, the lowest often bent outwards, with a few teeth. Teeth and tips of lobes acute. Stem-leaves paired, gradually decreasing in size upwards, usually with 5 divisions, their stipules sometimes united in pairs for part of their length. Plant rather densely covered with soft eglandular hairs. Branches paired or solitary. Inflorescence diffuse. Peduncles 1.5–8cm. Pedicels mostly 1½–2½ times as long as sepals. Flowers slightly recessed in the centre. Sepals 9–12mm; mucro 1–2mm. Petals 17–22 × 9–13mm, just over 1½ times as long as broad, broadest above the middle, tapered evenly or nearly so to base, rounded at apex, deep purplish magenta with dark violet feathered veins almost throughout, white at base, or the ground-colour sometimes much paler; base with a tuft of hairs from side to side across front surface and with marginal fringes beyond this. Stamens longer than sepals, curving outwards when functional; filaments rather abruptly enlarged at extreme base, base white, otherwise coloured like the petals, with a fine even hair fringe on margins in lower ⅓–½, becoming coarse at bases of outer filaments, inner with a row of bristly hairs down the middle at extreme base; anthers bluish. Each nectary topped by a hair-tuft. Style 7–10mm.

Figure 9.39 *G. wlassovianum*, Hull B.G., 1971, × ½

Stigmas 3.5–5.5mm, deep red to pink. Immature fruits erect on spreading or deflexed pedicels. Rostrum 20–24mm, including stylar portion 2–3mm. Mericarps 3.5–4.5mm. Discharge: seed-ejection (bristles).

East Siberia, Mongolia, Far Eastern part of USSR, N. China.

In its native lands this species grows in damp situations. In cultivation in Britain it grows moderately well even in dry ground in full sun. The form of it in general cultivation in Britain is rather compact in growth and has deep purplish flowers of slightly varying shades, but usually rather a sombre colour. At Cambridge we also grow a looser-growing plant (less satisfactory in this respect) with larger pale pink, white-centred flowers in which the strong veining of the petals is retained. It came from the University Botanic Garden of Tomsk, W. Siberia, USSR.

The hair-clothing and much more veiny petals distinguish G. wlassovianum from 34. G. palustre. It also has some resemblance to 22. G. wallichianum but does not have the black anthers and stigmas of that species, nor the large, fully united stipules.

36. G. donianum Sweet (G. multifidum D.Don, not Sweet; G. stenorrhizum Stapf) (Figure 9.40)

Perennial up to 40cm tall but sometimes dwarfed, with thick compact rootstock. Leaves 5–10cm wide, marbled, divided at least as far as $^4/_5$ into 5 or 7; divisions broadest at or near apex, palmately lobed; lobes usually 2 to 4 times as long as wide, with a few teeth. Teeth and tips of lobes acute or sometimes obtuse. Stem-leaves similar to the basal, few, paired. Hairs eglandular, coarse, sparse or sometimes dense enough to give a silky effect. Inflorescence diffuse. Flowers erect or upwardly inclined, funnel-shaped. Sepals about 8–11mm; mucro about 1mm. Petals about 13 to 19mm, varying from 1¼ to more than 1½ times as long as broad, rounded or notched at apex, attenuate at base, deep reddish purple or magenta; base with hairs on margin and front surface. Filaments more or less abruptly enlarged and hairy at base, dark purple. Style about 6mm. Stigmas about 3–4mm. Rostrum not more than 12mm, Mericarps between 2 and 4mm. Discharge: seed-ejection (bristles).

Figure 9.40 G. donianum, cult, Jack Drake, 1983, coll. Nepal: Iswa Khola (L.W. Beer), × ²/₃

Himalayas (widespread), S.W. China (Dad-jiang lu in Sichuan), Tibet.

There are two dried specimens of cultivated material of this species in the Kew Herbarium, and a painting made from one of them. One was grown at Kew in 1934, and the other, the subject of the painting, was grown by Sir Frederick Stern at Highdown, Goring-by-Sea, Sussex, in 1932. The species was introduced again by L.W. Beer from Iswa Khola, Nepal, probably collected during his reconnaissance for the Beer, Lancaster and Morris expedition of 1971. This collection is cultivated by Mr Jack Drake of Aviemore, Inverness-shire. The same introduction was germinated at Cambridge but failed to become established. As the earlier introductions seem to have died out it looks as if the species is difficult to cultivate. It is widespread and variable, so possibilities exist for the introduction of more amenable stocks. It is a desirable plant for the rock garden. Wild-flower seed merchants in India and Sikkim offer seed of G. donianum but in my experience send only G. polyanthes (no. 79).

The name G. multifidum was published by different authors for different species on the very same day, so one had to be re-named. Later, Dr Otto Stapf of Kew attempted to separate dwarf alpine states with relatively obtuse leaf-lobes as a separate species under the name *G. stenor-rhizum,* but other Kew botanists did not support the distinction, and nor can I. The leaves of *G. donianum* recall those of 43. *G. pylzowianum* but the habit is different, both above-ground and below. *G. donianum* differs from 15. *G. collinum* in the intensely coloured funnel-shaped flowers, the hairs spread across the front surface of the petals, and in the small leaves with the divisions broadest near the apex.

37. *G. shikokianum* Matsumura (Figure 9.41)

Bushy perennial with leaves rather deeply and coarsely lobed and cut, sometimes marbled; flowers more or less funnel-shaped, 25–30mm in diameter, pink with large white centre and a network of fine purple veins. Woodland or partial shade. July to September.

Perennial usually 20–40cm tall, with compact rootstock. Leaf-blades matt and faintly or distinctly marbled above, very shiny beneath. Basal leaves few. Blades of main leaves mostly between 5 and 10cm wide, divided as far as about $^5/_6$ into 5 or 7; divisions tapered both ways from about the middle, or sometimes very abruptly to the apex from above the middle, lobed half-way to the midrib or for $^1/_3$ of their length; lobes about $1^1/_2$ times as long as broad, with 1–3 teeth, the outermost teeth curving outwards. Teeth and tips of lobes more or less acute. Stem-leaves paired, decreasing gradually in size and length of stalk upwards, their stipules fused in pairs for most of their length, green. Hairs eglandular. Branches paired or solitary, forming a diffuse inflorescence. Peduncles mostly 4–6cm but lowest up to 16cm. Pedicels 2–3$^1/_2$ times as long as sepals. Flowers funnel-shaped. Sepals 8–9mm with scattered, long, fine, tapered, bristly hairs; mucro 1.5–2mm. Petals 16–18 × 10–12mm, broadest above the middle, rounded at apex, evenly tapered to base, pink with $^1/_3$ or more of their length at the base white, with reddish purple net-veining; base without hairs all across front surface, margins with a dense tuft and beyond this a fringe. Stamens divergent; filaments abruptly widened at base, white or tinged with pink towards tips, with or without a fringe of fine hairs in the lower part, inner with a tuft of hairs at base over each nectary; anthers bluish. Style 6mm. Stigmas 4.5mm, green, yellowish or pinkish. Immature fruits erect on reflexed pedicels. Rostrum 18mm, including stylar portion 1–2mm. Mericarps 4.5mm. Discharge: seed-ejection (bristles).

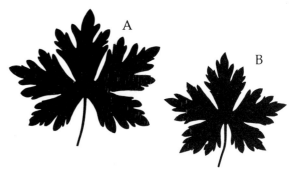

Figure 9.41 *G. shikokianum*: (A) Wisley Garden, 1975, *ex* Dr Rokujo, *per* K.A. Beckett; (B) var. *quelpaertense*, Wisley Garden, 1975, coll. Japan: Quelpart Island (Dr Rokujo, *per* K.A. Beckett), × $^1/_2$

Southern Japan, Korea (Quelpart Island).

G. shikokianum is probably best suited to partial shade. It is easily propagated by division and at times the rootstock seems to break up spontaneously. The white-centred, net-veined flowers are pleasing. This character of the petals is stated by Ohwi (1965) to occur only in 40. *G. krameri* and the related *G. yoshinoi* Nakai among Japanese species, but it is clear from the leaves that our plant really is *G. shikokianum*. The species was introduced to Britain by Mr K.A. Beckett, two stocks having been given him by the Japanese horticulturist Dr Rokujo. One is looser in growth and less hairy and has very attractive leaf-marbling. The other is from Quelpart Island and is:

G. shikokianum var. *quelpaertense* Nakai, (Figure 9.41B), described as smaller, lower-growing, more densely covered with spreading hairs than var. *shikokianum* and found only in Quelpart Island.

The Stapfianum Group

Plant dwarf with slender underground stolons. Hairs eglandular. Petals notched at apex, with a tuft and a fringe of hairs on each edge at the base but without hairs spread across surface. Filaments not enlarged at base. Nectary surmounted by a tuft of hairs. Style not longer than sepals. Stigmas rather long. Immature fruits erect on spreading or reflexed pedicels.

One species in S.W. China. *G. stapfianum* is

difficult to place in relation to any other species. It is here positioned after The Palustre Group because that group includes one species (37. *G. shikokianum*) without hairs across the front surface of the petals and one with notched petals (36. *G. donianum*); its long stigmas associate it with both The Palustre Group and The Krameri Group.

38. G. stapfianum Handel-Mazzetti (*G. forrestii* Stapf, not Knuth) (Figure 9.42, Plate 21)
Dwarf alpine plant with marbled leaves, red stems, leaf-stalks and leaf-margins and upwardly inclined flowers 25–35mm in diameter; petals notched, reddish purple, with red veins converging to a red patch at base. Alpine house, rock garden. June.

Perennial with an elongated scaly rootstock and extensive slender underground stolons; roots not thickened. Plant to about 15cm high with stems, leaf-stalks and margins of leaves red. Blades of basal leaves not more than 5cm wide, kidney-shaped in outline, marbled above, divided as far as $^1/_5$ into 5 or 7; divisions broadest at apex, sometimes overlapping, lobed at apex for ¼ to nearly ½ their length; lobes up to twice as long as broad, sometimes with 1 or 2 teeth. Teeth and tips of lobes obtuse or acute. Stem-leaves similar, only one or two pairs present or sometimes none. Plant without glandular hairs. Inflorescence of only 1 or 2 cymules, sometimes emerging directly from the rosette. Peduncles 2–10cm. Pedicels 2–3 times as long as sepals. Flowers saucer-shaped. Sepals 7.5–9mm, more or less flushed with dark red; mucro about 0.5mm. Petals 12–20 x 11–14mm, almost oblong in shape, notched at apex, deep magenta with darker red slightly feathered veins reaching nearly to apex and converging at base to form a red patch; base with a dense tuft of hairs on either edge and a sparse fringe above this, without hairs all across front surface. Stamens as long as sepals, uniformly tapered from base to apex, diverging from near the base, dark red but paler towards base, finely hairy at base; anthers dark reddish. Nectaries each surmounted by a tuft of hairs. Style 6–9mm, deep red. Stigmas 3.5–4mm, dark red. Immature fruits erect on spreading or reflexed pedicels. Rostrum 15–16mm, including stylar portion 2–3mm. Mericarps 2.5mm. Discharge: seed-ejection (bristles).

Figure 9.42 *G. stapfianum*, J. Stephens, 1969, *ex* Wisley Garden, × $^2/_3$

S.W. China (Yunnan, Sichuan), S.E. Tibet.

G. stapfianum occurs in open stony alpine pastures and on boulders and cliffs at altitudes from 10,500 to 17,000 feet (3,200 to 5,200m). It has been abundantly collected and looks most striking on the herbarium sheet. In cultivation it is disappointing in that its flowers are few and produced over a short period. It should, however, be tried out in scree conditions in the cooler parts of the British Isles.

The Cambridge stock of *G. stapfianum* was obtained from Mr Jan Stephens in 1969. He had received it from The Royal Horticultural Society's Garden, Wisley, Surrey, as *G. collinum* (no. 15), said to have been collected in Nepal, which must have been a mistake. Because of its rhizomatous growth it is easy to work up a large stock of it quickly but some unknown affliction destroyed all but a vestige of my stock one autumn. It recovered and was planted out on some rock-work, but disappeared in a dry summer. Fortunately, seeds had been saved and we started it off again. The species was known in cultivation to Stapf (1926) and a photograph of it under the name *G. pylzowianum* (no. 43) appeared in *Gardeners' Chronicle*, 90, 361 (1931). The main colour of the petals is HCC 32/1 Petunia Purple, which best matches RHSCC Purple Group 78B.

The Krameri Group

Perennials with compact rootstock and usually weak stems. Main leaves divided as far as $^5/_6$ or more into 5 or 7, their lobes about twice as long as broad or more. Hairs eglandular. Pedicel-length variable. Petals pink to reddish, usually with hairs on front surface at base between lateral tufts and scattered more extensively over front surface. Stamen-filaments enlarged at base, with or without a tuft of hairs over each nectary. Style considerably shorter than sepals (except, apparently, in small-flowered forms of 41. *G. dahuricum*). Stigmas 3–6mm. Immature fruits erect on usually spreading or reflexed pedicels.

Like The Palustre Group, this group has been tentatively assembled for the purpose of this book. The species are native to E. Asia, including Japan. All four species included here have (or can have) hairs scattered over the front surface of the petal well above the base, unlike those of The Palustre Group, but like those of The Pylzowianum Group. Other species which are to be included are *G. yoshinoi* Nakai, from Japan, and several Chinese species, some of which are as yet un-named.

39. *G. soboliferum* Komarov (Figure 9.43)
Small compact perennial with ferny leaves and deep magenta, somewhat veiny, flowers about 30mm in diameter; petals rounded at apex; stigmas about 5mm long; pedicels of immature fruits erect. Rock garden, perhaps water garden. July to September.

Rootstock thick, compact. Plant usually about 30–40cm in cultivation. Blades of basal leaves divided nearly to the base into 7; divisions broadest below or above the middle, usually overlapping their neighbours, pinnately dissected into segments only 3–9mm wide; lobes 4–6 times as long as broad, parallel-sided, with teeth up to about 6 times as long as wide. Teeth and tips of lobes acute. Stem-leaves similar, paired, decreasing gradually in size and abruptly in length of stalk upwards, their stipules united in pairs, more or less persistently green. Hairs eglandular. Branches mostly paired. Inflorescence rather dense. Peduncles 4–6cm. Pedicels mostly 1–1½ times as long as sepals. Flowers saucer-shaped. Sepals 8–9mm; mucro about 1mm. Petals 16–18mm, 1½ times to nearly twice as long as broad, broadest above the middle, rounded at apex, rather sharply widened just above base, deep reddish purple with darker veins; base with a tuft of hairs towards either edge and none or few on front surface between tufts, but with scattered long hairs arising from the veins on the front surface for nearly half the length of the petal. Filaments strongly curved outwards, more or less abruptly enlarged at base, similar in colour to petals, pale

at base, edges in basal ⅓ with a fringe of fine hairs, bases of inner with a tuft of hairs over each nectary; anthers bluish. Style 5–6mm, red. Stigmas 5–6mm, red. Immature fruits erect on erect pedicels. Rostrum 14–16mm, including stylar portion about 1mm. Mericarps 2.5mm. Discharge: seed-ejection (bristles).

USSR (Ussuria, on Pacific coast), Manchuria, mountains of C. and S. Japan.

The name of this species refers to its ability to produce some kind of runner. These I have never seen and Bobrov (1949) says they are rarely seen in herbaria. At Cambridge we grow a compact form, obtained as seed from the University Botanic Garden, Copenhagen. I have grown it only in frames, but from its behaviour I suspect it needs full sun and very moist soil. A second stock, sent from Japan by Professor T. Shimizu, has been kept in shade and its habit in full sun is unknown.

Figure 9.43 *G. soboliferum*, T. Shimizu, 1976, coll. Japan: Nagamo Pref., × ⅔

The showy inflorescence and finely cut leaves make this plant distinctive and it may have garden value, though the flower colour is rather harsh. It is propagated by division or from seed.

40. *G. krameri* Franchet & Savatier (Figure 9.44)
Perennial with compact rootstock. Stems up to 80cm but usually collapsing at base. Basal leaves between 5 and 20cm wide, like those of 42. *G. yesoense*. Stem-leaves decreasing abruptly in length of stalk upwards, mostly stalkless or nearly so, distinctive in shape; lower stem-leaves divided as far as about ⅚ into 5; divisions long, rather narrow, the basal widely splayed, all with 3 elliptic or triangular lobes at apex, the middle lobe much the longest and usually shallowly 2-toothed, the lateral toothless, bent outwards, margins of untoothed part

of divisions straight or concave; upper stem-leaves divided into 3, middle division much the largest. Teeth and tips of lobes acute. Hairs eglandular. Flowers flat. Petals about 11–14mm, about 1⅓ times as long as broad, slightly concave, rounded at apex, light pink with darker, scarcely feathered veins; base with a dense tuft of erect white hairs on front surface, lower ⅓–½ with scattered hairs on front surface. Style about 5mm. Stigmas 4.5–5mm. Immature fruits erect on reflexed pedicels. Rostrum 18–22mm, its stylar portion about 1.5mm. Mericarps 2.5mm. Discharge: seed-ejection (bristles). Partial shade. July to September.

N. China (S. to W. Hubei), Far Eastern part of USSR (south), Korea, Japan (C. and S.).

I have grown this species since 1978 but have only one plant and have been unable to divide it. Its behaviour in shade, where I grow it, suggests that it would prefer partial shade. It seems unlikely that it has garden value. It is distinctive in its leaf-shape. The straight line of erect hairs across the petal-bases forms a pentagonal palisade around the stamens.

Figure 9.44 *G. krameri*, Aritaki Arboretum, 1978, coll. Japan: Yamanashi Pref., × ½

41. G. dahuricum De Candolle (Figure 9.45)
Slender sprawling perennial with small finely cut leaves and a diffuse inflorescence; flowers on very slender pedicels, about 28mm in diameter; petals light pink, with fine dark red unfeathered veins; stigmas 3–3.5mm. Wild garden, rock garden, sun. June to August.

Rootstock thick; stems thin, attaining about 50cm in length but collapsing before this to

make a low bushy plant. Undersides of leaf-blades matt. Basal leaves few at flowering time, often red-edged, between 5 and 10cm wide, divided as far as ¾ or ⁶/₇ into 7; divisions broadest just below the apex, 3-lobed for more than ⅓ of their length, the middle division often small and the basal pair particularly large; lobes up to 2½ times as long as broad, with 0–2 teeth, not bent outwards. Teeth and tips of lobes acute, or tips of lobes bluntish. Stem-leaves sometimes less than 5cm wide, paired, numerous, divided as far as ⁶/₇ into 5 or 7; divisions tapered both ways from above the middle, their lobes often far apart, the lateral bent outwards; segments usually 3–5mm wide, rather narrower than those of basal leaves. Upper leaves with the basal divisions widely splayed and the uppermost stalkless. Stipules of stem-leaves sometimes united in pairs. Hairs eglandular, rather dense on the leaves, but everywhere fine, appressed on the veins beneath and nowhere widely spreading except sometimes on sepals when old. Branches paired or solitary. Inflorescence diffuse. Peduncles mostly 2–8cm. Pedicels 3–6 times as long as sepals and sometimes longer than peduncles. Flowers saucer-shaped. Sepals 5–9mm; mucro 0.75–1.75mm. Petals 13–14 × 9–10mm, not more than 1½ times as long as broad, broadest above the middle, rounded at apex, rather broad at base, light pink with fine dark red veins over about ⁴/₅ of their length; base densely hairy on front surface and margins, the hairs extending upwards on the surface for ⅓–½ the length of the petal and on the edge for half its length or all round. Filaments abruptly enlarged at the base, with fine hairs on the margin in the lower part and a few hairs on the back at the extreme base of at least the inner filaments; anthers bluish. Style 6–7mm. Stigmas 3–3.5mm, reddish. Immature fruits erect on spreading or reflexed pedicels. Rostrum 14–17mm, without an evident stylar portion. Mericarps about 2.5mm. Discharge: seed-ejection (bristles).

Continental N.E. Asia from E. Siberia and Mongolia to the Pacific, extending southwards in W. China to Sichuan.

G. dahuricum is one of those persistent flowerers that scarcely draw attention to themselves but may be of some use for the sake of having something in flower in the rock garden at

Figure 9.45 *G. dahuricum*, Uppsala B.G., 1973, coll. China: Chihli Prov. (H. Smith 21569), × ²/₃

an awkward season. With its slender stems and deeply cut leaves it never approaches coarseness. The newly emerging leaves come up pink and yellow. The rootstock is easily divided and plants can be raised from seed. I know only one stock in cultivation but have seen a moderate number of herbarium specimens which suggest that the species is rather uniform.

    G. dahuricum is so similar to 42. *G. yesoense* that I have not been able to provide a satisfactory distinguishing character in the dichotomous key (chapter 8). The relationship of the two plants is further discussed under *G. yesoense*.

42. G. yesoense Franchet & Savatier (Figure 9.46) Perennial of more or less bushy growth with leaves sharply and deeply cut, and scattered pink or rarely white flowers about 22–28mm in diameter; petals, if coloured, with darker veins, rounded at apex; stigmas 3.5–4.5mm. Wild garden, water garden. June to August.

Perennial similar to 41. *G. dahuricum*, to about 40cm high with compact rootstock. Undersides of leaf-blades usually shiny. Blades of basal leaves between 5 and 10cm wide, divided as far as ⁵/₆ or more into 7; divisions tapered both ways from above the middle, pinnately or palmato-pinnately lobed, varying from rather narrow to very wide and overlapping their neighbours; lobes mostly 2–3 times as long as broad, with 0–4 teeth which are up to 3 times as long as broad, the lateral lobes or their outer teeth bent outwards. Teeth and tips of lobes acute. Stem-leaves similar to basal, changing gradually upwards, their stipules free or some of them united in pairs. Hairs of the lower and middle stems reflexed and appressed, those of the leaf-

undersides spreading, usually coarser than those of 41. *G. dahuricum*. Flowers saucer-shaped or slightly funnel-shaped. Sepals 6–10mm; mucro 1–2mm. Petals 15–20 × 8–13mm, 1¹/₃–2 times as long as broad, tapered almost uniformly to the base, pink with fine darker veins or white; base hairy across front surface and on margins, a few hairs sometimes scattered some way along the veins and margins. Style 5–6mm, usually red. Stigmas 3.5–4.5mm, red or pink. Rostrum 15–29mm, including stylar portion about 1mm. Mericarps 2.5–4.5mm. Discharge: seed-ejection (bristles). Other characters as in 41. *G. dahuricum*.

    C. and N. Japan, Kuril Isles.

    G. yesoense has deeply cut foliage and often a bushy habit, in both of which characters it recalls 45. *G. sanguineum*. It differs from it, however, in having paired flowers and no hair-tufts over the nectaries, like 34. *G. palustre*, as well as in the paler flowers. It is a plant of no great horticultural interest, but certainly does not deserve Ingwersen's (1946) ferocious condemnation which, judging by the description, could have been based on 47. *G. thunbergii*, another Japanese species.

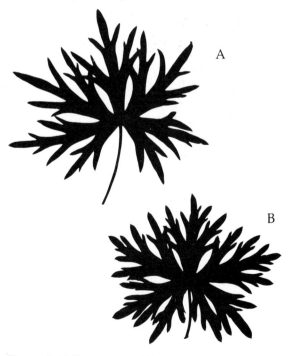

Figure 9.46 *G. yesoense*: (A) Sendai B.G., 1980; (B) T. Shimizu, 1976, coll. Japan: Nagamo Pref., × ²/₃

Through an unfortunate error, this species has recently been offered commercially in Britain under the name *G. palustre*.

I have grown six stocks: five have pink flowers and vary in flower and fruit size, habit and the nature of the leaf-cutting. The fifth is white-flowered and has broad crumpled petals; it is low-growing and its leaves and sepals are densely covered with the kind of hairs found on the sepals of 37. *G. shikokianum*. It was sent by Dr V.I. Safonov of the Sakhalin Complex Research Institute, Novoalexandrovsk, who collected it on the South Kuril Isles (immediately north of Japan). Ohwi (1965) recognises three varieties of *G. yesoense*; my white-flowered one belongs to var. *yesoense*, while the pink ones, being less hairy, are probably referable to var. *nipponicum* Nakai.

For distinctions betwen *G. yesoense* and 15. *G. collinum*, see under the latter. Although it is normally possible to distinguish *G. yesoense* from 41. *G. dahuricum* without difficulty, the differences are quite trivial and few of them are constant. In *G. yesoense* the plants are usually coarser; the basal leaves differ from those of the stem less than in *G. dahuricum*, their divisions having spreading lobes, while the upper leaves do not usually have splayed basal divisions; the hairs of the undersides of the leaves are coarse and spreading and the surface is usually shiny; the petals are often longer and relatively narrower; the stigmas are longer on average; and the rostrum includes a short stylar portion instead of none. These differences do not justify specific separation but I consider it inadvisable to make the necessary nomenclatural combinations of the varietal names of *G. yesoense* with *G. dahuricum* without personally studying the variation in *G. yesoense*. The *status quo* must therefore remain for the time being and it will not cause problems in horticulture if it does.

The Pylzowianum Group

Small alpine plants with small underground tubers interlinked by slender stolons; stems and leaf-stalks slender, sinuous, coming up from the buried tubers. Stem-leaves mostly solitary. Hairs eglandular. Flowers few. Petals with hairs on front surface in basal ¼ or more. Filaments enlarged at base. Immature fruits erect on more or less reflexed pedicels.

Apparently three species from W. China, two described here, the other (not yet named) known to me from a single herbarium sheet. The absence of glandular hairs, the development of hairs on the front surface of the petals in all three species, and the long stigmas of *G. orientalitibeticum* suggest a close relationship with The Krameri Group. The shortness of the stigmas in *G. pylzowianum* is probably connected with a rather specialised pollination arrangement, in which the clawed petals and narrow base of the flower also participate (see under 44. *G. orientalitibeticum*).

43. *G. pylzowianum* Maximowicz (Figure 9.47)

Dwarf perennial with underground runners and tiny tubers; blades of basal leaves not much more than 5cm wide, divided nearly to the base, divisions wedge-shaped, deeply cut into narrow lobes and teeth; flowers few to a stem, 27–32mm in diameter, trumpet-shaped, deep rose-pink with a greenish centre, with short stamens and stigmas. Rock garden, sun. May, June.

Plant reaching 12–25cm, with small tubers, about 5 × 3mm, deep underground and connected in chains by thread-like stolons. Leaf-stalks and stems coming up individually from the tubers, slender, sinuous. Blades of basal leaves less than or little more than 5cm wide, divided nearly to the base into 5 or 7, kidney-shaped or semicircular with basal divisions widely splayed and the middle one short, or pentagonal with the divisions more evenly arranged and more equal in size; divisions broadest near apex, palmato-pinnately lobed; lobes mostly 1½–4 times as long as broad, with 0–3 teeth. Teeth and tips of lobes acute or sometimes obtuse. Stem-leaves mostly solitary, stalked, smaller than the basal. Hairs eglandular. Inflorescence composed usually of up to 3 cymules, cymules occasionally emerging direct from tubers. Peduncles mostly 4–10cm. Pedicels mostly 3½–6 times as long as sepals. Flowers widely trumpet-shaped. Sepals 7–9mm, moderately divergent; mucro 0.5–1mm. Petals 16–23mm, and 1½ times to nearly twice as long as broad, narrowed into a claw at base, blade broad with rounded or faintly notched apex, deep rose-pink except for a whitish base, with fine dark almost unbranched veins; base with rather long hairs on front surface and margins for about ¼ the length of the petal, densest below. Filaments 6–8mm, curving outwards at tip when functional, distinctly but evenly enlarged towards base, white, sometimes pink towards tips, lower part generally covered with small hairs. Anthers before bursting cream with violet-blue edges. Style 5–7mm. Stigmas 2.3–2.8mm, pink to orange-red. Immature fruits erect on more or less reflexed pedicels. Rostrum 16–18mm, including stylar portion 1–2mm, Mericarps about 2.5mm. Discharge: seed-ejection (bristles).

Figure 9.47 G. pylzowianum, J. Stephens, 1966, × ²/₃

W. China (Gansu, Shaanxi, Sichuan, Yunnan).

This is a charming scree-plant, dwarf, with large rose-pink flowers (RHSCC Purple-Violet Group 80C) with the small stamens and stigmas crowded into the narrow throat in which the green colour of the sepals is visible. Although not a dominating plant it will invade its neighbours, and Ingwersen (1946) recommends putting it in a self-contained pocket in the rock garden.

At Cambridge we at one time had two significantly different stocks. The one now lost was the smaller in leaf, with elliptic, obtusish, rather than linear, acute leaf-lobes and teeth. According to Stapf (1926) G. pylzowianum was introduced into cultivation by Messrs Veitch, having been collected by William Purdom in the Taipei Shan (Tsin Ling range) in Shensi (Shaanxi) in 1910; one might suspect that as it grew to a large size in cultivation (up to 30cm high) it was really the next species, G. orientalitibeticum. However, I have seen Purdom's original specimen in the Kew Herbarium and identified it as G. pylzowianum. Later introductions were made by Farrer (his no. 170, from Kansu, 1914, which was mixed with G. farreri (Stapf, 1926)) and by Dr Alan Leslie (in 1981).

The natural habitat of G. pylzowianum is alpine pastures and meadows and rock ledges,

at an altitude of 8,000 to 14,000 ft (2,400 to 4,250 m).

44. G. orientalitibeticum Knuth (Figures 9.48 & 9.49, Plate 19)
Dwarf perennial with underground runners and small tubers like those of 42. G. pylzowianum but larger; leaf-blades deeply cut and strongly marbled in two shades of green, those of basal leaves up to 10cm wide; flowers few to a stem, 23–27mm in diameter, flat but with a cup-shaped white centre, the outer parts of the petals rather deep purplish pink; stamens and stigmas longer than in 42. G. pylzowianum. Rock garden, sun. June, July.

Plant similar to 42. G. pylzowianum but with tubers 5–10 × 4–6mm, and usually 20–35cm tall; leaf-blades strongly marbled, with lobes not more than 2½ times as long as broad, their tips and teeth often more or less obtuse; with up to 5 cymules in the inflorescence; pedicels mostly 2–3½ times as long as sepals; petals 16–22mm, 1¼–1⅓ times as long as broad, triangular at base, not clawed, crumpled, basal ⅓ white, remainder purplish pink, hairs on front surface spread all over the white area and beyond for ⅓–½ the length of the petal; filaments 7.5–9.5mm; style 6mm, stigmas 3–6mm, rostrum 19–21mm, mericarps 3–4mm. Discharge: seed-ejection (bristles).

S.W. China (Sichuan, in the neighbourhood of Dajian lu).

A scree-plant, closely related to 42. G. pylzowianum, differing from it in its mostly larger vegetative parts and fruits, marbled leaves with broader, blunter lobes, smaller flowers of a deeper pink, with a bowl-shaped white centre and longer stamens and stigmas, the petals being claw-less. Compared with G. pylzowianum it is more likely to smother other plants on the rock garden if allowed to invade them. It grows in scrub at altitudes of 7,500 to 9,000 feet (2,250 to 2,750 m), and is found only in the neighbourhood of Tatsien lu (Dajian lu) which is also called Kangding (variously spelt). The petal colour appears to me bluer than that of G. pylzowianum but reference to a colour chart has shown that it is merely darker (RHSCC Purple-Violet Group 80B).

I have received G. orientalitibeticum from a

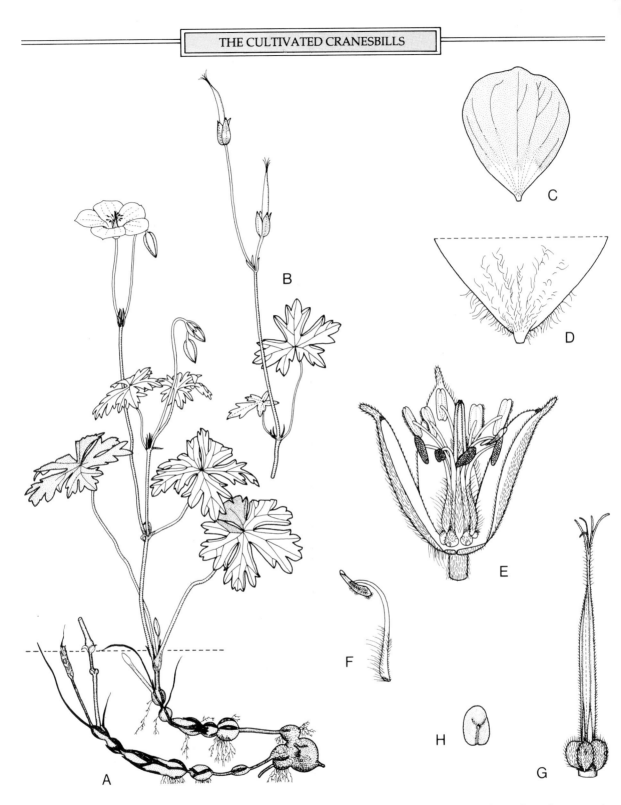

Figure 9.48 *G. orientalitibeticum* (J. Stephens, 1968). (A) plant beginning to flower, × ²/₃ ; (B) portion of inflorescence with mature fruit, × ²/₃ ; (C) petal, with pigmentation, × 2; (D) base of front surface of petal, × 4; (E) flower in male stage with petals and two sepals removed, × 4; (F) stamens of outer whorl, seen obliquely from back, × 4; (C) mature fruit, × 2; (H) seed, × 4

Figure 9.49 *G. orientalitibeticum*, H.E. Guinness, 1960, × ²/₃

number of sources, usually named *G. stapfianum roseum*, a name which is scarcely to be found in the literature, and which certainly has no botanical standing. Its only resemblance to 38. *G. stapfianum* is in the marbled leaves. After making allowance for certain deficiencies in the original description, I have recently come to the conclusion that this plant is the mysterious *G. orientalitibeticum* (Yeo, 1984a, in which the captions to the colour plates have been interchanged). Knuth must have had a specimen without the characteristic stolons and tubers, while the leaf-marbling is easily lost in drying; also, he must have had an exceptionally tall specimen because he gives the height as 50cm (I have a shade-grown specimen over 40cm). The type specimen was burnt in Berlin in 1945 but there are other specimens from the same area and collector, namely J.-A. Soulié, which are this species. These are labelled 'Thibet Oriental', because Dajian lu was at that time in Tibet.

Like 42. *G. pylzowianum*, *G. orientalitibeticum* was introduced into cultivation by Messrs Veitch, there being a specimen in the Kew Herbarium cultivated at Glasnevin Botanic Garden, Dublin, the label of which states that the plant (seed?) came from Veitch in 1914. Possibly it was E.H. Wilson's no. 3300, collected in July 1903, which I have seen in herbaria.

The differences in floral details between this species and 42. *G. pylzowianum* clearly relate to differences in pollination arrangements. I suspect that the short stamens and stigmas crowded into the narrow throat of the flower of the former are intended to brush the face of a short-tongued insect, whereas the stamens and stigmas over-arching the central bowl of the flower of *G. orientalitibeticum* may act by rubbing the proboscis of some larger insect, thrust between them.

The Sanguineum Group

Rhizomatous perennials with very few basal leaves and bushy growth of long-lived, leafy, flowering stems. Hairs eglandular. Leaf-blades deeply and rather narrowly divided and lobed; lobes and teeth few. Cymules 1-flowered. Flowers large; petals usually slightly notched and with hairs all across front surface between lateral tufts at base; stamens shorter than sepals; filaments enlarged at base; style shorter than stamens, with long stigmas.

One species from Europe (including Caucasia) and adjacent Turkey. It has much in common with The Krameri Group (nos. 39–42) but has no scattered hairs on the front surfaces of the petals, thus resembling The Palustre Group (nos. 34–37). It is the only large-flowered species of *Geranium* in this book which consistently has 1-flowered cymules, apart from the hoary-leaved *G. traversii* (no. 50).

45. *G. sanguineum* Linnaeus (Figure 9.50)

Low bushy perennial with leaves cut nearly to the base into rather narrow, deeply lobed divisions; inflorescence diffuse, leafy; cymules 1-flowered; flowers 25–42mm in diameter, erect, purplish red or various shades of pink or white. Border, rock garden, sun. May to August.

Perennial with shortly spreading underground rhizomes. Rosette leaves few, differing from stem-leaves in being less deeply divided and in having obtuse tips of lobes. Stem-leaves paired, stalked, their blades less than 5cm wide or between 5 and 10cm, divided as far as ¾ or ⁷/₈ into 5 or 7; divisions mostly deeply 3-lobed for ⅓ or ½ their length, the lobes entire or with 1 or 2 teeth, 2–4 times as long as broad, the middle lobe much the longest, the laterals curving outwards. Tips of teeth and lobes acute. Some of the stipules fused in pairs for most of their length. Hair-clothing bristly, eglandular. Branches solitary or paired, forming a very diffuse and leafy inflorescence of long duration. Cymules 1-flowered. Peduncles mostly 4–7cm. Pedicels mostly 2–5 times as long as sepals. Flowers saucer-shaped, more or less erect. Sepals 6.5–10mm; mucro 1.5–3.5mm. Petals 14–21 × 13–17mm, not much longer than broad, heart-shaped, usually with a shallow notch at apex, less commonly with a deep one or none, tapered almost evenly to the base, intense purplish red, white at extreme base, usually with darker veins; base with a dense tuft of hairs on either edge and usually with hairs across front surface between the tufts. Stamens shorter than sepals; filaments considerably but gradually enlarged towards the base, coloured more or less like the petals at their tips, edges fringed with hairs, sometimes minute, in the lower half, and with a few hairs on the back; anthers bluish. Style about 5mm. Stigmas 3.5–4.5mm, red or flesh-coloured. Immature fruits erect on erect pedicels. Rostrum 22–32mm, including stylar portion 1–2mm. Mericarps 4–4.5mm. Discharge: seed-ejection (bristles).

Figure 9.50 G. sanguineum, × ²⁄₃

Most of Europe, Caucasus, N. Turkey.

A plant of dry scrubby situations in nature, and in Britain found chiefly on limestones and coastal rocks and dunes. G. sanguineum has few basal leaves, most of its foliage being in the inflorescence, which continues to grow even after flowering has ceased, sometimes sending out new shoots from nodes which earlier bore only one branch. It varies greatly in the size of the flowers, the form of the leaves, density of hair-clothing and compactness of habit. The

foliage of G. sanguineum usually colours well in autumn. The largest-flowered plant of normal colouring known to me is an old stock at Cambridge, with flowers up to 42mm in diameter.

The typical flower-colour of G. sanguineum (RHSCC Purple Group 78C) is too fierce for the taste of many gardeners, but a good range of other shades is now available. Of these, 'Jubilee Pink' and 'Shepherd's Warning' were raised by Mr Jack Drake, of Inshriach Nursery, Aviemore, Inverness-shire, from open-pollinated seed of var. striatum, which itself is flesh-pink, and which was growing in the nursery with the typically coloured forms. G. sanguineum var. striatum is the correct name for the plant usually known as var. lancastriense.

G. sanguineum 'Album' is white-flowered, with no trace of pink or purple in any part of the flower; flower diameter 42mm; begins flowering in June and is of relatively tall, loose habit.

G. sanguineum 'Glenluce' was found on a cliff near Glenluce, Wigtownshire, Scotland, by A.T. Johnson (Johnson, 1937); it has 'large blooms of an exquisite wild-rose pink'; Johnson says it is 20 in (50cm) tall with silky leaves, but his garden was shady and Thomas (1976, 1982) says it is of compact growth. Petal colour: HCC Mauve, 633/1, RHSCC Violet Group 84B.

G. sanguineum 'Holden' has a spreading habit, small leaves and bright rose-pink flowers; it was raised before 1975 by Mr R. Milne-Redhead (Clifton, 1979) at Holden Clough Nursery, Bolton-by-Bowland, Lancashire.

G. sanguineum 'Jubilee Pink' is a rather compact plant with flowers 38mm in diameter of a magenta-pink (RHSCC Red-Purple Group 68A), beginning to flower in June. At the Wisley Trial in 1976 it received a First Class Certificate, the only variant of G. sanguineum to receive this highest award (see, however, 'Shepherd's Warning'); it was raised by Mr Jack Drake (see above under G. sanguineum).

G. sanguineum lancastriense is a synonym of G. sanguineum var. striatum.

G. sanguineum 'Minutum' grows only a few cm high and has leaves 1–2.5cm wide and flowers 3cm wide; it is offered by Ingwersen's of East Grinstead, Sussex. They received it from Mr W. Halstead of Haywards Heath, Sussex, who had received it from 'the late Mr Archer'. The Latin-form cultivar epithet may be illegitimate (see also the next).

G. *sanguineum* 'Nanum', offered formerly by Ingwersen's, was described as dwarf and compact, with rose-red salver-shaped flowers (Clifton, 1979). The name is apparently illegitimate. Mr Will Ingwersen tells me that 'Minutum' is far more compact and that it appears to come true from seed.

G. *sanguineum* 'Plenum' is dwarf, dark-flowered, and with wrinkled petals; it has some extra petals but is not a full double; I saw it at Bressingham Gardens, Diss, Norfolk, in 1979.

G. *sanguineum* 'Roseum' is a name first published by J. Stormonth in his 1928 catalogue for plants with a spreading habit and bright rose flowers (Clifton, 1979). However, Clifton also states that it is the same as 'Splendens' but this belongs under G. *sanguineum* var. *striatum* (see below).

G. *sanguineum* 'Shepherd's Warning' has flowers of RHSCC Red-Purple Group 67C, flushed with 67B (deeper), that is, they are a little deeper and redder than in 'Jubilee Pink'. Its origin is the same as that of 'Jubilee Pink' but at the Wisley Trial it received an inferior award (Highly Commended instead of a First Class Certificate). However, Mr Drake, writing to Mr Clifton in 1979, said that he now considered 'Shepherd's Warning' superior because of its compact habit (it was apparently less compact at Wisley) and he mentioned that it is a marvellous wall plant.

G. *sanguineum* var. *striatum* Weston (G. *sanguineum lancastriense* G. Nicholson; G. *sanguineum* var. *lancastrense* (Miller) Druce) (Plate 20) is quite distinct in its pale flesh-pink flowers (the colour is HCC Roseine Purple, 629/3, which matches RHSCC Red-Purple Group 73D); this colour is produced by rather faint, diffuse veining on a blush ground. The Wisley Trial Report assesses the colour of the veins (RHSCC Red-Purple Group 72D), not the overall effect; the Report makes clear the wide variation in habit and leaf-colour within the variety, which is native to Walney Island off the coast of North Lancashire (now Cumbria), England. The habit varies from dwarf to very dwarf. Plants begin to flower in May. Another name sometimes applied to the Walney Island plant is G. *sanguineum* var. *prostratum* (Cavanilles) Persoon, but it is also sometimes applied to dwarf plants regardless of flower-colour and it does not have priority over var. *striatum*.

G. *sanguineum* var. *striatum* 'Farrer's Form' (var. *lancastrense* 'Farrer's Form') is, according to Clifton (1979), the same as 'Form 1' in the Wisley Trial Report; it combines compactness (8in or 20cm tall) with dark green leaves. I saw it at Kew in 1971 and noted its compactness.

G. *sanguineum* var. *striatum* 'Splendens' (var. *lancastrense* 'Splendens') was described in the Wisley Trial Report as 17in (45cm) tall with very slightly serrated petals, pale pink with deep pink main veins, and with secondary veins RHSCC Red-Purple Group 72D, and beginning to flower in June.

The Columbinum Group

Annuals with deeply and finely divided leaves, cymules longer than subtending leaves, funnel-shaped flowers with broad-based sepals which enlarge conspicuously in fruit, narrow petals with a tuft of hairs on each margin at the base, stamen-filaments enlarged at base and a distinct style.

Perhaps two species in Europe and W. Asia, although G. *schrenkianum* Becker (mainly in Kazakhstan), which is smaller-flowered and more delicate than 46. G. *columbinum*, is included within the latter in *Flora Europaea* (Webb & Ferguson, 1968).

46. *G. columbinum* Linnaeus (Figure 9.51)

Annual with blades of basal leaves less than 5cm wide or a little more, divided to the base or nearly so into 5 or 7; divisions broadest at or above the middle, deeply lobed; lobes rather few, mostly 2–4 times as long as broad, widely spreading except in some of the first-produced leaves, with a few widely spreading teeth, some of which are deep. Leaf-segments of all orders nearly parallel-sided. Teeth and tips of lobes more or less obtuse. Stem-leaves paired, similar, smaller, with narrower and more acute lobes and teeth. Hairs eglandular, mostly appressed. Inflorescence diffuse. Cymules much longer than the subtending leaves. Flowers funnel-shaped. Sepals 6–8mm, enlarging to 8–9mm in fruit; mucro 2mm. Petals 8.5–12mm, wedge-shaped, about 3 times as long as broad, blunt or notched at apex, pale to deep reddish pink, white at base, veins sometimes darker. Stamens $^2/_3$ as long as sepals; filaments greatly enlarged at base, slightly hairy. Anthers bluish. Stigmas reddish, hairy. Rostrum 16–17mm, with a distinct stylar part 4mm long. Mericarps 3–4mm. Discharge: seed-ejection (bristles).

A

B

Figure 9.51 *G. columbinum*, P.F. Yeo, 1977, coll. Corsica: central valley: (A) stem-leaf; (B) basal leaf, × ²/₃

Europe, W. Asia.

A graceful annual with sometimes moderately conspicuous flowers. It is a native of local occurrence on limestones in Britain. Another annual with similar leaves is 64. *G. dissectum*; this has some of the hairs glandular, cymules shorter than the subtending leaves, much shorter petals and different seed-retention (prong).

The Sibiricum Group

Perennials with ill-defined and ill-protected rootstock. Leaf-blades divided into 3, 5 or 7. Stipules broad-based and drawn out into long points. Glandular hairs confined to the inflorescence or absent. Flowers small, with petals 10.5mm or less. Petal-bases with hairs on margins and sometimes also on front surface. Stamens and style very short. Stamen-filaments much enlarged at base, hairy. Stigmas short, hairy on outer surfaces. Immature fruits erect on usually spreading or reflexed pedicels. Pedicels thickened under the calyx when fruit is ripe.

Six species in S. and E. Asia and two in Africa (one extending into S.W. Asia). The above details are taken from the three species described here. The pale-flowered forms of these have a 'red-white-and-blue' effect because the anthers are blue and the stigmas red.

47. ***G. thunbergii*** Lindley & Paxton (*G. nepalense* Sweet var. *thunbergii* (Lindley & Paxton) Kudo) (Figure 9.52)

Sprawling, noticeably hairy perennial, with usually light green leaves; blades of stem-leaves mostly between 5 and 10cm wide, with 5 broad, pointed divisions, the basal widely splayed, or the upper with 3 almost diamond-shaped divisions; inflorescence diffuse; flowers normally 12–15mm in diameter; petals rounded or scarcely notched, white to deep pinkish purple; anthers blue; stigmas red. Ground-cover. July or August to October.

Perennial with a small rootstock. Stems trailing, sometimes rooting. Leaves mostly light green; some present in winter, these being darker green and almost always with bold brownish purple marks in the notches. Blades of basal leaves divided as far as ²/₃ or ³/₄ into 5; divisions broad, shortly tapered both ways from about the middle, coarsely and shallowly lobed in the apical ¹/₃ or ¹/₄; lobes not longer than broad, shallowly toothed. Teeth and tips of lobes obtuse with a small point, or acute. Stem-leaves paired, the lower with 5 divisions, of which the basal pair are usually rather small and widely splayed; upper with 3 broadly elliptic but pointed divisions with a few coarse lobes and sometimes shallow teeth, those of a pair noticeably unequal. Plant covered with spreading eglandular hairs; some glandular hairs present on sepals, rostrum and mericarps, and sometimes the pedicels. Inflorescence diffuse; cymules 2-flowered, longer than the subtending leaves. Sepals about 5–6mm, enlarging to 6.5–7mm in fruit; mucro 1mm or less. Petals 7–10.5 × 4–6mm, rounded or scarcely notched at apex, white or pale to deep purplish pink, with purple veins; base with a hair-fringe on either edge and a few hairs across the front surface. Filaments 4–5mm, enlarged at base, with numerous hairs on back and margins. Anthers violet-blue. Stigmas 1–2mm, flesh-pink or red. Immature fruits erect on erect, spreading or rarely reflexed pedicels. Rostrum 13–18mm with virtually no stylar portion. Mericarps 2.5–3mm. Discharge: seed-ejection (bristles).

N. China, Taiwan, Japan and neighbouring archipelagoes.

G. thunbergii is an almost weedy species that just gains a place in gardens, preferably as ground-cover. Although it produces great quantities of seed I have never seen much spontaneous germination in Cambridge. It is closely related to 48. *G. nepalense* and has been treated as a variety of it. Named thus, it sometimes loses its varietal name and becomes "*G. nepalense*". I have received it under this name from Mrs E. Smallbone of Strathfield, New South Wales, where it is one of the few *Geranium* species so far found to have garden value in the Sydney area. This particular form is more compact and has darker green leaves than usual, and deep purplish pink flowers. For a comparison of *G. thunbergii* wtih *G. nepalense*, see under the latter.

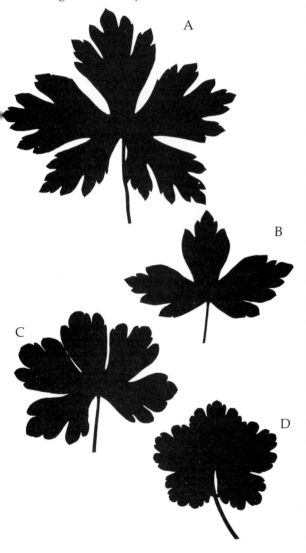

Figure 9.52 *G. thunbergii*, Kyoto B.G., 1965: (A) basal leaf; (B) stem-leaf; (C) Y. Fukuda, 1975, coll. Japan: Shiobara Pref.; (D) Mrs E. Smallbone, 1981, cult. in Sydney area, NSW, Australia; all × ²/₃

G. thunbergii is in circulation also under the name *G. wilfordii* Maximowicz. This is a related species with only 3 well-developed leaf-divisions which are tapered to a rather long point and evenly toothed rather than lobed and toothed. I have not seen living plants, but the species has been found as an alien in the Warsaw Province of Poland (Rostanski & Tokarski, 1973).

48. *G. nepalense* Sweet (Figure 9.53)

Similar to 47. *G. thunbergii* but with a slenderer stem and smaller darker green leaves, flowers 10–12mm in diameter, petals white to pale pink, rarely deep pink, with darker veins. Leafy in winter. Weed.

Perennial with slender rootstock and erect or prostrate stems, usually becoming bushy. Leaves rather dark green, often slightly marbled, and often purple beneath and brownish above. Blades of basal leaves 5–10cm wide or sometimes less, divided as far as ¾ or ⁵/₆ into 5 or 7; divisions shortly tapered both ways from above the middle, with 3 or 5 lobes at apex; lobes not longer than broad, toothed. Teeth and tips of lobes acute or obtuse. Stem-leaves paired, stalked, with 3 or 5 more gradually tapered divisions and usually acute teeth and tips of lobes. Hairs eglandular. Inflorescence diffuse. At least some cymules in each plant 2-flowered but 1-flowered cymules not infrequent. Sepals 4.5–5mm, becoming 5–6.5mm in fruit; mucro 1mm or less. Petals 5–8.5mm long, rounded or notched at apex, with 5 purple veins. Anthers violet-blue. Stigmas 0.5–1mm, red. Immature fruits erect on reflexed pedicels. Rostrum 10–13mm with stylar portion about 0.5mm. Mericarps 3–3.5mm. Discharge: seed-ejection (bristles).

East Afghanistan, Himalayas, peninsular India, China (Yunnan, Sichuan, Hubei, Henan, Guangxi).

This species is sometimes introduced by purchase of wild-flower seed from commercial collectors in the Himalayan region but it is a weed and can be quite persistent out of doors in Cambridge. The flower colour may range from pale pink to white in the same plant according to environmental conditions, but there is some inherent variation also. When the name *G. nepalense* was first published it was accompanied by a not very good plate of a plant with deep red flowers (which I have never seen in this species).

Figure 9.53 *G. nepalense:* (A) R. Gorer, 1974, coll. by G. Ghose of Darjeeling, India; (B) S.K. Raina, 1981, coll. India: Srinagar, Kashmir, × ²/₃

G. nepalense differs from 47. *G. thunbergii* in the lack of any glandular hairs, and in being slenderer, smaller-leaved and slightly smaller-flowered. It is rather variable in stature and leaf-form, certain forms approaching 47. *G. thunbergii* in these characters.

49. *G. sibiricum* Linnaeus (Figure 9.54)
Sprawling perennial with pale green foliage; leaf-divisions long, with rather deep, sharp, forwardly directed lobes and sharp teeth; cymules 1-flowered; flowers 9–10mm in diameter; petals white or nearly so with dark veins. Weed.

Perennial with slender rootstock and sprawling stems. Foliage pale green. Basal leaves few. Lower stem-leaves between 5 and 10cm wide, divided as far as about ⁵/₆ (sometimes much more); divisions rather narrow, gradually tapered both ways from about the middle, with rather numerous lobes, nearly straight-sided in the unlobed part; lobes divergent from midrib of the division at a small angle, up to about twice as long as broad, rather shallowly toothed. Teeth and tips of lobes acute. Divisions of upper stem-leaves untoothed and with the lobes forming a coarse saw-edge. Stem-leaves paired, stalked. Hairs eglandular. Inflorescence diffuse. Cymules 1-flowered, sometimes with no pedicel. Sepals 4mm, enlarging to 5 or 6mm in fruit; mucro about 0.75–1.25mm. Petals about 5–7mm, wedge-shaped, rounded or notched at apex, white or pale pink with 3 or 5 purple veins. Anthers violet-blue. Stigmas about 1mm, pink. Rostrum 10–13mm, the stylar portion about 1mm. Mericarps 3–3.5mm. Discharge: seed-ejection (bristles).

East and C. Europe (where it is spreading westwards), most of Asiatic USSR, China, Japan, W. Himalayas; introduced into N. America.

G. sibiricum is a weed, resembling an annual in habit though in fact a perennial. It grows in disturbed ground and, in continental climates, in lawns. In its small whitish flowers it resembles 48. *G. nepalense* but is distinguished from it by the sharply lobed, narrow leaf divisions and constantly 1-flowered cymules. Even when grown in the greenhouse this species goes dormant in winter.

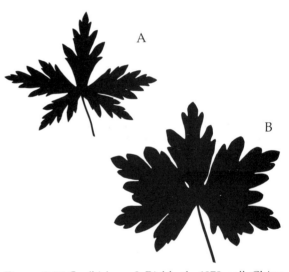

Figure 9.54 *G. sibiricum*, J. Rishbeth, 1978, coll. China: Kirin Prov.: (A) middle leaf; (B) lower leaf, × ²/₃

The Sessiliflorum Group

Perennials with well-developed rosette leaves and with bushy or trailing, diffuse inflorescences. Blades of lower leaves rounded in outline with divisions broadest at or near apex and with shallow lobes and teeth. Hairs eglandular. Cymules 1-flowered. Pedicels longer than peduncles. Stamen-filaments enlarged at base. Stamens and style not much more than half the length of the sepals. Rostrum without a distinct stylar portion.

This description covers the Australasian plants described as nos. 50 and 52. They are probably closely related to other species of Australasia and they also have connections with S. America (see no. 52).

50. *G. traversii* J.D. Hooker var. *elegans* Cockayne (Figure 9.55A)

Greyish-hairy, low-growing; basal leaves long-stalked, rounded in outline with shallow obtuse lobes and teeth; cymules 1-flowered; flowers held just above basal leaves, 26–29mm in diameter, opaque (milky) pink. Rock garden, sun. June to September.

Perennial with compact rootstock. Basal leaves numerous, long-stalked, their blades between 5 and 10cm wide, often broader than long, divided as far as $^3/_5$ into 7; divisions broadest almost at the apex, giving a scarcely angled outline to the whole blade, 3-lobed for about $^1/_4$–$^1/_3$ of their length; lobes broader than long, often with 1 or 2 small teeth. Teeth acutish, tips of lobes obtuse or broadly pointed. Stem-leaves paired, becoming reduced in size rather rapidly upwards, the upper with 5 divisions which are less enlarged towards the tip than those of basal leaves, giving the blade a more angular outline. Stipules not united, finely tapered. Hairs eglandular, dense, fine, clothing the whole plant in a greyish hoariness. Branches mostly paired, forming a diffuse inflorescence which becomes bushy and collapses, so that flowers are carried only a little above the basal leaves. Cymules 1-flowered. Flowers saucer-shaped. Sepals about 6.5–8mm; mucro 0.5–1mm. Petals 12–13mm long and almost as broad, rounded at apex, contracted at base into a short triangular claw, opaque (milky) pink, fading at the edges, with fine darker veins on lower half of blade and a whitish claw; base with evident hairs at the sides and a few fine hairs on veins of front surface of claw and base of blade (difficult to see). Stamens about $^2/_3$ as long as sepals; filaments enlarged at base, white, finely hairy in lower part; anthers yellow with pink edges. Stigmas 1.5mm, pinkish, hairy on outer surfaces. Immature fruits erect on erect pedicels. Rostrum 8–11mm, without a distinct stylar portion. Mericarps about 3mm. Discharge: seed-ejection (bristles).

Chatham Islands (nearly 400 miles (640 km) east of New Zealand).

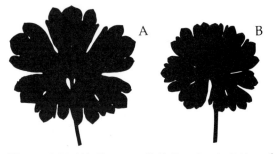

Figure 9.55 (A) *G. traversii*, F. Beanland, 1982, × $^2/_3$; (B) *G. sessiliflorum* subsp. *novaezelandiae* × *G. traversii*, K.A. Beckett, 1981, × $^2/_3$

In nature *G. traversii* grows on coastal cliffs. When first discovered it was described as having white flowers and the white form was known to Bowles (1914) and to Ingwersen (1946), who feared it was becoming extinct in our gardens, and this fear seems to have been realised. Its correct name is *G. traversii* var. *traversii*. Although plants cultivated in Britain are very uniform, Dr David Given tells me that in nature *G. traversii* is extremely variable, with great variation in leaf shape and colour, flower size and colour and vigour. The pink-flowered plant grown as var. *elegans* would therefore be better treated at the rank of forma or even regarded as a cultivar, but this matter had best be handled by New Zealand botanists.

G. traversii grows well in England but it is easily lost in severe winters and perhaps also through winter damp. However, it regenerates naturally from seed as a rule. The old inflorescences are said to bend down and take root, giving a 'hen-and-chickens' effect (Allan, 1961). I have not seen this but Farrer (1919) mentions striking cuttings in autumn as a precaution against loss in winter.

G. traversii is on the whole coarser in growth than the grey-leaved members of The Cinereum Group (nos. 104–110) and it differs from them in fruit-discharge type.

HYBRIDS. Has crossed with the European *G. endressii* to produce *G.* × *riversleaianum* (no. 3), and with *G. sessiliflorum* to produce no. 51.

51. *G. sessiliflorum* Cavanilles subsp. *novaezelandiae* Carolin × *G. traversii* J.D. Hooker var. *elegans* Cockayne (Figure 9.55B)

Plant with basal leaves slightly smaller than those of 50. *G. traversii* and with tiny stem-leaves 2cm or less wide in a profusely branched trailing inflorescence; flowers about

15mm in diameter, white, more or less flushed rose. Rock garden. June to autumn.

Perennial with blades of basal leaves thick, about 5cm wide, not much different in shape from those of 50. *G. traversii,* but divisions crowded and not lying flat; stem-leaves paired or solitary, less than 2cm wide, with 5 divisions which are sometimes unlobed. Plant less hairy than 50. *G. traversii,* the leaves being bright green. Flowers shallowly funnel-shaped. Sepals about 5mm, flushed with brown-purple, densely covered in short hairs and with some bristly hairs in addition; mucro 1mm or slightly more. Petals about 10 × 8mm, opaquely white or nearly so in summer, pale pink with white base in cooler weather. Filaments white; anthers cream with violet edges. Stigmas yellowish, Rostrum about 10mm.

This hybrid readily arises in gardens where the parents grow together and is sometimes fertile. The above description is based on specimens gathered in Mr and Mrs K.A. Beckett's garden at Stanhoe, near King's Lynn, Norfolk. I have also seen it at Kew (in 1971) and at Bressingham Gardens, Diss, Norfolk (in 1979), where, in a private area, there was an apparent 'hybrid swarm' of this cross. Mr Beckett's clone is now being grown at Cambridge and is distinctive and attractive. On the question of fertility, see Chapter 7.

52. G. sessiliflorum Cavanilles subsp. **novae-zelandiae** Carolin (Figure 9.56)
Dwarf perennial, sometimes carpeting, with green or dark brown leaves and white flowers about 10mm in diameter, scarcely if at all raised above the foliage. Rock garden. June onwards.

Perennial with a compact rootstock, stout for the size of the plant. Blades of basal leaves about 1.5–3cm wide, rounded in outline, divided as far as ½ or ³/₅ into 5 or 7; divisions broadest at the apex, shallowly 3-lobed at apex; lobes broader than long, obtuse, rarely toothed. Stem-leaves solitary, mostly 1–1.5cm wide, with 5 or 7 divisions, some of which may be unlobed; lobes obtuse or acutish. Hairs eglandular. Inflorescence diffuse, upper internodes short, causing flowers to be held at about the level of the blades of the basal and lower stem-leaves; cymules 1-flowered, the first ones often arising from the rosette; flowers erect, funnel-shaped. Sepals 3.5–6mm, brownish green, covered with long spreading hairs. Petals 6.5–7.5 × 3mm, broadest at apex, white; base with a few hairs on each edge and an occasional hair on the front surface; filaments just over ½ as long as sepals, enlarged at base, white, fringed with minute hairs in the lower part; anthers yellowish. Stigmas 1.5mm, whitish. Immature fruits erect on mostly spreading or reflexed pedicels. Rostrum about 8mm, with no stylar part. Mericarps about 2.5mm. Discharge: seed-ejection (bristles).

New Zealand (N. and S. Islands).

A rather insignificant species, of which Carolin (1964) recognised three subspecies, the others being *sessiliflorum* in S. America and *brevicaule* (J.D. Hooker) Carolin from Tasmania and the S.E. highlands of continental Australia. Two forms of subsp. *novaezelandiae,* one with green and one with dark bronzy leaves, are cultivated and are mentioned by Allan (1961), who says that where they occur together in nature intermediate colours may be found.

G. sessiliflorum subsp. *novaezelandiae* 'Nigricans' is the name I have adopted for the dark-leaved form mentioned above. The name appeared in the autumn supplement to the 1967 catalogue of The Plantsmen, Sherborne, Dorset, but it was applied to a plant received at Cambridge from Mr Jan Stephens in 1964; if it was published before 1959 it will be legitimate. Soon after they unfold, the leaves become olive green or bronzy above and when dying they turn orange; the basal ones tend to be circular in outline rather than kidney-shaped, as they are in a green-leaved stock grown at Cambridge (Figure 9.56 C & D).

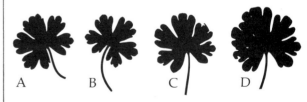

Figure 9.56 *G. sessiliflorum* supsp. *novaezelandiae*: (A) & (B) Lausanne B.G., 1958; (C) & (D) 'Nigricans', J. Stephens, 1964, × ¾

HYBRIDS. Can cross with 50. *G. traversii* (see no. 51); in occurrences known to me the hybrids show no sign of bronziness in the leaves. This has, however, appeared in the cross with 3. *G. endressii* (= 4. *G.* 'Kate').

The Incanum Group

Perennials with divided stipules and leaf-blades divided to the base or nearly so and having approximately linear segments. Inflorescence diffuse. Petals notched. Stamen-filaments enlarged at the base.

Southern Africa. The species of this region are not well known to me and the above description covers only certain of them, including those described below. A taxonomic revision has been undertaken by O.M. Hilliard and B.L. Burtt.

53. *G. incanum* N.L. Burman (Figure 9.57)

Bushy perennial with all leaves divided to the base and their divisions, lobes and teeth all 1mm or less in width; inflorescence diffuse; flowers 27–35mm in diameter; petals deep reddish purple with darker veins and a narrow apical notch. Rock garden, patio, sun. June to autumn.

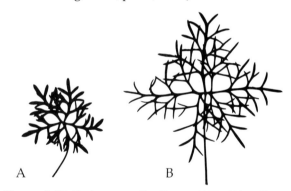

Figure 9.57 *G. incanum*, R. Gorer, 1975: (A) coll. in June; (B) coll. in November, × ²/₃

Perennial with aromatic herbage and no clear distinction between flowering and non-flowering shoots; stems branched below and becoming woody, closely leafy below, less so above. Leaves mostly solitary, some of the upper paired; blades less than or slightly more than 5cm wide, divided to the base into 5, green above, silky white-hairy beneath; divisions pinnately lobed and some of the lobes toothed; segments about 1mm wide or less. Stipules narrow, acute, deeply cut into 2 or 3 segments. Hairs eglandular, appressed. Peduncles mostly 6–14cm. Pedicels mostly 3–7cm. Sepals 5–6mm, silvery-silky; mucro 1mm. Petals 13–18 ×

9–14mm, approximately heart-shaped, with a narrow notch, deep magenta-pink with darker veins and a white V-shaped mark at the base; base with a dense tuft of hairs at either edge and a small group of hairs on middle of front surface between the tufts. Filaments enlarged and hairy on the edges below, white at base, pink above; anthers cream with purple edges. Stigmas 3–3.5mm, flesh-pink, hairy on outsides. Immature fruits erect on more or less reflexed pedicels. Rostrum about 22mm, including stylar portion 2–2.5mm. Mericarps about 4.5mm. Discharge: seed-ejection (bristles).

South Africa.

This is a distinctive and showy species for a warm situation. It is not hardy in severe winters in Britain but regenerates reliably from seed. It may also be propagated from stem-cuttings and maintained under glass through the winter. The description above refers to the form commonly cultivated in Britain, which is *G. incanum* var. *multifidum* (Sweet) Hilliard & Burtt; *G. incanum* var. *incanum* has smaller and paler (usually white) flowers.

Two other plants which I have grown belong to two closely related species dealt with below.

53a. *G. magniflorum* Knuth

Rootstock producing crowded short stems with rosette-like clusters of leaves. Divisions of leaves with central segments about 2mm wide; lobes about 1.5mm wide, few, toothless. Stipules cut into 3 or more segments. Glandular hairs present on upper stems, cymules, sepals and rostra. Inflorescence with branches and peduncles often widely divergent. Peduncles 1.5–7cm. Pedicels 1.5–4cm. Sepals about 5.5mm; mucro almost none. Petals about 10 × 8mm, heart-shaped with a wide notch, plum-purple with darker veins and a very clear white or greenish basal area; base with very weak hair-tufts at the sides and a few hairs in middle of front surface. Filaments white; anthers bluish. Stigmas 2mm, reddish. Rostrum about 18–22mm, including stylar portion about 3mm. Mericarps about 3.5mm.

South Africa (Drakensberg in southern Natal).

This was received from Mr Jan Stephens in 1967 as *G. thodei* Knuth. The petal colour matches HCC 31 Orchid Purple, a very intense colour, not far from RHSCC Purple Group 87A.

The plant is quite dwarf and is suitable for the rock garden. The plant has finally been lost at Cambridge after dying and being re-started several times from seed. A very similar plant collected at 9,000 ft (2,750 m) on the Drakensberg in 1970 by Sir Peter Watkin Williams had a much shorter life at Cambridge. It is *G. drakensbergense* Hilliard & Burtt, a new species which is expected to have received formal description by the time this book is published. Compared with *G. magniflorum* its flowers were larger, sparser and less intensely coloured and were produced in October. Its petal-bases had distinctive features. I am grateful to Mr B.L. Burtt for the identification of all three representatives of The Incanum Group described here.

The Maculatum Group

Annuals or perennials. Upper parts usually with glandular hairs. Sepal mucro $1/5$ or more as long as sepal. Petals without hairs across front surface (except in 56. *G. bicknellii*). Stamen-filaments enlarged at base. Pedicels of immature fruits erect. Rostrum with an evident stylar portion.

North America. The group comprises the four species described here and one or perhaps two additional species closely related to 57. *G. carolinianum*.

54. *G. maculatum* Linnaeus (Figure 9.58)

Perennial 50–70cm tall, sparsely leafy; main leaves with the divisions narrowly diamond-shaped and with very acute lobes and teeth; flowers partly in umbel-like clusters, about 30mm in diameter; petals pale to deep pink, rounded or slightly notched at apex; pedicels of immature fruits erect. Border, wild garden, sun or partial shade. May to July.

Rootstock compact and stout. Blades of basal leaves 5–20cm wide, divided as far as about $9/10$ into 5 or perhaps 7; divisions rather solid in outline but with rather wide notches between them, gradually tapered both ways from about the middle, the basal untoothed part of the margin long and nearly straight; lobes about 1½ times as long as broad, diverging from midrib of the division at a narrow angle, toothed. Teeth and tips of lobes very acute. Stem-leaves paired, few, lowest sometimes more than 20cm wide, widely spaced by the long stem-internodes,

decreasing rapidly in size and length of stalk upwards, the uppermost stalkless and with 3 divisions. Hairs mostly eglandular, those of the stem appressed to the surface; very long, small-headed glandular hairs sometimes present on sepals and at base of rostrum. Inflorescence of a few very long-peduncled lower cymules and groups of flowers without peduncles. Flowers upwardly inclined, shallowly bowl-shaped. Sepals 8–10mm; mucro 2–3.5mm. Petals 18–19 × 10–12mm, broadest near the tip, apex rounded or shallowly notched, base abruptly widened, bright or pale pink, fading to white at base, veins translucent; base with a tuft of hairs at either side, fringed above the tufts, without hairs all across front surface. Stamens loosely spreading when functional; filaments slightly shorter than sepals, pink, abruptly enlarged and with marginal hair-fringes at the base; anthers greyish. Each nectary with a tuft of hairs at the top. Style about 8.5mm. Stigmas 2–3mm, flesh-pink. Immature fruits erect on erect pedicels. Rostrum 23–25mm, including stylar portion about 4mm. Mericarps 4–5mm, blackish. Discharge: seed-ejection (bristles).

Figure 9.58 *G. maculatum*, Alpine Garden Soc., 1969, coll. USA: N. Carolina, × ½

East North America (westwards to Manitoba and Kansas).

A rather tall perennial of moderate appeal, it is naturalised at Wisley along the stream, where I have seen only pale-flowered plants. The deeper-coloured one grown at Cambridge seems preferable. Its natural habitat is 'fields, meadows and open woods' (Jones & Jones,

1943). The rootstock is easily divided.

On comparing the short description with that of 9. *G. sylvaticum* it will be seen that *G. maculatum* differs in being sparsely leafy and in having narrowly diamond-shaped leaf-divisions. These are also untoothed from about the broadest part downwards. Apart from this, *G. maculatum* has larger, typically pink, petals, without hairs across the front surface.

55. *G. oreganum* Howell (Figure 9.59)

Perennial about 60cm tall with leaves recalling those of 16. *G. pratense*; inflorescence not very dense; flowers 43–47mm in diameter; petals deep purplish pink, rounded at apex; immature fruits erect on erect pedicels. Border. June, July.

Perennial with a compact rootstock. Blades of basal leaves 10–20cm wide, divided nearly to the base into 7; divisions tapered both ways from above the middle, broad but rather open in outline, deeply and coarsely pinnately lobed; lobes up to 2 or 2½ times as long as broad, sometimes curving outwards, with few or several teeth. Teeth and tips of lobes acute. Stem-leaves paired, decreasing in size abruptly after the first few pairs. Glandular hairs present on upper stems, sepals and rostra. Inflorescence rather diffuse. Flowers saucer-shaped, upwardly inclined. Peduncles mostly 4–11cm. Pedicels mostly 1½–2½ times as long as sepals. Sepals about 10mm; mucro 2.5–4.5mm. Petals up to 23 × 21mm, rather evenly tapered to the base, deep purplish pink; base with a dense tuft of hairs on either edge and beyond that a fringe, but without hairs across front surface. Filaments curving outwards, abruptly enlarged at base and there with minute hair-fringes, pink; anthers yellow with purple edges. Each nectary topped by a dense hair-tuft. Style 9–11mm. Stigmas 2.5–3mm, reddish. Immature fruits erect on erect pedicels. Rostrum about 30mm, including stylar portion 3–4mm. Mericarps 4.5mm. Discharge: seed-ejection (bristles).

West USA (S. Washington, Oregon, N. California).

The above description is taken from plants growing at Cambridge which were received as seed in 1959 from Edinburgh. This is a lovely species with very large flowers, and should be better known. I have raised new plants from seed, but the species should be easy to prop-agate by division.

G. oreganum has some resemblance to 16. *G. pratense* but the leaf-cutting is coarser, the typical flower colour is different (HCC 32/1 Petunia Purple, similar to RHSCC Purple Group, betwen 78B and 78C), the stamens curve outwards all the time the flower is open, the flower is upwardly inclined and the immature fruits are erect on erect pedicels.

56. *G. bicknellii* Britton (Figure 9.60A)

Spring annual or overwintering annual. Blades of basal leaves not more than 10cm wide, dark green, firm in texture, divided nearly to the base into 7; divisions broadest above the middle, deeply 3-lobed; lobes about twice as long as broad, with several more or less deep teeth. Teeth and lobes almost parallel-sided, obtuse or acute at tips, the teeth often bent outwards. Stem-leaves similar to the basal. Stems usually three from the rosette or from a short erect central stem, regularly forked, producing a diffuse leafy inflorescence. Glandular hairs present on upper stems, sepals and rostra. Cymules in fruit normally with at least one pedicel twice as long as sepals. Flowers somewhat funnel-shaped, about 9mm in diameter. Sepals 4–5mm; mucro about 1mm. Petals about 7 × 3.5mm, notched, pale pink with darker forked and almost looped veins; base with a tuft of hairs on either side and hairs between tufts across front surface. Filaments enlarged and with fine hair-fringes at base; anthers bluish. Stigmas less than 1mm, crimson. Immature fruits erect on erect pedicels. Rostrum 16–17mm, including a distinct stylar

Figure 9.59 *G. oreganum*, Edinburgh B.C., 1959, × ½

portion 2–3mm. Mericarps about 2.5mm, black. Discharge: seed-ejection (bristles).

North America (Canada, E. United States).

A species with small pink flowers and distinctive thickish, dark green, slightly shiny leaves. The leaf-divisions are not as blunt as those of the round-leaved Eurasian annuals, 87. *G. molle*, 85. *G. pusillum* and 8. *G. rotundifolium*, and not as finely dissected as those of 46. *G. columbinum* and 64. *G. dissectum*. The flowers appear quite deep reddish pink because of the strong veining.

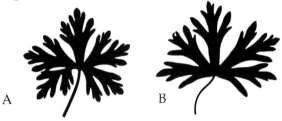

A   B

Figure 9.60 (A) *G. bicknellii*, Vancouver B.G., 1978, × ²⁄₃ ; (B) *G. carolinianum*, Antwerp B.G., 1971, × ²⁄₃

HYBRIDS. For a possible hybrid with 1. *G. endressii*, see that species. A hybrid with 57. *G. carolinianum* was found in the Cambridge Botanic Garden in 1981. The upper leaves appeared intermediate between those of *G. bicknellii* and the upper rosette leaves of *G. carolinianum*. The inflorescence did not contain umbel-like clusters but was crowded. The petals were paler pink than those of *G. bicknellii* and slightly larger than in either parent. There was no fruit development whatever.

57. *G. carolinianum* Linnaeus (Figure 9.60B)
Annual, usually behaving as a spring annual. Blades of basal leaves about 5cm wide, those produced first rounded in outline, divided as far as about ½ into 7; divisions broadest at the apex, some unlobed, some very shallowly 3-lobed. Blades of later rosette-leaves and of stem-leaves divided as far as ¾ or ⁶⁄₇ into 5 or 7; divisions like those of *G. bicknellii*. Stem with a very long first internode, then a few solitary and paired, or only paired, leaves. The paired leaves subtend branches producing dense umbel-like clusters of flowers, sometimes with one or two perfect cymules. Glandular hairs present on pedicels, sepals and rostra. Pedicels in fruit about ½–1½ times as long as sepals. Flowers

funnel-shaped. Sepals 5–8mm, sometimes very broad; mucro about 1.25mm. Petals 5 × 2mm or sometimes considerably larger, white or pale pink; base with a few hairs on the margins. Stigmas about 1mm. Immature fruits erect on erect pedicels. Rostrum about 12–13mm including a distinct stylar portion 1.5mm long. Mericarps 3–3.5mm, black. Discharge: seed-ejection (bristles), empty mericarps usually shed.

North America (Canada, E. and S. United States, N.W. Mexico). Introduced in China.

This annual usually has insignificant white flowers. It differs considerably from 56. *G. bicknellii* in habit though certainly closely related to it. In readily shedding its empty mericarps it resembles The Tuberosum Group and The Platypetalum Group. This condition has probably evolved independently in this case; it prevents the interference with discharge in other flowers in the crowded inflorescence that would be caused by retention of empty mericarps.

The above-described plant, with dense inflorescences, is known as var. *confertiflorum* Fernald; the var. *carolinianum* has a more open inflorescence.

HYBRIDS. For a possible hybrid with 1. *G. endressii* and for a hybrid with 56. *G. bicknellii*, see those species.

The Fremontii Group

Perennials with a thick rootstock. Blades of basal leaves divided as far as about ⁴⁄₅; divisions rather broad, with few coarse shallow lobes and teeth. At least the upper parts of the plant strongly glandular-hairy. Flowers strictly erect, usually pink or purplish, their stamens and long stigmas (4–6mm) curving outwards above the petals which are hairy across the front surface for about ¼ to ½ their length. Sepals with mucro not more than ¹⁄₈ of their length. Immature fruits erect on spreading or reflexed pedicels.

West North America, mainly in the Rocky Mountains but in the south spreading westwards and entering Mexico in Baja California. There are several species but the taxonomy of the group is difficult. The three species covered here are all said to have the hairs on the front surface of the petals restricted to the basal quarter (Jones & Jones, 1943) but this limit is commonly exceeded. The Richardsonii Group, which follows, is closely related.

58. G. nervosum Rydberg (*G. strigosum* Rydberg not N.L. Burman; *G. strigosius* St John; *G. viscosissimum* Fischer & Meyer var. *nervosum* (Rydberg) Hitchcock) (Figure 9.61)
Sticky-hairy aromatic perennial with rather broad leaf-divisions, usually with a single flowering stem, forking above; inflorescence diffuse; flowers erect, 24–40mm in diameter, pink or purplish red; petals notched, with dark veins and with hairs across front surface for about ⅓ of their length; stamens and stigmas curving outwards above the petals; immature fruits erect on erect, spreading or reflexed pedicels. Border, wild garden, sun. May onwards.

Perennial with a very stout deep woody rootstock. Blades of basal leaves 5–20cm wide, light green, divided as far as about ⁴/₅ into 7; divisions broadest above the middle, palmately lobed at apex, unlobed part of margin nearly straight; lobes up to 1½ times, or the central lobe twice, as long as broad, toothed, the outer teeth often bent outwards. Teeth and tips of lobes acute. Stem-leaves few, paired or the first two solitary, much smaller than the basal, the lowest with 5 divisions which are broadest about the middle, their lobes and teeth spreading or incurved, sometimes both on the same plant. Plant rather strongly hairy, hairs on upper parts mostly glandular and sticky, not purple. Stem solitary with a very long first internode, forming a diffusely branched inflorescence above. Peduncles mostly 1–3cm. Pedicels mostly 1–2 times as long as sepals. Flowers erect, flat. Sepals 7–10mm; mucro about 0.5–1.25mm. Petals 13–22 × 7–16mm, from about 1¼–2 times as long as broad, some of them more or less notched at apex, abruptly enlarged just above the base, pale or deep pink, usually fading to white at base, with weak or strong darker, forking veins; base with a dense tuft of hairs on the sides and on front surface and with more scattered hairs extending over basal ⅓–½ of front surface. Filaments slightly longer than sepals, curving outwards above, slightly and evenly enlarged towards base, pink, bearing rather coarse hairs over most of their length; anthers yellow with purple edges, or pink. A more or less distinct tuft of hairs present over each nectary. Style about as long as sepals; stigmas 4–6mm, reddish, widely spreading. Immature fruits erect on erect, spreading or reflexed pedicels. Rostrum 21–35mm, including stylar portion 2–5mm. Mericarps about 5.5mm. Discharge: seed-ejection (bristles).

Figure 9.61 *G. nervosum*, Vancouver B.G., 1978, coll. Canada: Botanic Valley, British Columbia, × ½

West North America (British Columbia and Alberta to N. California and Colorado).

This species is of moderate interest for the border and, in its smaller forms, for the larger rock garden. It is very variable; thus the leaf-shape may vary, the lower stem hairs may be spreading or appressed, and the petals have a large range in size and they vary in shape independently of this. The name *G. incisum* (Torrey & Gray) Brewer & Watson belongs strictly to 55. *G. oreganum*, but for a long period American authors applied it in error to the present plant, which doubtless explains why Bloom's Nurseries, of Diss, Norfolk, have offered *G. nervosum* as *G. incisum*. Bloom's stock is a rather small neat form with the hairs of the lower parts appressed, those of the upper parts short, and with well-coloured flowers of moderate size; it is certainly the most garden-worthy variant out of four that I have seen. I have had it in flower as early as May and as late as November.

Propagation of *G. nervosum* is by seed or by division of the rootstock; it may not be possible to obtain pieces with adequate young root-growth, and careful nursing will then be necessary.

59. *G. viscosissimum* Fischer & Meyer (Figure 9.62)

Similar to 58. *G. nervosum* but stems glandular-hairy from the base up, basal leaves apparently larger; inflorescence beyond the first fork with some greatly contracted branches and suppressed peduncles, producing umbel-like clusters of flowers accompanied by cymules with more or less reduced peduncles; pedicels longer, 4–8 times as long as sepals, strongly reflexed under the erect immature fruits; sepals to 12mm, with mucro 1–1.5mm. Stylar portion of rostrum about 6mm. Discharge: seed-ejection (bristles). June and again later.

Figure 9.62 *G. viscosissimum*, Alpine Garden Soc., 1965, coll. USA: Wyoming, × ²/₃

West North America (British Columbia and Alberta to N. California and South Dakota).

My acquaintance with this species is limited to one stock obtained from the Alpine Garden Society in 1965, originating from seed collected in Wyoming. It is a most beautiful plant, at least in the earlier stages of flowering, as it has large flattish pale pink, finely veined flowers with a white centre. The petals are up to 23 × 19mm. It may flower repeatedly through the season. Because of the amount of variation in both *G. viscosissimum* and *G. nervosum*, it is said by

American authors that the two cannot always be distinguished, and some prefer to treat *G. nervosum* as a variety of *G. viscosissimum*.

60. *G. fremontii* Gray (*G. parryi* (Engelmann) Heller) (Figure 9.63, Plate 22)

Sticky-hairy, unpleasantly scented perennial; blades of main leaves divided as far as ¾; divisions with few coarse lobes and teeth at apex; inflorescence diffuse, leafy, prolifically branched; flowers 35–40mm in diameter, like those of 58. *G. nervosum*. Border, sun. June onwards.

Perennial with thick rootstock, more branched than in 58. *G. nervosum* and 59. *G. viscosissimum*. Blades of basal leaves 5–10cm wide, divided as far as ¾ into 5 or 7; divisions broadest near apex, sides of the three middle ones concave in the lower unlobed part, lobed at apex for ¹/₅–¹/₄ of their length; lobes mostly broader than long, usually with one or two teeth of which the outermost on each division are bent outwards. Teeth and tips of lobes obtuse or acute. Stem-leaves numerous, paired or the first one or two solitary, decreasing gradually in size and length of stalk upwards, with 3 or 5 very coarsely lobed divisions. Hairs glandular except on upper leaf-surfaces and sometimes stalks of basal leaves and lower internodes. Flowering stems usually several together, with mostly paired branches, forming an extensive and diffuse inflorescence. Cymules sometimes 3-flowered, upper often with short or suppressed peduncles. Pedicels mostly 2½–4 times as long as sepals. Flowers the same as those of 58. *G. nervosum*, with petals not less than 16mm, sometimes clearly notched. Immature fruits erect on

Figure 9.63 *G. fremontii*, P.F. Yeo, 1973, coll. USA: Colorado, × ²/₃

spreading or strongly reflexed pedicels. Rostrum about 18mm, including stylar portion about 3mm. Mericarps 4.5mm. Discharge: seed-ejection (bristles).

West North America (Wyoming to New Mexico and Arizona).

I have grown two stocks of this species from the Rocky Mountains in the neighbourhood of Boulder, Colorado, one collected by me in 1973 and one by the late Professor H.E. Moore at the same time; the first had strongly coloured and veined flowers, and the second rather washy pink flowers. I have only grown them in open beds in dry Cambridge soil. They make big root-stocks, partly above the ground, and these tend to die off in parts, sometimes leaving the surviving crowns imperfectly rooted. Frequent re-planting therefore seems advisable to keep the plants in good growth. *G. fremontii* can be quite showy, and flowers for a long time, but is rather ungainly in habit.

I have indicated *G. parryi* as a synonym of *G. fremontii*, of which it was originally described as a variety. The distinguishing characters given by Jones & Jones (1943) are mixed contrarily in my plants, which seems to rule out recognition of *G. parryi* not only as a species but also as a variety.

The Richardsonii Group

Similar to The Fremontii Group but leaf-divisions tending to be more gradually tapered beyond the widest part, and with lobes and teeth not curved outwards. Sepal mucro usually more than 1/8 the length of the sepal. Petals white to lavender, hairs on front surface extending from base for 1/2–3/4 the length of the petal. Stigmas 3–5mm.

West North America from British Columbia to Mexico.

Jones & Jones (1943) deal with two Californian species that they consider closely related to *G. richardsonii*. Moore (1943) mentions one Mexican species (*G. albidum* Hanks & Small) as being closely related to *G. richardsonii*; this itself is a member of his series *Lata*, containing four species. Thus there could be seven species in the group. The white petals of *G. richardsonii* turn pale yellow on drying, but I do not know whether this is true of other white-flowered members of the group.

61. *G. richardsonii* Fischer & Trautvetter (Figure 9.64, Plate 23)

Perennial, 30–60cm tall, with bright green, slightly glossy and inconspicuously hairy leaves. Inflorescence diffuse. Flowers about 24–28mm in diameter; petals white or tinged pink, usually lightly purple-veined, not usually notched. Stigmas greenish or yellowish. Wild garden, water garden, sun. May onwards.

Perennial with a thick rootstock. Blades of basal leaves 5–10cm wide, divided as far as 2/3 or 5/6 into 5 or 7; divisions tapered gradually or abruptly both ways from above the middle, lobed at apex for 1/3 of their length or slightly more; lobes slightly shorter to slightly longer than broad, sparsely toothed. Teeth and tips of lobes broadly pointed to acute, rather symmetric. Stem-leaves paired or the first one solitary, numerous, decreasing gradually to a very small size, divisions 5 or 3, then with the middle one much the largest. Plant less hairy than species 58.–60.; non-glandular hairs more or less appressed; glandular hairs red-tipped, dense in the inflorescence. Stems solitary or few together, rather regularly forking, forming an extensive and diffuse inflorescence. Peduncles mostly 2–6cm. Pedicels mostly 1½–4 times as long as sepals. Flowers erect, flat. Sepals about 6mm; mucro about 1.5mm. Petals 12 × 6–18 × 15mm (i.e. variable in shape), rounded at apex, white or sometimes pale pink, with or without faint purple veins; base strongly hairy all over front surface, hairs sparser upwards but extending 1/2–3/4 the length of the petal. Filaments curving outwards above, moderately and evenly enlarged towards base, bearing rather coarse hairs over most of their length. Anthers lilac or greyish. Stigmas 3–4mm, greenish or yellowish. Immature fruits erect on erect, spreading or reflexed pedicels. Rostrum 13–17mm, including stylar portion about 1mm. Mericarps about 3.5mm. Discharge: seed-ejection (bristles).

West North America (British Columbia and Saskatchewan to South Dakota, New Mexico and California).

Two stocks are known to me from cultivation in Cambridge. One was received from Mr Jan Stephens in 1969 and is the same as a plant I saw at Kew in 1971: it is relatively low-growing and bushy, but has small flowers with narrow petals, which have the veins translucent pink. The other was grown from seed collected by me in Colorado in 1973; it has much finer flowers with broad rounded petals and a taller habit.

Figure 9.64 *G. richardsonii*, P.F. Yeo, 1973, coll. USA: Colorado, × ½

In nature *G. richardsonii* is decidedly variable; it grows in damp places and should be tried in water gardens in this country. The rootstock tends to develop in the same way as that of 60. *G. fremontii* and re-planting should therefore be carried out with similar frequency.

The Bellum Group

Perennials with few or no basal leaves. Blades of main leaves divided nearly to the base into 3, 5 or 7; divisions pinnately lobed; lobes sometimes pinnately toothed. Hairs eglandular. Inflorescence diffuse. Petals rounded or slightly notched; hairs at the base variable. Stigmas 3–7mm.

South and Central Mexico and Guatemala.

Moore (1943) named informally a series *Bella* comprising seven species including *G. schiedeanum*, described here. I have followed him in basing the name of this group on *G. bellum* Rose. Some other species of this group, together with *G. alpicola* Loesener in Moore's series *Nivea*, could be useful rock garden plants.

62. *G. schiedeanum* Schlechtendal (*G. purpusu* Knuth) (Figure 9.65)

Rather low-growing perennial; blades of principal leaves 5–10cm wide, their divisions narrow at base and enormously widened at the middle or above, pinnately lobed and with the teeth arranged pinnately on the lobes, wrinkled and slightly glossy above, very pale beneath and made more so by the dense hair-clothing;

flowers about 30mm in diameter; petals not notched, lavender. Rock garden, front of border, ground-cover, sun. June to September.

Rootstock thick, forming short horizontal rhizomes and bearing large swollen roots. Basal leaves few; basal and lower stem-leaves rounded or kidney-shaped in outline, divided into 5 or 7, the middle division free nearly to the base, the others separated for ²/₃–¾ of their length; divisions overlapping one another, broadest near the middle, pinnately lobed, margins of unlobed portion with concave profile; lobes about 1½ times as long as wide, widely spreading, enormously increasing the width of the division, most of them pinnately toothed with teeth of almost equal size on either side; upper surface slightly glossy, wrinkled, recurved at edges, lower very pale, not entirely on account of the dense hair-covering running along veins and margins. Teeth and tips of lobes acute or blunt with a small point. Stem-leaves mostly paired, upper similar to lower, lobes of basal divisions often without teeth. Plant without glandular hairs. Stems slender, reddish; branches solitary, paired or in threes, forming a diffuse inflorescence. Cymules with one or, usually, two flowers. Peduncles mostly 6–12cm but up to 18 or even 28cm. Pedicels 1–4 times as long as sepals. Flowers erect. Sepals 6–7mm; mucro 1–1.5mm. Petals about 15–16 × 12–13mm, broadest near apex, rounded or faintly notched, evenly tapered to base, medium purplish violet, white at extreme base, veins pink; base with a

Figure 9.65 *G. schiedeanum*, Logan B.G., 1974, × ¾

well-developed tuft of hairs on either edge and sometimes a few hairs in a narrow band across front surface. Filaments slightly longer than sepals, curving outwards above, white, slightly enlarged at base and here stiffly hairy. Style less than $^2/_3$ as long as sepals. Stigmas 3.5–4mm, pink and with a few coarse hairs on back, yellowish on front. Immature fruits erect on usually erect pedicels. Rostrum about 18mm, with stylar portion scarcely 1mm. Mericarps 3–4mm. Discharge: seed-ejection (bristles).

Mexico (San Luis Potosí to Vera Cruz and Oaxaca).

The natural altitudinal range of G. schiedeanum is 3,500–11,000 feet (1,050–3,350m), with most occurrences between 6,000 and 10,000 feet (1,800 and 3,050 m).

Moore (1943) described considerable variation in G. schiedeanum and placed four other specific names as synonyms of it. The leaves are not always twice pinnately cut, as described here, and the flower colour can be purple, red-purple, and perhaps white, as well as lavender as in our plant (which is near RHSCC Violet Group 87B).

The plant cultivated at Cambridge was first seen by me in 1974; it was then growing un-labelled at Logan Botanic Garden, Wigtown-shire, Scotland, a satellite of the Royal Botanic Garden, Edinburgh. The above description is almost entirely based on this cultivated material.

G. schiedeanum is a rather attractive plant, and suitable for a warm situation on the rock garden. In the spring of 1979 it was very late in starting into growth; as we had had severe cold and a long period of repeated thawing and freezing I suspect the only surviving growth at the end of the winter was several inches below ground. In 1982 the plant came up at a normal time despite lower temperatures in the preceding winter, and I believe this was caused by the long-lasting snow-cover. The rootstock can easily be divided. I have never been able to obtain viable seed from plants growing at Cambridge.

A plant with leaves like ours was cultivated at Darmstadt, Germany, early in the present century, and was made the basis of G. purpusii Knuth, one of the names reduced to the synonymy of G. schiedeanum by Moore (1943).

Section Dissecta, The Dissectum Section

Plants annual, biennial or perennial. Retention of seed in mericarp during the pre-explosive interval by a part of the mericarp wall which projects as a prong. Awn remaining attached to central column of rostrum after discharge.

Three species of Europe and W. Asia.

63. G. asphodeloides N.L. Burman

Biennial or perennial with stout rootstock and many thick roots. Blades of leaves divided as far as $^2/_3$ or $^5/_6$ into 5 or 7; divisions broadest above the middle, sometimes at the apex. Stem-leaves paired. Plant with at least some glandular hairs. Inflorescence diffuse, leafy. Flowers 23–34mm in diameter. Sepals 6–8mm, noticeably narrow; mucro from less than 1mm to 2mm. Petals 1½–2½ times as long as wide; base with a dense tuft of hairs on either edge but without hairs across front surface. Filaments distinctly enlarged below and with fine hair-fringes towards the base. Stigmas about 1mm or less. Rostrum 14–19mm including distinct stylar portion 4–5mm long. Mericarps 2.5–3mm. Discharge: seed-ejection (prong).

As this species is divisible into three subspecies, a condensed description, intended to distinguish it from other species, is given above. The three subspecies are treated below in accordance with their horticultural importance.

63a. G. asphodeloides subsp. asphodeloides (G. pallens Bieberstein) (Figure 9.66, Plate 24)

Perennial with bushy growth; stem-leaves with irregularly and sharply cut divisions; petals usually 2–3 times as long as broad, pale to deep pink, with usually strong darker veins, or white. Rock garden, wild garden, sun. June to August.

Basal leaves few, their blades up to about 8cm wide, divided as far as $^2/_3$–¾ into 5 or 7; divisions broadest at or near apex, lobed at apex for about ⅓ of their length, broad, straight-sided; lobes shallowly toothed. Teeth and tips of lobes obtuse or obtusish. Stem-leaves numerous, usually divided as far as $^4/_5$–$^5/_6$ into 5; divisions broadest above the middle, usually 3-lobed; lobes up to about 2½ times as long as wide, acute, more or less toothed; teeth acute. Eglandular hairs mostly small and appressed; glandular hairs with red tips present on pedicels, sepals and rostra, sometimes also on peduncles or all stems and leaf-stalks. Flowers flat. Sepals 6–7mm, widely spreading, more or less flushed with pink; mucro usually 1mm or less. Petals 10–15 × 4.5–7mm, twice as long as wide or more, rarely up to 8.5mm wide and only 1½ times as long as wide, not so widely spreading as sepals, rounded or faintly notched at apex, broadest at middle or apex, usually pale pink with darker veins running most of their length but also deep pink or white. Filaments coloured as the petals; anthers bluish. Stigmas red.

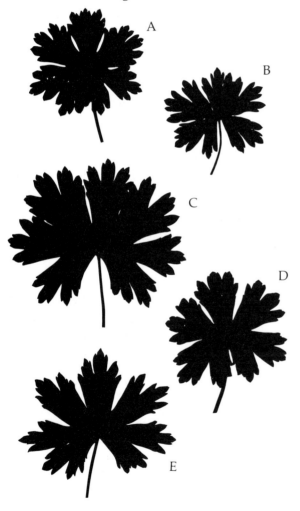

Figure 9.66 G. asphodeloides subsp. asphodeloides, E.M. Rix, 1971, coll. Turkey: Cankiri Prov. (Fraser-Jenkins 2188); (A) & (B) two plants, May; (C) & (D) two plants, November; (E) R. Gorer, 1974, coll. Greece: Lower Pindus; all × ²⁄₃

South Europe from Sicily eastwards to Crimea and Caucasus; N. Iran; Turkey; absent from Crete and Cyprus.

G. asphodeloides is easily distinguishable as being the larger-flowered of the only two widespread species with the prong arrangement for retention of the seed in the pre-explosive phase of discharge. However, it is also distinctive in the narrow sepals which, together with the stamens and style, seem small in relation to the size of the petals, and in its short stigmas. The plant forms big clumps, easily divided up. It flowers abundantly despite the diffuse inflorescence, and has a long season.

Subspecies *asphodeloides* is the most common and widespread subspecies of *G. asphodeloides* and is highly variable. In a sample grown from seed collected in Çankiri Province, Turkey, by Dr C.R. Fraser-Jenkins, in 1970, I raised plants with pink petals of differing shades and with white petals, and with varying shapes, colours and textures in the leaves. Mr Richard Gorer collected a vigorous, dark-flowered, broad-petalled plant at Karpenisi in the Lower Pindus of Greece and presented it to Cambridge in 1974. Perhaps the most beautiful form is one obtained by Mr Jan Stephens from Mrs B.C. Rogers as *G. pallens* and passed on to Cambridge in 1970; it has pale lilac petals with fine dark stripes. It is also unusual in that its stems and leaf-stalks are glandular-hairy throughout. *G. pallens* is the name used for *G. asphodeloides* in *Flora of the USSR* (Bobrov, 1949).

63b. G. asphodeloides subsp. *crenophilum* (Boissier) Bornmüller (Figures 9.67 A & B)
Differs from 63a. subsp. *asphodeloides* in having more erect stems, numerous basal leaves, often more than 10cm wide, with blades almost circular in outline, and stem-leaves similar to the basal, with divisions broadest at the apex and lobes up to only about 1½ times as long as broad; in having glandular hairs on all vegetative parts and on the sepals and rostra, the hairs not being tipped with red; and in having the flowers slightly funnel-shaped at the base, the sepals 7–8mm long and the petals broad and deep rose-pink.

Lebanon, Syria.

Superficially quite a lot different from subsp. *asphodeloides*, this subspecies tends to build its rootstock up above ground and needs re-planting from time to time. It can be propagated by division or seed. It seems quite hardy out of doors at Cambridge. In the form of its flowers it might be judged better than the starry subsp. *asphodeloides* but it lacks the individuality of the latter. It was twice collected in the Kidisha Gorge, Lebanon, by the late Mr W.K. Aslet.

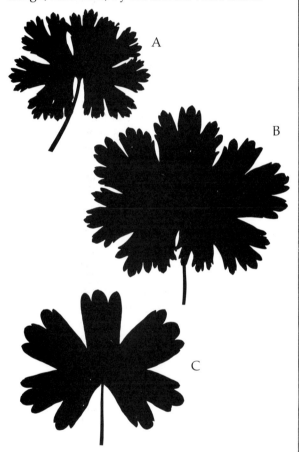

Figure 9.67 *G. asphodeloides*: (A) subsp. *crenophilum*, J. Stephens, 1969, coll. Lebanon: Kidisha Gorge (Aslet), March (greenhouse), × ²/₃ ; (B) the same, a larger leaf, May (greenhouse), × ¹/₂; (C) subsp. *sintenisii*, Mrs J. Forty, 1980, from a young fast-growing plant, × ²/₃

63c. G. asphodeloides subsp. sintenisii (Freyn) Davis (Figure 9.67C)
Perennial, forming a mass of leaves with blades between 5 and 20cm wide. Basal leaves rather like those of subsp. *crenophilum*, stem-leaves more different from the basal than in the latter, less so than in subsp. *asphodeloides*; stems, leaf-stalks, undersides of leaves, sepals and rostra

more or less covered with red-tipped glandular hairs. Inflorescence very prolific. Petals up to 13mm long, pale pink or sometimes deep purple.

North Turkey.

I received seeds of the pink form of this from Mrs Joy Forty in 1980. They were sown that autumn and some plants were exposed to the winter but none flowered in 1981, though all did in 1982. However, seeds sown in 1982 produced flowering plants in 1983. The flowers were pale pink and the petals wrinkled.

HYBRIDS. A reported hybrid of *G. asphodeloides* with 76. *G. bohemicum* (in section *Tuberosa*) is discussed in Chapter 7. Within *G. asphodeloides*, hybrids between subsp. *asphodeloides* and subsp. *crenophilum* have occurred spontaneously at Cambridge; except in flower-colour (see Chapter 7) they were intermediate between the parents; their glandular hairs were partly red-tipped and partly not.

64. G. dissectum Linnaeus
A low-growing annual with stem-leaves deeply cut into narrow segments. Cymules not longer than subtending leaves (a distinction from 46. *G. columbinum*). Glandular hairs usually present above. Petals 6mm or less, deeply notched, usually deep pink. Weed.

Annual, usually overwintering. Blades of basal leaves not usually more than 5cm wide, divided as far as ¾ or ⁵/₆ into 7; divisions broadest at apex. Stem-leaves paired, their blades not more than 10cm wide, divided into 5 as far as ⁷/₈ or nearly to the base, deeply cut into segments 2–10mm wide; divisions broadest about the middle, pinnately lobed; lobes about 3–10 times as long as broad, with teeth of similar proportions. Glandular hairs usually present in upper parts. Inflorescence made up of dense clusters. Cymules (excluding rostra) not longer than the subtending leaves. Lower peduncles up to about 5cm, upper about same length as pedicels. Pedicels 1–1½ times, or the lowest up to 2½ times, as long as sepals. Sepals 5–6mm; mucro about 1–1.5mm. Petals about 4.5–6 × 3mm, deeply notched at apex, deep pink or occasionally pale pink; base with hairs on either edge but not across front surface. Filaments about ²/₃ as long as sepals, greatly enlarged downwards from a point just below the apex, with fine hair-fringes on enlarged part. Anthers bluish. Stigmas less than 0.5mm, reddish. Rostrum 12–13mm, with a distinct stylar portion 1–2mm long. Discharge: seed-ejection (prong).

Europe and W. Asia; widely naturalised elsewhere.

G. dissectum is reliably distinguished from other small species with similar leaves which occur in various parts of the world by the fruit-type. It has no garden value.

Section Tuberosa, The Tuberosum Section

Annual, biennial or perennial. Eglandular hairs of sepals much longer than half the width of the sepal. Petals more or less notched, base without hairs across front surface but with a tuft of fine hairs (rarely a mere fringe) on either edge. Stamen filaments with large hairs. Immature fruits erect on erect pedicels. Stigmas not more than 2.5mm. Retention of seed in the mericarp during the pre-explosive interval by a twist at the junction of awn and mericarp, so that the orifice faces sideways. Awn not remaining attached to central column after discharge.

Mediterranean Region, W. Asia as far as Kashmir; annual and biennial species extending north to S. Scandinavia.

The section is easily divided into two groups which are best characterised separately.

Subsection Tuberosa, The Tuberosum Group

Perennial. Rootstock an underground tuber, usually horizontal; adjacent tubers linked together by slenderer sections of rhizome. Plants becoming dormant in summer after flowering. Leaf-blades deeply cut, at least the incisions on either side of the middle division usually reaching to top of leaf-stalk, middle division usually distinctly smaller than those on either side of it; segments mostly narrow. Most of the cymules without peduncles. Petals usually pink. Filaments rather evenly enlarged towards base, usually with moderate-sized hairs on margins in addition to the large ones.

Ten species in the Mediterranean Region and W. Asia. Some are sometimes treated as subspecies, as here, reducing the number to a minimum of six. Of these, four are treated here.

The members of this group occur naturally in areas of summer drought; they are precociously flowering, coming up rapidly in spring and typically producing the first cymule at the first or second node. Examples grown at Cambridge seem to be infertile to their own pollen. Davis (1970) states that several species are composed of both normal, hermaphrodite, plants and female plants (the condition called gynodioecism). In this connection, see remarks under 65. *G. tuberosum.*

65. *G. tuberosum* Linnaeus (*G. stepporum* Davis) (Figure 9.68A)

Leaves with at least the three middle divisions free to the base or nearly so; divisions deeply cut into numerous narrow entire or narrowly toothed lobes; flowers about 20–30mm in diameter; petals purplish rose with darker veins, notched; stylar portion of rostrum about 1mm. Leafy in spring. Rock garden. May.

Tuber 7–15mm thick. Blades of basal leaves 5–10cm wide, with 7 divisions, the middle one free to the base, and usually also those either side of it, deeply cut into segments 3mm wide or less; divisions broadest about the middle, overlapping, pinnately lobed throughout most of their length; lobes numerous, about 2–4 times as long as broad, the larger ones with scattered narrow teeth. Teeth and tips of lobes acute. Stem-leaves paired, those at the first or first and second nodes usually similar to the basal, thereafter nearly or quite stalkless and with narrowly lanceolate divisions with scattered narrow lobes or close-set short lobes forming a saw-edge, decreasing in size gradually. Plant without glandular hairs. Stems erect. Branches partly paired and partly solitary. All or most of the cymules with the peduncle suppressed. Pedicels about 1½–3½ times as long as sepals. Sepals 5–8mm, flushed with purple, especially within; mucro 1mm or less. Petals 9–17 × 7–13mm, broadest well above the middle, deeply notched between rounded lobes, bright rose-purple, with dark veins slightly forking at tips; base with a tuft of hairs on either edge but without hairs across front surface. Filaments considerably but evenly enlarged towards base, about the same colour as veins of petals, with rather sparse large hairs. Fertile anthers dark bluish. Stigmas about 2.5mm, usually strongly coiled, crimson. Rostrum about 17mm, stylar portion about 1mm, indistinct. Discharge: seed-ejection (twist).

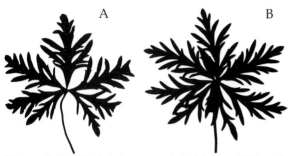

Figure 9.68 (A) *G. tuberosum*, A.P. Vlasto, 1963, coll. Yugoslavia: Zaroukhla valley, × ²/₃ ; (B) *G. macrostylum*, Miss J. Robinson, 1980, *ex* Sir Cedric Morris, × ²/₃

Mediterranean Region eastwards to W. Iran.

This is a common and variable species which behaves as a weed in cornfields and vineyards. The tubers multiply rapidly, and in Turkey are used for food. The above description is based on plants at Cambridge collected by Dr A.P. Vlasto in 1963 at Zaroukhla in Yugoslavia. A wide range of petal-sizes has been observed in this stock, which is probably one clone. The smallest flowers which I have seen on it appeared in 1971; none of them had well-formed anthers. In 1972 all flowers were larger than those of 1971 but some which had most of the anthers fertile were larger than the others. In this stock the petals do not overlap and are somewhat contracted towards the base, revealing the coloured sepals between them.

European plants belong to subsp. *tuberosum* which, however, occupies most of the range of the species. Overlapping with its W. Asiatic range, but extending further east, is *G. tuberosum* subsp. *linearifolium* (Boissier) Davis, in which the lobes of the basal leaves are untoothed. The name *G. stepporum* Davis refers to this latter plant, but after publishing it the author chose, on the basis of further study, to treat it as a subspecies (Davis, 1967). Another subspecies, *G. tuberosum* subsp. *micranthum* Schönbeck-Temesy, was described in *Flora Iranica* (Schönbeck-Temesy, 1970).

66. G. macrostylum Boissier (Figures 9.68B & 9.69)

Similar to 65. *G. tuberosum*, but covered in the upper parts with glandular hairs and with smaller leaves and flowers, the latter about 20mm in diameter; petals pale pink, with darker base; stylar portion of rostrum 1.5–2.5mm. Leafy in autumn, winter and spring. Rock garden. May.

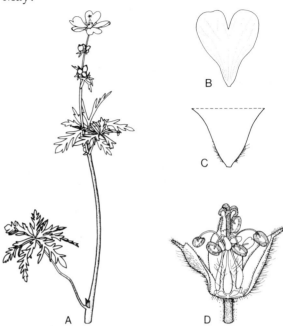

Figure 9.69 *G. macrostylum* (Miss J. Robinson, 1980, *ex* Sir Cedric Morris). (A) shoot at beginning of flowering, × ¹/₂ ; (B) petal, showing dark pigmentation,×1¹/₂ ; (C) base of front surface of petal,×3¹/₂ ; (D) flower in male stage with petals and two sepals removed,×3¹/₂; the anthers of the outer whorl of this flower were abortive

Differs from 65. *G. tuberosum* as follows: tubers mostly elongated, 5–10mm thick; blades of basal leaves scarcely more than 5cm wide; stem-leaves above the first or second nodes not more than about 1cm long; upper parts of plant covered with red-tipped glandular hairs; sepals 4–5mm; petals about 8mm, flimsy, pale pink with indistinct veins converging to form a darker zone at base; rostrum with stylar portion 1.5–2.5mm. Discharge: seed-ejection (twist).

Greece, Albania, S. Yugoslavia, C. and S.W. Turkey.

A pretty species which I have grown only in pans. It came from Miss J. Robinson of Boxford, Suffolk, who regards it as a pest in her garden, the tubers being small and easily scattered. The same stock was naturalised in the garden of the late Sir Cedric Morris at Hadleigh, Suffolk. My description is based only on the above stock, except for that of the fruit which is taken from the literature.

67. *G. linearilobum* De Candolle (Figure 9.70)

Blades of basal leaves with the middle division free to the base and often particularly small, the lateral joined for about $^{1}/_{6}$–$^{1}/_{4}$ of their length, divisions very variable; stem with one or two solitary leaves before the first pair, flowers about 30mm in diameter; petals deeply notched, pink, strongly veined; rostrum with stylar portion 1.5–3mm. Leaves present in spring. Rock garden. May.

Blades of basal leaves up to 10cm wide, with 7 or 9 divisions, middle one particularly small, free to the base, others joined for about $^{1}/_{6}$–$^{1}/_{4}$ of their length; divisions either (a) pinnately lobed with few, widely divergent untoothed lobes up to about 6 times as long as wide, the lowest lateral ones arising just below the middle of the division and being not more than half as long as the central one, or (b) pinnately lobed only above the middle with less divergent lobes up to about 4 times as long as wide and usually toothed, the lateral much more than half as long as the central. First one or two stem-leaves solitary, others paired, usually changing gradually in form, size and length of stalk upwards, their lobes without teeth, the divisions of the uppermost without lobes. Plant without glandular hairs. Cymules mostly or all stalkless. Sepals about 6.5mm, green; mucro 1mm or less. Petals 13–15 × 12–13mm, overlapping at their widest part, bright pink with bold, slightly forked, darker veining. Stamens, when not aborted, pink. Stigmas dark red. Rostrum up to 18mm with stylar portion 1.5–3mm. Discharge: seed-ejection (twist).

Southern Russia, Caucasus, N. and W. Iran, E. Turkey, Soviet Central Asia.

This species was introduced by Mr R.F. Hunter in 1980; he collected it in the Tschim Gan (Chimgan) Valley near Tashkent, and again about 6 miles (10 km) south of Alma Ata. Dr Martyn Rix took a photograph of it at the former locality (see Rix & Phillips, 1981, p. 65); this shows basal leaves of the type (b) of my description, but extraordinarily different stem-leaves with entire divisions 10 or 12 times as long as wide, which have not appeared on the plant in

cultivation (and are not mentioned in the above description). The basal leaves are the same as on the cultivated plant and fall within the range of variation described by Davis (1970) for *G. linearilobum* subsp. *transversale* (Karelin & Kirilow) Davis. The leaves of type (a) in my description are found on Mr Hunter's Alma Ata plant; they correspond with Davis' description of subsp. *linearilobum*, but that subspecies occurs only in the western part of the range of the species, and these specimens were collected near its eastern limit. However, I have not studied herbarium specimens of this subspecies and, on account of their origin, both cultivated stocks ought to be referred to subsp. *transversale* for the present. For horticultural purposes it may eventually prove unimportant to distinguish

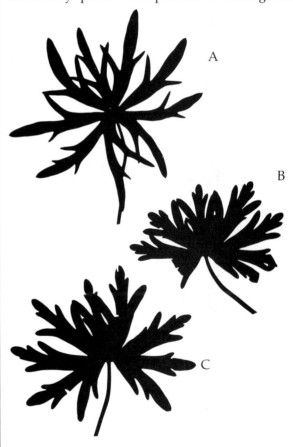

Figure 9.70 *G. linearilobum* subsp. *transversale*: (A) R.F. Hunter, 1980, coll. USSR: S. of Alma Ata, Kazakhstan; (B) & (C) R.F. Hunter, 1980, coll. USSR: Tschim Gan (Chimgan), near Tashkent, × $^{2}/_{3}$

subspecies within *G. linearilobum* (which, incidentally, is not to be confused with *G. tuberosum* subsp. *linearifolium* (Boissier) Davis).

68. *G. malviflorum* Boissier & Reuter (Figure 9.71, Plate 25)

Blades of basal leaves mostly 6–10cm wide (larger than in other members of The Tuberosum Group), the middle division free to the base, the others shortly joined; divisions freely pinnately lobed from near the base, and the lowest lobes pinnately toothed; flowers about 35–45mm in diameter; petals heart-shaped, violet-blue or purplish, veiny. Leaves present in spring, sometimes also in autumn and winter. Rock garden, border. April, May.

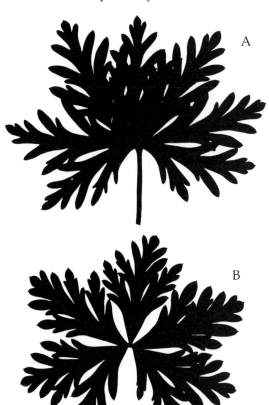

Figure 9.71 *G. malviflorum*, J. Stephens, 1966, as *G. atlanticum*: (A) March; (B) November, × ²/₃

Tubers up to 6 × 1.5cm, spindle-shaped. Blades of basal leaves mostly between 10 and 15cm wide, with 7 divisions, the middle one free to the base; divisions broadest about the middle, overlapping, pinnately lobed to within 3–1.5mm of the midrib for most of their length or from just below the middle; lobes numerous, mostly 2–5 times as long as broad, the lower ones pinnately toothed, some without teeth. Stem-leaves paired, the first pair similar to the basal, thereafter abruptly reduced in size and in complexity of lobing, and stalkless or nearly so. Plant without glandular hairs. Stems erect. Branches paired, the first pair subtended by the first leaves. Many of the cymules without peduncles. Pedicels up to about 3 times as long as sepals. Flowers saucer-shaped at first. Sepals 7–9mm, flushed with violet; mucro about 1.5mm. Petals 16–22mm, about ⁴/₅ as broad as long, heart-shaped, overlapping or contiguous, violet-blue or violet, with strong darker veins forking near tips, obliterated towards the base; base with a tuft of hairs on either edge but without hairs across front surface. Filaments purplish, evenly enlarged towards base, with rather sparse large hairs. Anthers cream with black edges, becoming blue-black. Stigmas about 1.5mm, deep red. Rostrum 20–22mm, with stylar portion 3–5mm. Discharge: seed-ejection (twist).

S. Spain, Morocco, Algeria.

This magnificent blue-flowered species often goes under the name *G. atlanticum* Boissier, having been illustrated under that name in error in the authoritative *Curtis's Botanical Magazine* (Hooker, 1879). Most plants in cultivation, including a stock at Cambridge, are probably a clone descended from the Algerian plant there depicted. Leaf-divisions which are pinnately lobed only from just below the middle upwards instead of from near the base appear on these plants in autumn. A second clone grown at Cambridge was collected by Mr Richard Gorer in Ronda, S. Spain. It differs in not sending up its leaves until early spring, and in having the sides of the lobes and teeth edged with purplish brown, in flowering later and in having the flowers less blue. Regardless of when the leaves come up, *G. malviflorum* becomes dormant after flowering. The amount of flower produced in cultivation may vary from year to year, and in some situations is persistently small. Other introductions, by Professor P.H. Davis, are cultivated at Edinburgh.

The true *G. atlanticum* is not a member of The Tuberosum Section and is not in cultivation in Britain at present.

Subsection Mediterranea, The Platypetalum Group

Annual, biennial or perennial, the last either green all summer or summer-dormant. Blades of main leaves not usually divided beyond $^7/_8$. Some of the cymules often without pedicels. Petals usually blue, with darker, usually feathered or netted veins. Filaments rather abruptly enlarged towards base, with minute hairs on enlarged part as well as the large, more generally distributed hairs.

Ten or eleven species, the perennials confined to Greece, Turkey, the Levant and the Caucasus; the one annual and one biennial scattered in S. and E. Europe and N.W. Africa.

69. G. platypetalum Fischer & Meyer (Figures 9.72 & 9.73)
Noticeably hairy perennial, up to about 40cm; main leaves rounded in outline, divided about half-way into 7 or 9; divisions broadest near apex with short, broad, freely toothed lobes; inflorescence dense; floral axis horizontal; flowers 30–45mm in diameter; petals usually notched, deep violet-blue with darker veins. Border, sun or partial shade. June and sometimes later.

Perennial with thick compact rootstock. Blades of basal leaves between 10 and 20cm wide, rounded, sometimes broader than long, wrinkled above, divided as far as about $^1/_2$ into 7 or 9; divisions broadest near apex, broader than long, lobed at apex for about $^1/_3$ of their length, sides of unlobed part convex to concave; lobes broader than long, mostly with a tooth on each side. Teeth and tips of lobes obtuse or broadly pointed. Stem-leaves paired, or a solitary one sometimes present near base, the upper with 3 or 5 divisions broadest near the middle, gradually reduced in size and length of stalk upwards. Glandular hairs of mixed lengths, some very long, present on much of the plant, exceeded in length by the eglandular hairs, but these scarce in the more glandular parts except for the sepals. Inflorescence dense, some or all the peduncles suppressed, longest up to 8cm. Pedicels not more than 3 times as long as sepals, both in one cymule sometimes shorter than sepals. Bracteoles 7–15mm. Floral axis horizontal. Flowers flat or saucer-shaped. Sepals 9–12mm; mucro 2–4.5mm. Petals 16–22 ×

13–19mm, notched or feebly 3-lobed at apex, broadest and sometimes recurved near apex, deep violet or blue-violet, usually slightly paler and pinkish at base, with very dark violet, embossed, glossy and forking veins. Filaments slightly curved outwards at tips at first, arching back towards petals later, with many long hairs, coloured like the petals, paler at base, which is distinctly enlarged and bears few or many minute hairs. Anthers blue-black. Stigmas about 2.5mm, dark red. Immature fruits erect on erect pedicels. Rostrum about 24–30mm, with stylar portion 4–5mm. Mericarps about 5mm. Discharge: seed-ejection (twist).

Caucasus Region, including N.E. Turkey and N.W. Iran.

Figure 9.73 G. platypetalum, E.M. Rix, 1971, coll. Turkey: Rize Prov. (Fraser-Jenkins 2355), × ½

G. platypetalum in Turkey grows in spruce woods and hazel scrub (Davis, 1967). Certain forms of this species in which the flowers are not too flat or too sombre make attractive perennials which may flower two or three times in a season.

HYBRIDS. G. platypetalum is a parent of the very commonly grown sterile hybrid, 71. G. ×magnificum. A hybrid with 73. G. renardii (q.v.) has also been found.

70. G. ibericum Cavanilles subsp. **ibericum** (Figure 9.74, Plate 26)
Noticeably hairy perennial, up to about 50cm; main leaves angular in outline, divided as far as $^2/_3$–$^7/_8$ into 9 or 11; divisions broadest near middle, overlapping, with deep complex lobing; flowers 40–48mm in diameter; petals

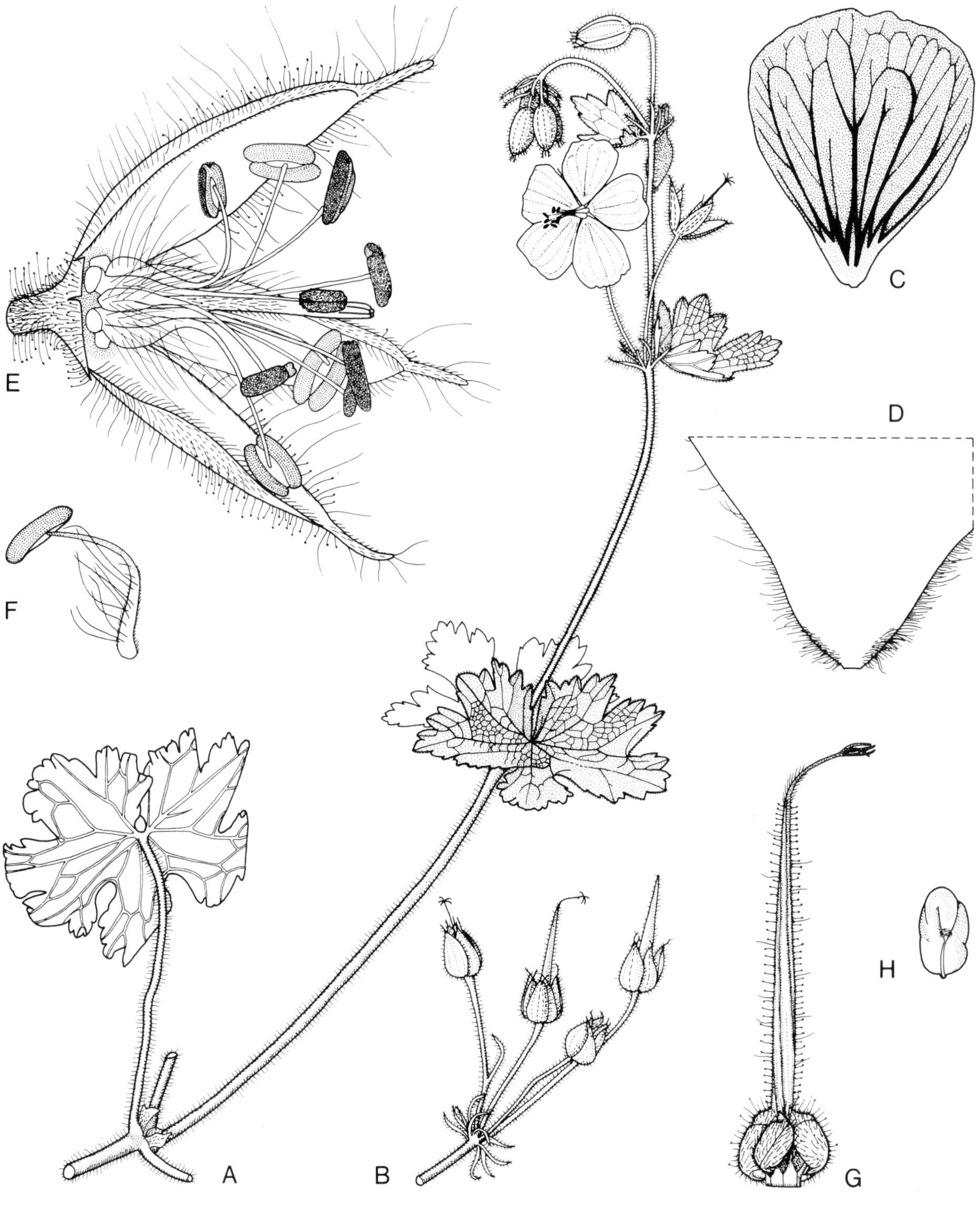

Figure 9.72 *G. platypetalum* (J. Stephens, 1969, *ex* Kew B.G.). (A) portion of flowering shoot, × ²/₃ ; (B) portion of inflorescence with immature fruit, × ²/₃ ; (C) petal, with pigmentation, × 2; (D) base of front surface of petal, × 4; (E) flower in male stage with petals and two stamens removed, × 4; (F) stamen of outer whorl seen obliquely from the back, × 4; (G) fruit in pre-explosive interval, × 2; (H) seed × 4

notched, violet-blue with feathered purplish veins. Border, sun. June.

Differs from 69. G. *platypetalum* in having blades of basal leaves divided as far as ¾–⁷/₈ (occasionally only ²/₃) into 9 or 11, divisions broadest just above the middle, palmato-pinnately lobed, the main lobes themselves lobed, the lobing and toothing continued down the sides of the divisions nearly to the base, the lobes about 1–2 times as long as broad, toothed, often turned outwards, teeth and tips of lobes acute; and in having stalkless upper stem-leaves, no glandular hairs, bracteoles 4.5–9mm long, few or no peduncles, upwardly inclined flowers, sepal mucro only 2–3mm, relatively narrower petals (about 24–26 x 16–17mm) and rostrum 27–35mm with stylar portion 4–7mm. Discharge: seed-ejection (twist).

Figure 9.74 G. *ibericum* subsp. *ibericum*, × ½

N.E. Turkey, Caucasus, perhaps N. Iran.

This plant is probably adapted to drier conditions than 69. G. *platypetalum*; it is perhaps handsomer too, partly because the flowers face upwards; it was highly commended at the Wisley Trial. At Cambridge there is an old stock of unknown origin and another from Western Armenia, supplied by the Erevan Botanic Garden. The latter tends to build its rootstock up above ground-level and to need occasional re-planting.

G. *ibericum* subsp. *ibericum* is not difficult to distinguish from 69. G. *platypetalum* but the situation is complicated by the existence of the hybrid between the two (71. G. ×*magnificum*) and of G. *ibericum* subsp. *jubatum* (see below).

The distinctions between subsp. *ibericum* and 71. G. ×*magnificum* are mentioned under the latter. G. *ibericum* subsp. *jubatum* (Handel-Mazzetti) Davis is not much (if at all) different in its leaves from subsp. *ibericum*; the bracts and sepal mucros are about the same length as in that and the petals are the same shape. However, the hairs on the pedicels are like those of G. ×*magnificum* and the stock at Cambridge resembles the typical clone of G. ×*magnificum* in having the floral axis horizontal and the petals bluer than in subsp. *ibericum*. The Cambridge plant of subsp. *jubatum* was collected in N.E. Turkey by Mr A.W.A. Baker, who presented a root to Cambridge in 1981. The subspecies is widespread in northern Turkey.

HYBRID. G. *ibericum* × G. *platypetalum* is dealt with next.

71. G. ×*magnificum* Hylander (Figures 9.75, 9.76 & 9.77, Plate 27)

Perennial up to 50–70cm or even more; similar to 70. G. *ibericum* subsp. *ibericum* but sterile (no ripe seed formed), petals a rich purplish violet, pedicels with rather uniform-length glandular hairs; distinguished from G. *ibericum* subsp. *jubatum* (see under no. 70) mainly by its sterility and greater vigour. Border, ground-cover, sun or partial shade. June.

Blades of basal leaves less angular than in 70. G. *ibericum* subsp. *ibericum*, sometimes broader than long (thus approaching 69. G. *platypetalum*), divisions very like those of G. *ibericum*, sometimes more abruptly tapered beyond the the widest part. Upper parts of stem and pedicels covered with both very long eglandular hairs (such hairs very sparse in 69. G. *platypetalum*) and abundant glandular hairs less than half their length (not of very variable length, as in G. *platypetalum*). Bracteoles 5–9mm. Floral axis horizontal to nearly erect. Flowers saucer-shaped. Petals 22–24 × 16–22mm, often with a point in the notch (its presence or absence varies from flower to flower). Stamens either normal or sometimes with yellowish anthers which do not burst. Some of the rostra often partly developed but not usually reaching full size and seeds not ripening; stylar portion 4–7mm.

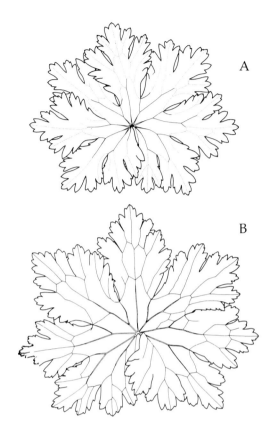

A

B

Figure 9.75 *G* × *magnificum*: (A) clone 'A', B. Wurzell, 1972; (B) clone 'C', cult. P.F. Yeo, 1983, × ½

Evidently a hybrid between 69. *G. platypetalum* and 70. *G. ibericum* subsp *ibericum*, but the time and place of its origin are unknown.

The foliage of this hybrid is very like that of *G. ibericum* and the plant is best distinguished by its failure to ripen seed. The mixture of moderately long glandular and very long eglandular hairs on the pedicels is also a good character provided one is comparing it with the eglandular *G. ibericum* subsp. *ibericum* and not with *G. ibericum* subsp. *jubatum* (see no. 70). *G. platypetalum* (no. 69) is moderately distinct in its leaves; its pedicels bear glandular hairs of very variable length, while the eglandular hairs among them that are longer than the glandular are very sparse. The petals of the hybrid range from a little wider than those of *G. ibericum* to about as wide as those of *G. platypetalum*. The very fine flower-colour no doubt reflects the qualities of both parents.

G. ×*magnificum* is perhaps the commonest member of its genus in gardens. It will gradually spread to fill the space available and may be left for years without attention. It produces a magnificent display when it is in flower but the season is rather short and I have never seen it flower a second time. The leaves may colour well in autumn, however. I know of three clones which I describe below after giving the history of the plant.

The name *G.* ×*magnificum* was given to this plant in 1961 by the late Dr Nils Hylander, of the Uppsala Botanic Garden, Sweden. In the course of building up a collection of *Geranium* he repeatedly obtained it under the name *G. platypetalum*, while the true *G. platypetalum* arrived from various botanic gardens under assorted names. Having noted its sterility and compared it with *G. platypetalum* and *G. ibericum* he concluded that it was a hybrid between the two. His published account of his investigations (Hylander, 1961) includes valid publication of the name for the hybrid. He obtained evidence from his own observations and from books and periodicals that *G.* ×*magnificum* was cultivated in various countries, including Britain. He could not find out when it first appeared but the earliest evidence for its existence was a herbarium specimen gathered in 1871 in the Botanic Garden of Geneva and preserved in the Botanical Museum at Uppsala.

Rather curiously, Hylander never went into the question of chromosome numbers, yet they had been investigated by Warburg (1938) working at Cambridge. Warburg found 28 chromosomes in *G. platypetalum* and 56 in a plant received as *G. ibericum* var. *talyshense* (this is a tetraploid but Warburg erroneously referred to it as a hexaploid). He also had what he called 'sterile *G. platypetalum*', different from the one with 28 chromosomes and, he stated, known in gardens as *G. ibericum*, *G. ibericum* var. *platypetalum* or *G. platypetalum*. He said he had never observed seed on this plant, and had failed to induce seed formation by pollinating it with other species. He considered that it agreed with the description of *G. platypetalum* but I feel no doubt that he had *G.* ×*magnificum*. It had 42 chromosomes (triploid) and from their behaviour Warburg thought it was a triploid derived by the crossing of two species (an allotriploid).

Figure 9.76 *G × magnificum*, clone 'B', Kew B.G., 1972, *ex* G.S. Thomas as *G. ibericum* var. *platypetalum*, × ½

In 1973 I obtained evidence that there are two clones of *G. ×magnificum* growing in Britain. When studying the living collection of *Geranium* at Kew in 1972 I had found a plant that had been received under the name *G. ibericum* var. *platypetalum* from Mr Graham Thomas. Suspecting that it was *G. ibericum* subsp. *jubatum* I requested a root, which was kindly sent to Cambridge early the following year. I grew it near a clump of what I regarded as *G. ×magnificum* and in 1973 I examined the chromosomes in the pollen mother-cell meiosis of both plants. Both were triploids, both showed chromosome behaviour which indicated allotriploidy (hybridity) and both were sterile.

In 1983 I became aware of the existence of a third clone, which appears to be less common than the first one described below (which may be called clone 'A') but more common than Mr Thomas's clone (clone 'B'), which I have not encountered again. I first noticed it in Mrs Joy Forty's garden at Woking and shall refer to it as clone 'C'.

Clifton (1979) proposed cultivar names ('Hylander' and 'Peter Yeo') for the two clones known to me at that time, but confused the characters of the plants (including that of the point in the notch of the petals which I mentioned to him but now think too variable for use). The two most widespread clones 'A' and 'C', are the most distinct; if in the future it is felt that they should be named, it will be important to choose names which are both apposite and internationally acceptable.

I am fairly certain that the apparently most widely distributed clone ('A') is the one which Hylander described as *G. ×magnificum* (he included a photograph of a herbarium specimen in his article), but it is difficult to give the characters of one clone without reference to the others, as is done below.

Clone 'A' (Figures 9.75A & 9.77A): blades of basal leaves very like those of *G. ibericum*, more deeply divided compared with clone 'B', with the divisions more gradually tapered beyond the widest part, deeper green, more wrinkled than in 'B' and 'C'; flowers more obviously grouped into clusters than in 'B' and 'C', with axis horizontal, petals broader and more overlapping than in 'B', less so than in 'C', but slightly recurved towards apex and margins, their dark-coloured veins less bold and more profusely branched than in 'C'; filaments white at base.

Clone 'B' (Figures 9.76 & 9.77B): blades of basal leaves with the shape of the divisions intermediate between those of clones 'A' and 'C', and perhaps less profusely toothed, less wrinkled and paler than those of 'A'; flowers less obviously grouped into clusters than in 'A', more like those of *G. ibericum* than are those of 'A' and 'C', with axis upwardly inclined or erect and with narrower, scarcely recurved, straighter-sided petals, the veins of which are less profusely branched than those of clone 'A', more so than those of clone 'C'; filaments almost white at base.

Clone 'C' (Figures 9.75B & 9.77C, Plate 27): of the three clones, this has the basal leaves the most like those of *G. platypetalum*, the divisions being much more abruptly tapered beyond the middle (the middle ones apparently overlapping less) and the teeth and tips of lobes being blunter, and it shows an obvious corresponding difference in the upper leaves (Figure 9.77); the surface of the leaves is only shallowly wrinkled; the flowers are not obviously clustered and they have the axis horizontal; it has the broadest, most strongly overlapping petals with the most strongly curved sides of the three clones and they are often both lobulate and undulate at the apex; the petals are bluer, and have bolder but less profusely feathered veins than those of clones 'A' and 'B'; the filaments are pink at the base.

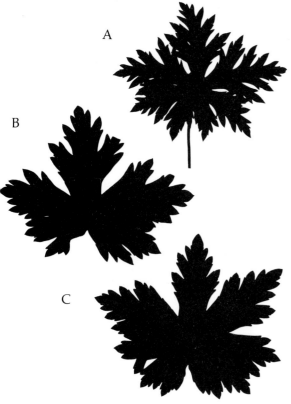

Figure 9.77 *G* × *magnificum*, upper leaves: (A) clone 'A'; (B) clone 'B'; (C) clone 'C', sources as in Figures 9.75 & 9.76, × ²⁄₃

Hylander suspected that the photograph accompanying the report of the Award of Garden Merit to *G. ibericum* (*Journal of the Royal Horticultural Society*, 67, fig. 130, 1942) (also published in Synge & Platt, 1962), was truly that species, especially as there was mention of abundant seed-production. However, I am certain the plant illustrated is *G.* ×*magnificum,* and while I consider that the latter deserves the A.G.M., I do not think *G. ibericum* does or would have obtained it.

72. *G. gymnocaulon* De Candolle

Inconspicuously hairy, slender perennial to about 35cm tall; blades of basal leaves not wrinkled, between 5 and 10cm wide, cut rather like those of 70. *G. ibericum* but less complex; inflorescence dense; floral axis horizontal; flowers about 35mm in diameter; petals notched, violet-blue, with darker, slightly forked veins. Rock garden. July, August.

Perennial with thick rootstock, developing above ground for several centimetres. Blades of basal leaves between 5 and 10cm wide, angular in outline, divided as far as about ⁶⁄₇ into 7; divisions broadest about the middle, palmato-pinnately lobed, lobing and toothing continued down the sides below the middle but not nearly to the base; lobes about twice as long as broad, the lateral sometimes curving outwards, toothed, the teeth sometimes widely spreading. Teeth and tips of lobes very acute. Stem-leaves similar, decreasing gradually in size and length of stalk upwards, all stalked, the first one or two solitary, others paired. Sepals and rostrum with long eglandular hairs, hairs otherwise minute, crisped, eglandular. Stems slender, with the first two internodes very long, the solitary leaves accompanied by a pair of branches or a branch and a cymule, paired leaves mostly with a pair of branches and a cymule. Inflorescence dense but peduncles not suppressed, mostly not more than 4cm and often shorter than pedicels. Pedicels mostly 1–1½ times as long as sepals. Floral axis more or less horizontal. Flowers almost flat. Sepals 7–10mm, flushed with purple; mucro 2–3mm. Petals up to 18 × 14mm, broadest near apex, notched, rather deep violet-blue with darker, forking veins, reaching about ²⁄₃ of the way to the apex, pale at extreme base. Filaments at first divergent, later recurved, lilac-pink with white base, with long coarse hairs and minute hairs on the enlarged base; anthers bluish. Stigmas about 1.5mm, dull pink. Rostrum about 25mm with stylar portion about 3mm. Mericarps about 4.5mm. Discharge: seed-ejection (twist).

N.E. Turkey, S.W. Caucasus.

This species has probably been introduced on a number of occasions but is apt to die out. A group of plants was raised at Cambridge from seed from Nalchik Botanic Garden in the Caucasus in 1965 and did well on the rock garden until 1977 when they unaccountably died. Quantities of seeds were set in some years but I never saw any germinating near the parent plants. Some which I sowed produced only a handful of seedlings and I failed to raise any to maturity. It is said to be in cultivation at Edinburgh. It is an unassuming but quite attractive plant, flowering later than its allies.

73. G. renardii Trautvetter (Figure 9.78, Plate 28)
Low-growing perennial with rounded sage-textured leaves, shallowly divided and lobed; inflorescence dense; petals wedge-shaped, notched, white, with bold, slightly forked violet veins. Rock garden, wall, patio, sun or partial shade. June.

Perennial with thick woody rootstock trailing above ground. Blades of basal leaves up to 10cm wide, grey-green, finely wrinkled, divided as far as 1/2 into 5 or 7; divisions broader than long, usually with spaces between them and with a wide space between the basal pair, scarcely tapered below the middle, roughly semicircular above it, with shallowly 3-lobed or 5-lobed apex; lobes shorter than broad, toothed. Teeth and tips of lobes obtuse. Stem-leaves paired, sometimes one pair not much smaller than basal, otherwise abruptly reduced in size and length of stalk and much altered in shape. Hairs eglandular or those of the pedicels sometimes glandular, those of leaf-blades short, forming a deciduous felt on upper surfaces and a thick persistent felt on lower surfaces. Stems slender, usually once or twice forked, the tips of the branches bearing dense umbel-like clusters of flowers, usually without peduncles. Pedicels 1–1½ times as long as sepals. Floral axis horizontal. Flowers flat. Sepals 7–9mm; mucro about 0.5mm. Petals about 15–18 × 9–10mm, 1½–2 times as long as wide, wedge-shaped, notched, not contiguous, white or bluish white, boldly marked with violet feathered veins. Filaments with long coarse hairs below, moderately enlarged at base, there white, otherwise deep violet; anthers yellow with violet edges. Stigmas about 2mm, dull reddish, style the same colour. Immature fruits erect on erect pedicels. Rostrum about 25mm with stylar portion 4–5mm. Mericarps about 4mm. Discharge: seed-ejection (twist).

Caucasus.

An attractive and unmistakable plant, unique in its foliage and flowers. It was introduced by Walter Ingwersen in 1935 (Ingwersen, 1946) and he says that the ground-colour of the petals is 'pastel-lavender', while Bobrov (1949) says it is pale pink. Ingwersen found the plant on rock-cliffs and recommends that it should never be grown in 'fat' soil, but should be provided with a meagre diet and wedged between rocks to maintain its dwarf and compact habit. It grows and flowers particularly well in Scotland and northern England, despite general neglect of Ingwersen's advice.

G. renardii 'Walter Ingwersen' is a name applied to the stock which received an Award of Merit at the Wisley Trial in 1976, as it was considered desirable to specify that it was Ingwersen's own introduction (the specific epithet was omitted from the name in the report of the trial). I do not know of any variation in this species in cultivation and therefore cannot characterise the cultivar.

HYBRID. A description by Y.N. Woronow of a hybrid with 69. *G. platypetalum* is quoted by Bobrov (1949); the hybrid was found in nature at two localities.

74. G. peloponnesiacum Boissier (Figure 9.79, Plate 29)
Perennial about 60cm tall with glandular hairs above; blades of basal leaves 10–20cm wide, divided as far as 3/4 or less into 7; divisions diamond-shaped, with rather solid outline, cut half-way to the midrib; flowers 38–43mm in diameter, in loose umbel-like clusters on tall stems; petals notched, porcelain-blue, with slightly

Figure 9.78 *G. renardii* T. Watson, 1955 *ex* Munich B.G., × 2/3

smudgy feathered or netted dark veins; plant dormant after flowering. Leaves present in winter. Border, rock garden. May.

Perennial from a thick rhizome. Basal leaves appearing in autumn; their blades (in spring) wrinkled, 10–20cm wide, divided as far as ²/₃ or ¾ into 5 or 7; divisions broad, tapered both ways from about the middle, with entire, straight or concave sides below the broadest part, palmato-pinnately lobed, edges of lobes and divisions often faintly marked with a wide brown band; lobes about as long as broad, toothed. Teeth and tips of lobes mostly obtuse. Stem-leaves paired, with 3 or 5 divisions, the lowest larger than the basal, gradually reduced in size and length of stalk upwards, the upper-most almost stalkless. Hairs mostly straight and spreading; upper parts of plant with glandular hairs but these few on the sepals. Stems with long internodes. Some peduncled cymules present but most flowers in umbel-like clusters and then on long pedicels, 3–5 times as long as sepals, so that inflorescence is not dense. Flowers upwardly inclined, shallowly funnel-shaped. Sepals 9–12mm; mucro 1–1.5mm. Petals up to about 25 × 17mm, deeply notched, straight-sided, rather pale violet-blue with darker but not sharply drawn feathered or slightly netted veins, ground-colour often paler

Figure 9.79 *G. peloponnesiacum*, Wisley Garden, 1971, coll. Greece: Lower Pindus (R. Gorer), × ²/₃

towards base, front surface with or without occasional hairs towards base. Filaments straight when anthers are functional, purplish pink. Anthers cream with blue edges. Stigmas about 1mm, greenish. Rostrum about 22mm including stylar portion 2–3mm. Discharge: seed-ejection (twist).

Greece.

This species was not introduced until about 1972 when Mr Richard Gorer collected seed at Karpenisi in the Lower Pindus mountains. I saw young plants at Wisley in 1973 and was allowed to take three back to Cambridge.

G. peloponnesiacum is a lovely plant, producing sprays of large pastel-blue flowers in May on long stalks which sway in the breeze. Despite its height, I suggest that it may be acceptable on the rock garden because of its summer dormancy.

75. G. libani Davis (*G libanoticum* (Boissier) Boissier, not Schenk; *G. peloponnesiacum* Boissier var. *libanoticum* Boissier) (Figure 9.80)
Perennial about 40cm tall; blades of basal leaves glossy above, divided as far as ²/₃ or ¹/₅ into 5 or 7, with rather broken outline; flowers about 28–32mm in diameter; petals notched, medium violet-blue or violet, with more or less smudgy, slightly feathered veins. Plant dormant in summer. Leaves present in winter. Rock garden. April, May.

Differs from 74. *G. peloponnesiacum* in its lesser height, glossy upper leaf-surfaces, more open (gappy) leaf division and lobing, the lateral lobes of the divisions curving outwards, abrupt decrease in size of stem-leaves after the first pair, absence of glandular hairs, pedicels about twice as long as sepals, shorter sepals (7–9mm), shorter petals (17–20mm), and longer rostrum (30–35mm) with stylar portion only about 3mm. Discharge: seed-ejection (twist).

Lebanon, western Syria, central southern Turkey.

This species reached Cambridge in 1978 from two sources, and the plants are rather different. Kew (Wakehurst) sent plants collected in 1974 at the source of the Kidisha River, Mount Lebanon, and Mr Andrew Clarke gave me a clone obtained from Miss J. Robinson. No locality is available for the latter but Miss

Robinson received it from an acquaintance who was known to have visited Lebanon.

The Kew plant has broader leaf-divisions and lobes and broader, bluer, petals, making a more desirable type of flower. Mr Clarke's plant has narrower and more violet petals but is much more free-flowering. I saw a fine clump of it flowering in light shade at Bressingham Gardens, Norfolk, in 1983.

The synonymy of this species shows firstly that it has been called *G. libanoticum*, a name which it cannot retain because *G. libanoticum* Schenk has priority (the name applies to a species that belongs to The Tuberosum Group which is not in cultivation) (Davis & Roberts, 1955) and, secondly, that Boissier considered it sufficiently similar to *G. peloponnesiacum* to treat it as a variety of the latter.

76. *G. bohemicum* Linnaeus (Figure 9.81A)
Sprawling, hairy biennial; blades of main leaves wrinkled, divided as far as about ¾ into 5 or 7 broadly diamond-shaped, closely toothed and lobed divisions. Lobes and teeth very short, more or less acute. Glandular hairs present on leaf-stalks, stems, peduncles, pedicels, sepals and rostra. Inflorescence diffuse, leafy, with long-stalked leaves. Flowers up to about 23mm in diameter. Sepals about 6mm, enlarging to 9mm; mucro 1.5–2mm. Petals about 9–11 x 8–9mm, notched, moderately strongly violet-blue with darker, forked veins, these converging to a pinkish zone at base; base with hairs on each side forming a small tuft. Stamens and styles just under ²/₃ as long as sepals. Stigmas green or whitish. Rostrum about 22mm, without a distinct stylar portion. Mericarps about 5mm, black. Seeds mottled in light and dark brown. Cotyledons with a notch on each side. Discharge: seed-ejection (twist).

East and C. Europe, north to southern Scandinavia.

Among annual and biennial species of *Geranium* only two, *G. bohemicum* and 77. *G. lanuginosum*, have blue flowers. Those of *G. bohemicum* might be considered just big enough to give the plant some appeal, at least to the more ardent devotees of the genus. *G. bohemicum* was

the subject of detailed investigation by the Swedish botanist Hedlund (1901) who studied especially its rather peculiar seed-ejection arrangement which, we now know (Tokarski, 1972), is common to The Tuberosum and Platypetalum Groups. He also noted that its occurrence is very sporadic and associated with the sites of fires (see Chapter 2). The character of the notched cotyledons is shared only with the two species of Section *Divaricata* in Subgenus *Robertium* (see 83. *G. albanum*).

HYBRID. Another Swedish botanist, K.V.O. Dahlgren (1923, 1925), carried out crossing experiments between *G. bohemicum* and 77. *G. lanuginosum* and obtained sterile hybrids with marbled leaves (see Chapter 7).

77. G. lanuginosum Lamarck (*G. bohemicum* Linnaeus subsp. *depraehensum* Almquist) (Figure 9.81B)

Sprawling, glandular-hairy annual, forming a rosette when over-wintering, similar to 76. *G. bohemicum*; leaves not wrinkled, marbled, with lobes and teeth finger-like, being deeper than those of *G. bohemicum* and parallel-sided with rounded tips. Flowers up to 16mm in diameter. Sepals 3.5–5mm in flower, enlarging to about 8mm. Petals 8–9 × 6–7mm, campanula-blue but pale pinkish white between veins in basal half; base with hairs on each side forming a sparse fringe. Stigmas purplish pink. Rostrum about 18mm. Seeds uniformly brown. Cotyledons not notched. Discharge: seed-ejection (twist).

Mediterranean Region, including N.W. Africa, Sweden (where it is perhaps introduced).

This species, of no garden value, is included here because it is so like 76. *G. bohemicum* that it could be taken for it by anyone unaware that it existed.

HYBRID. Has been artificially crossed with the preceding species, q.v.

78. G. gracile Nordmann (Figure 9.82)

Noticeably hairy perennial to about 40cm tall, with light green wrinkled leaf-blades, the basal divided as far as ²/₃ or ¾ into 5 or 7; divisions scarcely lobed, more or less saw-edged; flowers deeply funnel-shaped; petals narrow, notched, pink, with white base and eyelash-like veins. Woodland. June onwards.

Plant with a thick, much-branched rootstock. Blades of basal leaves light green, wrinkled, up to 20cm wide, divided as far as ²/₃ or occasionally ¾ into 5 or 7; divisions diamond-shaped or broadly elliptic, tapered both ways from above the middle, with teeth continuing down the sides well below the broadest part, scarcely lobed but with numerous regular or alternately large and small teeth. Teeth incurved, highly asymmetric, more or less acute. (Another type of leaf with more distinct lobes and very few coarse teeth may be produced under conditions favouring very rapid growth.) Stem-leaves paired, similar to the prevalent type of basal leaf but with 3 or 5 divisions, decreasing gradually in size and length of stalk upwards. Upper parts of plant, apart from leaves, with glandular hairs. Stem forking repeatedly, forming inflorescences of prolonged growth, leafless in the upper parts, never densely flowered. Peduncles mostly 2–4cm. Pedicels about 1½–2½ times as long as sepals. Flowers erect, funnel-shaped. Sepals 6–7mm; mucro 1.5–2mm. Petals about 21 × 9mm, wedge-shaped, notched, erect at base, flared above, bright pink with white basal third, the lower part of the coloured zone with short purple veins; base with a sparse hair-fringe on either side. Filaments of the inner and outer whorls more unequal than usual, tinged pink, basal enlargement inconspicuous, large hairs more restricted to base than in other members of The Platypetalum Group. Anthers cream with blue edges. Stigmas deep flesh-pink. Rostrum about 23–26mm with stylar portion about 4mm but not well demarcated. Mericarps about 4.5mm, dark brown. Discharge: seed-ejection (twist).

N.E. Turkey, S. Caucasus, N. Iran.

Plants growing at Cambridge were collected by Mr Roy Lancaster in woodland below the Sumena Monastery, South of Trabzon, N.E. Turkey in 1977 (no. L. 79). I supposed this to be a new introduction but while writing this book I discovered a dried specimen cultivated at Cambridge in 1900 and another grown at Kew in 1930.

This species has attractive foliage and charming flowers (especially in clones with well-developed 'eyelash' marks on the petals); in hot dry conditions smaller flowers of paler colour are produced.

Figure 9.82 *G. gracile*, cult. P.F. Yeo, 1983, coll. Turkey: Trabzon Prov. (Lancaster 79), × ⅓

Superficially *G. gracile* is extraordinarily like a hairy version of 6. *G. nodosum* (of The Endressii Group) and quite unlike all other species of The Platypetalum Group. Like *G. nodosum* it is a woodland plant, and the similarity is a testimony to the forces of natural selection operating in similar environments. Presumably the type of leaf seen in these two plants is well adapted to woodland conditions, and the resemblance in the flowers suggests that both have been forced to adapt themselves to similar types of pollinating insect. Gone are the blues of the flowers of most members of the group, and their dense inflorescences, while the hairs on the petals and filaments and the basal enlargements of the filaments are reduced, these being evidently unnecessary in the deeply funnel-shaped flowers.

G. gracile is unequivocally placed in The Platypetalum Group by its fruit, but it also shows affinity with its true relatives in the form of the exceptional basal leaves mentioned in the description and in having very long hairs on its sepals. Although the fruit-type distinguishes it from members of The Endressii Group, additional characters are mentioned in discussion under nos. 1, 2, 5 and 6.

Subgenus II Robertium

Plants annual or perennial. Fruit-discharge by carpel projection; each carpel is thrown off explosively with the seed in it and the awn drops away at the moment of explosion. Base of mericarp rounded, without a horny point or blunt tubercle.

Section Polyantha, The Polyanthes Group

Perennial plants with a thick knobbly rootstock. Petals rounded at apex. Style not more than 6mm, stigmas less than 2mm. Mericarps 4–5mm, acute at apex, blunt at base, with netted ribs.

Six species from the Himalayas and the mountains of Burma and S.W. China.

79. G. polyanthes Edgeworth & J.D. Hooker (Figure 9.83, Plate 30)
Perennial, 20–45cm tall, with slightly succulent rounded leaves, the lobes and teeth confined to the apices of the divisions. Flowers partly in umbel-like clusters, about 2.5cm wide, funnel-shaped, deep pink, reminiscent of *Oxalis*. Rock garden. July.

Rootstock thick, knobbly, tuber-like. Leaves slightly succulent, often narrowly edged with red. Blades of basal leaves up to 5cm wide, occasionally more, rounded in outline, divided as far as ⅔ or ⅘ into 7 or 9; divisions broadest at the apex where they are lobed for ⅕ of their length; lobes mostly with a few small teeth. Teeth and tips of lobes acute or obtuse with a small point, all reaching about the same level. Stipules about 6mm broad, ovate, sometimes toothed at the top. Stem-leaves similar, but the upper with fewer and narrower divisions; lower solitary; uppermost paired, some of these almost without stalks and with unequal lobes. Cymules without peduncles; pedicels hairy; flowers partly in umbel-like clusters, erect, funnel-shaped. Sepals 6–7mm, hardly at all spreading, green, flushed with purplish red, densely covered with glandular hairs; mucro 0.75mm or less. Petals about 12–15mm, about 1½ times as long as broad, bright purplish pink with fine, slightly feathered veins, a glistening texture and pale base, rounded at apex, gradually tapered at base; base with a tuft of fine hairs on margins but no hairs on front surface. Filaments 4.5mm, white. Anthers about 0.7mm, yellow. Style about 3mm; stigmas 1.5mm, yellowish, tipped with pink. Immature fruits and pedicels erect. Rostrum with no stylar portion. Mericarps 4mm, with a network of raised veins, finely hairy, acute at apex. Discharge: carpel-projection.

Figure 9.83 *G. polyanthes*, O. Polunin, 1978, coll. India: Sikkim/Nepal border, Uttar Pradesh, × ½

Himalayas from Nepal eastwards, S.W. China (Yunnan).

This is an attractive plant but it seems to be temperamental in cultivation, though not difficult to establish initially, nor to increase by division. Its natural habitat is alpine meadows. It begins growth very late — perhaps in May. *G. polyanthes* has been repeatedly introduced from the Himalayas, and is often sold by local dealers in wild-flower seeds, sometimes as *G. donianum* (no. 36). The two species can be distinguished by their seeds, *donianum* having seeds that are ejected from the carpel and appear smooth, whereas *polyanthes* seeds are shed (and therefore despatched) in their carpels, showing the raised network of veins and coat of fine hairs. *G. donianum* differs also in having deeply lobed leaf-divisions.

Section Trilopha, The Trilophum Group

Annuals with no rosette, the stem internodes all elongated. Inflorescence diffuse. Some of the flowers cleistogamous (i.e. self-fertilised in the bud and never opening), these with shortened pedicels and no peduncles. Flowers usually with a dark eye and always with dark stamens and stigmas. Pollen white. Mericarps either with a pattern of ribs and an acute apex, or with a large toothed crest round the edge.

Five species of East Africa and the Arabian Peninsula, one of which extends outside this area. They are not important in cultivation and

are variable within themselves; the presentation of the species here has been varied according to need.

80. *G. trilophum* Boissier (*G. omphalodeum* Lange) (Figure 9.84)
Slender annual with pink flowers, 14–18mm wide, with a slightly darker area at base of petals formed by convergence of veins. Mericarps with a toothed ridge down the middle and a wide recurved and toothed wing round the edge. Discharge: carpel-projection.

I know this species in two considerably different forms, here designated (a) and (b).

(a). (Figure 9.84A). Leaf-blades not more than 5cm wide, divided as far as ⅚ into 5; divisions coarsely and deeply pinnately lobed; lobes with an occasional tooth. Flowers 14mm in diameter; petals 8mm long, strongly overlapping, deep pink, slightly paler towards base, with dark veins in basal half which become much stronger at base. Stamens (except at extreme base) and stigmas deep purplish violet. Mericarps 4–4.75mm, rather dark brown, apex extending beyond the lateral wings.

This plant is in circulation among botanic gardens under the name *G. trilophum*. It rarely produces open flowers in Cambridge but I once saw a clump of it flowering freely in the Copenhagen Botanic Garden (this stock has been tried at Cambridge) so at least somewhere in Europe it will behave as a decorative annual. It corresponds to *G. omphalodeum* Lange, described from plants in the Copenhagen Botanic Garden in 1865, and it has every appearance of being

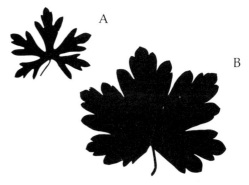

Figure 9.84 *G. trilophum*: (A) Amsterdam B.G., 1970; (B) A.G. Miller, 1981, coll. Oman: Jebel Qara, Dhofar (2376), × ⅔

specifically distinct from form (b) but I cannot match it with wild plants in the Kew Herbarium. East African examples of *G. trilophum* approach it more closely than do those from the Arabian Peninsula and on present knowledge it cannot in fact be accepted as a distinct species.

(b). (Figure 9.84B). Leaf-blades often more than 5cm but less than 10cm wide, divided as far as ½ or just beyond into 5; divisions shallowly 3-lobed at the top; lobes frequently toothed. Flowers 18mm in diameter; petals 10mm, not or only slightly overlapping, rose-pink with a transverse band of white just below the middle and below this a lilac-pink area darkened by diffuse veins; stamens blackish except at base; stigmas blackish with nearly white tips. Mericarps 6mm, pale brown, apex overtopped by lateral wings.

I received this at Cambridge in 1981 from Dr A.G. Miller of the Royal Botanic Garden, Edinburgh. He collected it at Dhofar, Oman, at an altitude of 3,000 ft (900 m). I have so far only grown it in a greenhouse; the flowers are beautiful and reasonably freely produced at the beginning of the year, but the seeds do not germinate readily.

81. G. ocellatum Cambessèdes (Figure 9.85)
Annual with rather profusely lobed and toothed leaf-divisions. Flowers 16–18mm in diameter, deep pink with a black eye. Mericarps horizontally ribbed.

Mountains of W. Africa, E. Africa, Arabian Peninsula, Himalayas, S.W. China.

The following is a description of the most desirable of three forms which I have grown (Figure 9.85D).

Leaf-blades not more than 10cm wide, divided as far as ²/₃ or slightly more into 5 or 7; divisions tapered both ways from above the middle; lobes about as long as broad, usually with 2 teeth; tips of lobes and teeth obtuse to acute. Petals about 9.5mm long, about 1½ times as long as wide, not overlapping, deep pink with a black triangle at the base; stamens blackish except at extreme base; stigmas dark red. Mericarps about 2.5mm, with a raised midrib and about 9 transverse ribs on either side, all ribs covered with minute hairs. Discharge: carpel-projection.

I received this at Cambridge in 1981 from Dr A.G. Miller of the Royal Botanic Garden, Edinburgh. He collected it at Shibam in the Yemen Arab Republic. It produces a small number of open flowers out of doors and perhaps rather more in the greenhouse. Stocks of *G. ocellatum* grown from two other areas differ in various ways; one flowers rarely (Figure 9.85C) and the other has not yet flowered except cleistogamously in Cambridge (Figures 9.85A & B).

82. G. biuncinatum Kokwaro (*G. yemense* in the sense of Knuth) (Figure 9.86, Plate 31)
Annual very similar to the plant described under no. 81, but with petals up to 10.5mm, ¾ as wide as long, overlapping, the basal triangle with a fine white border, mericarp body 6.5mm long

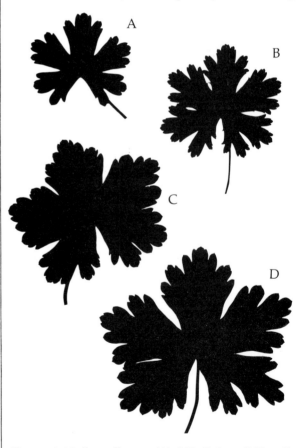

Figure 9.85 *G. ocellatum*: (A) S.K. Raina, 1981, coll. India: Udampur, Jammu, grown in cool conditions; (B) the same, tropical conditions; (C) Stockholm B.G., 1972, coll. Angola: Huila Distr. (Kers 3298); (D) A.G. Miller, 1981, coll. Yemen Arab Republic: Shibam (Miller & Long 3372), × ²/₃

(excluding the hooks), with raised midrib and a wide recurved and toothed wing round the edge like that of 80. *G. trilophum* but continued at the top into a hook on either side looking like a pair of horns. Discharge: carpel-projection.

East Africa, Arabian Peninsula.

Seed of this was collected by J.R.I. Wood at Jebel Bura', Yemen, and given to Cambridge in 1981 by the Royal Botanic Gardens, Kew. It has only been grown in the greenhouse so far. It flowers quite freely at the beginning of the year and has the largest flowers of its group, as well as most remarkable fruits.

Figure 9.86 *G. biuncinatum*, Kew B.G., 1981, coll. Yemen Arab Republic: Jebel Bura' (Wood 3126), × ⅔

Section Divaricata, The Albanum Group

Annual or perennial plants. Cotyledons notched. Petals more or less notched at apex. Pollen bluish. Rostrum of fruit slender; discharge mechanism inoperative. Mericarps bristly, ribbed or crested.

Two species of N.W. Africa, S. Europe and W. and C. Asia, a perennial, described below, and an annual with very small flowers, *G. divaricatum* Ehrhart. The only other species of *Geranium* known to have notched cotyledons is 76. *G. bohemicum.*

83. G. albanum Bieberstein (Figure 9.87, Plate 32)

Perennial with leaves present through the winter. Leaves rounded in outline. Inflorescence diffuse, flowers 22–25mm in diameter with pink, veiny, slightly notched petals. Herbaceous border, ground-cover, wild garden. June, July.

Rootstock compact, much branched. Blades of basal leaves 10–20cm wide, rounded in outline, divided as far as about ½ into 9; divisions broad, tapered towards base from near the slightly rounded apex, lobed at the apex for ¼–⅓ of their length; lobes with up to about 5 unequal teeth. Tips of teeth and lobes obtuse or some of the teeth acute. Stipules of basal leaves thin, blunt, brown. Stem leaves paired, stalked, divided more deeply than the basal into 5 or 7, with rather narrower, often divergent, lobes and teeth. Plant conspicuously clothed with spreading eglandular hairs; glandular hairs sometimes also present. Stems trailing, up to 1m long, forming diffuse inflorescences. Peduncles commonly 4–8cm; pedicels commonly 2.5–4cm, widely divergent. Flowers more or less erect. Sepals 6–7.5mm at flowering time, with mucro about 0.5mm, 7–9mm in fruit, green, flushed with purplish red. Petals about 10–12mm, lightly notched at apex, bright pink with slightly branched deep magenta veins; base with a few hairs on the surface and a small dense tuft at either side. Filaments magenta-pink; anthers violet-blue. Stigmas 1.5mm, deep pink. Immature fruits erect on more or less reflexed pedicels. Rostrum not becoming thickened, 6–8mm. Mericarps 4–4.5mm, broadest near the apex, upper half with a network of raised veins, produced into a crest of bristly teeth at the top. Mericarps, containing the seeds, remaining on plant long after death of calyx and rostrum.

Figure 9.87 *G. albanum*, × ⅔

South-east Caucasus and the adjacent part of Iran.

Grows in shrubby vegetation below the tree-line. An undistinguished but very reliable and reasonably floriferous plant with a long flowering period. When among tall herbs or shrubs it scrambles. The name of the species derives from Albania, the Latin name for the Caspian province of the Caucasus, today called Daghestan.

Section Batrachioides, The Pyrenaicum Group

Annual or perennial, softly hairy plants. Sepal mucro very small. Petals notched. Pollen bluish. Immature fruits erect on reflexed pedicels. Mericarps ribbed, though sometimes only faintly and only near the midrib at the top.

Four or perhaps 5 species in Europe and W. Asia.

84. G. pyrenaicum N.L. Burman (Figure 9.88A)

Slender perennial with leaves present throughout the year. Leaves rounded in outline. Inflorescence diffuse, flowers about 12–18mm in diameter, with purplish pink (occasionally white) deeply notched petals. Woodland and wild garden. May–October.

Perennial with ill-defined and ill-protected rootstock. Blades of basal leaves up to about 10cm wide, rounded in outline, sometimes broader than long, divided as far as about $1/2$–$2/3$ into 7 or perhaps 9; divisions broadest at the apex, lobed at the apex for about $1/3$ of their length; lobes as broad as or broader than long, usually with 2 lateral teeth but in earliest leaves without teeth. Teeth and tips of lobes obtuse. Stipules of basal leaves ovate, acute, crimson. Stem-leaves paired, like the basal, becoming gradually reduced in size and length of stalk upwards, the uppermost with narrower, acute, toothless lobes. Minute glandular and eglandular hairs forming a dense clothing, usually accompanied by an abundance of long eglandular hairs, but these sometimes absent except on leaf-blades. Stems trailing, up to about 70cm, forming a diffuse inflorescence. Peduncles mostly 1.5–5cm, slender; pedicels mostly 1–2cm, very slender. Sepals 4–5mm, green, with a very small mucro. Petals not more than 10mm, finely pointed at base, notched for $1/3$–$2/5$ of their length at apex, deep purplish pink, tending towards violet, except for white base; veins slightly darker than ground-colour; base with a small dense tuft of hairs towards either edge and a

narrow hairless zone on the front surface between the tufts. Filaments pale pink, at least at the tips; anthers bluish. Stigmas about 1.5mm, pale yellow, sometimes tinged with pink. Immature fruits erect on sharply reflexed pedicels. Rostrum 12–13mm; stylar portion not more than 0.5mm. Mericarps about 2.5mm, with short appressed hairs and a few raised ribs in the immediate vicinity of the midrib at the top. Discharge: carpel-projection.

S.W. and W. Europe, east to the Caucasus, introduced further north and naturalised in the British Isles.

Grows in meadows, on roadsides and on disturbed ground. A quite attractive plant for the wild garden, tolerant of moderate shade.

G. pyrenaicum forma albiflorum Schur has the petals and stamen-filaments white or, in cool weather, faintly tinged with pink.

HYBRIDS. Said to have hybridised naturally with 87. G. molle and 85. G. pusillum (see Chapter 7).

85. G. pusillum Linnaeus (Figures 9.88C & D)

Annual with blades of lower leaves not more than 5cm wide, rounded in outline, divided as far as $2/3$ or $3/4$ into 9; divisions lobed for $1/3$–$1/2$ of their length; lobes toothed; lobes and teeth obtuse to acute, the lateral curved outwards; notches marked with a small crimson spot. Stem-leaves paired, stalked. Hairs eglandular, those of stems and leaf-stalks very short. Flowers extremely small; sepals about 2.5mm; petals about 4mm, notched at apex, lilac, not as widely spreading as the sepals; anthers only 5, bluish. Rostrum about 7mm, without a stylar portion. Mericarps about 2mm, otherwise like those of 84. G. pyrenaicum. Discharge: carpel-projection.

Europe, N. and W. Asia; introduced elsewhere.

A weed with an apparent preference for sandy soils. Superficially similar to 87. G. molle but differing in the short hairs on the stems, paired stem-leaves, smaller flowers and unribbed, hairy mericarps.

HYBRID. Said to have hybridised naturally with 87. G. molle (see Chapter 7).

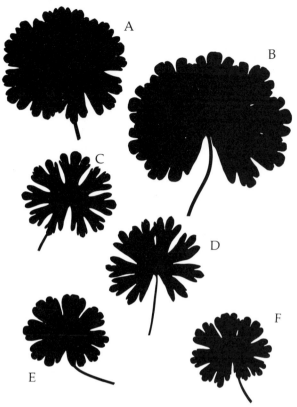

Figure 9.88 (A) *G. pyrenaicum*, S.M. Walters, 1975, coll. USSR: Caucasus (75/457): (B) *G. brutium*, K.A. Beckett, 1981, coll. Yugoslavia: Montenegro; (C) & (D) *G. pusillum*, weed in Cambridge B.G.; (E) & (F) *G. molle*, P.F. Yeo, 1977, coll. Corsica: SE Mts, × ²/₃

86. *G. brutium* Gasparrini (Figure 9.88B)

Annual with rounded leaves, with blades less deeply divided than those of 84. *G. pyrenaicum* but having more lobes and teeth when of comparable size. Flowers similar to those of 84. *G. pyrenaicum* but up to 25mm in diameter and with bright rose-pink petals. Mericarps hairless, closely ribbed. Rock garden or border. Summer.

Blades of basal leaves between 5 and 10cm wide, divided nearly as far as ½ into 9; divisions lobed for ⅓ or less of their length; lobes often with one tooth; teeth and tips of lobes blunt. Stem-leaves solitary, becoming rapidly reduced in size and length of stalk upwards. Hair-clothing nearly the same as in 84. *G. pyrenaicum*. Stems erect, up to about 30cm, becoming bushy, or up to 50cm and trailing, forming diffuse inflorescences which nevertheless produce a profusion of flowers. Peduncles and pedicels very

slender. Sepals 4–6mm, with hardly any mucro. Petals 8–12.5mm (varying greatly according to conditions), gradually tapered or distinctly constricted at base, notched at apex for about ¼ of their length, with indistinct darker veins; base with a rather dense fringe of wavy hairs on either side. Filaments the same colour as the petals; anthers blue-black. Stigmas 1.5mm or slightly more, pink or purple. Immature fruits erect on sharply reflexed pedicels. Rostrum 7–9mm. Mericarps 2–2.5mm, acute at apex, hairless, densely covered with fine slanting ribs. Discharge: carpel-projection.

S. Italy, Sicily, Balkan Peninsula, Turkey.

A showy and apparently easily grown annual. The above description is based on an introduction from the Pindus of Greece by Mr A.W.A. Baker and another from Yugoslavia by Mr K.A. Beckett. In the solitary stem-leaves and ribbed mericarps it resembles 87. *G. molle*.

87. *G. molle* Linnaeus (Figures 9.88E & F)

Annual with blades of lower leaves up to about 8cm wide, rounded in outline, divided as far as ½ or ³/₅ into 9; divisions lobed for ⅓–²/₅ of their length; lobes often with 1 or 2 teeth on their sides, the lateral scarcely curved outwards; tips of lobes obtuse, teeth often acute. Lowest stem-leaves paired, others solitary, stalked. Hairs eglandular, many of them long. Sepals 3–5mm. Petals 4–6mm, notched at apex for about ¹/₅–¼ of their length, purplish pink with white base, pale pink or white, widely divergent; base with a fringe of wavy hairs on either side; anthers bluish. Stigmas about 1mm, crimson. Rostrum 5–8mm, stylar portion about 0.5mm. Mericarps like those of 86. *G. brutium* but only 1.5mm long and more nearly spherical. Discharge: carpel-projection.

Europe, W. Asia, extending to the Himalayas.

A weed of lawns and disturbed places on roadsides and hill pastures, *G. molle* is superficially similar to 85. *G. pusillum* but most of its stem-leaves are solitary and it has larger, spreading and more deeply notched petals and hairless, ribbed mericarps. Closely related to 86. *G. brutium* but smaller in all parts (except upper leaf-stalks) and less erect.

HYBRIDS. Said to have hybridised naturally with 85. *G. pusillum* and 84. *G. pyrenaicum* (see Chapter 7).

Section Unguiculata, The Macrorrhizum Group

Plants perennial. Stems and leaves slightly succulent. Hairs mostly glandular. Sepals erect, usually forming a swollen calyx. Petals with a distinct claw and blade, not appreciably notched at apex. Pollen yellow. Style hairless. Immature fruits and their pedicels erect. Mericarps with a pattern of ridges, obtuse at apex, hairless.

Five species in the mountains of the Mediterranean Region, of which four are cultivated.

88. G. glaberrimum Boissier & Heldreich (Figure 9.89, Plate 33)
Dwarf aromatic perennial with small, almost hairless kidney-shaped leaves with blunt lobes and teeth. Flowers about 23mm in diameter, erect, bright pink. Petals with a claw at base. Stamens and style about twice as long as sepals. Alpine house and probably rock garden. June and again later.

Rootstock thick, developing above ground. Blades of main leaves not more than 5cm wide, wider than long, divided as far as $^3/_5$ or nearly so into 7 or 9; divisions tapered towards the base from near the rounded and shallowly 3-lobed apex; lobes mostly with a tooth on one side or both. Teeth and tips of lobes obtuse or acute. Upper stem-leaves similar, decreasing rapidly in size upwards, stalked; all stem-leaves paired, members of pairs unequal. Plant covered with minute glandular hairs but without large hairs. Stems forking regularly, forming inflorescences up to about 25cm tall. Sepals about 9mm long, erect, the outer ones with longitudinal ribs with small cross-connections; mucro 1mm or slightly more. Petals about 20mm, with a claw and a blade; blades less than 16mm, broadest near the

tip, bright pink, with paler veins near base; claws hairy along the edges, each with a double ridge abutting a stamen so that the petals form 5 nectar-passages of approximately circular section. Filaments 17mm, deep pink; anthers red. Style 16mm, red; stigmas less than 1mm, red. Immature fruits and their pedicels more or less spreading. Rostrum about 17mm, including stylar portion 10mm. Mericarps 4–4.5mm, narrow, with a network of raised ribs. Discharge: carpel-projection.

Mountains of S.W. Turkey.

Grows in rock fissures at 4,250–6,000 ft (1,300–1,800 m) altitude. A very attractive plant for the alpine house which will probably prove itself satisfactory on the rock garden also. This plant has been established at Cambridge from a single seedling raised from seed sent by Professor G.G. Guittonneau in 1976 (his no. 73.06.26.03) and at Kew from a plant collected by Mr Brian Mathew in 1980. The Kew plant has more acute leaf-teeth and more rounded and overlapping petal-blades than the Cambridge one. Pieces of the above-ground rootstock seem unwilling to root but the species can be increased by seed.

89. G. macrorrhizum Linnaeus (Figure 9.90A)
Rhizomatous sticky and aromatic perennial. Leaves 10–20cm wide, with shallow rounded lobes. Flowers 20–25mm in diameter, with axis horizontal. Calyx reddish, inflated. Petals pink to purplish or white, with a claw at base. Stamens and style more than twice as long as sepals, sinuous. Rock garden, border, wild garden, ground-cover. Leafy in winter. May–June and usually again later.

Plant up to 30 or 50cm tall, with fleshy underground rhizomes and thick ascending, above-ground stems lasting several years. Lowest leaves 10–20cm wide, divided as far as $^2/_3$–$^3/_4$ into 7; divisions tapered both ways from above the middle, shallowly palmato-pinnately lobed; lobes about as long as broad, with several teeth. Teeth and tips of lobes obtuse or the teeth acute. Stems with 1–3 pairs of leaves, these similar to the lower but decreasing rapidly in size and length of stalk upwards. Plant densely clothed with minute glandular hairs and usually more or less densely covered also with long glandular and eglandular hairs, these occasionally almost absent. Inflorescence dense, usually with

Figure 9.89 *G. glaberrimum*, G.G. Guittonneau, 1976, coll. Turkey: Icel Prov. (73.06.26.03), × $^2/_3$

umbel-like clusters above the first few flowering nodes. Pedicels shorter than or little longer than the sepals. Floral axis horizontal. Sepals 7–9mm, reddish, forming a bladdery calyx; mucro ¼–½ as long as sepal. Petals 15–18mm, with a claw and a blade; blades rounded, usually purple, slightly asymmetrically spreading in the flower; claws wedge-shaped, half the total length of the petal, with two rounded ridges and a central channel, hairy on the back and on the front at the sides, the hairs sometimes extending on to the tops of the ridges and overhanging the channel. Filaments 18–24mm, displaced to the lower side of the flower and slightly turned up at the tips, usually purplish red; anthers orange-red to dull red. Style about 22mm, growing rapidly, purplish red, displaced and curved like the filaments; stigmas 1–1.5mm, yellowish. Immature fruits and their pedicels erect. Rostrum about 30–34mm, stylar portion about 18mm. Mericarps 2.5–3mm, with wavy horizontal ribs. Discharge: carpel-projection.

South side of the Alps, Apennines, Balkan Peninsula, S. and E. Carpathians; often naturalised elsewhere in Europe.

This species grows among rocks and scrub (usually in shade) in mountains, and in subalpine woodlands, and has potential for drought-resistance. It has long been used for medicinal purposes and as a source of oil of geranium which is used in perfumery (now superseded in the latter role by *Pelargonium* species and hybrids). It has also been used in tanning. It is quite frequently introduced from the wild and the introductions show a good deal of variation in hair-clothing, petal colour and other details, which affect the plant's garden value. *G. macrorrhizum* is valuable for dry shady situations in the garden, but only certain of the cultivars qualify for a place in the herbaceous border or rock garden, though an Award of Merit was bestowed on the species at the Wisley Trial. The first flower-buds are often damaged by late frosts. Easily propagated from the rhizomes or by using the rosette-bearing stems as cuttings.

G. macrorrhizum 'Album' has white petals and pink calyces and stamens; it was introduced by Walter Ingwersen from the Rhodope Mountains of Bulgaria, and is relatively large-flowered. White petals are mentioned as occurring occasionally in this species by Gams (1923–4). Whether all British white-petalled material belongs to the Ingwersen clone I do not know. If not, the name 'Album' will inevitably be used for all white forms unless others appear which can be distinguished. Stocks at Cambridge lack hairs on the sides and front of the petal claws. 'Album' is a charming garden plant.

G. macrorrhizum 'Bevan's Variety' has deep red sepals and deep magenta petals of good form and size; it is the most intensely coloured variant but the colours of the sepals and petals clash. First distributed by Washfield Nurseries, Hawkhurst, Kent, having been collected by the late Dr Roger Bevan while on an excursion with Dr Giuseppi.

G. macrorrhizum 'Grandiflorum' was found as a seedling in cultivation by Ingwersen, having larger flowers than usual, 'fully an inch across' by which 'it has been lifted from mediocrity to the rank of a well-worth-while garden plant' (Ingwersen, 1946). It is apparently lost from cultivation.

G. macrorrhizum 'Ingwersen's Variety' is a fine pale pink form (RHSCC Purple Group 75A) with rather pale green and slightly glossy foliage; it was found as a single plant among typically coloured plants on Mount Koprivnik, Montenegro, Yugoslavia, by Walter Ingwersen in 1929, and is the best form for the herbaceous border.

G. macrorrhizum 'Spessart' is a cultivar of German origin said to have dark pink petals; the white-flowered plant circulating under this name in Britain is not 'Spessart'.

G. macrorrhizum 'Variegatum' has the leaves irregularly variegated with cream; the flowers are a fairly typical shade of purplish pink.

HYBRID. See 90. *G. × cantabrigiense.*

90. *G. × cantabrigiense* Yeo (Figure 9.90C, Plate 34)

Aromatic carpeting plant to about 30cm tall; foliage light green, appearing hairless (the hairs present being minute); leaf-blades not more than 10cm wide, intermediate in size and shape between those of 89. *G. macrorrhizum* and 91. *G. dalmaticum.* Flowers about 25–28mm in diameter, formed and held like those of *G. macrorrhizum*; petals bright pink or white. Rock garden, front of border, ground-cover. Sun or shade. June to July.

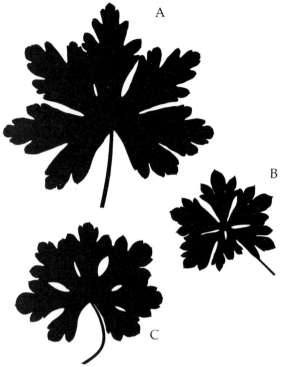

Figure 9.90 (A) *G. macrorrhizum* 'Bevan's Variety', J. Stephens, 1969; (B) *G. dalmaticum*, Miss E.M. Savory, 1958; (C) *G × cantabrigiense*, Miss H.E.M. Kiefer, 1974 × ²/₃

Plant with long-lived trailing stems like those of 91. *G. dalmaticum*. Blades of main leaves 3–9cm wide, divided as far as ¾ or ⁴/₅ into 7; divisions broadest well above the middle, with 3 short broad lobes each with 1 or 2 teeth, or some of them without teeth; teeth and tips of lobes rounded and mucronate. Flowering stems with leaves at the first and sometimes the second node; inflorescence of 1 cymule at the first fork and 5–10 flowers at the tip of each of the 2 branches. Flowers like those of 89. *G. macrorrhizum* and 91. *G. dalmaticum*, intermediate in most of the details in which these differ, but like *G. dalmaticum* in having hair-tipped teeth on the filaments. Petals bright pink or white, tinged with pink at base of blade. Sterile.

A hybrid between 89. *G. macrorrhizum* and 91. *G. dalmaticum*.

This hybrid has arisen independently on a number of occasions. In 1974 Dr Helen Kiefer, working at Cambridge, made reciprocal pollinations between the two parent species; 31 flowers were pollinated in each direction; with *G. dalmaticum* as the female parent three seeds were produced but none germinated, and with *G. macrorrhizum* as female parent five seeds were obtained, one of which germinated. This plant grew on and was finally planted in the Geranium Display Bed, where it grew extremely rapidly. It makes a more or less weed-proof carpet of pleasantly light green scented foliage and in some years the leaves can hardly be seen when it is in full flower. The colour of the petals is RHSCC Purple-Violet Group between 80B and 80C. In winter the leaves appear attractively glossy. The rostra mostly remain undeveloped.

Reports have been made of spontaneous occurrence of pink-flowered forms of this hybrid in gardens, and plants have been collected together for evaluation. The following white-flowered one was found in nature:

G. × cantabrigiense 'Biokovo' has runners that creep further than those of the Cambridge clone and consequently it forms a less dense mat; the petals are white with a tinge of pink at the base of the blade. The rostrum usually develops, but no seed is formed. This clone was found near Makarska in the Biokova (Biokovo) mountains of southern Dalmatia, Yugoslavia, by the nurseryman Mr Hans Simon of Marktheidenfeld, West Germany, who named it and introduced it into cultivation.

91. G. dalmaticum (Beck) Rechinger (Figures 9.90B & 9.91, Plate 35)
Fragrant rhizomatous dwarf carpeting plant, with glossy hairless leaves not more than 4cm wide. Flowers formed and held like those of 89. *G. macrorrhizum* but calyx less red; petals shell-pink or white. Rock garden in sun or light shade, ground-cover. June–July.

Plant up to about 15cm tall, with trailing stems lasting several years which ascend at tips and bear leaf-rosettes. Blades of leaves up to 4cm wide, divided as far as ⁴/₅–⁶/₇ into 5 or 7; divisions wedge-shaped, mostly 3-lobed for ¼–⅓ of their length, with the middle lobe the largest; lobes broad, abruptly pointed, usually without teeth. Flowering stems sometimes with one pair of leaves and with small bracts at higher nodes, or with bracts only. Plant hairless except for fine hairs on lower flowering stems and glandular hairs on pedicels and sepals. Inflorescence long-

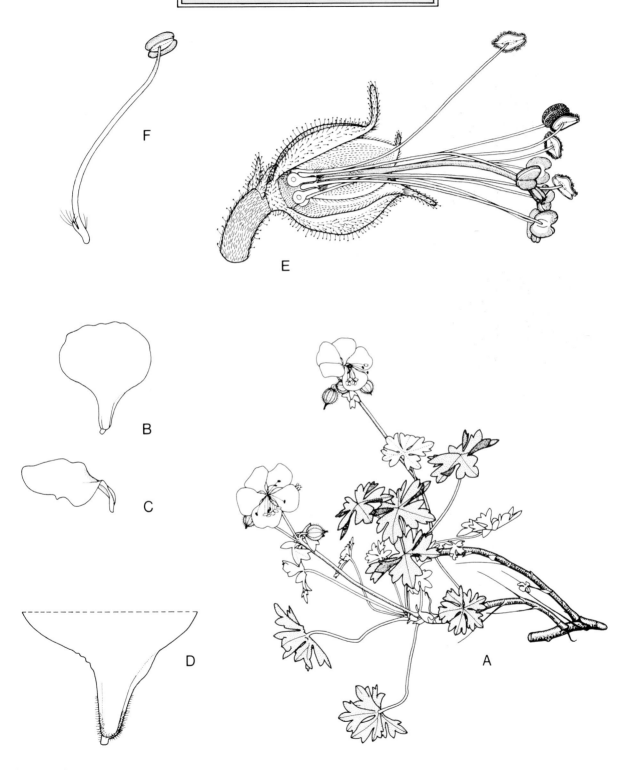

Figure 9.91 *G. dalmaticum* (Miss E.M. Savory, 1958). (A) portion of plant beginning to flower, × ²/₃ ; (B) petal, × 2; (C) petal, seen from side, × 2; (D) base of front surface of petal, × 4; (E) flower in male stage with petals and two stamens removed, × 4; (F) stamen of outer whorl, × 4

stalked, dense, few-flowered, many of the bracts barren. Pedicels shorter than calyx. Floral axis horizontal. Sepals 6–6.5mm, green with translucent pink margins, forming a bladdery calyx, the outer with raised ribs near the edges; mucro about ¼ as long as sepal. Petals 18mm long and up to 12mm wide, with a claw and a blade; blades broadly rounded, bright pink; claws wedge-shaped, about ⅓ of the total length of the petal, woolly on back and sides and in a strip across the front above the base, without central ridges. Filaments 15mm, displaced to the lower side of the flower and slightly turned up at the tips, each with a pair of hair-tipped teeth at the base; anthers red. Style about 18mm, growing rapidly, crimson towards tip, displaced and curved like the stamens; stigmas 1.5mm, crimson. Rostrum about 33mm, including stylar portion 14mm. Mericarps 2.5–3mm, with lateral ribs slanting and occasionally forking or merging. Discharge: carpel-projection.

South-west Yugoslavia and Albania.

This species was first introduced into cultivation by the late Mr Walter Ingwersen in 1947 and by 1949 it had already received an Award of Merit of the Royal Horticultural Society. The cultivar 'Album' was commercially introduced in 1956. G. dalmaticum is a delightful plant, easy to grow and to propagate — by cuttings from the rhizomes. At Wisley it grows on the vertical face of a retaining wall. It is less floriferous in the North of Britain than in the South unless given maximum exposure to the sun.

G. dalmaticum 'Album' has white petals and is slightly less vigorous than the type; it appears to have arisen in cultivation and was shown at a Royal Horticultural Society meeting in July 1956 by Bloom's Nurseries, Diss, Norfolk.

HYBRID. See 90. G. ×cantabrigiense.

92. G. cataractarum Cosson (Figure 9.92, Plate 36) Dwarf aromatic perennial with leaves divided to the base into 3 and nearly into 5, recalling those of 95. G. robertianum. Flowers 17–19mm in diameter, funnel-shaped, inclined upwards. Calyx inflated. Petals bright pink. Stamens less than twice as long as sepals; anthers red. Rock garden. Leaves present in winter. June onwards.

Rootstock thick, developing above ground. Blades of basal leaves not more than 10cm wide, divided to the base into 3, and nearly to the base into 5; divisions stalked, broad, more or less fan-shaped, deeply pinnately lobed; lobes 1–1¾ times as long as broad, with several teeth. Teeth and tips of lobes obtuse. Stem-leaves paired, members of pairs unequal, lateral divisions stalkless. Plant more or less covered with very small-headed glandular hairs. Flowering stems with shorter eglandular hairs on one side, forking unequally, making a fairly dense inflorescence up to about 30cm tall. Flowers upwardly inclined. Sepals 5–6mm, enlarging to 7–8mm, making an inflated calyx; mucro 0.5mm or less. Petals 15 × 7–8mm, with a claw and a blade; blades bright pink, flat-ended; claws narrow, ⅓ of total length of petal, without hairs or central ridge. Filaments 7mm, projecting out of throat of flower, hairless, pink-tipped. Style about same length as filaments, reddish at tip; stigmas 1mm, flesh-pink on back and white on front. Rostrum 17mm; stylar portion 6–7mm. Mericarps about 3.5mm, with a network of ribs, those in the lower ²/₃ mostly directed lengthwise. Discharge: carpel-projection.

South Spain, Morocco.

G. cataractarum grows naturally on damp or shady limestome rocks. My description is based entirely on a stock originating from a cliff near

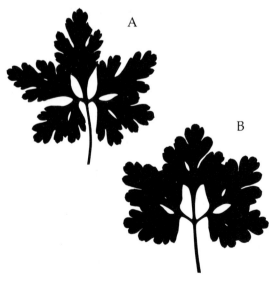

Figure 9.92 (A) G. cataractarum, R.C. Barneby, 1970, coll. Spain: Jaén Prov. (B) G. cataractarum subsp. pitardii, G.G. Guittonneau, 1977, coll. Morocco: Moyen Atlas (72.07.08.01), × ²/₃

the source of the Guadalquivir river, Province Jaén, Spain, collected by Dr Rupert C. Barneby in 1967. The plant is completely hardy in Cambridge but has not proved as attractive on the rock garden there as it did in Dr Barneby's garden at Greenport, New York, as evidenced by a colour transparency he sent me. Possibly it needs frequent renewal. I also grow at Cambridge *G. cataractarum* subsp. *pitardii* Maire (Figure 9.92B), which is the Moroccan representative of the species. It was collected in the Middle Atlas by Professor G.G. Guittonneau in 1972, cultivated by him, and sent to me as seed in 1976. It is slightly smaller in all parts than Dr Barneby's plant, and has narrower and paler petal-blades, fading nearly to white at the base. *G. cataractarum* is easily propagated by cuttings from the above-ground stock and from seed.

HYBRID. See 93. *G. cataractarum* × *G. maderense*.

Figure 9.93 *G. cataractarum* × *G. maderense*, P.F. Yeo, 1971, × ½

Section Unguiculata × Section Anemonifolia

93. *G. cataractarum* Cosson × *G. maderense* Yeo (Figure 9.93)

Perennial with a rosette-bearing stem 10–20cm tall, branching after flowering. Leaf-blades more than 10cm and sometimes more than 20cm wide, divided to the base into 3 and nearly to the base into 5; divisions stalked, pinnately lobed nearly to the midrib, the lobes themselves with secondary, toothed lobes, those of both orders curving outwards. Inflorescence about 25cm tall, held well above the leaves (which become reflexed), dense, leafy in the lower part, bracteate in the upper. Flowering stems forking regularly, borne in a group at the top of the rosette. Flowers upwardly inclined, 3cm in diameter at first, more splayed later. Petals about 18 × 12mm, with a claw about ⅕ of their length; blades deep reddish pink with raised veins paler than the ground-colour, and a streak of darker red in the centre of the lower third. Filaments deep pink, anthers yellowish; stigmas deep pink.

This hybrid is almost exactly intermediate between the parents. It is quite sterile but can be propagated by the rooting of branches which form after flowering has taken place. Well-grown specimens are highly decorative, and if a system of management could be worked out it might make a fine conservatory plant. It was raised at Cambridge, where it has been grown only under glass. The cross was made by me in 1971 and by Dr Helen Kiefer in 1974; it was successful only when *G. maderense* was the female parent. The main petal colour is HCC Phlox Purple, between 632 and 632/1.

Section Lucida, G. lucidum

Plants annual. Stem and leaves slightly succulent. Hairs mostly glandular. Sepals erect, with lengthwise keels and transverse flaps between these. Petals hairless, with a distinct claw and blade; claws ridged so as to form nectar-passages; blade not notched at apex. Pollen yellow. Style minutely bristly. Immature fruits and their pedicels erect. Mericarps with lengthwise ridges bearing glandular hairs, obtuse at apex.

One species.

94. *G. lucidum* Linnaeus (Figures 9.94)

Erect annual up to 50cm tall, with succulent red stems and slightly succulent glossy leaves. Leaf-blades about 5cm wide, rounded in outline, divided as far as about ⅔ into 5. Divisions broadest near the apex which is shallowly 3-lobed; lobes usually with a few teeth. Teeth and tips of lobes obtuse. Stem-leaves paired, stalked. Flowers erect, not more than 10mm in diameter. Sepals about 5mm. Petals 8–9mm, with a very small deep pink (rarely white) blade shorter than the claw. Stamens and style reaching about 1mm beyond throat of flower. Rostrum about 11mm, its stylar portion 4mm. Mericarps about 2.2mm, broadest at the top, with a network of raised ribs which run parallel and vertically at the top. Discharge: carpel-projection. Wild garden, walls. Spring and summer.

Europe, N. Africa, S.W. and C. Asia.

This plant is attractive for its glossy green foliage and for the red colouring which develops when it is old. Plants arising from autumn germination form stronger rosettes and grow to a larger size than those germinating in spring.

Figure 9.94 *G. lucidum*, × ²⁄₃

HYBRID. A natural hybrid with 95. *G. robertianum* has been reported (see Chapter 7).

Section Ruberta, The Robertianum Group

Plants annual, biennial or perennial. Stems and leaves slightly succulent. Hairs mostly glandular. Leaves divided to the base. Petals hairless, with a distinct claw and blade; claws ridged so as to form nectar-passages of approximately circular cross-section; blade not appreciably notched at apex. Pollen yellow. Style hairy. Rostrum hairless. Mericarps with a pattern of ridges, obtuse at apex.

Four species from the North Atlantic islands, Europe, Asia and Africa. *G. canariense,* included here, was formerly treated as a member of Section Anemonifolia (Yeo, 1973). The one species not described below is *G. purpureum* Villars, which is similar to *G. robertianum* but with much smaller flowers (petal-blades up to 2.5mm wide).

95. *G. robertianum* Linnaeus (Figure 9.95)
A usually over-wintering evil-smelling annual with leaves divided to the base into 3 and nearly to the base into 5, the divisions stalked, much cut. Flowers 11–16mm in diameter, pink or white. Petals with a claw at base. Wild garden,

shade or sun, perhaps rock garden. Spring, summer, autumn.

A rosette-forming succulent annual, usually over-wintering, often strongly pigmented with red or brown. Blades of basal leaves up to about 11cm wide, divided to the base into 3 and nearly to the base into 5; divisions stalked, ovate or diamond-shaped, pinnately lobed almost or quite to the midrib; lobes less than twice as long as broad, toothed or with secondary, toothed, lobes. Teeth and tips of lobes obtuse, often with a distinct mucro. Stems leafy, the leaves decreasing gradually in size, complexity of lobing and length of stalk upwards, and becoming acutely toothed. Plant sparsely to densely beset with large, glistening, glandular and eglandular hairs. Flowering stems arising in a cluster from the rosette or in one or more whorls on a central stem emerging from the rosette, forking regularly but slightly unequally below, more unequally above, forming a diffuse inflorescence. Sepals 4–6mm, erect; mucro about 0.75–1.25mm. Petals 10–14mm, with a claw and a blade; blades 3.5–5.5mm wide, deep pink with paler veins towards base; claws slightly shorter than the blades, each with a double ridge abutting a stamen so that 5 nectar passages of approximately circular cross-section are formed. Stamens projecting about 1.5mm from throat of flower; anthers red to pinkish orange. Stigmas 0.5–1.5mm. Rostrum 12–15mm; stylar portion 4–5mm. Immature fruits and their pedicels upwardly inclined. Mericarps 2–2.8mm, with a network of ribs, sparse towards the base, and 1 or 2, sometimes 3, collar-like rings round the apex, hairless or finely hairy, each with 2 bundles of hair-like fibres ('tangle-strands') near the top. Discharge: carpel-projection.

Europe, N.W. Africa, Canary Isles, W. Asia, Himalayas, S.W. China. Probably an introduction in E. North America.

This is the familiar hedge-bank flower, Herb Robert. Some of its variation has been described by Yeo (1973) and Baker (1956) while more detailed researches are reported by Bøcher (1947) and Baker (1957). I found that different samples grown under similar conditions differed considerably in leaf-size and flower-size and somewhat in flower-colour. The smallest-flowered forms tend to be compact and prostrate, unlike the small-flowered *G. purpureum* (see under Section *Ruberta)*, which tends to be erect or straggling. It is essentially a species for the wild garden and shady corners, though compact forms may be risked on the rock garden. All stocks which I have grown, except for cultivar 'Album', have to grow through the winter before they will flower. The species is mainly self-pollinating and different stocks grown near together remain distinct. This fact was noted by Bowles (1914) with regard to the two common white-flowered cultivars, 'Album' and 'Celtic White'. However, when these are crossed, all the progeny in the first generation have the normal pink wild-type flower (see below under 'Hybrids').

Figure 9.95 *G. robertianum*, Besançon B.G., 1969, coll. France?, × ½

G. robertianum 'Album' is a trailing, thin-stemmed plant, very strongly pigmented with red-brown in the vegetative parts, having rather large flowers with white or nearly white petals, attractively set off by the brown sepals; it flowers in the first year from seed and it may continue to flower late into the autumn, survive the winter and begin again early in spring. The botanical name *G. robertianum* forma *bernettii* A. Schwarz is said by Gams (1923–4), to apply to a plant with this colouring but whether it has the same growth behaviour is unknown. The cultivar name is that given by Ingwersen (1946). There are specimens of *G. robertianum* 'Album' in the herbarium of the University Botanic Garden, Cambridge. I have seen it from several sources. Mr G.E. Barrett has recently sent me a plant similar to this which differs in requiring to be over-wintered before it will flower.

G. robertianum subsp. *celticum* Ostenfeld (*G. robertianum* var. *celticum* (Ostenfeld) Druce) occurs in W. Ireland and S. Wales; its red-brown pigmentation is restricted to nodes and bases of leaf-stalks, and its flowers are pale pink. It is apparently not at present in cultivation (but see next).

G. robertianum 'Celtic White' is a dwarf, compact albino with at most a tinge of brown at the nodes, varying in its hairiness, and having bright green leaves and rather small flowers with pure white petals; it is called var. *celticum* in gardens but, as explained by Baker (1956), it is not that (see above), and I therefore propose this cultivar name; there are herbarium specimens dated 10/6/1966, 14/6/1968 and 23/7/1970 in the herbarium of the University Botanic Garden, Cambridge. Bowles (1914), in attempting to trace the origin of this plant, was always led to one Sir Charles Isham, but he could not find out where *he* got it.

G. robertianum 'Cygnus' is a name proposed by Clifton (1979) for white-flowered plants with rather little brown pigment, to which the botanical name *G. robertianum* forma *leucanthum* Beckhaus has been applied (Baker, 1956); the original description of the latter merely stated that the flowers were pure white with scarlet-red anthers and it was based on plants found in North Germany, and the application of the name is therefore uncertain.

G. robertianum subsp. *maritimum* (Babington) H.G. Baker is a name applied by Baker (1956) to coastal plants; the variation in the species seems, however, to cut across the coast/inland boundary.

HYBRIDS. I have crossed *G. robertianum* 'Album' with 'Celtic White' in both directions; the resulting plants are normal (like the wild form) in flower-size, flower-colour and in vegetative colouring; in genetical terms this can be explained by saying that the characters of each cultivar are determined by different recessive genes, the respective dominant ('wild-type') alleles of which are found in the other cultivar. Crossing 'Celtic White' with a normal wild form also gives only pink-flowered progeny. Sterile hybrids have been obtained by crossing this species with 99. *G. maderense, G. purpureum* and 96. *G. rubescens;* reports of natural sterile hybrids with 94. *G. lucidum* and 16. *G. pratense* are dubious (see Chapter 7).

96. *G. rubescens* Yeo (Figure 9.96)

A biennial, looking like a large form of 95. *G. robertianum,* with beetroot-red lower stems and leaf-stalks and with flowers 22–33mm in diameter. Sun or shade. May or June onwards.

Plant similar to 95. *G. robertianum* and having stems up to 60cm; stems and leaf-stalks much thicker than those of *G. robertianum;* leaf-blades up to 23cm wide with more generally acute teeth which are more prominently mucronate. Sepals 7–8mm, with mucro about 2mm. Petals 18–22mm; claws about half as long as blades; blades 7–13mm wide, bright purplish pink with paler veins near base; throat of flower dark red. Mericarps 3.3–3.7mm, with 1 or 2 collar-like rings at the top and no hairs or tangle-strands. Stylar portion of rostrum 6–7mm. Discharge: carpel-projection.

Figure 9.96 *G. rubescens,* × ½

Madeira.

The evidence which justified the treatment of this plant, which has long been known, as a distinct species was collected by Mr W. Jackson and published by Yeo (1973). *G. rubescens* is very hardy and forms magnificent over-wintering rosettes. It is useful for sheltered, partly shaded corners. In gardens it is often called *G. anemoni-*

folium (a synonym of 98. *G. palmatum*) or *G. lowei,* a name which has no botanical standing.

HYBRIDS. Sterile hybrids with 95. *G. robertianum* have been raised and have occurred spontaneously at Cambridge. Fertile hybrids with 97. *G. canariense* have been raised at Cambridge and at the University of California, Berkeley (see Chapter 7).

97. *G. canariense* Reuter (Figure 9.97)

A fragrant evergreen short-lived perennial with rosettes on a stem usually 5–15cm tall. Leaf-blades up to 25cm wide, succulent, divided to the base into 3 and nearly to the base into 5, divisions much cut, not stalked. Flowers 23–36mm in diameter, deep pink. Petals with a claw at base, not clasped by the sepals, and a narrow blade. Stamens about twice as long as sepals. Greenhouse or sheltered corners out of doors. Spring onwards.

Figure 9.97 *G. canariense,* Barcelona B.G., 1966, *ex* La Orotava B.G., × ½

Perennial with a rosette on a distinct above-ground stem which may become branched, and is commonly 5–15cm tall but in old, protected, plants up to 30cm. Flowering stems and leaves more or less succulent. Leaf-blades up to 25cm wide, divided to the base into 3 and nearly to the base into 5; divisions not stalked, deeply pinnately lobed; lobes 1½–3 times as long as broad, themselves with secondary, toothed, lobes. Teeth and tips of lobes obtuse or acute. Leafstalks dull brownish to purplish. Stem-leaves paired, rapidly decreasing in size, complexity of lobing and length of stalk upwards. Flowering stems arising from neighbouring axils of the rosette or, in old plants, terminally, forming a dense inflorescence up to 45cm in height, its upper parts thickly covered with purple glandular hairs. Floral axis horizontal. Sepals 8–10mm, divergent; mucro about 1mm. Petals 17–24mm, with a claw and a blade; blades 6–9mm wide and 1¾–2½ times as long as wide, deep pink; claws half as long as blades or less, each with a double ridge abutting a stamen so that 5 nectar-passages of approximately circular cross-section are formed. Throat of flower pale or dark. Filaments about twice as long as sepals; anthers scarlet or dark red. Styles about as long as stamens, white; stigmas about 2mm long, pink or white. Immature fruits slightly nodding on spreading or deflexed pedicels. Rostrum about 30mm, including stylar portion 16–18mm. Mericarps about 3.5mm, with a uniform network of ribs and 1 or 2, sometimes 3, small collar-like rings at apex, hairless or with fine hairs at the top. Discharge: carpel-projection.

Canary Isles (Tenerife, Palma, Gomera and Hierro).

A plant for sheltered situations, preferably in the milder west, or for the greenhouse. I have had three accessions of G. canariense of known wild origin and two the same as each other from botanic gardens. The last was the neatest in habit and flower-form and is the one illustrated in colour by Yeo (1970). Some stocks are spoiled by minor deformities of the leaves and flowers, probably caused by a virus. Propagated by seed.

HYBRIDS. Fertile hybrids with 96. G. rubescens have been raised at Cambridge and at the University of California, Berkeley (see Chapter 7).

Section Anemonifolia, The Palmatum Group

Giant rosette plants behaving as short-lived perennials. Stems and leaves slightly succulent. Hairs mostly glandular. Leaves divided to the base. Petals hairless, with a distinct claw and blade; claws ridged so as to form nectarpassages of elongated cross-section; blade rounded at apex. Pollen yellow. Style hairy at base. Rostrum hairless. Mericarps with a pattern of ridges, obtuse at apex.

Two species in Madeira.

98. G. palmatum Cavanilles (G. anemonifolium L'Héritier) (Figure 9.98)
Plant like 97. G. canariense but with hardly any development of stem except in old plants, and with leaves up to 35cm wide, their middle division stalked. Flowers distinctive, 33–45mm in diameter, with sepals clasping petal-claws and petals slightly oblique in posture, broadbladed. Stamens twice as long as sepals. Greenhouse or sheltered corner out of doors. Summer.

Perennial with a massive rosette on a condensed stem. Lower stems and leaves more or less succulent. Leaf-blades up to 35cm wide, divided and lobed much as in 97. G. canariense but with middle division distinctly stalked and the lobes up to 4 times as long as broad, light green. Leaf-stalks green or pink-flushed. Stemleaves as in G. canariense. Flowering stems axillary, forming a dense inflorescence up to 1.2m in height, covered with purple glandular hairs except at the base. Floral axis horizontal. Sepals 7–10mm, appressed to the petal-bases and curved outwards at the tips; mucro 1–2mm. Petals 20–30mm long, arranged slightly obliquely, with a claw and a blade; blade 13–18mm wide and slightly longer than wide, purplish rose shading to deep crimson in the basal ⅕, giving the flower a dark throat; claws ¼–⅕ as long as blade, each with a double ridge abutting a stamen so that 5 nectar passages of narrowly elongate cross-section are formed. Filaments about twice as long as sepals, slightly displaced to the lower side of the flower, deep magenta; anthers cream or yellow, sometimes tinged with pink. Styles like the filaments in length, position and colour. Stigmas 3–4mm, purplish crimson. Immature fruits and their pedicels downwardly inclined. Rostrum about 28mm, including stylar portion about 13mm. Mericarps 3.2–3.4mm, with a network of ribs, these closer towards apex where there are 1 or 2 collar-like rings, hairless. Discharge: carpelprojection.

Madeira.

G. palmatum has been cultivated in Europe since the eighteenth century but has usually been known by the name *G. anemonifolium* which was published two years later than *G. palmatum*. The petal-colour is RHSCC Purple Group 77C, with base Red-Purple Group 71B. Different accessions received at Cambridge have differences in habit which affect the value of the plant. The best I have had, from this point of view, was received from Mr Jan Stephens in 1964, though I do not believe he introduced it from Madeira, as stated by Clifton (1979). The species may be used in the same way as *G. canariense* and propagation is by seed.

HYBRIDS. Fertile hybrids with 99. *G. maderense*, using the latter as female parent, have been raised at Cambridge (see Chapter 7).

99. *G. maderense* Yeo (Figure 9.99, Plate 37)
A giant aromatic rosette plant, often dying after flowering, with a distinct erect rosette-stalk. Leaves even larger than in 98. *G. palmatum*, with distinctive pale brown stalks. Flowers about 35mm in diameter, with sepals clasping petal-claws; petals broad-bladed, purplish pink with a network of pale elevated veins, dark towards base. Stamens about as long as sepals. Greenhouse or sheltered position out of doors in areas with very mild winters. February or March onwards under glass.

Rosette-bearing stem up to 60cm tall and 6cm in diameter, either dying after flowering or continuing to grow by means of lateral branches. Flowering stems and leaves more or less succulent. Leaf-blades up to 60cm wide, divided and lobed much as in 97. *G. canariense* but with the middle division stalked, the lobes up to 4 times as long as broad and the secondary lobes rather far apart in the larger examples. Teeth and tips of lobes acute. Leaf-stalks dull reddish brown, hoary from the minute glandular hairs but without large hairs. Inflorescence arising from the centre of the rosette, consisting of a short central stem bearing 1 or 2 whorls of branches which give rise to a great mound of flowers above the leaves; lower parts coloured like the leaf-stalks, upper parts thickly covered with purple glandular hairs; branches regularly forking, sometimes some of the internodes suppressed. Stem-leaves decreasing in size rapidly

Figure 9.98 *G. palmatum*, J. Stephens, 1964, × ½

upwards, becoming 3-lobed and the middle lobe becoming dominant. Floral orientation indefinite. Sepals 8–10mm, appressed to the petal-bases which are divergent; mucro about 1mm. Petals 19–21mm long, with a claw and a blade; blade 13–18mm wide and about as long or slightly longer, purplish pink with a network of pale elevated veins, darker towards throat which is blackish purple; claws only about 2.5mm, each with a double ridge abutting a stamen so that 5 nectar-passages of elongate cross-section are formed. Filaments about as long as sepals, purplish or dark red, curved outwards at the tips; anthers dark red. Styles and stigmas dark red; stigmas 2.5mm. Immature fruits indefinitely orientated, approximately in line with their pedicels. Rostrum about 20mm, including stylar portion 7mm. Mericarps 4–4.5mm, with a network of ribs and 1–3 collar-like rings at the top, hairless. Discharge: carpel-projection.

Figure 9.99 *G. maderense*, C.H.C. Pickering, 1967, × ½

Madeira.

This is the largest of all *Geranium* species, growing to about 1.5m in height, having the largest leaves of any species and producing an immense inflorescence of purplish flowers surrounded by the purple haze of its glandular hairs. The petal colour is RHSCC Purple Group 77C, passing through Red-Purple Group 72B towards the base which is 77a. In the parts of Britain where winters are cold it needs a greenhouse, but it may be grown out of doors on the Atlantic coast. In the greenhouse it requires two years to mature, and will only do this if potted on very rapidly or planted out. Some plants have been raised to flowering out of doors in 12 months. Its introduction is due to the late Major C.H.C. Pickering, who observed it in cultivation in Madeira and traced a natural population in the 1950s; only two or three restricted colonies are known. Pickering asked me for a taxonomic evaluation of it and I confirmed that it was specifically distinct from *G. palmatum*; he also sent it

to many other countries and it is now widely cultivated. It grows mainly in the winter months and is able to withstand severe summer drought, so it would seem best suited to areas with a Mediterranean climate. The leaf-stalks are persistent and become reflexed, propping up the otherwise top-heavy rosette; they also store water and starch. To display this plant in a natural condition the leaf-stalks should not be tidied away.

HYBRIDS. Fertile hybrids have been raised at Cambridge by pollinating *G. maderense* with 98. *G. palmatum*, and sterile hybrids by pollinating it with 92. *G. cataractarum* and 95. *G. robertianum*.

Subgenus III Erodioideae

Plants perennial. Fruit-discharge of the Erodium-type; carpel containing the seed discharged together with the awn as one unit; awn becoming coiled after discharge. Mericarps 5mm or more long; base tapered and terminating in a horny point which is glossy on the back and covered with bristles at the sides.

Section Erodioideae, The Phaeum Group

Tall branching plants. Main leaves with the divisions tapered towards the tip, freely toothed. Flowers nodding, with widely spreading or reflexed petals. Apex of mericarp conical, with 3–5 keels or ridges around it.
Three species, all cultivated.

100. G. phaeum Linnaeus (Figures 100, 101 & 102, Plate 38)
A medium-sized leafy perennial with the leaves not deeply cut, but copiously toothed. Flowers about 22–25mm in diameter, nodding, flat, approximately circular, but often with a little point on each petal, in sombre shades of purplish red or a soft pale lilac, in either case with a white base; inflorescence-branches one-sided. Developing fruits upwardly inclined. Shade or semi-shade. Ground-cover. Leafy in winter. May–June and often again.

Perennial with stout rootstock growing on the soil surface, and oblique, often purple-dotted, stems reaching 40–80cm. Basal leaves mostly 10–20cm wide, divided as far as $^3/_5$–$^2/_3$ or occa-

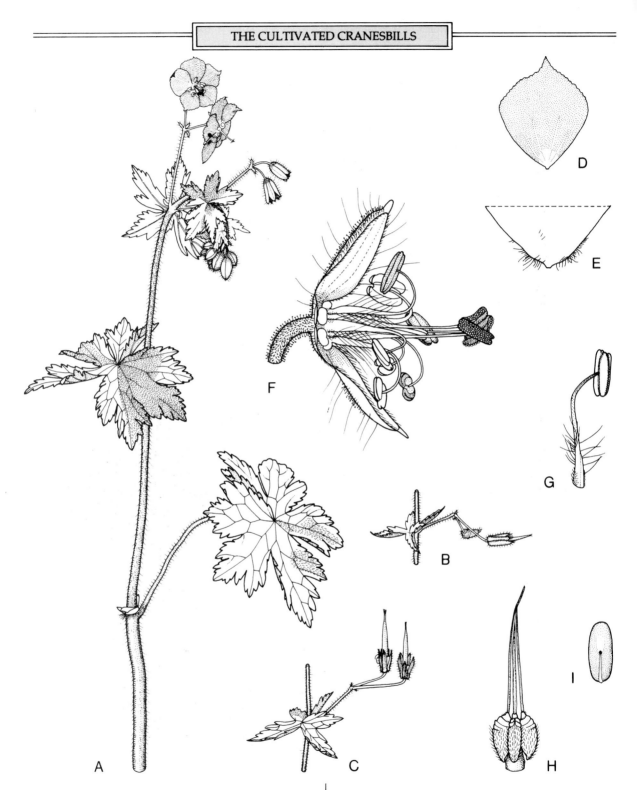

Figure 9.100 *G. phaeum* var. *phaeum* (Liège B.G., 1979, coll. France: Hautes Pyrenées) (A) shoot beginning to flower, ×²/₃ ; (B) & (C) cymule with immature and mature fruit, respectively, × ²/₃; (D) petal, with pigmentation, ×2; (E) base of front surface of petal, × 4; (F) flower in male stage with petals and three sepals removed, ×4; (G) stamen of outer whorl seen obliquely from back, ×4; (H) fruit in pre-explosive interval, × 2; (I) seed, × 4

sionally $^4/_5$ into 7 or 9, upper surface often blotched with purplish brown in the notches; divisions tapered both ways from about the middle, rather solid in outline; lobes about as long as broad, straight or curved outwards, with 2–5 or more teeth, a proportion of these usually very shallow. Teeth and tips of lobes acute or obtuse. Stipules of basal leaves large, thin and rounded. Stem leaves, and sometimes the lower inflorescence leaves, solitary; upper inflorescence leaves paired, unequal, more or less stalkless, often with lobes up to 1½ times as long as broad and very sharp teeth. Stipules of stem-leaves thin, brownish, conspicuous, usually slashed at the tip. Minute glandular hairs (see Chapter 4) larger than usual, dense. Inflorescence loose, with one'or few long branches, with recurved tips, each with only one or two flowers open at a time, the flowers directed to one side. Peduncles and pedicels upwardly inclined. Flowers nodding or with axis horizontal. Sepals 6–11mm, usually purplish at the base; mucro 0.5mm long or less. Petals usually 11–14mm, nearly as wide as long or wider, somewhat ruffled and/or lobulate round the edge, sometimes with a triangular point at the tip, widely spreading above the very shortly erect base, dull lilac or pinkish to deep violet, dull purple, maroon or nearly black, with a distinct whitish base; base with at least a few hairs across front surface and moderately tufted hairs at the sides. Filaments curved outwards at first, becoming appressed to the style as the anthers open but still spreading at the tips, coloured like the petals towards their tips, bearing very long spreading and glistening hairs with recurved tips in their lower halves. Anthers whitish with purplish edges. Stigmas 1.25–2mm, yellowish or greenish. Immature fruit upwardly inclined, pedicels likewise or sometimes more nearly horizontal. Mericarps 5–5.5mm, bristly, with 4 or 5 keels or ridges around the top. Stylar portion of rostrum 3–4mm. Discharge: Erodium-type.

Mountains of S. and C. Europe from the Pyrenees through the Alps to N. Yugoslavia, S.E. Germany, Czechoslovakia, Poland and Western USSR. Often naturalised outside this range, especially northwards.

G. phaeum grows in damp meadows, and along wood margins and shady road verges in high hills and at the lower levels of the moun-

tains. It is very suitable for cultivation in shade or semi-shade in Britain and its stout rhizomes enable it to withstand some dryness. It carries a good crop of basal leaves with which it covers the ground for most or all of the year. The flowers of var. phaeum are unusual in their dark colouring; the lighter flowers of var. lividum are more colourful but never vivid. A range of intermediates between the two varieties can be seen in some gardens. 'It is a quaintly handsome plant and will appeal to those who have an eye for unusual and quiet charm' (Ingwersen, 1946).

G. phaeum 'Album' is a name applied by Ingwersen (1946) to a white-petalled G. phaeum of tall growth and large flower-size collected in Switzerland, though it is not practicable to restrict it to this. White mutants appear among seedlings in cultivation occasionally. They appear to cross with var. phaeum or var. lividum to produce plants with faintly bluish flowers.

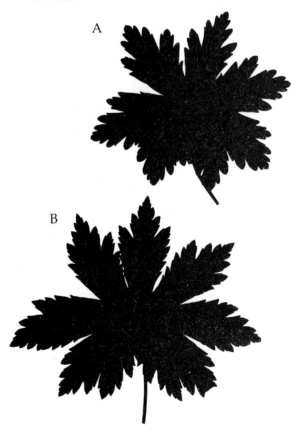

Figure 9.101 G. phaeum var. lividum: (A) B. Wurzell, 1972; (B) 'Majus', Mrs B.C. Rogers, 1966, × ½

G. phaeum 'Lily Lovell' was raised and introduced by Trevor Bath, of Woking, Surrey, and described as 'larger and earlier than the type, the flowers a beautiful deep mauve, contrasting well with the distinctive light green leaves'.

G. phaeum var. *lividum* (L'Héritier) Persoon (Figure 9.101A, Plate 38) has the petals

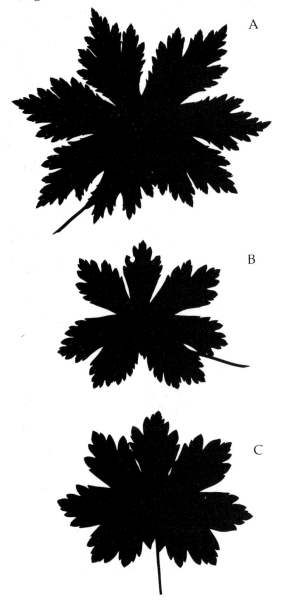

A

B

C

Figure 9.102 *G. phaeum* var. *phaeum*: (A) Liège B.G., 1979, coll. France: Hautes Pyrenées; (B) Dresden B.G., 1980, coll. Czechoslovakia: Belaer Tatra; (C) R.P. Dales, 1979, *ex* Margery Fish Nursery, × ½

rounded and bluish, lilac or pink, rather pale, and with a white base smaller than in var. *phaeum*; the base and the lowest part of the coloured portion are traversed by short bluish or violet veins which become diffuse (smudged) as they enter the coloured zone, giving rise to a bluish halo, which forms a straight border with the white base; above the blue halo there is usually another whitish halo; in the principal colour there may be a noticeable change from pink towards blue during the life of each flower. This variety extends from Croatia westwards along the southern side of the Alps, reaching the French Alps, and replacing var. *phaeum* throughout this area. The leaves are usually unblotched; Clifton (1979) notes that when dying they turn primrose yellow.

G. phaeum var. *lividum* 'Majus' (Figure 9.101B) is the name under which a particularly tall and large-flowered clone (petals to 16mm long) was received at Cambridge from Mrs B.C. Rogers of Bromley, Kent, in 1966.

G. phaeum var. *phaeum* (Figures 9.100 & 9.102, Plate 38) has the petals cuspidate or sometimes lobulate and dark pinkish lilac to nearly black, with silvery white or nearly white bases; the white area has a jagged edge and the flower by transmitted light thus has a star-shaped white centre. In the least dark forms there may be dark veins just above the whitish base. The leaves may be blotched or unblotched. This variety occupies the greater part of the natural range of the species.

G. phaeum var. *phaeum* 'Variegatum' has irregular pale yellow variegation towards the leaf-margins, the variegated areas usually somewhat curled; in the absence of a variegated form of var. *lividum* the name may be written as *G. phaeum* 'Variegatum'.

HYBRID. See 101. *G.* ×*monacense*.

101. G. ×*monacense* Harz (*G. punctatum* of gardens) (Figures 9.103 & 9.104, Plate 38)
Intermediate between 100. *G. phaeum* and 102. *G. reflexum* in colour and shape of petals (1½ times as long as broad) and the degree to which they are reflexed. Immature fruits and their pedicels upwardly inclined. Like 100. *G. phaeum* in requirements and behaviour.

Like 100. *G. phaeum* and 102. *G. reflexum* in vegetative parts, with or without brown blotches on the leaves. Petals 11–14mm, strongly reflexed, about 1½ times as long as broad, sometimes obscurely lobed at the tip, dark dull purplish red or pinkish lilac with a white basal zone and, above this, a dull bluish violet zone which is traversed by darker violet veins; margins at the base with a dense hair-tuft, as in G. reflexum. Stamens with long or very long hairs as in G. phaeum. Immature fruits and their pedicels slightly deflexed or the immature fruits inclined slightly upwards.

Evidently a spontaneous garden hybrid between 100. G. phaeum and 102. G. reflexum.

Plants of this hybrid were found growing near the parents by Dr K. Harz in his garden in Upper Bavaria, and named G. ×monacense after the city of Munich. However, the hybrid has evidently arisen in different places and at different times, for different clones exist, as mentioned below, and apparent intermediates between G. phaeum and G. reflexum were noted by Bowles (1914).

The description above is based on three stocks grown at Cambridge. Two of these have purplish red petals, a little paler and more obviously purplish than those of G. phaeum var. phaeum, which is evidently one of their parents. One of them, which has strongly blotched leaves, was received from Mr G.S. Thomas in 1974 as G. punctatum, a name which is not to be found in botanical literature and rarely even in print (e.g. Johnson, 1937, p. 187) except in nursery catalogues. The other is like the first but with only weak blotches on the leaves. The third stock has lilac-pink petals (darkening slightly with age), and unblotched leaves. The petal-colour is intermediate between that of G. reflexum and G. phaeum var. lividum (as grown at Cambridge), and the latter is presumably one of its parents (it was given to me by Professor R.P. Dales of Horsham, East Sussex). The first two stocks (with darker flowers) represent nothovar. monacense and the third represents nothovar. anglicum. Quite a lot of apparently good seed is produced by these hybrids but I have never sown any.

Attention was drawn to the name G. ×monacense by Clement (1976, p. 24) as a result of the discovery by Mr Patrick Roper of a plant escaped from cultivation at Hurst Green, East Sussex. That plant was brought back into cultivation and has reached me via Mrs J. Forty; it proves to be a second clone of nothovar. anglicum.

Figure 9.103 G × monacense nothovar. anglicum, R.P. Dales, 1979, ex Alan Bloom, as G. phaeum, × ½

G. ×monacense nothovar. anglicum Yeo (Figure 9.103, Plate 38) is the hybrid in which G. phaeum var. lividum has participated; the main petal colour is pinkish lilac and the whitish petal-base is small and straight-edged, while the bluish violet zone above it is wide, conspicuous and strongly veined. In the two clones known to me (see above) the leaves are unblotched, their divisions are

Figure 9.104 G × monacense nothovar. monacense, G.S. Thomas, 1974, as G. punctatum, × ½

comparatively long and narrow, each having the main pair of lobes noticeably divergent, and the teeth and tips of lobes are mostly obtuse. Professor Dales' plant was received from Bloom's of Bressingham, Diss, Norfolk (as *G. phaeum*) where I have seen it myself. The Hurst Green plant has been assigned a cultivar name (see below).

G. ×*monacense* nothovar. *anglicum* Yeo 'Eric Clement' can be written "*G* ×*monacense* 'Eric Clement' ": it applies to the Hurst Green plant (Clifton, 1979, and ms notes). It differs from the Bressingham clone in being slightly more vigorous and in having slightly larger petals, more obviously lobed at the tip and with the edges curved forwards instead of being flat. The leaves do not turn yellow when dying (Clifton, 1979).

G. ×*monacense* nothovar. *monacense* (Figure 9.104, Plate 38) is the hybrid in which *G. phaeum* var. *phaeum* has participated (this is indicated by the way in which Harz described *G. phaeum* when publishing *G.* ×*monacense*). The main petal colour is purplish red (RHSCC Red-Purple Group 64B) and the whitish petal-base is relatively large and has a toothed edge, while the bluish violet zone above it is inconspicuous. Brown blotches are present in the notches of the leaves, the latter being conspicuously yellow when young.

G. ×*monacense* nothovar. *monacense* 'Muldoon' (Clifton, 1979) which may be shortened to "*G.* ×*monacense* 'Muldoon' ", applies to a clone with strongly blotched leaves, presumably the one mentioned above that was received at Cambridge from Mr G.S. Thomas, and often called *G. punctatum*. (The name 'Muldoon' does not apply to the weakly spotted Cambridge clone.)

102. G. reflexum Linnaeus (Figure 9.105, Plate 38) Like 100. *G. phaeum* in vegetative characters. Petals much narrower (twice as long as broad), very strongly reflexed (making flowers only 13–16mm in diameter), rose-pink with a more distinct white base. Immature fruits downwardly inclined. Like *G. phaeum* in requirements and behaviour.

Vegetatively almost identical with 100. *G. phaeum*; leaves usually strongly blotched with brown where the divisions, and sometimes the lobes, meet. Flowers more or less inverted.

Sepals like those of *G. phaeum* but more or less red-flushed. Petals 11–13mm, twice as long as broad or more, sometimes with a triangular point and often with one or more incisions at the tip, very strongly reflexed a short way above the erect base, the tips more spreading where they are pressed outwards by the sepals, bright rose-pink with a white base occupying about ¼ of the petal's length, and with a bluish band between the white and pink areas, without hairs across front surface at base and with a strong tuft at either side (better developed than in *G. phaeum*). Filaments appressed to the style, bordered at the base with very small fine hairs. Immature fruits deflexed or horizontal on deflexed or horizontal pedicels. Mericarps with 3 or 4 keels or ridges around the top. Discharge: Erodium-type.

Figure 9.105 *G. reflexum*, Marburg B.

Italy (in the Apennines from Abruzzo to Marche and Umbria); Yugoslavia (Croatia) to N. Greece (Thessaly).

A plant of similar garden value to 100. *G. phaeum*. The flowers are brighter in colour but appear rather small. Because of its close similarity to *G. phaeum* some authors have treated it as a variety of that. It is more distinct, however, from varieties *phaeum* and *lividum* than they are from one another.

HYBRID. See 101. *G.* ×*monacense*.

103. _G. aristatum_ Freyn (Figure 9.106, Plate 39)

A greyish-hairy perennial of medium size with rather large, coarsely lobed and toothed leaves. Flowers about 22–28mm in diameter, nodding with reflexed oblong petals, nearly white or lilac-pink at tips but with lilac veins becoming merged to a lilac zone at the base. Sepal mucro half as long as sepal body or more. Sun or light shade. Leafless in winter. June onwards.

Figure 9.106 _G. aristatum_, Kew B.G., 1976, × ½

Perennial with a stout rootstock emerging above the surface and nearly erect stems to about 60cm. Basal leaves mostly 15–20cm wide, divided as far as ¾ into 7 or 9, rather pale green; divisions tapered both ways from well above the middle, rather solid in outline; lobes about as long as broad, straight with V-shaped notches between them, and usually with 2–5 unequal teeth. Teeth and tips of lobes acute. Stipules of basal leaves about 2cm, very narrow, tapered to a long point. Stem-leaves paired, usually with five divisions diverging widely from each other, and few coarse lobes and teeth. Stem with branches mostly paired. Plant covered in long hairs, those of the upper parts mostly glandular. Inflorescence loose. Cymules often 3-flowered. Flowers nodding. Sepals 9mm, flushed with pink, reflexed, with a mucro ½–¾ as long as body of sepal. Petals 13–16mm, about twice as long as broad, strongly reflexed just above the base, nearly square-ended but slightly lobed or with a projecting triangular point at the tip, the greater part nearly white or lilac, with ill-defined, slightly netted, lilac-pink veining which coalesces to form a darker blotch on basal ⅓ of petal, without hairs on front surface at base but a dense tuft on either side. Filaments pink at base, white towards tips, appressed to the style, with divergent stiff hairs in the lower half. Anthers cream, becoming pale brown. Nectaries each with a canopy of white hairs. Immature fruits erect on reflexed pedicels. Mericarps about 6mm, with 4 or 5 keels or ridges around the top. Stylar portion of rostrum not distinct. Discharge: Erodium-type.

Mountains of S. Albania, S. Yugoslavia and N.W. Greece.

A fine plant, completely unmistakable, though evidently allied to _G. phaeum,_ etc. Old inflorescences may be cleared away through the long flowering season to keep it looking fresh.

Section Subacaulia, The Cinereum Group

Compact alpine plants with silvery, hoary or greyish green foliage. Main leaves with the divisions not or scarcely tapered to the tip, their lobes usually with few or no teeth. Plants without glandular hairs. Inflorescence with few or no well-developed leaves, with relatively few flowers (often 12 or fewer). Flowers erect. Sepals and petals not reflexed. Apex of mericarp compressed, with 1–3 ribs (occasionally none) around it. Stylar portion of rostrum not distinct.

The number of species is in doubt. The group occurs in the Atlas Mountains of Morocco, in S.E. and N. Spain, in the Pyrenees, French Alps, Apennines, East Italian Alps and Balkan Peninsula, and throughout Turkey, extending thence into Transcaucasia, Syria and Lebanon.

There is a long tradition of recognising two species, _G. argenteum_ and _G. cinereum,_ and accepting a great deal of variation in the latter. The various forms of _G. cinereum_ occurring in Turkey and adjoining countries are particularly difficult to classify and are usually treated as varieties. Davis and Roberts (1955) and Davis (1967), proposed that the uniform Pyrenean representatives of _G. cinereum_ should be treated as subsp. _cinereum_ and that the varieties from further east should be assembled to constitute a second subspecies, _subcaulescens._ The two subspecies were to be distinguished by the single character of the absence of long hairs on the sepals in subsp. *cinereum* and their presence (usually) in subsp. *subcaulescens*. In fact, long hairs can be found on the sepals of the Pyrenean plant, and subsp. *subcaulescens*, being so variable, is a rather meaningless entity. For horticultural purposes it is the varieties that are significant. Conveniently, the International Code of Botanical Nomenclature does not oblige one to allocate the varieties to their respective subspecies if one does not want to, otherwise the names would be cumbersome.

Whereas the variation in the East is catered for mainly by varietal names, that in the West is covered by specific names (one for N.W. Africa and three for Spain apart from the Pyrenees). A second specific name for a Balkan taxon has recently been published (Franzén, 1983). So far, none of the western plants bearing specific names has been introduced into cultivation apart from *G. cinereum* in the original sense.

All members of the group that have been cultivated at Cambridge readily produce hybrids among themselves, and tradition is, I fear, the only justification for retaining *G. cinereum* as a distinct species from *G. argenteum*.

Although, as explained above, the overall pattern of variation in the group causes difficulties in classification, the differences in botanical and horticultural characteristics that occur in *G. cinereum* are so pronounced that the varieties are here numbered separately. The members of the Cinereum Group treated here are listed below, together with their most important cultivars.

104. *G. argenteum*
105. *G.* ×*lindavicum* (*G. argenteum* × *G. cinereum*)
    (a) *G. argenteum* × *G. cinereum* var. *cinereum* with 'Apple Blossom'
    (b) *G. argenteum* × *G. cinereum* var. *subcaulescens* with 'Alanah', 'Gypsy', 'Lissadell' and 'Purpureum'
106. *G. cinereum* var. *cinereum* including 'Album'
107. *G. cinereum* 'Ballerina' together with 'Artistry' and 'Lawrence Flatman' (var. *cinereum* × var. *subcaulescens*)
108. *G. cinereum* var. *obtusilobum*
109. *G. cinereum* var. *palmatipartitum*
110. *G. cinereum* var. *subcaulescens* including 'Giuseppii' and 'Splendens'

104. *G. argenteum* Linnaeus (Figure 9.107A)

A rosette plant with silvery-silky leaves divided nearly to the base, with the lobes not lying flat. Flowers 20–25mm in diameter. Petals more or less notched, pale pink to white with more or less definite, sometimes netted, veins. Rock garden. June–July.

Rootstock compact, covered with rather large hoary stipules. Leaf-stalks and stems greyish with appressed hairs. Blades of basal leaves not more than 5cm wide, divided nearly to the base into 7; divisions usually 3-lobed to beyond the middle; lobes more or less acute, without teeth, not lying flat. Leaf-blades silvery-silky on both sides, the lower surface slightly more thickly clad than the upper. Stems with 1 or 2 solitary leaves and 1 or 2 pairs of leaves; stem leaves smaller and with fewer lobes than the basal. Inflorescence normally with fewer than 10 flowers. Sepals 5.5–8.5mm, silky; mucro about 1mm. Petals about 12–14mm, nearly as broad as long, more or less notched, pale pink to white, often with faint or distinct, more or less netted, darker veins; base with hairs across front surface and a dense tuft on either edge. Filaments white or green; anthers pinkish orange. Stigmas 1–1.5mm, yellow. Immature fruits erect on more or less reflexed pedicels. Mericarps 6–6.5mm. Discharge: Erodium-type.

French Alps (Depts. Hautes Alpes and Basses Alpes), Italy (S. Tirol; Etruscan Apennines), Yugoslavia (Julian Alps).

Somewhat variable in ways which affect its garden value. Propagation is by division, cuttings or root cuttings. One year at Cambridge we attempted to gather seeds from a clonal colony but could find none. Next year, when *G. cinereum* var. *cinereum* was placed beside it, many seeds were formed but all seedlings raised (about 10) proved to be hybrids.

HYBRIDS. See 105. *G.* ×*lindavicum* and remarks on Section *Subacaulia*.

105. *G.* ×*lindavicum* Knuth

This name covers all hybrids between 104. *G. argenteum* and *G. cinereum*, regardless of variety, though it was originally proposed for a cross involving *G. cinereum* var. *subcaulescens*. Because the varieties of *G. cinereum* are so different no common description is given here for *G. argenteum* × *G. cinereum*.

(a). *G. argenteum* × *G. cinereum var. cinereum*. Rather more vigorous than either parent. Leaves slightly silky with slightly or considerably deeper lobes than those of *G. cinereum* var. *cinereum;* lateral divisions not lying flat. Inflorescences long and trailing. Petals 15–19mm, strongly net-veined on a pink or sometimes white ground, rounded or notched at apex. Filaments greenish white; anthers pale yellow with violet edges and yellow pollen. Style tinged with pink; stigmas yellowish.

This description is based on plants raised at Cambridge as described under 104. *G. argenteum*. The cross was previously reported without description by Sündermann in 1906; a description, based on information supplied by Sündermann, was published by Knuth (1912) under the illegitimate name *G. ×intermedium*, attributed to Sündermann (see Appendix I).

G. ×lindavicum 'Apple Blossom' (syn, 'Jenny Bloom') (Figure 9.107B) is low-growing, with silver-grey leaves, the divisions cut for nearly half their length into three lobes with obtusish tips; the petals are not very broad and are rounded a the apex; they are almost white and lightly veined, the veins being faintly netted; stigmas nearly white. This is possibly a back-cross to *G. argenteum*. It was raised by Bloom's Nurseries, Diss, Norfolk.

(b). *G. argenteum* × *G. cinereum* var. *subcaulescens* (De Candolle) Knuth. Plant more or less erect, up to 30cm tall. Leaves greyish-velvety, the divisions lobed for half their length or more. Inflorescences erect (at least at first), leafy, many-flowered. Petals 13–15mm, rounded or weakly notched at apex, rather strong purplish pink, with dark red, slightly feathered veins; these become more diffuse (smudgy) towards the base, broadening into a dark patch with a toothed edge. Filaments red-purple; anthers black. Stigmas dark red.

This description is based on plants raised at Cambridge in 1973 by Mr R. F. Hunter. The plants varied somewhat in habit and persistence but all are now dead. This suggests that if reliable plants are wanted, numerous progeny should be grown and tested. The cross was first raised by Sündermann at Lindau, on the German side of Lake Constance, and it was to this that the name *G. ×lindavicum* was originally applied when published by Knuth (1912).

Figure 9.107 (A) *G. argenteum*, W. Ingwersen, 1958; (B) *G × lindavicum* 'Apple Blossom' (= A × E, probably × A), cult. Harlow Car Gardens, 1983; (C) *G. lindavicum* 'Gypsy' (= A × E × H), cult. Mrs J. Forty, 1983; (D) *G. cinereum* 'Ballerina' (= E × F), R.F. Hunter, 1972; (E) *G. cinereum* var. *cinereum*, Spetchley Park Gardens, 1960; (F) *G. cinereum* var. *subcaulescens*, Alan Bloom, 1957; (G) the same, lateral divisions of one side; (H) *G. cinereum* var. *subcaulescens* 'Splendens', Wisley Gardens, 1976; (I) *G. cinereum* var. *subcaulescens*, J. Akeroyd, R. Mellors & C. Preston, 1976, coll. Greece: Mt Parnassos, × ²⁄₃

G. ×lindavicum 'Alanah' (*G. argenteum* 'Alanah') was described by Ingwersen (1946) as just slightly less silvery in the foliage than *G. argenteum*, and extremely free in the production of its vivid crimson-purple flowers; he said it had been raised by Sir Jocelyn Gore-Booth in his garden at Lissadell in Ireland as a cross of *G. argenteum* with a very fine form of *G. cinereum* var. *subcaulescens*. There do not seem to be any plants in circulation under the name 'Alanah' at present, but it is mentioned here because Ingwersen thought it was the same as 'the plant known as *G. argenteum* var. *purpureum*' (see *G.* ×*lindavicum* 'Purpureum'). Clifton (1979) gives a different story, apparently obtained from an early twentieth-century catalogue of J. Stormonth, according to which the parentage is *G. argenteum* 'Purpureum' × *G. traversii*, which is very improbable. See also *G.* ×*lindavicum* 'Lissadell'.

G. ×*lindavicum* 'Gypsy' (Figure 9.107C, Plate 40) is fairly low-growing; the upper surface of the leaf-blade is grey-green and only sparsely hairy; the leaf-divisions are broad at the tips, lobed for ⅓–½ their length and toothed also, the teeth and tips of lobes being acute; the petals are rounded and irregularly lobed or with a small narrow notch, of a brilliant pink-cerise shot with carmine, fading to white just above the maroon, butterfly-shaped blotch at the base, and closely net-veined with maroon; the anthers are black and the filaments and stigmas much the same colour as the petal-blotch. The colour of the flowers is not like that of any other *Geranium* I know: a flamboyant gypsy! The plant was raised in the 1970s by Eric Smith, partner with J.C. Archibald in 'The Plantsmen', a now defunct firm at Buckshaw Gardens, Sherborne, Dorset, where the cross was made; it is believed to be from *G.* ×*lindavicum* 'Lissadell' pollinated with *G. cinereum* var. *subcaulescens* 'Splendens' (in which case it is a back-cross to *G. cinereum* var. *subcaulescens*).

G. ×*lindavicum* 'Lissadell' is similar to 'Alanah'; Clifton (1979) states that it has a beautiful silvery leaf and rich wine-coloured flowers. I have no detailed notes on 'Lissadell' but I saw it at Wisley in 1971 and observed that the leaf-lobes were narrower than those of 'Purpureum' (below).

G. ×*lindavicum* 'Purpureum' (*G. argenteum* 'Purpureum') was considered by Ingwersen (1946) to be the same as *G.* ×*lindavicum* 'Alanah', in which case the description quoted above for that applies here. Plants are probably still current under the present name; one I saw at Wisley in 1971 appeared to be the present hybrid, and I noted that 'Lissadell' was very similar except in the width of the leaf-lobes (see above).

106. G. cinereum Cavanilles var. **cinereum** (Figures 9.107 E & 9.108, Plate 41)
A rosette plant with grey-green leaves divided as far as ⁴/₅ of their radius. Flowering stems trailing. Flowers about 33mm in diameter. Petals notched, white or pink with a strong network of very fine pinkish purple veins or entirely white. Rock garden. June–August.

Rootstock compact, covered with relatively small stipules. Blades of basal leaves not more than 5cm wide, divided as far as ¾ or ⁴/₅ into 5 or 7; divisions wedge-shaped, usually 3-lobed for ¹/₅–⅓ of their length, the lobes about as broad as long, more or less acute, without teeth, the lateral more or less bent upwards. Leaf-blades greyish green, an effect not produced by hairs, which are small and sparse. Stem-leaves paired, smaller and with fewer lobes than the basal. Stems with up to 5 pairs of leaves but inflorescence usually with 10 or fewer flowers. Sepals 7.5–9.5mm; mucro 1mm or less. Petals about 17mm, notched, translucent white or pale pink with a dense network of fine, sharply defined, pinkish purple veins; base with a few hairs across front surface and a dense tuft on either edge. Filaments white; anthers yellowish. Stigmas 2mm, green. Immature fruits erect on more or less reflexed pedicels. Mericarps about 5.5mm. Discharge: Erodium-type.

Central Pyrenees.

Can be propagated by division or from seeds if grown in isolation from other members of the *G. cinereum* group. The strongly coloured plants which are recommended to be grown by Ingwersen (1946) must be hybrids, though a degree of variation in the ground-colour occurs naturally.

G. cinereum var. *cinereum* 'Album' has completely white flowers.

HYBRIDS. See 105. *G.* ×*lindavicum* and 107. *G. cinereum* 'Ballerina' and remarks on section *Subacaulia*.

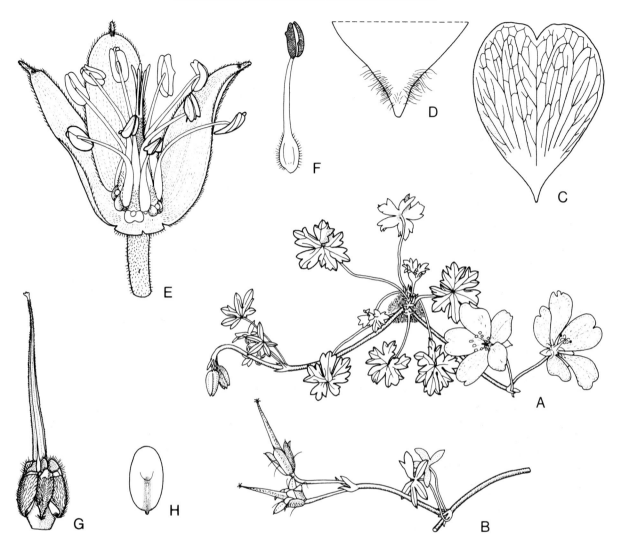

Figure 9.108 G. *cinereum* var. *cinereum* (Spetchley Park Gardens, 1960). (A) plant beginning to flower, × ²/₃ ; (B) branch bearing cymule with immature fruit, × ²/₃ ; (C) petal, with pigmentation, × 2; (D) base of front surface of petal, × 4; (E) flower in male stage with petals and two sepals removed, × 4; (F) stamen of outer whorl, × 4; (G) fruit in pre-explosive interval, × 2; (H) seed, × 4

107. G. cinereum Cavanilles 'Ballerina' (Figure 9.107D, Plate 42)

Like G. *cinereum* var. *cinereum* in habit, with slightly grey leaves. Flowers up to 32mm across; petals notched, of a rather sombre purplish pink with a close network of dark red veins and a dark patch at the base. Rock garden. June onwards.

Blades of basal leaves not more than 5cm wide, divided as far as ⁴/₅ or ⁵/₆ into 7; divisions lobed for ⅓ to nearly half of their length, the lobes often with a tooth; tips of lobes and teeth obtuse. Leaf-blades a slightly greyish green. Stem leaves paired, rather well developed, with 5 divisions, their lobes occasionally toothed, more or less acute. Stems with about 4 pairs of leaves and about 8 flowers. Sepals 7–10mm, recurved at tips, with mucro about 0.5mm. Petals 18 x 16mm, drawn out into a long point at base, narrowly notched at apex, ground-colour pale purplish pink, fading towards base, marked with a close network of strong, fine, dark red veins which converge to form a very dark red V-shaped basal zone; base with hairs across front and a strong tuft on either edge. Stamens blackish red. Stigmas red.

An outstanding hybrid between *G. cinereum* var. *cinereum* and var. *subcaulescens,* raised by Bloom's Nurseries, Diss, Norfolk. It received a Preliminary Commendation of the Royal Horticultural Society in 1961 and an Award of Merit in 1976. Although a few good seeds are formed the plant seems to be largely sterile, which may partly account for its prolonged flowering season. The flowers are dramatically rather than vividly coloured. 'Ballerina' is easily propagated by cuttings or by division. Bloom has introduced two other cultivars of the same parentage, 'Artistry', with a clearer pink ground-colour in the flowers, and 'Lawrence Flatman', which is very similar to 'Ballerina' but more vigorous, with less regular petals in which there is a triangle of darker ground-colour at the apex with its tip pointing towards the base; this is not present in all flowers, presumably depending on age.

108. *G. cinereum* Cavanilles var. *obtusilobum* (Bornmüller) Yeo (Figure 9.109A)

Rosette plant with very small, soft, pale green leaves with blunt lobes. Flowers bowl-shaped, about 28mm in diameter. Petals oblong, notched, white, tinged with pink, with fine slightly feathered veins. Rock garden. June onwards.

Rootstock prolifically branched, covered with pale brown papery stipules. Leaf-blades not more than 3cm wide, divided as far as about $^2/_3$ into 5 or 7; divisions 3-lobed for $^1/_3$ of their length, the lobes obtuse or, in late-season growth, more or less acute. Leaf-blades light green, velvety above, more or less woolly beneath. Peduncles emerging directly from the rootstock at the beginning of the season, borne

Figure 9.109 (A) *G. cinereum* var. *obtusilobum,* W.K. Aslet, 1974, coll. Lebanon: Mt Lebanon; (B) *G. cinereum* var. *palmatipatritum,* E.M. Rix, 1972, coll. Turkey: Sivas Prov., × $^2/_3$

on few-branched stems later. Flowers bowl-shaped. Sepals 6.5–8.5mm; mucro 0.5mm or less. Petals about 17mm, tending to be oblong, apex notched, ground-colour white, faintly tinged with pink around the edges, inconspicuously marked with fine reddish purple veins, forking towards their extremities; base with a few hairs across front and a small tuft on either edge. Filaments white; anthers yellowish brown. Stigmas pink. Mericarps about 5.5mm. Discharge: Erodium-type.

Lebanon, Syria.

This variety was introduced by the late Mr Ken Aslet from Mount Lebanon about 1974. One wonders whether he knew of Walter Ingwersen's commendation of it as a desirable plant (Ingwersen, 1946), which proved to be fully justified. In colouring it recalls *G. cinereum* var. *cinereum* but is quite different in character, with its tiny blunt-lobed leaves and flowers held well above them. The rootstock is profusely branched and propagation is very easy. It is reproducible from seed by self-fertilisation.

HYBRIDS. At Cambridge this has produced hybrids with other members of the *G. cinereum* group when seed has been sown, and from self-sown seed.

109. *G. cinereum* Cavanilles var. *palmatipartitum* Knuth (Figure 9.109B)

Rosette plant with greyish, acutely lobed leaves. Flowers somewhat bowl-shaped, about 27–30mm in diameter, pink with large white centre; stigmas and tips of stamens purple (not blackish). Rock garden. June onwards.

Stems erect or ascending. Leaf-blades not more than 5cm wide, divided as far as about $^4/_5$ into 7; divisions lobed for about $^1/_3$ of their length, the lobes entire, acute, variable in breadth, unequal, sometimes tending to be considerably reduced or occasionally suppressed so that the division is narrowly elliptic instead of wedge-shaped. Leaf-blades generally silver-grey and velvety. Inflorescence usually with 6 or 8 flowers. Sepals 8–11mm; mucro 0.5–1mm. Flowers somewhat bowl-shaped. Petals about 18mm, varying in width, not significantly notched, clear rose-pink in the outer half, fading gently to nearly white about the middle, marked with fine dark veins which are slightly feathered towards the tips; base without hairs across front but with a weak tuft on either edge. Filaments white at base, coloured more darkly than the petals at the tips; anthers purplish red. Stigmas 1.5–2mm, dull crimson. Mericarps 7.5mm. Discharge: Erodium-type.

East Central Turkey.

This variety is not securely established in cultivation but is included here for two reasons. The first is that in 1972 Dr Martyn Rix collected three plants from a single population in the Province of Sivas (Rix 2038) and presented them to the Cambridge Botanic Garden. All were different in details of leaf lobing, intensity of flower-colour and breadth of petals. Only one has survived but fortunately it is the handsomest in flower. The details of the colouring of the flowers are the same as in the herbarium specimens of the only two previously known gatherings of the variety. The second reason is that *G. cinereum* var. *elatius* Davis, which is so closely related to var. *palmatipartitum* that it is doubtful whether it merits varietal separation, was grown at Edinburgh from the time of its collection in 1952 at least until 1956, when specimens were prepared for distribution to herbaria. This plant has large leaves (between 5 and 10cm wide) with occasionally toothed lobes, and quite robust stems to 50cm long. The flowers have the same colouring as those of Rix's plant but the petals are narrower.

The surviving plant at Cambridge is a beautiful thing but we have not succeeded in propagating it either by shoot or root cuttings (but the latter were not attempted at the best time). All seedlings raised, with one possible exception (which does not match the parent in beauty), have been hybrids, and it is probable that this variety is self-incompatible. If the variety should ever be collected again a number of clones should be obtained (or seeds collected), and once plants are established they should be pollinated among themselves in isolation from other members of the *G. cinereum* group before the collection is dispersed.

HYBRIDS. See remarks on section *Subacaulia*.

110. G. cinereum Cavanilles var. **subcaulescens** (De Candolle) Knuth (*G. subcaulescens* De Candolle) (Figures 9.107F, G & I, Plate 43)
Rosette plant with rather dull dark green leaves. Flowers 22–25mm in diameter. Petals brilliant deep purplish red, with a distinct black triangle at the base or at least a very dark area where the veins converge; stamens and stigmas black or nearly so. Rock garden. May–June and usually again later.

Rootstock covered with dark brown stipules and ranging from very compact to quite elongated. Blades of basal leaves not more than 5cm wide, divided as far as ¾ or nearly to the base into 5 or 7; divisions lobed for ⅓–½ their length; lobes as broad as long and obtuse or up to two or more times as long as broad and acute, with occasional teeth. Leaf-blades rather dark green, with minute or quite long and loose hairs. Peduncles emerging from the rootstock or borne on stems with solitary or paired leaves. Inflorescences with 6 or 8 flowers. Sepals 6–8mm; mucro 0.5–1mm. Petals 12–15mm, nearly as wide as long, notched or rounded at apex, triangular or constricted at base, brilliant deep purplish red, often paler towards base but with a blackish, rayed spot at the base, or with a dark red zone at base formed by the converging veins; veins very dark red, reaching ½–¾ of the way up the petal, sometimes netted; base without hairs across front surface but with a small tuft on each edge. Filaments blackish red; anthers black. Stigmas black or nearly so. Mericarps 5–6mm. Discharge: Erodium-type.

Balkan Peninsula and C. and N.E. Turkey.

A really splendid plant for those not afraid to admire a dazzling colour. However, to quote Ingwersen (1946) 'some assert that the typical plant verges dangerously on magenta, a barbaric colour disliked especially by ladies'. He then recommended the var. *grandiflorum* (which I do not know) as offering no danger in this respect.

G. cinereum var. *subcaulescens* is extremely variable, but in my view it comprises all forms with rather dark leaves, deep purplish red petals, more or less dark at the base, and blackish stamens and stigmas. Plants from southern Italy appear to have rather paler petals and still paler stamens and stigmas, and I have therefore omitted this area from the statement of natural distribution. It is remarkable that plants with black-centred flowers re-appear in central and eastern Turkey; they are assigned by Davis and Roberts (1955) partly to var. *subcaulescens* (which also, in their view, includes paler-flowered plants from S.W. Turkey) and partly to var. *ponticum* Davis & Roberts.

The plant was cultivated in Central Europe at the beginning of the twentieth century, having been used by Sündermann in a cross with *G. argenteum* (Knuth, 1912). It was brought to Britain independently by two expeditionary parties in 1929, one composed of Mr Walter Ingwersen and Dr P.L. Giuseppi, who collected it at Korab, and the other of Dr R. Seligman and H.R.S. (?H.R. Spivey), who collected it on Mount Kaimachkalan in Serbia (*Alpine Garden Society Bulletin, 2,* 195, 1934). This is doubtless the reason why there is even now a clone in circulation named after Dr Giuseppi, although when the name was first coined I do not know. A second cultivar, 'Splendens', has emerged comparatively recently. The latter is grown at Cambridge and is distinct from three other stocks also grown there, namely one supplied by Mr Alan Bloom (Figure 9.107F, Plate 43), one collected by Dr Alexis Vlasto near Tetovo in Yugoslavia (his no. 28, 1959), and one collected as seed by Akeroyd, Mellors & Preston (no. 375, 1976) (Figure 9.107I).

All stocks seem to be propagated quite easily from cuttings or divisions, and at least Dr Vlasto's reproduces itself from seed.

G. cinereum var. *subcaulescens* 'Giuseppii' has the petals moderately broad and varying from rounded to weakly notched at the apex even in the same flower, not quite magenta in colour, and with no distinct black basal spot, but merely a dark area formed by the convergent bases of the veins; the ground-colour becomes pale just above the base. The name is persistently mis-spelt as 'Guiseppii'; it is sometimes applied to plants in which there is no fading of the ground-colour towards the dark basal area but I suspect that this is incorrect. (For origin, see above.)

G. cinereum var. *subcaulescens* 'Splendens' (Figure 9.107H, Plate 44) has broad, rounded, weakly notched petals of a brilliant but not harsh colour, slightly iridescent, with a distinct blackish red basal blotch, well-marked dark veins and a white zone along each margin for a short distance above the basal blotch; the leaves have shallow blunt lobes, some of them toothed, also bluntly. A most charming plant, but not so easily suited in cultivation as other forms. Said by Clifton (1979) to have been introduced by J. Stormonth about 1936 and offered again in 1974 by Stanton Alpine Nurseries.

HYBRIDS. See 105. *G.* ×*lindavicum* and 107. *G. cinereum* 'Ballerina'.

Glossary

This glossary defines terms as they are used in this book or as they apply to *Geranium*. Some of the definitions do not have validity in a wider context, while some terms have additional or wider meanings not mentioned here. Reference to Chapters 4 or 5 means that the term is defined or illustrated there; when this is the case only terms that can be explained simply are defined here.

annual a plant which completes its life-cycle from seed to seed in less than a year.

anther the terminal part of a stamen, containing the pollen.

anthocyanin a class of plant pigments, ranging in colour from blue through purple to red, imparting these colours to flowers and often suffusing the chlorophyll-containing (green) parts of the plant.

appressed pressed up against a surface (as hairs on a leaf, leaves on the ground) or organ (as stamens against the style).

awn in this book used for a particular floral part (Chapter 4, p. 28).

axil the angle between the base of a leaf and the part of the stem that forms the next internode above it.

axillary situated in an axil.

back-cross a cross between a hybrid and one of its parents; to make such a cross.

biennial a plant that completes its life-cycle from seed to seed in a period of more than one year but less than two.

bilaterally symmetric (of a flower) with a single plane of symmetry, along which it can be divided into halves which are mirror-images of each other.

bract a leaf found in the inflorescence and having a reduced size and modified shape (Chapter 4, p. 25).

bracteate furnished with bracts.

bracteole a small bract; in *Geranium* it applies to the small bracts at the bases of the pedicels in a cymule (Chapter 4, p. 27).

calyx collective term for all the sepals of one flower.

carpel one of the hollow structures in the centre of the flower that contain the ovules, each bearing a style.

carpel-projection a term adopted here for one of the methods of seed-dispersal found in *Geranium* (Chapter 5, p. 32).

central column (of a fruit) Chapter 4, p. 28.

chromosome one of the microscopic thread-like or rod-like bodies, consisting of nucleic acid and containing the genes, that appear in a cell-nucleus shortly before cell-division.

claw the stalk of a stalked petal (Chapter 4, p.27).

clone the sum-total of the plants derived from vegetative reproduction of an individual and having the same genetic constitution.

cotyledon one of the two leaves pre-formed in the seed.

cultivar a variant of horticultural interest that is not conveniently treated as one of the categories (such as subspecies, variety) in a botanical classification (its name is written in single quotation marks and with capital initial letters).

cuspidate with a sharp, shortly tapered point on an otherwise blunt apex.

cymule Chapter 4, p. 27.

dense (of an inflorescence) Chapter 4, p. 27.

diffuse (of an inflorescence) Chapter 4, p. 27; (of coloured veins on a petal) smudgy.

diploid a set of chromosomes the various members of which can be matched up in pairs; a diploid plant is one in which each of the vegetative cells contains a diploid chromosome set.

division (of a leaf) Chapter 4, p. 28.

eglandular hairs Chapter 4, p. 29.

endemic confined, as a native, to a named (usually small) area.

Erodium-type a term adopted here for one of the methods of seed-dispersal found in *Geranium* (Chapter 5, p. 32).

female stage (of a flower) Chapter 4, p. 27.

filament the slender part of a stamen which bears the anther at its tip (see *stamen*).

glandular hairs Chapter 4, Figure 4.5.

haploid a set of chromosomes, the members of which cannot be paired off; two haploid sets go to make a diploid set (see *diploid*).

hexaploid a set of chromosomes, the various members of which can be matched up in sets of six (compare *diploid*).

inflorescence Chapter 4, p. 26.

internode a length of stem extending from one node to the next.

inverted flowers Chapter 4, p. 30.

lobe (of a leaf) Chapter 4, p. 28.

lobulate bearing a series of small lobes.

male stage (of a flower) Chapter 4, p. 27.

mericarp Chapter 4, p. 28.

mucro (of leaf-teeth and lobes) a short narrow point at the tip; (of a sepal) in this book used of the narrow point at the tip, regardless of length.

mucronate provided with a short narrow point at the tip.

nectary Chapter 4, p. 27.

nectar passage a tube or orifice formed above each nectary by the shaping of the petal bases.

nodding flowers Chapter 4, p. 30.

node the point on a stem at which a leaf or pair of leaves is attached.

opposite (of leaves) Chapter 4, p. 25.

palmate a group of leaf-divisions, leaf-lobes or veins all radiating from the same point.

palmato-pinnate (of a leaf-division) Chapter 4, p. 29.

pedicel Chapter 4, p. 27.

peduncle Chapter 4, p. 27.

petal Chapter 4, Figure 4.5.

pinnate an arrangement in which leaf-lobes or veins arise at intervals on either side of a leaf-division or central vein.

radially symmetric (of a flower) with the parts alike and arranged in circles, so that the flower can be divided into identical halves, which are mirror-images of each other, along a number of planes passing through the centre (this number being five in the case of *Geranium* which has floral parts in fives).

rhizome a horizontal stem, situated underground or on the substratum, with roots arising from some or all of its nodes (see also *stolon*).

rootstock Chapter 4, p. 26.

rosette Chapter 4, p. 25.

rostrum Chapter 4, p. 28, 30.

seed-ejection a term adopted here for one of the methods of seed-dispersal found in *Geranium* (Chapter 5, p. 32).

segment (of a leaf) Chapter 4, p. 29.

sepal Chapter 4, Figure 4.5.

solitary (of leaves) Chapter 4, p. 26.

stamen the organ of the flower which produces the pollen, there being 10 of them in a flower of *Geranium* (Figure 4.5; see also *filament* and *anther*).

stigma Chapter 4, p. 27.

stipule one of the pair of small appendages found beside the base of the leaf-stalk.

stolon a far-creeping, more or less slender, above-ground or underground rhizome giving rise to a new plant at its tip and sometimes at intermediate nodes.

stylar portion (of the rostrum) Chapter 4, p. 30.

style Chapter 4, Figure 4.5.

subtending leaf the leaf in the axil of which a named organ is situated.

taxon a named assemblage of plants, regardless of rank, such as a family, species or variety (see Chapter 3, p. 21).

tetraploid a set of chromosomes, the various members of which can be matched up in sets of four (compare *diploid*).

triploid a set of chromosomes, the various members of which can be matched up in sets of three (compare *diploid*).

tuber a swollen underground stem or root used for food-storage.

type specimen see Chapter 3, p. 22.

umbel-like Chapter 4, p. 27.

whorl a circlet of 3 or more similar organs (e.g. petals, leaves) attached at the same level.

References

There are a number of small publications on *Geranium* produced by botanic gardens, horticultural societies and individuals. These are not obtainable through booksellers and they are distinguished here by the fact that the number of pages they contain is indicated.

Aiton, W. (1789) *Hortus Kewensis, 2*

Allan, H.H. (1961) *Flora of New Zealand, 1,* Wellington

Bailey Hortorium, USA (1976) *Hortus Third,* New York and London

Bailey, L.H. (1914–17) *Standard Cyclopedia of Horticulture* (4 vols.) (also in 3 vols. & 6 vols.; various later printings), New York and London

Baker, H.G. (1956) 'Geranium purpureum Vill. and G. robertianum L. in the British flora. II. *Geranium robertianum*', Watsonia, 3, 270–9

——(1957) 'Genecological studies in *Geranium* (Section Robertiana). General considerations and the races of G. purpureum Vill.', *New Phytologist, 56,* 172–92

Berrisford, J.M. (1963) *Gardening on Lime*, London

Bobrov, E.G. (1949) 'Geraniaceae' in B.K. Shishkin & E.G. Bobrov, *Flora of USSR, 14*, Moscow and Leningrad

Bocher, T.W. (1947) 'Cytogenetic and biological studies in *Geranium robertianum*', *Biologiske Meddelelser, 20 (8)*

Bowles, E.A. (1914) *My Garden in Summer*, London

——(1921) 'Hardy geraniums for the wild garden, woodland and border', *The Garden, 85*, 308, 321, 344–5, 369

Brickell, C.D. *et al.* (1980) *International Code of Nomenclature for Cultivated Plants — 1980, Regnum Vegetabile, 104*, Utrecht, 32 pages

Burman, J. (1738–9) *Rariorum africanorum plantarum*, Amsterdam

Carolin, R.C. (1964) 'The genus *Geranium* L. in the south western Pacific area', *Proceedings of the Linnean Society of New South Wales, 89*, 326–61

Chittenden, F.J. (ed.) (1951) *Royal Horticultural Society Dictionary of Gardening*, 4 vols., Oxford

Clement, E. (1976) 'Adventive news 5', *BSBI News, 13*, 33–4

Clifton, R. (1979) *Hardy Geraniums (Cranesbills) Today*, Farnham, Surrey (British Pelargonium and Geranium Society), 16 pages

——(1982) '*Geranium traversii* — hybrids and cultivars', *Geraniaceae Group News, 6*, 3–4

——(1984) Geranium Family, Species Check List, 3rd edn, Part 2, *Geranium*, 55 pages

Crann, M. (1982) Harlow Car Publications, no. 1: *Geraniums*, Harrogate, 12 pages

Crichton, V. & Crawford, M. (1979) *Green Pages*, London, etc.

Dahlgren, K.V.O. (1923) '*Geranium bohemicum* L. × *G. bohemicum* *deprehensum Erik Almq., ein grün-weiss-marmorierter Bastard', *Hereditas, 4*, 239–49

——(1925) 'Die reziproken Bastarde zwischen *Geranium bohemicum* L. und seiner Unterart *deprehensum Erik Almq.', *Hereditas, 6*, 237–56

Davis, P.H. (1967) '*Geranium*' in P.H. Davis, J. Cullen and M.J.E. Coode (eds.), *Flora of Turkey, 2*, 451–74, Edinburgh

——(1970) '*Geranium* sect. *Tuberosa*, revision and evolutionary interpretation', *Israel Journal of Botany, 19*, 91–113

Davis, P.H. & Roberts, J. (1955) 'Materials for a Flora of Turkey, I — Geraniaceae', *Notes from the Royal Botanic Garden Edinburgh, 22*, 9–27

De Candolle, A.P. (1824) *Prodromus Systematis Naturalis Regni Vegetabilis, 1*, Paris

Drabble, E. & Drabble, H. (1908) '*Geranium pratense* × *Robertianum*', *Journal of Botany, London, 46*, 301

Edgeworth, M.P. & Hooker, J.D. (1874) 'Geraniaceae' in J.D. Hooker, *Flora of British India, 1*, 426–40, London

Everett, T.H. (1981) *New York Botanical Garden Encyclopedia of Horticulture, 5*, New York, London

Farrer, R. (1917) *On the Eaves of the World, 2*, London

——(1919) *The English Rock Garden*, 2 vols., London and Edinburgh (several subsequent impressions appeared)

Folkard, O.G. (1974) 'A Geranium hybrid', *Journal of the Royal Horticultural Society, 99*, 316–17 & fig. 145

Forty, J. (1980) 'A survey of hardy Geraniums in cultivation', *The Plantsman, 2*, 67–78

——(1981) 'Further notes on hardy geraniums', *The Plantsman, 3*, 127–8

Franzén, R. (1983) '*Geranium thessalum*, sp. nov. from northern Greece,' *Nordic Journal of Botany, 2 (6)*, 549–52

Gams, H. (1923–4) 'Geraniaceae' in G. Hegi, *Illustrierte Flora von Mittel-Europa*, 1st edn, *IV (3)*, 1656–1725, Munich

Grigson, G. (1955) *The Englishman's Flora*, London

Hardy Plant Society (1982) *The Hardy Plant Directory, Silver Jubilee Edition*

Harz, K. (1921) '*Geranium phaeum* L. + *G. reflexum* L.=*G. monacense* Harz', *Mitteilungen der Bayerischen Botanischen Gesellschaft, 4*, 7

Hedlund, T. (1901) 'Om frukten hos *Geranium bohemicum*', *Botaniska Notiser, 1901–1902*, 1–39

Hooker, J.D. (1879) '*Geranium atlanticum*', *Curtis's Botanical Magazine, 105*, tab. 6452

Hylander, N. (1960) *Vara Prydnadsväxters Namn*, revised edn, Boras

——(1961) 'Kungsnävan, vara trädgardars praktfullaste *Geranium*', *Lustgarden, 1961*, 109–14

Ingwersen, W. (1946) *The Genus Geranium*, East Grinstead, 31 pages

Jeffrey, C. (1977) *Biological Nomenclature*, 2nd edn, London

——(1982) *An Introduction to Plant Taxonomy*, 2nd edn, Cambridge

Johnson, A.T. (1937) *A Woodland Garden*, London, New York

Jones, G.N. & Jones, F.J. (1943) 'A revision of the perennial species of *Geranium* of the United States and Canada', *Rhodora, 45*, 5–53

Knuth, R. (1912) 'Geraniaceae' in A. Engler, *Das Pflanzenreich, 1V. 129*, Leipzig

Kokwaro, J.O. (1971) 'The family "Geraniaceae" in North-east Tropical Africa', *Webbia, 25*, 623–69

Lawrence, G.H.M., Buchheim, A.F.G., Daniels, G.S. & Dolezal, H. (eds.) (1968), *B-P-H, Botanico-Periodicum-Huntianum*, Pittsburgh

Lawrence, W.J.C. (1948) *Practical Plant Breeding*, 2nd edn, London

Linnaeus, C. (1753) *Species Plantarum*, 2 vols.

Llewellyn, J., Hudson, B. & Morrison, G.C. (1981) *Growing Geraniums and Pelargoniums in Australia and New Zealand*, Kenthurst

Loudon, J.C. (1830) *Hortus Britannicus* (and 2nd edn, 1832)

Lundström, E. (1914) 'Plantae in horto botanico bergiano annis 1912–1913 critice examinatae, *Geranium' Acta Horti Bergiani, 5* (3), 50–77

McClintock, D. (1980) *A Guide to the Naming of Plants with Special Reference to Heathers*, 2nd edn, Leicester, 37 pages

Moore, H.E. (1943) 'A revision of the genus *Geranium* in Mexico and Central America', *Contributions from the Gray Herbarium, 146*

——(1963) '*Geranium campii* and *G. durangense* — two new species', *Brittonia, 15*, 92–5

Nasir, Y.J. (1983) 'Geraniaceae', in E. Nasir & S.I. Ali, *Flora of Pakistan, 149*, 1–43, Islamabad

Nicholson, G. (1884–7) *Dictionary of Gardening*, 4 vols., London

Ohwi, J. (1965) *Flora of Japan*, Washington

Paterson, A. (1981) *Plants for Shade*, London.

Rix, M. & Phillips, R. (1981) *The Bulb Book*, London

Robertson, K.R. (1972) 'The genera of Geraniaceae in the southeastern United States', *Journal of the Arnold Arboretum, 53*, 182–201

Rostański, K. & Tokarski, M. (1973) '*Geranium wilfordii* Maxim. an ephemerophyte new to the Polish flora', *Fragmenta Floristica et Geobotanica, 19*, 385–8 (in Polish with English summary)

Rowley, G.D. (1980) *Name That Succulent*, Cheltenham

Royal Horticultural Society Colour Chart (1966), London

Sansome, F.W. (1936) 'Experiments with *Geranium* species', *Journal of Genetics, 33*, 359–63

Schönbeck-Temesy, E. (1970), 'Geraniaceae' in K.H. Rechinger (ed.), *Flora Iranica, 69*, 1–67, Graz

Stace, C.A. (1975) *Hybridization and the Flora of the British Isles*, London, New York, San Francisco

Stafleu, F.A. & Cowan, R.S. (1976–83), *Taxonomic Literature*, 2nd edn, vols. 1–4 (incomplete), Utrecht, Antwerp, The Hague, Boston

Stapf, O. (1926) '*Geranium farreri*', *Curtis's Botanical Magazine, 151*, tab. 9092

Stephens, J. (1967) 'A new hybrid Geranium', *Journal of the Royal Horticultural Society, 92*, 491

Stungo, R. (1982) 'National Reference Collections', *The Garden, 107*, 462–4

Sweet, R. (1820–30) *Geraniaceae*, 5 vols. London

Synge, P.M. & Platt, J.W.O. (1962) *Some Good Garden Plants*, new edn, London

Thomas, G.S. (1958) *The Modern Florilegium*, Windlesham, Surrey (Sunningdale Nurseries), 80 pages

——(1960) 'Geraniums for ground cover', *Gardeners Chronicle, 147*, 480–1, 504, 508–9

——(1970) *Plants for Ground-Cover*, 1st edn, London

——(1976) *Perennial Garden Plants*, 1st edn, London

——(1977) *Plants for Ground-Cover*, 2nd edn, London

——(1982) *Perennial Garden Plants*, 2nd edn, London

Thompson, D. (1982) *Hardy Geraniums*, Seattle, 24 pages

Tokarski, M. (1972) 'Morphological and taxonomical analysis of fruits and seeds of the European and Caucasian species of the genus *Geranium* L.' *Monographiae Botanicae, 36* (in Polish with English captions and summary)

Veldkamp, J.F. & Moerman, A. (1978) 'A review of the Malesian species of *Geranium* L. (Geraniaceae)', *Blumea, 24*, 463–77

Voss, E.G., *et al.* (1983) *International Code of Botanical Nomenclature*, Utrecht, etc.

Walters, S.M. *et al.* (eds.) (1984) *The European Garden Flora, 2*, Cambridge, London, New York, New Rochelle, Melbourne, Sydney

Warburg, E.F. (1938) 'Taxonomy and relationship in the Geraniales in the light of their cytology', *New Phytologist*, 37, 130–59, 189–210

Webb, D.A. & Ferguson, I.K. (1968) 'Geraniaceae' in T.G. Tutin *et al.* (eds.), *Flora Europaea*, 2, 193–204, Cambridge

Wilson, R.F. (1939 and 1942) *Horticultural Colour Chart*, 2 vols., London

Wolley Dod, C. (1903) 'Geraniums', *Flora and Sylva*, 1, 54–7

Yeo, P.F. (1970) 'The *Geranium palmatum* group in Madeira and the Canary Isles', *Journal of the Royal Horticultural Society*, 95, 410–14, and correction (1971), ibid., 96, 44

——(1973) 'Geranium procurrens', *Curtis's Botanical Magazine*, 139, tab. 644

——(1975) 'Geranium species from Mount Victoria, Burma', *Notes from the Royal Botanic Garden Edinburgh*, 34, 195–200

——(1977) *A Guide to Cranesbills* (Geranium), Cambridge University Botanic Garden, 14 pages, 2nd revision, 1981, 16 pages

——(1983) 'Geranium candicans and G. yunnanense of gardens', *The Garden*, 109, 36–7

——(1984a) 'Geranium pylzowianum, the rice-grain geranium and its mysterious ally', *Kew Magazine*, 1, 111–18 (colour plates have captions transposed)

——(1984b) 'Fruit-discharge type in *Geranium* (Geraniaceae): its use in classification and its evolutionary implications', *Botanical Journal of the Linnean Society*, 89, 1–36

Appendix I

Place of Publication and Meaning of Scientific Names

Numbers in bold type are those of species (etc.) in Chapter 9; the 'equals' sign (=) indicates a synonym mentioned under the number cited. Author citations are given in full; elsewhere in the book author-names followed by 'ex' or preceded by 'in' are omitted. I have seen all references except those asterisked.

G. aconitifolium L'Héritier, in Aiton, *Hort. Kew.*, 2, 435 (1789), = **10** (with leaves like *Aconitum*, Monkshood)

G. albanum Bieberstein, *Fl. Taur.-Cauc.*, 2, 137 (1808), **83** (pertaining to Albania, Roman province on Caspian Sea, now Daghestan)

G. albidum Rydberg ex Hanks & Small, *N. Amer. Fl.*, 25, 19 (1907), before **61** (whitish)

G. albiflorum Ledebour, *Icon. Fl. Pl. Ross.*, 1, 6 (1829), **12** (white-flowered)

G. alpestre Schur, *Verh. Mitt. Siebenb. Ver. Naturw.*, 10, 131 (1859), not Chaix (1785), = **9** (found in the lower alps)

G. alpicola Loesener, *Bull. Herb. Boiss., ser. 2, 3*, 92 (1903), before **62** (an inhabitant of alps)

G. anemonifolium L'Héritier, in Aiton, *Hort. Kew.*, 2, 432 (1789), = **98** (anemone-leaved)

G. angulatum Curtis, *Bot. Mag.*, 6, tab. 203 (1792), = **9** (angled, referring to the stem)

G. argenteum Linnaeus, *Cent. Pl.*, 2, 25 (1756), **104** (silvery, referring to the leaves, etc.)

G. aristatum Freyn & Sintenis ex Freyn, *Bull. Herb. Boiss.*, 5, 587 (1897), **103** (bristled, referring to sepal-mucro)

G. armenum Boissier, *Fl. Or.*, 1, 878 (1867), = **13** (pertaining to Armenia, territory in N.E. Turkey and S.W. Transcaucasia)

G. asphodeloides N.L. Burman, *Spec. Bot. Geran.*, 28 (1759), **63** (like asphodel, referring to the roots)

G. asphodeloides N.L. Burman subsp. *crenophilum* (Boissier) Bornmüller, *Feddes Repert. Beih.*, 89 (3), 134 (1938), **63b** (spring-loving; 'spring' in the sense of a source of water)

G. asphodeloides N.L. Burman subsp. *sintenisii* (Freyn) Davis, *Notes Roy. Bot. Gard. Edinb.*, 28, 36 (1967), **63c** (P.E.E. Sintenis, plant-collector, Germany)

G. atlanticum Boissier, *Diagn. Pl. Or. Nov.*, 1 (1), 59 (1843), under **68** (pertaining to the Atlas Mountains, N.W. Africa)

G. backhousianum Regel, *Acta Horti Petrop.*, 2, 432 (1873), = **13** (James Backhouse, nursery-man, Britain)

G. bellum Rose, *Contr. U.S. Nat. Herb.*, 10, 108 (1906), before **62** (beautiful)

G. ×bergianum Lundström, *Acta Horti Berg.*, 5 (3), 69 (1914) (from the Latin name of Stockholm Botanic Garden: Hortus Bergianus)

G. ×besseanum Camus ex Gams in Hegi, *Ill. Fl.*

Mitteleur., 4 (3), 1715 (1923–4) (not validly published) (Maurice Besse, Canon of Grand Saint Bernard and amateur botanist, Switzerland)

G. bicknellii Britton, *Bull. Torrey Bot. Club*, 24, 92 (1897), **56** (E.P. Bicknell, botanist, USA)

G. biuncinatum Kokwaro, *Webbia*, 25, 639 (1971), **82** (two-hooked, referring to the mericarps)

G. bohemicum Linnaeus, *Cent. Pl.*, 2, 25 (1756), **76** (pertaining to Bohemia)

G. bohemicum Linnaeus subsp. *depraehensum* Almquist, *Svensk Bot. Tidskr.*, 10, 411 (1916), = **77** (detected, discovered, presumably as distinct from *G. bohemicum* proper)

G. brutium Gasparrini, *Rendic. Accad. Sci. (Napoli)*, 1, 49 (1842), **86** (the Bruttii or Brutii, inhabitants of S. Italy)

G. caeruleatum Schur, *Enum. Pl. Transs.*, 136 (1866), under **10** (made blue)

G. canariense Reuter, *Cat. Graines Jard. Bot. Genève, 1857*, no. 3 (1858), **97** (inhabiting the Canary Isles)

G. candicans Knuth, in Engler, *Pflanzenreich, IV, 129*, 580 (1912), = **32;** under **23** (becoming pure white)

G. ×cantabrigiense Yeo, this volume, Appendix II, **90** (inhabiting Cambridge)

G. carolinianum Linnaeus, *Sp. Pl.*, 682 (1753), **57** (pertaining to Carolina, part of USA)

G. carolinianum Linnaeus var. *confertiflorum* Fernald, *Rhodora*, 37, 298 (1935), **57** (densely flowered)

G. cataractarum Cosson, *Not. Pl. Crit.*, 3, 99 (1851), **92** (of cataracts)

G. cataractarum Cosson subsp. *pitardii* Maire, *Bull. Soc. Hist. Nat. Afr. Nord*, 15, 96 (1924), **92** (J.C.M. Pitard, botanist, France)

G. christensenianum Handel-Mazzetti, *Symbolae Sinicae*, 7 (3), 621 (1933), before **22** (C.K.A. Christensen, botanist, Denmark)

G. chumbiense Knuth, *Feddes Repert.*, 19, 228 (1923), = **23** (inhabiting Chumbi, part of Tibet between Sikkim and Bhutan)

G. cinereum Cavanilles, *Monad. Class. Diss. Dec.*, 4, 204 (1787), **106–110** (ashy in colour, referring to the leaves, etc.)

G. cinereum Cavanilles var. *elatius* Davis, *Notes Roy. Bot. Gard. Edinb.*, 28, 36 (1967), under **109** (taller)

G. cinereum Cavanilles subsp. *nanum* (Cosson) Maire, *Mém. Soc. Sci. Nat. Maroc, nos. 21–22*, 29 (1929) (dwarf, adj.)

G. cinereum Cavanilles var. *obtusilobum* (Born-

müller) Yeo, this volume, Appendix II, **108** (blunt-lobed, referring to the leaves)

G. cinereum Cavanilles var. *palmatipartitum* Knuth, in Engler, *Pflanzenreich IV, 129*, 94 (1912), **109** (palmately split, referring to the leaves)

G. cinereum Cavanilles var. *ponticum* Davis & Roberts, *Notes Roy. Bot. Gard. Edinb.*, 22, 23 (1955), under **110** (pertaining to the Pontus, Latin name of a region of N.E. Turkey)

G. cinereum Cavanilles var. *subcaulescens* (L'Héritier ex De Candolle) Knuth, in Engler, *Pflanzenreich, IV, 129*, 92 (1912), **110** (slightly stem-forming)

G. clarkei Yeo, this volume, Appendix II, **18** (C.B. Clarke, botanist, Britain)

G. collinum Willdenow, *Sp. Pl.*, 3, 705 (1800), **15** (of hills)

G. columbinum Linnaeus, *Sp. Pl.*, 682 (1753), **46** (pertaining to a dove, the foot of which is supposedly resembled by the leaf)

G. crenophilum Boissier, *Diagn. Pl. Or. Nov.*, 2 (8), 117 (1849), = **63b** (spring-loving; 'spring' in the sense of a source of water)

G. dahuricum De Candolle, *Prodr.*, 1, 642 (1824), **41** (Dahuria, a Latinised name for a region of S.E. Siberia, USSR)

G. dalmaticum (Beck) Rechinger, *Magyar Bot. Lapok*, 33, 28 (1934), **91** (Dalmatia, Latin name for an Adriatic province now in Yugoslavia)

G. ×decipiens Haussknecht, *Mitt. Thür. Bot. Ver.*, 5, 65 (1893) (deceptive)

G. delavayi Franchet, *Bull. Soc. Bot. Fr.*, 33, 442 (1886), **29** (P.J.M. Delavay, missionary and plant collector, France)

G. dissectum Linnaeus, *Cent. Pl.*, 1, 21 (1755), **64** (cut-up, referring to the leaves)

G. divaricatum Ehrhart, *Beiträge zur Naturkunde*, 7, 164, (1792)

G. donianum Sweet, *Geraniaceae*, 4, sub tab. 338 (1827), **36** (D. Don, botanist, Britain)

G. drakensbergense Hilliard & Burtt, *Notes Roy. Bot. Gard. Edinb.*, 42, 190 (1985), under **53a** (inhabiting the Drakensberg, high mountain range in Republic of South Africa and Lesotho)

G. endressii Gay, *Ann. Sci. Nat.*, 26, 228 (1832), **1** (P.A.C. Endress, plant collector, Germany)

G. endressii Gay var. *armitageae* Turrill, *Gard. Chron.*, 85, 164 (1929), = **2** (Miss E. Armitage, horticulturist, Britain)

G. endressii Gay var. *thurstonianum* Turrill, *Jour. Bot. (London)*, 66, 46 (1928), = **2** (E. Thurston, horticulturist, Britain)

G. *erianthum* De Candolle, *Prodr.*, *1*, 641 (1824), **21** (woolly-flowered)

G. *eriostemon* Fischer ex De Candolle, *Prodr.*, *1*, 641 (1824), **20** (woolly-stamened)

G. *eriostemon* Fischer ex De Candolle var. *reinii* (Franchet & Savatier) Maximowicz, *Bull. Acad. Imp. Sci. Pétersb.*, *26*, 464 (1880), **20** (J.J. Rein, geographer and geologist, Germany)

G. *eriostemon* De Candolle var. *reinii* (Franchet & Savatier) Maximowicz forma *onoei* (Franchet & Savatier) Hara, **20** (M. Ono, botanist, Japan)

G. *farreri* Stapf, *Bot. Mag.*, *151*, tab. 9092 (1926), **33** (R.J. Farrer, plant collector and horticulturist, Britain)

G. *favosum* Hochstetter ex A. Richard, *Tent. Fl. Abyss.*, *1*, 117 (1847) (honeycombed, referring to the mericarps)

G. *forrestii* Knuth, in Engler, *Pflanzenreich, IV*, *129*, 578 (1912), = **29** (G. Forrest, botanist and plant collector, Britain)

G. *forrestii* Stapf, *Bot. Mag.*, *151*, sub tab. 9092 (1926), = **38** (G. Forrest, botanist and plant collector, Britain)

G. *fremontii* Torrey ex Gray, *Pl. Fendl.*, 26 (1849) (*Mem. Amer. Acad. ser. 2, 4, 26* (1849)), **60** (J.C. Frémont, explorer and plant collector, USA)

G. *glaberrimum* Boissier & Heldreich, in Boissier, *Diagn. Pl. Or. Nov.*, 2 (8), 116 (1849), **88** (quite without hairs)

G. *gracile* Ledebour ex Nordmann, *Bull. Sci. Acad. Imp. Pétersb.*, *2*, 314 (1837), **78** (slender, graceful)

G. *grandiflorum* Edgeworth, *Trans. Linn. Soc. London*, *20*, 42 (1846), not Linnaeus (1753), = **19** (large-flowered)

G. *grandiflorum* Edgeworth var. *alpinum* (Regel) Knuth, in Engler, *Pflanzenreich, IV*, *129*, 188 (1912), = **16c**; under **19** (alpine)

G. *grevilleanum* Wallich, *Pl. Asiat. Rar.*, *3*, 4 (1832), = **23** (R.K. Greville, botanist, Britain)

G. *gymnocaulon* De Candolle, *Prodr.*, *1*, 640 (1824), **72** (naked-stemmed)

G. *himalayense* Klotzsch, in Klotzsch & Garcke, *Bot. Ergeb. Reise Waldem.*, 122 (1862), **19** (inhabiting the Himalaya Mountains)

G. × *hybridum* Haussknecht, *Mitt. Geogr. Ges. Bot. Ver. Thür.*, *3*, 278 (1885), not Linnaeus (1767) (hybrid, adj.)

G. × *hybridum* F.A. Lees, *Bot. Loc. Rec. Club, Rep. 1884, 1885, 1886*, 118 (1887), not Linnaeus (1767) (hybrid, adj.)

G. *hyperacrion* Veldkamp, *Blumea, 24*, 470 (1978) (over the mountains)

G. *ibericum* Cavanilles subsp. *jubatum* (Handel-4, 209 (1790), **70** (Iberia, Latin name for Georgia in the Caucasus, now Gruziya)

G. *ibericum* Cavanilles subsp. *jubatum* (Handel-Mazzetti) Davis, *Notes Roy. Bot. Gard. Edinb.*, *22*, 24 (1955), **70** (maned, possibly from the very long hairs in the inflorescence)

G. *ibericum* Cavanilles var. *platypetalum* (Fischer & Meyer) Boissier, *Fl. Or.*, *1*, 876 (1867), = **69** (flat-petalled, referring to the petals of a flower collectively)

G. *incanum* N.L. Burman, *Spec. Bot. Geran.*, 28 (1759), **53** (white or hoary, referring to stems and undersides of leaves)

G. *incanum* N.L. Burman var. *multifidum* (Sweet) Hilliard & Burtt, *Notes Roy. Bot. Gard. Edinb.*, *42*, 197 (1985), **53** (much cleft, referring to the leaves)

G. *incisum* (Torrey & Gray) Brewer & Watson, *Bot. Calif.*, *1*, 94 (1880), not Andrews (1799), = **55**; under **58** (deeply cut, referring to the leaves)

G. × *intermedium* Sündermann ex Knuth, in Engler, *Pflanzenreich, IV*, *129*, 220 (1912), not Colla (1834), under **105a** (intermediate)

G. *kariense* Knuth, in Engler, *Pflanzenreich, IV*, *129*, 577 (1912), = **29** (inhabiting the Kari Pass, Yunnan, China)

G. *kishtvariense* Knuth, *Feddes Repert.*, *19*, 229 (1923), **26** district of Kishtwar in Kashmir)

G. *krameri* Franchet & Savatier, *Enum. Pl. Jap.*, *2*, 306 (1878), **40** (Kramer, collector for Savatier)

G. *lambertii* Sweet, *Geraniaceae*, 4, tab. 338 (1827), **23** (A.B. Lambert, botanist, Britain)

G. *lanuginosum* Lamarck, *Encycl. Méth. Bot.*, *2*, 655 (1788), **77** (woolly)

G. *libani* Davis, *Notes Roy. Bot. Gard. Edinb.*, *22*, 25 (1955), **75** (of Lebanon)

G. *libanoticum* (Boissier) Boissier, *Fl. Or.*, *1*, 877 (1867), not Schenk (1840), = **75** (Lebanese)

G. × *lindavicum* Sündermann ex Knuth, in Engler, *Pflanzenreich, IV*, *129*, 220 (1912), **105** (Lindau on Lake Constance)

G. *lindleyanum* Royle, *Ill. Bot. Himal. Mount.*, 150 (1835) (J. Lindley, botanist, Britain)

G. *linearilobum* De Candolle, *Fl. Fr., ed.3, 5*, 629 (1815), **67** (with linear lobes, referring to the the leaves)

G. *linearilobum* De Candolle subsp. *transversale* (Karelin & Kirilow) Davis, *Israel Jour. Bot., 19*, 105 (1970), **67** (transverse, possibly referring to the wide leaves)

G. londesii Fischer ex Link, *Enum. Hort. Berol. Alt., 2*, 196 (1822) under **15** (F.W. Londes, botanist, Germany/Russia)

G. lucidum Linnaeus, *Sp. Pl.*, 682 (1753), **94** (shining)

G. ×*luganense* Chenevard ex Schröter, *Ber. Schweiz. Bot. Ges., 14*, 121 (1904), not validly published (Lugano, Switzerland)

G. macrorrhizum Linnaeus, *Sp. Pl.*, 680 (1753), **89** (large-rooted)

G. macrostylum Boissier, *Diagn. Pl. Or. Nov., 1 (1)*, 58 (1843), **66** (large-styled)

G. maculatum Linnaeus, *Sp. Pl.*, 681 (1753), **54** (spotted, from the yellowish marks in the notches of the leaves)

G. maderense Yeo, *Bol. Mus. Munic. Funchal, 23*, 26 (1969), **99** (inhabiting Madeira)

G. ×*magnificum* Hylander, *Lustgarden, 1961*, 114 (1961), **71** (magnificent)

G. magniflorum Knuth, *Bot. Jahrb, 40*, 68 (1907), **53a** (large-flowered)

G. malviflorum Boissier & Reuter, *Pugillus*, 27 (1852), **68** (mallow-flowered)

G. maximowiczii Regel & Maack ex Regel, *Tent. Fl. Ussur.*, 38 (1861)*, under **21** (C.J. Maximowicz, botanist, Russia)

G. meeboldii Briquet, *Annu. Cons. Jard. Bot. Genève, 11/12*, 184 (1908), =**19** (Meebold, personal name, presumably Swiss)

G. melanandrum Franchet, *Pl. Delav.*, 112 (1889), = **30** (with black anthers)

G. molle Linnaeus, *Sp. Pl.*, 682 (1753), **87** (soft, referring to the hairiness of the plant)

G. ×*monacense* Harz, *Mitt. Bayer. Bot. Ges., 4 (1)*, 7 (1921), **101** (inhabiting Monachium, Latinised form of Munich or München)

G. ×*monacense* Harz nothovar. *anglicum* Yeo, this volume, Appendix II, **101** (English)

G. multifidum D. Don, *Prodr. Fl. Nepal.*, 207 (1825), =**36** (much cleft, referring to the leaves)

G. napuligerum Franchet, *Pl. Delav.*, 115 (1889), under **33** (bearing turnips, referring to the shape, but not the size, of the roots)

G. nepalense Sweet, *Geraniaceae, 1*, tab. 12 (1820), **48** (inhabiting Nepal)

G. nepalense Sweet var. *thunbergii* (Siebold ex Lindley & Paxton) Kudo, *Medic. Pl. Hokkaido*, tab. 55 (1922)*, =**47** (C.P. Thunberg, botanist, Sweden)

G. nervosum Rydberg, *Bull. Torrey Bot. Club, 28*, 34 (1901), **58** (nerved, probably referring to the petals)

G. niuginiense Veldkamp, *Blumea, 24*, 473 (1978) (inhabiting New Guinea)

G. nodosum Linnaeus, *Sp. Pl.*, 681 (1753), **6** (knotty, referring to the swollen joints of the stem)

G. ocellatum Cambessèdes, in Jacquemont, *Voy. Inde, 4 (Bot.)*, 33 (1841?)*, **81** (eyed or eye-letted, referring to the dark centre of the flower)

G. ×*oenense* Borbás, *Progr. Ober-Real Schule Innsbruck*, 53 (1891)* (an inhabitant of the River Inn or Innsbruck)

G. omphalodeum Lange, *Ind. Sem. Horti Haun.*, 27 (1865), **80a** (like *Omphalodes*, a genus of Boraginaceae, from the resemblance in the mericarps)

G. oreganum Howell, *Fl. N.W. Amer.*, 106 (1897), **55** (Oregon)

G. orientalitibeticum Knuth, *Feddes Repert., 19*, 230 (1923), **44** (East Tibet, now W. Sichuan)

G. ×*oxonianum* Yeo, this volume, Appendix II, **2** (pertaining to Oxford)

G. pallens Bieberstein, *Fl. Taur.-Cauc., 2*, 138 (1808), = **63a** (pale, referring to the flower-colour)

G. palmatum Cavanilles, *Monad. Class. Diss. Dec., 4*, 216 (1787), **98** (palmate, referring to the leaf-form)

G. palustre Linnaeus, *Cent. Pl., 2*, 25 (1756), **34** (found in marshes)

G. parryi (Engelmann) Heller, *Cat. N. Amer. Pl., ed. 2, 7* (1900), = **60** (C.C. Parry, Britain/USA)

G. peloponnesiacum Boissier, *Diagn. Pl. Or. Nov., 3 (1)*, 110 (1853), **74** (the Peloponnese, the part of Greece S. of the Gulf of Corinth)

G. peloponnesiacum Boissier var. *libanoticum* Boissier, *Diagn. Pl. Or. Nov., 3 (5)*, 73 (1856), = **75** (Lebanese)

G. phaeum Linnaeus, *Sp. Pl.*, 681 (1753), **100** (dusky)

G. phaeum Linnaeus var. *lividum* (L'Héritier) Persoon, *Syn. Pl., 2*, 235 (1806), **100** (livid)

G. platyanthum Duthie, *Gard. Chron., 39*, 52 (1906), = **20** (flat-flowered)

G. platypetalum Fischer & Meyer, *Ind. Sem. Horti Petrop., 1*, 28 (1835)*, **69** (flat-petalled, referring to the petals of a flower collectively)

G. platypetalum Franchet, *Pl. Delav.*, 111 (1889), = **28** (flat-petalled)

G. pogonanthum Franchet, *Pl. Delav.*, 111 (1889), **31** (with a bearded flower)

G. polyanthes Edgeworth & J.D. Hooker, in J.D. Hooker, *Fl. Brit. Ind., 1* 431 (1874), **79** (many flowered)

G. potentilloides L'Héritier ex De Candolle, *Prodr., 1*, 639 (1824) (like a *Potentilla*, presumably referring to the flowers)

G. potentilloides L'Héritier var. *abditum* Carolin, *Proc. Linn. Soc. N.S.W., 89*, 340 (1964) (removed)

G. pratenese Linnaeus, *Sp. Pl.*, 681 (1753), **16** (inhabiting meadows)

G. pratense Linnaeus forma *albiflorum* Opiz, *Seznam Rostlin Květeny České*, 47 (1852), **16** (white-flowered)

G. pratense Linnaeus var. *album* Weston, *The Universal Botanist and Nurseryman, 2*, 353 (1771), = **16** (white)

G. pratense Linnaeus subsp. *stewartianum* Y. Nasir, *Fl. Pak., 149*, 19 (1983) (R.R. Stewart, botanist, USA/Pakistan)

G. pratense Linnaeus subsp. *stewartianum* Y. Nasir var. *schmidii* Y. Nasir, *Fl. Pak., 149*, 21 (1983) (F. Schmid, botanist, Germany)

G. procurrens Yeo, *Bot. Mag., 179*, tab. 644 (1973), **25** (running forth)

G. pseudosibiricum J. Mayer, *Abh. Böhm. Ges. Wiss., 1786*, 238 (1786), **11** (false *sibiricum*)

G. psilostemon Ledebour, *Fl. Ross., 1*, 465 (1842), **13** (with bare, i.e. hairless, stamens)

G. purpureum Villars, in Linnaeus, *Syst. Pl. Eur., 1, Fl. Delph.*, 72 (1785), under and before **95** (purple)

G. purpusii Knuth, *Feddes Repert., 12*, 40 (1913), = **62** (C.A. Purpus, plant collector, Germany)

G. pusillum Linnaeus, *Syst. Nat., ed. 10, 2*, 1144 (1759), **85** (puny, slender)

G. pylzowianum Maximowicz, *Bull. Acad. Imp. Sci. Pétersb., 26*, 452, 466 (1880), **43**

G. pyrenaicum N.L. Burman, *Spec. Bot. Geran.*, 27 (1759), **84** (Pyrenean)

G. pyrenaicum N.L. Burman forma *albiflorum* Schur, **84** (white-flowered)

G. rectum Trautvetter, *Bull. Soc. Nat. Moscou, 33*, 459 (1860), **7** (straight, referring to the stem or the (sometimes) upright pedicels)

G. reflexum Linnaeus, *Mantissa Alt.*, 257 (1771), **102** (reflexed, referring to the sepals and petals)

G. refractum Edgeworth & J.D. Hooker, in J.D. Hooker, *Fl. Brit. India, 1*, 428 (1874), **30** (bent backwards, referring to the pedicels)

G. regelii Nevski, *Acta Inst. Bot. Acad. Sci. U.R.S.S., 4*, 304 (1937), **16c** (E. Regel, botanist, Switzerland/Russia)

G. renardii Trautvetter, in Trautvetter, Regel,

Maximowicz & Winkler, *Decas Pl. Nov.*, 5 (1882), **73** (K.I. Renard, naturalist, Russia)

G. richardsonii Fischer & Trautvetter, *Ind. Sem. Horti Petrop., 4*, 37 (1838)*, **61** (Sir John Richardson, explorer and naturalist, Britain)

G. ×riversleaianum Yeo, this volume, Appendix II, **3** (Riverslea Nursery near Christchurch, England)

G. rivulare Villars, *Prosp. Pl. Dauph.*, 40 (1779), **10** (found by rivers or streams, a misnomer)

G. robertianum Linnaeus, *Sp. Pl.*, 681 (1753), **95** (Robert or Ruprecht, see Chapter 1)

G. robertianum Linnaeus forma *bernettii* A. Schwarz, **95**

G. robertianum Linnaeus subsp. *celticum* Ostenfeld, *Rep. Bot. Exch. Club Brit. Is., 5*, 551 (1920), **95** (Celtic)

G. robertianum Linnaeus var. *celticum* (Ostenfeld) Druce, *Brit. Pl. List, ed. 2*, 21 (1928), **95** (Celtic)

G. robertianum Linnaeus forma *leucanthum* Dumortier ex Beckhaus, *Jahresb. Westfäl. Prov. Ver. Wiss. Kunst, 5*, 178 (1878), **95** (white-flowered)

G. robertianum Linnaeus subsp. *maritimum* (Babington) H.G. Baker, *Watsonia, 3*, 272 (1956), = **95** (maritime)

G. rotundifolium Linnaeus, *Sp. Pl.*, 683 (1753), **8** (round-leaved)

G. rubescens Yeo, *Bol. Mus. Munic. Funchal, 23*, 26 (1969), **96** (reddish or becoming reddish, referring to the stems and leaf-stalks)

G. rubifolium Lindley, *Bot. Reg., 26*, tab. 67 (1840), **27** (bramble-leaved)

G. sanguineum Linnaeus, *Sp. Pl.*, 683 (1753), **45** (bloody, blood-red, referring, inaccurately, to the colour of the petals)

G. sanguineum Linnaeus var. *lancastrense* (Miller) Druce, *List of British Plants*, 14 (1908), = **45** (Lancashire, English county) (later homonym of *G. s. lancastriense* G. Nicholson)

G. sanguineum Linnaeus *lancastriense* G. Nicholson, *Ill. Dict. Gard., 2*, 64 (1885), name published without indication of rank, = **45** (Lancashire, English county)

G. sanguineum Linnaeus var. *prostratum* (Cavanilles) Persoon, *Syn. Pl., 2*, 234 (1806), = **45** (prostrate)

G. sanguineum Linnaeus var. *striatum* Weston, *The Universal Botanist and Nurseryman, 2*, 353 (1771), **45** (striped, referring to the veiny petals)

G. schiedeanum Schlechtendal, *Linnaea, 10*, 253

(1836), **62** (C.J.W. Schiede, botanist and plant collector)

G. *schrenkianum* Trautvetter ex Becker, *Bull. Soc. Nat. Moscou, 57, 53* (1882), before **46** (A.G. von Schrenk, botanist)

G. *sessiliflorum* Cavanilles, *Monad. Class. Diss. Dec., 4, 198* (1787), **52** (sessile-flowered, referring to the pedicels arising from the rootstock)

G. *sessiliflorum* Cavanilles subsp. *brevicaule* (J.D. Hooker) Carolin, *Proc. Linn. Soc. N.S.W., 89,* 357 (1964), **52** (short-stemmed)

G. *sessiliflorum* Cavanilles subsp. *novaezelandiae* Carolin, *Proc. Linn. Soc. N.S.W., 89,* 356 (1964), **52** (of New Zealand)

G. *shikokianum* Matsumura, *Bot. Mag. Tokyo, 15,* 123 (1901), **37** (Shikoku, S. Japan, the smallest of the five main islands of Japan)

G. *shikokianum* Matsumura var. *quelpaertense* Nakai, *Bot. Mag. Tokyo, 26,* 260 (1912), **37** (Quelpart Island, S. Korea, also called Cheju do)

G. *sibiricum* Linnaeus, *Sp. Pl., 683* (1753), **49** (Siberian)

G. *sinense* Knuth, in Engler, *Pflanzenreich, IV, 129, 577* (1912), **28** (inhabiting Sina, Latinised form of China)

G. *soboliferum* Komarov, *Acta Horti Petrop., 18,* 433 (1901), **39** (bearing runners or long rhizomes, see Chapter 9)

G. *stapfianum* Handel-Mazzetti, *Symbolae Sinicae, 7 (3),* 620 (1933), **38** (O. Stapf, botanist, Germany/Britain)

G. *stenorrhizum* Stapf, *Bot. Mag., 151,* sub tab. 9092 (1926), = **36** (slender-rooted)

G. *stepporum* Davis, *Notes Roy. Bot. Gard. Edinb., 28, 35* (1967), = **65** (of steppes)

G. *striatum* Linnaeus, *Amoen. Acad., 4, 282* (1759), = **5** (striped)

G. *strigosius* St John, *Fl. S.E. Wash. Adj. Idaho,* 243 (1937), = **58** (more strigose; erroneously written *strigosior* when published. See *G. strigosum)*

G. *strigosum* Rydberg, *Bull. Torrey Bot. Club, 29,* 243 (1902), not N.L. Burman (1768), = **58** (with stiff appressed hairs)

G. *subcaulescens* L'Héritier ex De Candolle, *Prodr., 1,* 640 (1824), = **110** (slightly stem-forming)

G. *sylvaticum* Linnaeus, *Sp. Pl., 681* (1753), **9** (pertaining to woods)

G. *sylvaticum* Linnaeus forma *albiflorum* A.G. Blytt, *Haandb. Norges Fl.,* 478 (1905), **9** (white-flowered)

G. *sylvaticum* Linnaeus var. *alpestre* Thaiss. ex Domin & Podpęra in Polívka, Domin & Podpęra, *Klíç k Uplné Kvętene Republicky Çeskoslovenské, ed. 2,* 111 (1928), = **9** (found in the lower alps)

G. *sylvaticum* Linnaeus subsp. *caeruleatum* (Schur) Webb & Ferguson, *Feddes Repert., 74,* 25 (1967), under **10** (made blue)

G. *sylvaticum* Linnaeus subsp. *pseudosibiricum* (J. Mayer) Webb & Ferguson, *Feddes Repert., 74, 26* (1967), = **11** (false *sibiricum)*

G. *sylvaticum* Linnaeus subsp. *rivulare* (Villars) Rouy, *Fl. Fr., 4,* 81 (1897), = **10** (found by rivers or streams, a misnomer)

G. *sylvaticum* Linnaeus forma *roseum* Murr, **9** (rose-coloured)

G. *sylvaticum* var. *wanneri* Briquet, *Bull. Soc. Bot. Genève, 5,* 201 (1889), **9** (Monsieur Wanner, botanist, Switzerland)

G. *thodei* Schlechter ex Knuth, *Bot. Jahrb., 40, 70* (1907), under **53a** (J. Thode, collector for Schlechter)

G. *thunbergii* Siebold ex Lindley & Paxton, *Paxton's Flower Garden, 1,* 186 (1851), **47** (C.P. Thunberg, botanist, Sweden)

G. *transbaicalicum* Sergievskaya, *Sist. Zametki Mater. Gerb. Tomsk. Univ., 1,* 4 (1934), **16a** (beyond Lake Baikal)

G. *traversii* J.D. Hooker, *Handb. N. Zeal. Flora,* 726 (1867), **50** (W.T.L. Travers, ornithologist)

G. *traversii* J.D. Hooker var. *elegans* Cockayne, *Trans. N. Zeal. Inst., 34,* 320 (1902), **50** (elegant)

G. *trilophum* Boissier, *Diagn. Pl. Or. Nov., 1 (6),* 30 (1845), **80** (three-crested, referring to the mericarps)

G. *tuberosum* Linnaeus, *Sp. Pl., 680* (1753), **65** (tuberous)

G. *tuberosum* Linnaeus subsp. *linearifolium* (Boissier) Davis, *Notes Roy. Bot. Gard. Edinb., 22, 26* (1956), **65** (linear-leaved, but probably referring to the divisions of the upper leaves)

G. *tuberosum* Linnaeus subsp. *micranthum* Schönbeck-Temesy, in K.H. Rechinger, *Flora Iranica, 69,* 7 (1970), **65** (small-flowered)

G. *versicolor* Linnaeus, *Cent. Pl., 1,* 21 (1755), **5** (variously coloured)

G. *viscosissimum* Fischer & Meyer, *Ind. Sem. Horti Petrop., 9, suppl.,* 18 (1846)*, **59** (very sticky, from the glandular hairs)

G. *viscosissimum* Fischer & Meyer var. *nervosum* (Rydberg) C.L. Hitchcock, in C.L. Hitchcock et al., *Vasc. Pl. Pacific Northwest, 3,* 383 (1961),

= **58** (nerved, probably referring to the petals)

G. wallichianum D. Don, in Sweet, *Geraniaceae, 1*, tab. 90 (1821), **22** (N. Wallich, surgeon and botanist, Denmark/Britain/India)

G. wilfordii Maximowicz, *Bull. Acad. Imp. Sci. Pétersb., 26*, 453 (1880), under **47** (C. Wilford, botanist and plant collector, Britain)

G. wlassovianum Fischer ex Link, *Enum. Horti Berol. Alt., 2*, 197 (1822), **35**

G. yemense in the sense of Knuth, in Engler, *Pflanzenreich IV, 129*, 60 (1912), = **82** (inhabiting the Yemen)

G. yesoense Franchet & Savatier, *Enum. Pl. Jap.,* 2, 305 (1878), **42** (inhabiting Yeso or Yezo, old name of Hokkaido, the northernmost large island of Japan)

G. yesoense Franchet & Savatier var. *nipponicum* Nakai, *Bot. Mag. Tokyo, 26*, 266 (1912), **42** (Nippon, another name for Japan)

G. yoshinoi Nakai, *Bot. Mag. Tokyo, 26*, 258 (1912), under **37** (Z. Yoshino, botanist, Japan)

G. yunnanense Franchet, *Pl. Delav.*, 114 (1889), **32** (inhabiting Yunnan, China)

G. ×*zermattense* F.O. Wolf ex Gams in Hegi, *Ill. Fl. Mitteleur., 4 (3)*, 1715 (1923–4) (not validly published) (inhabiting Zermatt, Switzerland)

Appendix II

New Names

The following names are used for the first time in this book and are below validly published in accordance with the International Code of Botanical Nomenclature (Voss *et al.*, 1983). Binary names are not provided for all the interspecific hybrids in cultivation, but only in those cases where it seems they would be particularly useful. The Latin descriptions of the first three hybrids are similar in content to the English descriptions in Chapter 9 and are, therefore, not translated here.

1. Geranium ×*oxonianum* Yeo, nothospecies nova (Chapter 9, no. 2)

Hybridae mutabiles inter *G. endressii* Gay et *G. versicolorem* Linnaeus. Herba perennis, foliosa, c. 80cm attingens, parentibus frequenter elatior. Indumentum in partibus superioribus pro parte stipitato-glandulosum. Foliorum laminae 5–20cm latae, quinquepartitae, divisionibus minus attenuatis et minus profunde incisis quam in *G. endressii,* supra rugulosae sublucentaeque. Flores infundibuliformes, eis parentium saepe majores; sepala, mucrone excluso, usque 11mm longa; petala usque 26 × 15mm, cuneata, emarginata, colore rosea, plerumque reticulato-venosa. Fructus fertilis.

TYPE: Cult. Hort. Bot. Univ. Cantab., no. 24–74 G.S. Thomas, sub nomine *Geranium endressii* × *G. versicolor:* 'Claridge Druce', 13.vi.1974 lecta et in foliis herbarii duobus conservatur (CGG).

The name commemorates the city of Oxford and has been chosen in view of the history of the cultivar 'Claridge Druce' (see Chapter 9, no. 2).

2. Geranium ×*riversleaianum* Yeo, nothospecies nova (Chapter 9, no. 3)

Hybridae inter *G. endressii* Gay et *G. traversii* J.D. Hooker. Herba perennis indumento canescenti, caulibus longis ramosissimis procumbentibus inflorescentiam diffusam foliosam efformantibus. Foliorum principalium laminae 5–10cm latae, usque ad 2/3 vel 3/4 septempartitae, divisionibus supra medium latioribus in tertiam partem lobatis; lobi sparse dentati, ut dentes obtusi vel acuti. Cymuli biflori. Flores 20–32mm diametro, late infundibuliformes. Sepala, mucrone excluso, 6–7mm longa; mucro usque 1mm longus. Petala 14–17mm longa, paullo longiora quam lata, apice leviter emarginato, colore pallide rosea vel rubropurpurea, venis parum pinnatis modice obscurioribus. Petalorum basis in superficie et marginibus parce pilosis. Staminum filamenta quam sepala breviora, alba, pilosa. Stigmata 2–3.5mm longa, externe plus minusve setulosa. Fructus non accrescens, abortivus.

TYPE: Cult. Hort. Bot. Univ. Cantab., no. 172–74 G.S. Thomas, sub nomine *Geranium* 'Russell Prichard', 30. vii. 1975 lecta (CGG).

The clonal cultivar 'Russell Prichard' was raised early in the present century at Prichard's nursery, Riverslea, Hampshire.

3. Geranium ×*cantabrigiense* Yeo, nothospecies nova: (Chapter 9, no. 3)

Hybridae inter *G. dalmaticum* (Beck) Rechinger et *G. macrorrhizum* Linnaeus. Herba perennis, aromatica, stolonifera, usque c. 30cm alta. Folia puberula, vivide viridia; laminae 3–9cm latae, usque ad 3/4 vel 4/5 septempartitae, divisionibus cuneatis apicem breviter trilobatum versus dilatatis, lobis nonnullis dentibus sparse ornatis. Caules floriferi nodo primo et interdum secundo foliati. Inflorescentiae dibrachiatae, inter brachia cymula biflora praeditae et ad apicem utriusque rami floribus 5–10 instructae. Flores eis parentium similes, staminum filamenta ut in *G. dalmatico* dentibus duobus pilosis sub-basalibus instructa. Sepala rubro-tincta; petala rosea vel alba. Fructus abortivus vel accrescens sed constanter sterilis.

TYPE: Cult. Hort. Bot. Univ. Cantab., no. 232–74 Kiefer, sub nomine *G. dalmaticum* × *G. macrorrhizum* culta, 22.vi.1983 lecta et in foliis herbarii tribus (holotypus et duo isotypi) conservatur (CGG).

The name commemorates the city of Cambridge in which the deliberately raised clone which provided the type was produced (see Chapter 9, no. 90).

4. Variation within Geranium ×monacense *Harz* (Chapter 9, no. 101)

The above name was proposed by Dr Kurt Harz of Munich for a hybrid between *G. phaeum* Linnaeus and *G. reflexum* Linnaeus (Harz, 1921). Its name is based on 'Monachum', the Latin name for Munich.

In gardens one may find apparent hybrids of *G. reflexum* with, on the one hand, *G. phaeum* var. *phaeum* and, on the other, *G. phaeum* var. *lividum*. Both hybrids are intermediate in petal shape (though this is not easily appreciated unless the petals are detached and pressed flat) and in the degree of reflexion of the petals. It is in the details of the petal colouring that the influence of the two varieties of *G. phaeum* may be seen.

Below I name the hybrids arising from these two different crosses in accordance with Article H.11.2 (and other relevant articles) of the International Code of Botanical Nomenclature (Voss *et al.*, 1983).

The hybrid that Harz reported appeared in his garden near *G. reflexum* and *G. phaeum*. He described *G. phaeum* as having the petals roundly cuneate-ovate, weakly emarginate or rounded off at the outer end, otherwise almost entire-margined, dark brown-red, spread flat and later slightly bent backwards. The description of the colour makes it clear that he was growing *G. phaeum* var. *phaeum*. The hybrid to be named now is, therefore, that involving *G. phaeum* var. *lividum*.

(a). *Geranium* ×*monacense* Harz nothovar. *anglicum* Yeo, nothovar. nova.

Hybridae inter *G. phaeum* Linnaeus var. *lividum* (L'Héritier) Persoon et *G. reflexum* Linnaeus. Petalorum color principalis roseo-lilacinus; area basalis albidus parva, margine distali recto; zona intermedia caeruleo-violacea lata, conspicua, valde venosa.

Main petal colour pinkish lilac; whitish basal area small, straight-edged; intermediate bluish-violet zone wide, conspicuous and strongly veined.

TYPE: Cult. Hort. Bot. Univ. Cantab., no. 281–81 Forty, primo ex Hurst Green, East Sussex, a P. Ropero lecta, exsiccata sub nomine *G. phaeum* var. *lividum* 4. vi. 1982 lecta et in foliis herbarii duobus conservatur (CGG).

The naming and description of the above nothovariety automatically establishes the name *G.* ×*monacense* nothovar. *monacense,* used in Chapter 9. The characters of the plant are, for convenience of comparison, repeated here.

(b). *Geranium* ×*monacense* Harz nothovar. *monacense*

Hybrids between *G. phaeum* Linnaeus var. *phaeum* and *G. reflexum* Linnaeus. Main petal colour purplish red; whitish basal area relatively large, with a toothed edge; intermediate bluish-violet zone inconspicuous.

5. Geranium clarkei Yeo, species nova (Chapter 9, no. 18)

Herba perennis affinis *G. pratensi* Linnaeus, a quo rhizomatibus extensis, foliis caulibusque gracilioribus, inflorescentia minus densa, pedicellis longioribus, axibus florum ascendentibus, petalis majoribus violascentibus (aut albis reticulo ornatis) differt. A *G. himalayense* Klotzsch habitu erecto, foliis angustisectis, floribus sursum spectantibus, petalorum colore differt.

Rhizoma subterraneum plus minusve elongatum. Folia basalia numerosa, longe petiolata, stipulis angustis acutis usque 2cm longis et lamina 5–13cm lata fere ad basin septempartita instructa. Laminae divisiones circa in medio latiores, profunde pinnatilobatae; lobi plerumque 2–3plo longiores quam latiores, 1–2 dentati, sicut dentes acuti. Folia caulina similia, opposita. Caules usque 50cm alti, inflorescentiam ramosam plurifloram haud densam efformantes. Indumentum in partibus plantae inferioribus subappresse tomentosum, in ramis superioribus, sepalis et fructibus patente stipitato-glandulosum. Pedunculi 1.5–8cm longi; uterque pedicellus in una cymula calycibus longior. Flores suberecti, sepalis petalisque late divergentibus. Sepala, mucrone excluso, c. 11mm longa: mucro c. 1.5–2.5mm longus. Petala 22–24 × 16–18mm, basi late cuneata, apice rotundata, toto splendide purpureo-violascentes vel alba et pallide lilacino eleganter reticulata. Petalorum bases marginibus pilis densis et superficie interiore glabro vel interdum pilis perpaucis instructae. Staminum filamenta sepalis paullo breviora, basi ovate dilatata et pilosa. Stigmata 1.5–2mm longa. Fructus immaturi et pedicelli eorum divaricati, ascendentes vel inclinati. Rostrum 24–28mm longum, partem stylosam 6–8mm longam includens. Mericarpia 4–5mm longa.

TYPE: Hirpoor, Kashmir, 9 July 1876, C.B. Clarke, no. 28663A (K). Perennial herb related to *G. pratense* L., from which it differs in the elongate rhizomes, more graceful leaves and stems, less dense inflorescence, longer pedicels, ascending floral axis and larger violet, or white and net-veined, petals. Differing from *G. himalayense* Klotzsch in the erect habit, more narrowly cut leaves, the upturned flowers and colour of the petals.

Plant with a more or less elongate underground rhizome. Basal leaves numerous, long-stalked, with narrow acute stipules up to 2cm long and with a blade 5–13cm wide, divided almost to the base into 7. Divisions of the blade broadest about the middle, deeply pinnately lobed; lobes usually 2–3 times as long as wide, with 1 or 2 teeth, like the teeth acute. Stem-leaves similar, opposite. Stems up to about 50cm tall, forming a branched, many-flowered but not dense inflorescence. Hair-clothing of the lower parts rather densely felted, of the upper branches and parts of the flowers glandular. Peduncles 1.5–8cm long; both pedicels in each cymule longer than the calyx. Flowers with axis upwardly inclined and with widely divergent sepals and petals. Sepals c. 11mm long without the mucro; mucro c. 1.5–2.5mm long. Petals 22–

24 × 16–18mm, broadly wedge-shaped at the base, rounded at the apex, of a fine purplish violet colour or white with delicate pale lilac net-veining. Bases of the petals provided with dense hairs on the margins and sometimes a very few on the surface. Stamen filaments a little shorter than the sepals, ovately enlarged and finely hairy at the base. Stigmas 1.5–2mm long. Immature fruits and their pedicels spreading and ascending or slightly nodding. Rostrum 24–28mm long, including stylar portion 6–8mm long. Mericarps 4–5mm long.

This plant is named after C.B. Clarke (1832–1906), Superintendent of the Calcutta Botanic Gardens, President of the Linnean Society of London and substantial contributor to *Flora of British India;* he collected the earliest specimen of this *Geranium* that I could find in the Kew Herbarium, which I have designated as the type.

This plant now seems quite distinct enough to merit recognition as a species, though it is closely related to *G. pratense*, as shown by the fact that in the body of this book it is described by comparing it with that species. The part of *Flora of Pakistan* dealing with Geraniaceae (Nasir, 1983) does not account for *G. clarkei*, although it describes two new taxa in the *G. pratense* alliance. These are *G. pratense* subsp. *stewartianum* Nasir var. *stewartianum* and var. *schmidii* Nasir. I now have plants in cultivation, grown from two samples of seed sent from Kashmir by Dr S.K. Raina of Srinagar, which correspond with the first of these varieties. They are variable but differ in many points from *G. clarkei*, which I also have from Dr Raina as well as from Mr C.R. Lancaster. *G. pratense* subsp. *stewartianum* var. *schmidii* has petals only 12mm long with a narrow, hairy base, and I am doubtful about its true affinity.

6. *Geranium cinereum* Cavanilles var. *obtusilobum* (Bornmüller) Yeo, comb. nov.
BASIONYM: *G. subcaulescens* L'Héritier ex De Candolle var. *obtusilobum* Bornmüller, *Beihefte zum Botanischen Centralblatt, 31 (1)*, 197 (1913).
TYPE: *Geranium subcaulescens* L'Hérit. ∝ *obtusilobum* Bornm., Montium Libani borealis in decliv. alpinis Dahr-el-Kodib, 24–3500 m. s. m., 5.vii.1910, J. et F. Bornmüller, J. Bornmüller: Iter Syriacum II, no. 11540 (JE,!).

Index of Plant Names